THE CIVIL WAR
in
MIDDLE TENNESSEE
(In Four Parts)

(Originally published by *The Nashville Banner* as
four separate supplements, commemorating the
Civil War's Centennial years.)

By ED HUDDLESTON

Printed By

The Parthenon Press

Nashville, Tennessee

1965

The Nashville Banner and the author acknowledge with thanks the permission graciously granted them to quote from the following books:

The Army of Tennessee, by Stanley F. Horn, copyrighted 1941 by The Bobbs-Merrill Company, and *The Decisive Battle of Nashville*, also by Mr. Horn, Louisiana State University Press, 1956.

"First With the Most" Forrest, by Robert Selph Henry, McCowat-Mercer Press, Jackson, Tenn.; and *The Story of the Confederacy*, also by Mr. Henry, Bobbs-Merrill, 1931.

Steamboatin' on the Cumberland, by Judge Byrd Douglas, Tennessee Book Company, 1961.

The Attitude of Tennesseans Toward the Union, 1847-1861, by Mary Emily Robertson Campbell, Vantage Press, 1961 (especially concerning statistics portraying socio-economics of ante-bellum Tennessee).

A Different Valor, by Gilbert E. Govan and James W. Livingood, The Bobbs-Merrill Company, Inc., 1956 (particularly for the 1861 warning to Gen. Joseph E. Johnston from his wife, and Johnston's reply. To the same sources *The Banner* is grateful for quotations from the Gen. Johnston-Sen. Louis T. Wigfall correspondence. Additional thanks are expressed to the Henry E. Huntington Library and Art Gallery, San Marino, Calif., and to the Library of Congress, repositories for a number of the letters).

Education in Violence, the Life of George H. Thomas and the History of the Army of the Cumberland, by Francis F. McKinney. Reprinted by permission of the publishers, Wayne State University Press. Copyright (c) 1961 by Francis F. McKinney. All rights reserved. Library of Congress Catalog Number 61-6040.

(To Mr. McKinney and the Wayne State University Press, *The Banner* and the author are especially grateful for material and quotations concerning Gen. Thomas as a professional soldier, his family background and youth, interchanges with Gen. William T. Sherman in the closing months of 1864 and details of Gen. Thomas' final honors.)

The Gallant Hood, by John P. Dyer, Bobbs-Merrill Company, Inc., 1950 (especially concerning Gen. John B. Hood's youth and background and, in particular, the advice of Hood's father on Hood's departure for West Point).

A Diary from Dixie, by Mrs. Mary Boykin Chestnut (Ben Ames Williams, ed.), Houghton Mifflin Company, 1949 (particularly for intimate glimpses of the times, notable personalities and, specifically, Hood's Richmond convalescence and his romance with Sally Preston).

Morgan and His Raiders, by Cecil Fletcher Holland, The Macmillan Company, 1942 (particularly for permission to quote from the letters of Mattie Ready Morgan and a sister).

Messages of the Governors of Tennessee, 1857-1869, Vol. V, by Dr. Robert H. White, Tennessee Historical Commission, 1959 (especially concerning elections and other political actions in war-torn Tennessee, after its occupation by Federal forces).

A Diary from Dixie, by Mrs. Chesnut, Appleton, N.Y., copyright 1905, especially for the description of Gen. Stephen D. Lee's men in Chester, S.C. Appreciation is also expressed for permission to reproduce the picture of Sally Preston from the same work.

Gratitude is also expressed to Appleton-Century for generous permission to use many illustrations from *The Century War Book, 1861-1865*, edited by Robert Underwood Johnson and Cleburne Clough Buel, copyright 1884-'87-'88 and 1894, by The Century Co., (a condensation of the earlier *Battles and Leaders of the Civil War*).

In addition, scores of individual credits, for both narrative and pictorial material, appear throughout this book.

To

DeWitt (Dee) Smith Jobe

of

Coleman's Scouts,

Forgotten martyr of the Confederacy,

Middle Tennessee.

Many good men who passed the spot
Would think of Jobe and the deal he got,
    Or cross themselves like nuns.
And say, on nights when the dark clouds toss,
Can you hear the clatter of a runnin' hoss?
      Oh, Lawdy! What's the matter? But nobody talks.
      The clatter stops and the ghost hoss walks.
It's the Yankees teachin' Dee Jobe who's boss
    At the point of 15 guns.

                    —Part III

FOREWORD

This volume, commemorative of the Civil War in Middle Tennessee, is a compilation of a four-part series by the *Nashville Banner's* EDWIN HUDDLESTON.

In these pages, replete with authentic maps, drawings and photographs, Huddleston graphically pictures the Civil War in Middle Tennessee from the day of secession until sundown on that bloody Dec. 16, 1864, when Gen. John B. Hood's once glorious Army of Tennessee was driven from the battlefields of Nashville, symbolized by Shy's Hill, the deathbed of the Confederacy.

Huddleston has established himself not only as a competent historian but by his absorbing, exciting and imaginative style, a writer of distinguished accomplishment.

The Banner is happy to share in the Civil War's Centennial through this chronicle of events which marked Middle Tennessee as ground forever hallowed by the lives and deeds and memories of those brave men, North and South, who fought and died here.

James G. Stahlman

Publisher, Nashville Banner.

"LEAVING HOME"   **By Gilbert Gaul**

CIVIL WAR NASHVILLE
Capital of a "Border State" that changed her mind in a hurry. . . .

The CIVIL WAR In
MIDDLE TENNESSEE
Part I, 1861-1862

SECEDE or not?

It was Jan. 9, 1861, in Nashville. The crisis men had long feared was at hand.

Soon Tennessee must take her stand, one way or the other. She had 30 days in which to think it over. Then there would be a referendum, an election, Feb. 9. A lot can happen in 30 days.

A lot would happen.

Mississippi was voting on secession today; Florida tomorrow; Alabama the next day.

Nineteen days had passed since South Carolina left the Union, exultantly, Dec. 20. Many Tennesseans were irked with their sister state. They thought she had somewhat precipitated this latest crisis in her headlong rush from the Union. Older Nashvillians remembered that South Carolina had tried the same thing back in the 1830s. They recalled the presidential toast of a Tennessean, Andrew Jackson, who'd put a stop to the effort: *"Our Federal Union, it must be preserved."*

It was far more serious this time.

CHARLESTON
MERCURY

EXTRA:

Passed unanimously at 1.15 o'clock, P. M., December 20th, 1860.

AN ORDINANCE

To dissolve the Union between the State of South Carolina and other States united with her under the compact entitled "The Constitution of the United States of America."

We, the People of the State of South Carolina, in Convention assembled, do declare and ordain, and it is hereby declared and ordained,

That the Ordinance adopted by us in Convention, on the twenty-third day of May, in the year of our Lord one thousand seven hundred and eighty-eight, whereby the Constitution of the United States of America was ratified, and also, all Acts and parts of Acts of the General Assembly of this State, ratifying amendments of the said Constitution, are hereby repealed; and that the union now subsisting between South Carolina and other States, under the name of "The United States of America," is hereby dissolved.

THE
UNION
IS
DISSOLVED!

—Courtesy Rare Book Room, Library of Congress

EXTRA!
South Carolina has left the Union. The Charleston Mercury breaks the news.

CHARLESTON FOR SECESSION! Hats go into the air. The city rejoices. But Middle Tennessee is in no such mood. In Tennessee, opinion is sharply divided.

LESS than two months had passed since election of Abraham Lincoln as President, Nov. 6, 1860, with not one popular vote cast for him in 10 Southern States. The South, long accustomed to eminence in national politics, sensed a decline of her power. Had she lost her voice in national affairs? Were states' rights about to be lost too?

And what of Fort Sumter, in the center of Charleston harbor? She was Federal property, in a seceded state. Federal troops held her. Would she be evacuated? And given to South Carolina?

"No, my friend," many a Middle Tennessean might have answered. *"Don't you know that would wreck the Republican Party in the North?"*

Its man was Lincoln. He was at his home in Springfield, Ill., and since election he'd been inclined to keep silent.

The South felt his election had placed her at the mercy of a party hostile to her interests and institutions. One of these was slavery, long under fire by abolitionists—who weren't at all new to Tennessee. Another was the South's belief in states' rights.

These things, plus secession, were three big heaps of dry powder. They might not explode for years unless touched by the fire of coercion. In short, would Lincoln's administration try to force South Carolina back into the Union?

If he sent supplies to reprovision Fort Sumter; if he tried to strengthen her garrison, would South Carolina shoot? Or would she be allowed to call the fort her own and depart from the Union in peace?

Even Horace Greeley, the abolitionist, only two months ago had strongly insisted upon the rights of the Southern states to secede. On Nov. 9, just 41 days before South Carolina seceded, he had written in the *New York Tribune:*

"If the Cotton States shall become satisfied that they can do better outside the Union than in it, we insist on letting them go in peace. The right to secede may be a revolutionary one, but it exists nevertheless."

Was the Union doomed? Nerves were on edge. Gloom overlay the land. And what had brought such a situation about?

One factor was this, with a significance unrealized by many at the time: The Democratic Party, one of the great bonds holding North and South together, had ripped apart at its convention.

It had split into Northern and Southern Democrats, largely on the issue of slavery in the territories. Each faction had nominated a candidate. This not only widened the sectional breach. It had also made the Democratic defeat of November a certainty.

Anything could happen now, and the nation was eyeing Mississippi.

As the cold morning wind swept up Nashville's Union Street from the Cumberland River, dapper young men in tall hats were reading the latest telegram in the *Nashville Patriot.* It came from Jackson, Miss., and concerned the voting on secession there:

"The committee on the ordinance of secession is now in caucus. The excitement and anxiety is intense."

Before the day was done, Mississippi had left the Union by a vote of 84 to 15, the second state to secede. Fireworks lit her night skies. Cannon boomed in celebration.

On the same day in Charleston, an unarmed merchant vessel, the Star of the West, tried to land supplies and 200 artillerymen to reinforce Fort Sumter.

—Frank Leslie's Illustrated Weekly

ABRAHAM LINCOLN
Will the new President favor coercion?

A SOUTH CAROLINA BATTERY fires on the Star of the West, an action that preceded Fort Sumter. Many people consider this the first shot of the Civil War.

—Harper's Weekly

AGEING General-in-Chief Winfield Scott had sent the ship. But a jittery Washington had changed its mind and tried to call her back. It was too late. She was out of touch with land and sailed on, easing into Charleston harbor with her lights out. Her expected arrival was common gossip in the streets of Charleston hours before she appeared. She was fired upon by secessionist batteries and driven back. (Some regard this as the first actual shooting of the Civil War.)

Fort Sumter wasn't fired upon and her guns stayed silent.

The North didn't get excited, but the Cotton States picked up an idea: It looked like the beginning of a coercive policy. (Actually, at that moment, the North didn't positively know what her policy would be. An example of this had been the change of orders to the Star of the West. After Lincoln's inaugural, maybe things would clear up.)

Tennessee was a Border State. She called herself such. There was even talk that a Border States Confederacy should be formed, to stand between the anger of the South and the rising ire of the North.

Wouldn't such a course be wise for Tennessee, many asked, with the state's political views so mixed? Advocates of the plan were reminding that Tennessee's native son, John Bell of Nashville, had carried Tennessee, Kentucky and Virginia in the recent presidential election.

This was true. Tennessee had given 69,274 votes to Bell (whose brilliant mind has been called *"one of the ablest Tennessee ever produced"*). A moderation candidate in an immoderate day, Bell's ticket had appealed to the neutral element and proved stronger than was expected. He won 600,000 votes against 1,800,000 for Lincoln. Bell came in third in the four-man race.

But Tennessee had given nearly as many votes, 64,709, to John C. Breckenridge of Kentucky, pro-slavery candidate of the Southern Democrats. He won second place in the national count, with 845,000 votes. For Stephen A. Douglas, candidate of the Northern Democrats, who had boldly attacked disunion, Tennessee cast 11,350 votes. Douglas ran fourth.

Tennessee was unlike other Southern States. She was a long, long Border State, of three distinct divisions, with 1,109,801 inhabitants, 24 per cent slave.

She had little slave holders, big slave holders, many people who hated slavery, and 7,500 freedmen. Tennessee was herself and in no mood to be dragged anywhere by what South Carolina and Mississippi did or didn't do.

Across the South, not one white man in 10 owned a slave. In Tennessee, with 34,844 slave-holders, the average was far less. In 1860, one Tennessean did have 499 slaves. But 21 per cent of Tennessee slave-holders had only one slave each. This had led to better relations between slave and master than in the Cotton States where slave ownership was often concentrated and directed by overseers.

The ratio of Negroes to whites in Middle Tennessee was one to three; in East Tennessee, one to 12, and in West Tennessee, three to five.

West Tennessee, with her cotton economy, bore a close likeness to the Deep South and had 44,019 slaves worth $32,769,507.

Mountainous East Tennessee, with its many small farmers and yeomen, was pro-Union and abolitionist. It had 11,862 slaves worth $7,480,920.

Middle Tennessee, with commerce and industry, had larger estates than East Tennessee and many farms of middle-size. She was more moderate in her views than either East or West. But she had 63,407 slaves worth $42,069,296, and her upper-class slave-holding citizenry strongly inclined to the views of the South.

So, Tennessee differed sharply from the lower South, where 3,000 or 4,000 families owned most of the slaves and enjoyed three-fourths of the income. One Georgia man, for example, had 1,000 slaves and raised cotton on 10,000 acres.

Such a concentration of wealth also meant a concentrated intellectual leadership, without powerful dissenters. This was plainly showing in the next two days after Mississippi left the Union.

Florida seceded Jan. 10, and Alabama, Jan. 11. Three days later, Jan. 14, the Crittenden Compromise failed in the U.S. House of Representatives by a vote of 113 to 80. (It would fail in the Senate, March 2, by a vote of 20 to 19.) This was the last desperate effort of the South to avert secession and war.

Georgia seceded within a week, Jan. 19; Louisiana on Jan. 26, and Texas, Feb. 1. The Confederacy began.

But on Feb. 4 Virginia (which had gone for Bell, remember) voted to stay in the Union.

Nashville rejoiced at Virginia's action. *"Thirty-four guns were fired yesterday morning from the summit of Capitol Hill, in honor of the conservative men of Virginia,"* said a Nashville newspaper on Friday, Feb. 8.

Tennessee would vote next day. And she would not be *"coerced by South Carolina,"* said an editorial, *"or by the Northern Abolitionists."*

A telegram appeared in Friday's *Patriot*. It had been received by W. H. Polk of Columbia, brother of the late President.

Tennessee Library and Archives

JOHN BELL
Ran against Lincoln

WINFIELD SCOTT
U.S. General-in-Chief

—Courtesy of Mrs. W. M. Carr

THE DAVIDSON COUNTY COURTHOUSE during the Civil War. Can you see its shattered windowpanes? At the right is the old City Hotel.

GOV. ISHAM G. HARRIS
Tennessee's Civil War Governor

THE TELEGRAM said:

"Take hope from Virginia.
Save Tennessee and the Union is safe."

The signers were J. J. Crittenden, author of the compromise try, and Douglas, who had opposed Lincoln.

The night before election great crowds rallied around the Public Square and the Market House, surging to and fro in front of the balustraded City Hotel in which lived Gov. Isham G. Harris, ardent secessionist, sampling the political wind. Tennessee then had no governor's mansion, and besides, where could the public pulse be better felt than at the City Hotel?

Outside Harris' window drums were beating, American Flags waving. The city was in a "perfect blaze of enthusiasm." Did Harris wonder how long this mood would last?

(The hour was not yet, but Gov. Harris would become Tennessee's greatest natural party leader since Andrew Jackson.)

Saturday, as Tennessee voted, a provisional Constitution of the Confederacy was being set up in Montgomery with Jefferson Davis as president. The fever didn't reach Tennessee.

She voted to STAY IN THE UNION. For secession: 57,798. Opposed, 69,387. The secession convention had lost by 11,589.

The majority margin had been picked up principally in strongly pro-Union East Tennessee. Middle Tennessee went mildly pro-Union, West Tennessee heavily for secession.

Two days later Lincoln left Springfield, enroute to Washington and his inaugural, making speeches along the way.

Lincoln called the crisis "artificial." What he said often made an unfavorable impression in the South. The faint, recent glow of optimism in the Border States began to dim again.

Lincoln's inaugural address came two weeks later, March 4. It was conciliatory.

He disclaimed any intention to interfere with slavery in the states. He denounced secession as anarchy, the acts of secession as legally void, and exhorted the seceded states to return.

But what of Fort Sumter? Lincoln asked his cabinet for written advice. Should it be reprovisioned? Only two members favored this. Five counseled evacuation (although some later changed their minds).

Fort Sumter's supplies were running low. Should Lincoln send food? Reinforcements? Both?

Nashville's John Bell had been in Washington, trying desperately, to the very last, to promote a compromising spirit, a temperate policy, on the part of the new administration.

How best could Lincoln maintain the status quo without appearing warlike? He decided to replenish the fort's provisions, peaceably—but by force if necessary. Notice was served upon the governor of South Carolina. It sounded like an ultimatum. He informed the Confederate government.

It was April 8. That day the Confederacy cut off the fort's food supply from Charleston and seized its mail. A confiscated official letter confirmed the South's suspicions. It mentioned a Yankee "expedition," enroute. It was coming by sea, under cover of warships — just in case. Charleston readied its harbor guns.

Excitement soared. Hundreds crowded to Charleston housetops to witness the expected attack. *"A battle is expected hourly,"* Nashvillians read on the morning of April 12.

Even then it was happening. At daylight Confederate batteries opened fire. A hand jerked a lanyard and a 10-inch mortar belched a round shell. It arched across the waters and exploded over the fort's parade ground.

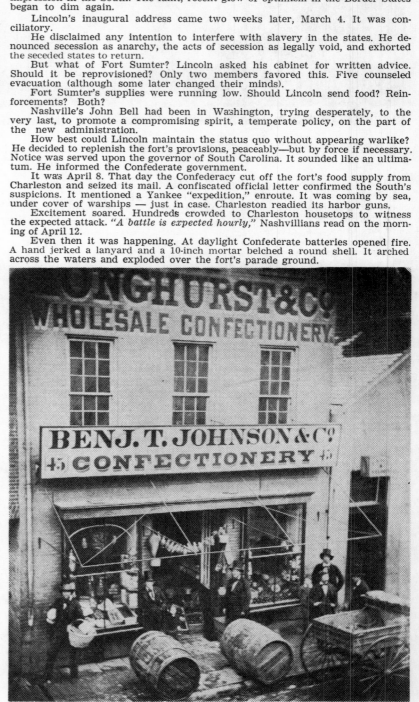

VENUS. "You say dey's fitin', 'Poleon."
NAPOLEON. "Yes, Marster say dey is, 'cause dey can't get no Coppermise."
VENUS. "Whar dey get dat?"
NAPOLEON. "In de Norf, I bl'ieve."
VENUS. "Well, my Lor! sooner en' to fite, dey better git de Coppermise, ef it cos' hundred Dollar; dis ting of Brudderin' fitin' is agin de Scripture!"

Fighting had begun when *Harper's Weekly* ran this cartoon. Slaves are discussing failure of the "Coppermise."

—Courtesy Tennessee Historical Society

Lower Union Street, Nashville, about 1859. Notice high hats of men. The barrels hold candy.

INTERIOR OF FORT SUMTER during bombardment. (In the final hours of defense, as her guns faltered, then fired again, Southern sympathizers cheered the Federals for their spunk.)

THE CIVIL WAR had begun. It was 4:30 a.m.

The Confederacy poured 2,500 rounds of shot and shell into the fort. She bravely returned the fire. Her barracks burned; she was badly damaged. Relieving ships could not enter the harbor. No fatality occurred on either side as a direct result of the bombardment.

On April 14, Fort Sumter surrendered. Rage swept the North. The Deep South celebrated, and Memphis joined in. In parts of the Border States, where armies must first collide, many persons were praying.

In neutral Kentucky, a Confederate flag went fluttering up at blue-blooded Lexington, over a hemp and wool factory owned by a 36-year-old veteran of the War with Mexico. He was a handsome six-footer with a Van Dyke beard and a taste for luxurious living. His name was John Hunt Morgan and before long his name would be a household word in Middle Tennessee. He let the flag stay up.

Next day Lincoln called for 75,000 volunteers, to serve three months. The news jangled on Southern nerves like an alarm-bell. Did it not suggest an invasion? But in his proclamation, Lincoln denied any such intention.

"For some time now," said a Nashville newspaper, "it has been a matter of considerable difficulty to determine Mr. Lincoln's policy . . . Let the Border States stand firm, as long as there is a plank left of the old Ship of State—"

Then Lincoln's Secretary of War asked Tennessee for two regiments.

That did it. Gov. Harris replied:

"Tennessee will not furnish a single man for purposes of coercion, but 50,000 if necessary for the defense of our rights and those of our Southern brothers."

In his anger, Harris almost wrote "75,000," then marked it out. (He could have written the bigger figure with accuracy. By the end of July he would turn over to the Confederacy 100,000 men.) It was April 17.

—Harper's Weekly

Charleston housetops during the bombardment of Fort Sumter. Men cheered. Women wept. War had begun.

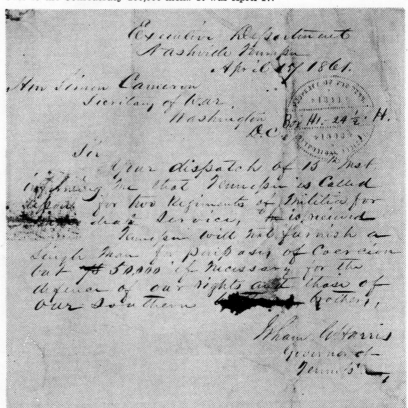

—Courtesy Tennessee Historical Society

Here you see a facsimile of Gov. Harris' historic letter of April 17, 1861: "Not a single man . . . for coercion. . . ."

13

GEN. ROBERT E. LEE
Beloved "Marse Robert"

A MILD SHOCK FOR OUR VIRTUOUS FRIEND, MR. JOHN BULL.

"NO MORE COTTON!" says Jack-in-the-box, to a startled John Bull, as the North begins her blockade of Southern ports. From *Harper's Weekly*.

THE HOUR had come for Tennessee. As many saw it, the North and the new administration had shown its hand — a coercive policy, which the South had suspected and feared since Lincoln's election.

For six months Tennessee had withheld judgment. Now doubt was gone. The call for troops; the attempt to relieve Fort Sumter — wasn't that proof? South Carolina and the others would not be allowed to depart in peace? Then goodbye to states' rights, if that's the ticket!

Before sunset, Virginia had seceded.

In the lightning-like change of public opinion, Tennessee's majority was ready to secede almost overnight. Harris knew it, and in those cataclysmic hours he would emerge as Tennessee's "strong man," the "War Governor," perhaps the most energetic of all Southern governors in promoting the military cause of the Confederacy.

As the political star of Harris soared toward its zenith, that of Bell began to set. Bell was a loyal Southerner, but he had hoped too long, trusted too long, that Lincoln's policy would be different.

That hope, that trust, had suddenly been jerked away, like a lifted gangplank from the Ship of State. Bell was left in political mid-air, falling—dropping into political obscurity.

Another boat was sailing. In Tennessee, for years, its captain would be Gov. Harris. On April 18, he called for the legislature to meet again, quickly, April 25, because of an *"alarming and dangerous usurpation of power by the President . . ."*

"The political excitement of the city continues unabated," a Nashville newspaper commented April 19. *"Business here is in a measure suspended. The people are congregating in the streets. Speeches are being made at many points. Every night large meetings are held, in which the general sentiment is that the Union is irretrievably at an end. Several volunteer companies are in the process of formation. Enlistments are rapid.*

"From all the surrounding counties in this division of the state, the people generally accept the issue of war as already determined, and are prepared to accept the consequences, whatever they may be . . ."

Before nightfall, all Southern ports had been ordered blockaded. If successful, this would shut off all supply of cotton to Great Britain, which the South hoped to have as an ally. (She seemed to forget that England would need Northern wheat about as much as Southern cotton.)

Events were coming like a rockslide now. In Virginia, Robert E. Lee was made a major general and placed in command of Virginia's forces. In Nashville, John Bell stood on the steps of the Davidson County Courthouse and made a speech, his political swansong.

It is night. The crowd is big, and it has great respect for whatever Bell may say.

His speech is to this effect:

I besought Mr. Lincoln not to misunderstand Tennessee's vote of Feb. 9. But neither Mr. Lincoln nor any member of his cabinet gave any definite assurance of the precise policy to be followed concerning the seceded states. Now that policy is obvious . . .

GOVERNOR MAGOFFIN'S NEUTRALITY means holding THE COCK OF THE WALK (*Uncle Sam*) while THE CONFEDERATE CAT (*Jeff Davis*) kills off his Chickens.

"Columbia Awake at Last"—This cartoon appeared in *Harper's* the week Tennessee voted to secede. Columbia, Constitution in hand, grabs the throat of a Rebel who is labeled "treason" and "secession."

Both sides violated and criticized Kentucky's early efforts at neutrality. Here *Harper's* accuses Kentucky's Gov. Beriah Magoffin of aiding the "Confederate Cat."

"A SHORT BLANKET" was the title *Harper's* gave this cartoon, ridiculing the Confederate Army as too small to defend its far-flung border and coasts. The foot of the Rebel is tagged "Savannah," a suggestion that the Georgia coast was exposed.

BELL, it seems, had bought a pig in a poke from Mr. Lincoln. And when Bell looked in the poke he found coercion.

Bell has had enough of Mr. Lincoln and his cabinet.

Bell is declaring himself a Rebel. He is casting his lot with the South, and what he says will be a terrific boost to the Confederate cause in Tennessee.

But in saying it, Bell is cutting his political throat. His change of view has come too late.

For Bell, the decision was enormous. It has even been said that it cost him the Presidency (but big "ifs" are involved in this view).

It has been written that, had Bell stuck to his long-held view of neutrality and moderation, the national situation would have put him on the ticket with Lincoln in 1864; that Bell would have become vice president and therefore, upon Lincoln's assassination in 1865, would have become president instead of another Tennessean, Andrew Johnson. (In this case, a national shrine might be on lower Broadway today, where Bell long lived. Instead, bring up his name and somebody will likely ask, "Who was John Bell, anyway?")

Soon, Harris asked the legislators for a "declaration of independence" from the Union. Should Tennessee join the Confederacy? He recommended both actions. The election was set for June 8. The legislators didn't wait for the balloting. Public opinion was storming on, at the heels of bellwether Harris.

On May 1, the legislature authorized him to enter into a military alliance with the Confederacy. Four days later it authorized the raising and equipping of 55,000 soldiers, with $5 million in bonds to foot the bill.

On June 6, Mayor R. B. Cheatham of Nashville ordered formation of a home guard (one company from each ward) because, he said, the country seems "*inevitably doomed to a general civil war . . .*" The election was two days ahead.

"*How will you vote today?*" a Nashville newspaper asked on June 8. "*The idea of an armed neutrality,*" it continued, "*has been demonstrated impracticable by the course of Kentucky . . . Tennessee cannot maintain an independent attitude. She must unite with the South eventually. Then why delay? Certainly our strength is in union with our friends.*" Nashville was bracing for war.

"Drums! Drums!" exclaimed an advertisement. One man on Union Street had 250 for sale. Down at a stable on Front Street, 80 cavalry horses were urgently wanted. And who had old rags to be made into paper for the South?

Also for sale were military books, a flood of them, "gray and blue cloth, and gold lace," army blankets, tin cups, skillets, army kettles. Some merchants were switching to a cash basis because of the war gamble. Trade went on.

A German baker was offering 12 loaves of bread for $1. "Several likely families" of Negroes were for sale down at the slave market, No. 8 Market St., (Second Avenue).

The voting in Nashville was quiet. But, "*in truth,*" one man wrote later, "*the public pulse was surging and the public brain was reeling.*"

The result surprised no one. Secede! Tennessee would become the last of 11 Confederate States to leave the Union. For separation, 102,172. Opposed, 47,238. What a change in just four months, since Feb. 9, when she had stood faithfully by the Federal Ship of State!

Biggest change of public opinion had come in Middle Tennessee — 57,767 for separation; opposing, 7,147. East and West Tennessee stood their earlier ground, but with bigger majorities — West Tennessee, four-to-one for secession (29,625 to 7,168); East Tennessee, more than two-to-one for sticking with the Union (32,923 to 14,780).

Items of war were being boldly advertised in Nashville newspapers June 8, 1861, as Tennessee voted for a second time on the issue of secession. The advertisements leave little doubt as to the public mood.

"*There never was a quieter election held in this city,*" one Nashville newspaper said next day. "*It showed the people were acting with calmness and determination — that they were not unmindful of the awful responsibility they had assumed . . .*"

Another let fly a broadside:

"*Who would have believed, even two months ago, that the great North . . . would soon make the humiliating discovery that it cannot live without the South? Why, we were, at best, a little fag-end of the nation. They had all the money, all the shipping, all the commerce, all the cities, the great men, the manufactures, the Constitution, the railroads . . .*"

"*But the very moment we begin to turn upon our heel, such another cry of distress is heard. Did you ever! The whole great North bellows and blubbers as if it had lost its Mammy! It can't live or get along without the dear blessed, rascally, villainous, fostering care of the South — Did you ever!*"

"FALL IN FOR SOUP!" From a drawing in *Century Magazine*. Notice the varying ages of the soldiers and the use of barrels as chimneys.

"WELL, DEAR sister North, you'll have to try it alone. We've made our arrangements to go. It's too late now. We have taken a through ticket and checked our baggage with the C.S.A. . . . So, goodbye. But such cries of distress! And then, don't you think, the jade wants to fight us as we go!"

A week later, about 4:30 p.m. on June 17, the Dunlap Zouaves lowered the American Flag on Capitol Hill and ran up the "Stars and Bars."

Next day Gov. Harris told the Tennessee Senate and House, "In obedience to your act of May 6th, I have caused to be organized . . . 21 regiments of infantry now in the field, 10 regiments of artillery companies now in the process of organization . . . and a sufficient number of cavalry companies to compose one regiment. Organization of an engineer corps is nearly completed. In addition, we have three regiments mustered into the service of the Confederate States, now in Virginia . . . and a number stationed at Pensacola . . ."

On June 24, Harris signed a proclamation that Tennessee was a "free and independent government." For four weeks thereafter, Tennessee would stand on her own feet, outside the Union and not yet formally within the Confederacy.

Meanwhile, 10 days earlier, on June 14, a swarthy, high-cheeked man, 40 years old, with wavy iron-grey hair, might have been seen enlisting as a private in Memphis. He had a short black chin beard, a quiet way of speaking, and wide-set eyes of deep gray-blue that held a calm and level look.

He was a wealthy planter and slave trader, worth perhaps $1½ million, and he'd made it himself, without benefit of "silver-spoon" background. His name was Nathan Bedford Forrest, born in Chapel Hill, Tenn., the son of a blacksmith. Gov. Harris "knew him well."

GEN. LEONIDAS POLK
The Bishop-General

DOUBTLESS Tennessee's governor knew the private very well indeed. Harris soon obtained permission, with the aid of Gen. Leonidas Polk, for Forrest to raise a cavalry battalion.

Forrest bought the equipment himself in Louisville. Out of "neutral" Kentucky he smuggled 500 pistols labeled "potatoes." (Eight companies would be ready to ride with him in October.)

"I went to war," Forrest would say years later, "because my vote had been unable to preserve the peace. I took a through ticket, and I fought and lost as much as anybody else — certainly as much as I could."

Five weeks after Forrest's enlistment, Tennessee was admitted to the Confederate States of America, July 22 — second day of the First Battle of Bull Run, near Manassas, Va.

Tennesseans were there, sent by Gov. Harris in response to Virginia's call for help. Yankee congressmen had come out from Washington to watch, expecting to see something of a picnic victory. Instead, Union troops panicked and streamed back toward Washington, nearly running over the congressmen. Union casualties were about 2,700. Confederate casualties, around 1,950.

The North was astounded. Yankee congressmen pulled themselves together and authorized a levy of 500,000 men.

Gen. Polk, Episcopal Bishop of Louisiana, had been placed in command of military operations in Tennessee by his West Point schoolmate, President Davis. The bishop-general (cousin of the late President Polk) donned uniform while the North cried out in shock that a bishop should do such a warlike thing. On July 13, Gen. Polk took over in Memphis and began to fortify strategic points on the Mississippi.

He foresaw the battleground agony that would be Tennessee's. He foresaw a struggle for her rivers and roads, her railroads and mountain passes. And he was right. In a short time Federal gunboats were assembling along the Ohio River.

—From "First With the Most" Forrest by
Robert Selph Henry, McCowat-Mercer Press
NATHAN BEDFORD FORREST
As a Civilian

—Courtesy National Archives, Photo by Mathew Brady
JEFFERSON DAVIS
President of the Confederacy

IT LOOKED like a plan to invade Tennessee through Kentucky, by the triple-track of rivers that led toward the heart of the South — the Tennessee, the Cumberland and the Mississippi. It looked like a plan to cut the Confederacy in half by controlling the Mississippi.

It was all these things, and it had to be thwarted.

A Confederate line of defense, the Line of the Cumberland, was established across the state in September by brilliant Gen. Albert Sidney Johnston (who had been Polk's roommate at West Point).

It ran directly east from Columbus on the Mississippi (in Kentucky) to Mill Springs on the Upper Cumberland, then southeast to Cumberland Gap in Union-minded East Tennessee where the terrain seemed to beckon invasion from the North. An approximate center would be established at Bowling Green.

Who, with the raw recruits available, could hold such a line — and have enough left to defend the Confederate coastline? With such a far-flung land to defend, how could the war last any time? (The North lampooned the idea with a cartoon of a grizzled man in bed, beneath a blanket far too short.)

In Memphis, Gen. Polk was eyeing Columbus as the keystone of Mississippi defense. Doing the same thing was a little-known Union general by the name of U.S. Grant, at Cairo, Ill. A Union fleet and army was there and Grant was in command. He meant to grab Columbus Sept. 4.

The Southern bishop-general beat him to it. Polk seized Columbus on the night of Sept. 3. Grant then took second choice, Paducah, Ky., at the mouth of the Tennessee. He also took Smithland at the mouth of the Cumberland.

The news made many a Middle Tennessean stop and think. But there was Fort Donelson on the Cumberland, Fort Henry on the Tennessee—just 12 miles apart — and incomplete Fort Heiman across the river from Henry. Why worry unduly?

ULYSSES S. GRANT
In the tumult of war, a new name . . .

GEN. FELIX ZOLLICOFFER
"Governor-maker"

—Courtesy Tennessee Library and Archives
Zollicoffer's home stood on the present site of the Andrew Jackson Hotel. From this house he went forth to war in East Tennessee, with 4,000 men.

POLK HAD 11,000 men at Columbus. The pro-South Kentuckian, Gen. Simon Bolivar Buckner (former West Point instructor) left Nashville Sept. 14 for Bowling Green, occupying it with 4,000 men four days later. Gen. Felix K. Zollicoffer had taken 4,000 men to Cumberland Gap a few weeks earlier.

Zollicoffer, a beloved Nashville journalist, former congressman and former state comptroller, had departed in August from his serene old house with an Old World air which stood on High Street (now Sixth Avenue N., where the Andrew Jackson Hotel stands). Handsome and magnetic, Zollicoffer was no professional soldier. He had other qualities, including diplomacy, which the Confederacy thought badly needed in the uplands which had voted a 20,000 Union majority. And his men "worshiped the ground he walked on."

A Whig orator and often called the "governor-maker," Zollicoffer had stumped New York in support of Bell for president. But after Lincoln's call for troops to coerce the South, Zollicoffer, like Bell, had become a "Rebel."

At midnight, Sept. 19, a Federal recruiting post moved quietly into Lexington, Ky., and occupied the fairgrounds there. It was whispered that certain members of the fashionable Lexington Rifles were to be arrested, including its captain. This was Morgan, the man who had been flying the Confederate Flag since Fort Sumter.

Hearing that Buckner had reached Bowling Green, Morgan began to make his plans. At dusk on Sept. 20, two wagon loads of hay moved down Lexington's Main Street. They rolled past Union soldiers who were strolling contendedly on the brick sidewalks. Deep in the hay were rifles. Morgan and his cavalry pals soon would be joining Buckner.

All words had failed.

The guns were waiting.

For Middle Tennessee, and for many friends in Kentucky, the big blue chips were down.

Across the land the leaves were turning gold. For many Tennesseans it would be the last autumn. For thousands more, ahead was heartbreak and hardscrabble for the remainder of their years upon earth.

As the leaves came down, hammers banged, saws whined. Mills were rising to make powder, guns, military stores. Since May, a farsighted Clarksville firm had been making serviceable cannon. Since June, 231 Nashville ladies had been working on contributions of all kinds, for the field, camp, hospitals.

Since mid-July Nashville factories had been making 100,000 percussion caps daily. By Oct. 1, a total of 250 guns and 1,300,000 percussion caps were being manufactured in the state.

ONE SOUTHERN man of every four would wear a uniform; in the North, one of every five. From farms and villages and towns they were coming, from mansions and modest homes and shanties, with whatever arms they had.

And why were they coming from modest homes and shanties, as well as from mansions? Why wasn't it a rich man's war? What was the nameless thing that bound them together, the slaved and slaveless? What was the magic of their common bond which lay like a light over both the Deep South and the Border States?

It was something which even the noble Lincoln, at the outset of war, apparently did not understand. It was that they were weary unto disgust of trying to live with the North. They wanted a bill of divorcement. They were sick of sharing the bed and willing to die to escape it. In today's terms, they were "fed up."

John Bell is a case in point.

Slavery was a factor, yes. But perhaps the very last Johnny Reb among them would have been startled if accused of going to war in defense of slavery. Far more was involved. Foremost in their minds was rage against coercion. Quit pushing!

The South, with 9,000,000 people — including 3,500,000 slaves — was going to war against 22,000,000 people in the North. The South, with 10,000 factories, was going to war against a region with 100,000 factories.

With $47 million in bank deposits, the South was going to war against a people who had $189 million on deposit. With $5.4 billion in property, the South was going to war against a people who had $11 billion in property.

"War'll be over in no time," said various Northern politicians. *"Ninety days ought to do it."*

They were poor prophets.

The war would last four years, almost to the day.

—Photograph by Thomas Nebbia, Copyright 1961, Courtesy **National Geographic** Magazine

A TIME OF PARTING . . .

END OF 1861

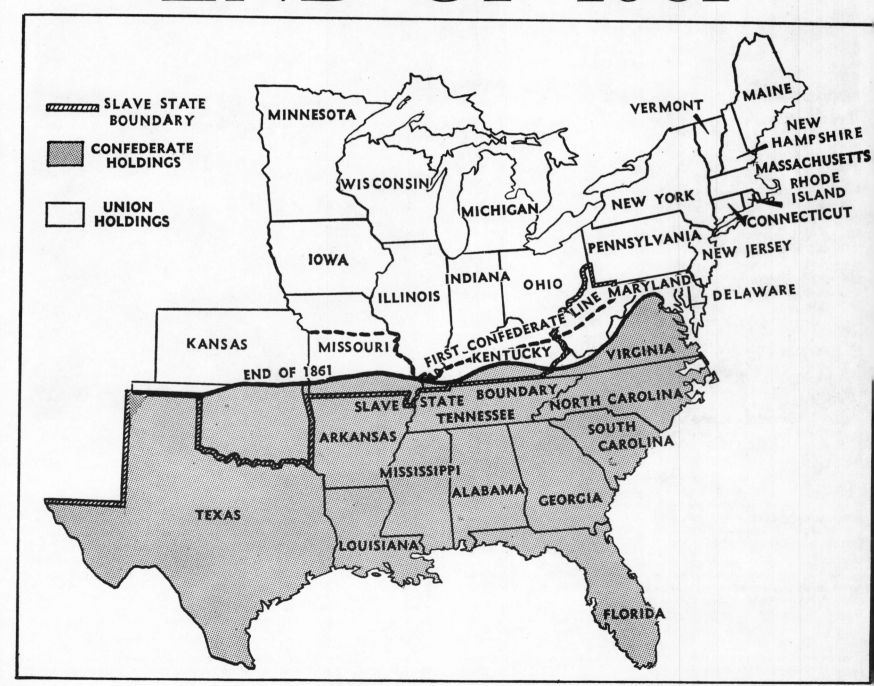

SLAVE STATE BOUNDARY

CONFEDERATE HOLDINGS

UNION HOLDINGS

THE YEAR 1862

IN SUCH A NIGHTMARE of rain and mud, Zollicoffer struck at the foe in Kentucky. This drawing, "Dragging Artillery," shows six-horse Federal units.

—Harper's Pictorial History of the Civil War

AHEAD was the foe, sound asleep.

Rain was pouring and the night pitch-black. Guns bogged in the deep sucking mud near Fishing Creek, Ky., just over the East Tennessee line.

Since midnight the Rebels had marched and struggled and sworn, dragging the guns on, six miles, toward Logan's Cross Roads on the north side of the Cumberland, across the river from Mill Springs.

It was far past midnight now, Jan. 19, 1862. Rain was sluicing from the white raincoat of their leader, Gen. Zollicoffer. He must have guessed that the darkness would be gone far too soon.

The rain began to slacken. Fog came in with the dawn. The Federal pickets of Gen. George H. Thomas were turning out for roll call as Zollicoffer delivered the first assault. He was well out in front with two regiments, his men strung out across a mile of mud behind him. Then the thunder and screams of battle for three hours.

At the height of it all Zollicoffer rode far ahead of his troops, squarely up against the enemy. He was near-sighted, and he turned to give a command— to a Federal colonel.

The colonel put a bullet in Zollicoffer's chest. Nashville's knight of honor fell, the first Confederate general to die in battle.

The news flashed through the cold and hungry ranks, to exhausted men with flintlocks already useless from rain. They broke, fell back. Behind them Confederate Gen. George B. Crittenden had thrown his full column into the fray. But the tide had turned with retreat of Zollicoffer's men. It couldn't be stopped.

They were fleeing and fast. The Federals, pausing to replenish their ammunition, couldn't overtake them. The Rebels were leaving their supplies, their wounded, their venerated dead.

Zollicoffer lay in a fence corner, his face mud-spattered, fog swirling about him. Yankees were rushing past. Some paused and snipped off locks of his hair. Others simply yanked out locks.

Gen. Thomas stopped the indignities. He ordered the body prepared for decent burial. Later, under a flag of truce, it would be sent through the lines to Lebanon. It would lie in state in Nashville, in the House of Representatives, while Nashville shuddered with grief and rage.

> *"First in the fight, and first in the arms*
> *Of the white-winged angel of glory—"*

The words would long be familiar to Middle Tennessee families, as a first two lines by Harry Flash, Confederate poet.

Nashville was staggered with shock. Shock at the fall of the right wing

—From a sketch in Frank Leslie's Illustrated Weekly

DEATH OF GEN. ZOLLICOFFER

of the Line of the Cumberland, and anger, too, at Crittenden. He was blamed.

Crittenden's East Tennessee army was reeling back, shattered, no longer an army, its horses, its guns, all behind in the mud and fog of Kentucky, and Crittenden was coming with them. (He would be bitterly criticized for it all, and unjustly, because Richmond, the Capital of the Confederacy, had sent him too late to correct the military misjudgments of the gallant Zollicoffer whose bright career had never included the checkmate trainings for war.)

Night came. A little steamboat put the remnants of the army of 4,000 back across the Cumberland, to the south side, where Crittenden had warned Zollicoffer to stay.

They lurched on deep into Tennessee, at last making camp at Chestnut Mound in Smith County, about 80 miles from Nashville. The Confederate right wing was no more.

Union gunboats advancing up the Tennessee River to attack Fort Henry. Puffs of smoke come from its guns.

Fort Henry is overwhelmed. Here you see its bombardment and capture, Feb. 6, 1862.

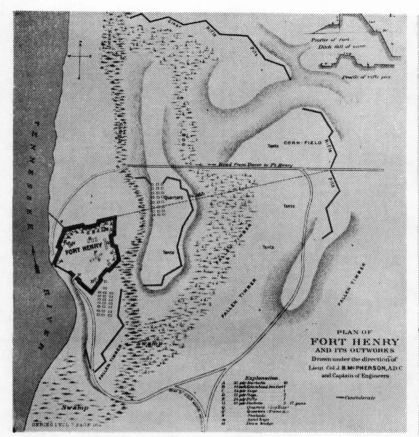

FORT HENRY. The double line curving northeast, then due east, is the road to Dover.

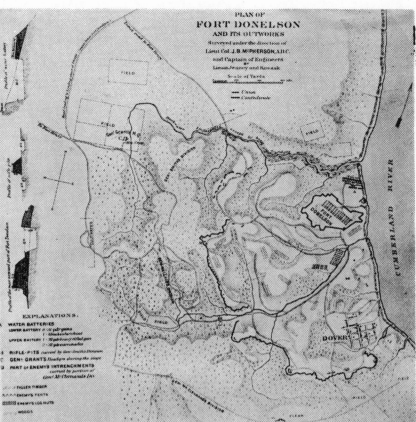

FORT DONELSON. The largest rectangle, upper left, indicates Grant's headquarters.

GEN. JOHNSTON now had only 14,000 men under his immediate command. They were facing 40,000 in Kentucky under Gen. Don Carlos Buell, newly placed in charge of the Federals' Department of the Ohio.

In the next few days, two grim messages would be sent. One went from Gen. Johnston, Jan. 22, to the Confederate capital: *"All the resources of the Confederacy are now needed for the defense of Tennessee."* But Richmond was preoccupied with the war in Virginia.

The other went from Gen. Grant at Cairo, Ill., Jan. 28, to Gen. Henry W. Halleck in St. Louis: *"With permission, I will take Fort Henry on the Tennessee . . ."*

Fort Henry and Fort Donelson were still incomplete. So was Fort Heiman in Kentucky, just across the river from Fort Henry. Not many miles away a fleet of Federal gunboats waited, under Adm. A. H. Foote. When rivers rose, the gunboats would strike.

The rivers were rising. Transports took Grant up the Tennessee with 17,000 men. It was Feb. 2. Along went seven gunboats.

The lookout at Fort Henry saw them coming. Through the morning mist of Feb. 4 the naval parade seemed endless. Grant sent 6,000 men up the west bank. They took unoccupied Fort Heiman. Its men had gone to reinforce Fort Henry. By dusk of Feb. 5, all other troops were ashore on the east bank. The gunboats eased up the flooded stream.

Guns of Fort Henry spoke, nine on the river side, four on the land. The gunboats moved back downstream. Darkness fell. The river still rose, inching toward the feet of men armed with shotguns, fowling pieces, and muskets used under Andrew Jackson in the War of 1812. Which would reach the men first, high water or the foe?

In Appreciation

For assistance in compiling Part I The Banner expresses its appreciation to Col. Campbell H. Brown, state executive director, Civil War Centennial Commission; Dr. Robert H. White, state historian; Robert T. Quarles Jr., former state archivist, retired; Mrs. Hermione Embry, Mrs. Gertrude Parsley and Miss Kendall Cram, of the Tennessee State Library; Miss Bettye Bell of the Tennessee Room, Nashville Public Library; to the Joint University Libraries and the Library of Congress.

Published works often consulted, which have been most helpful include:
The Army of Tennessee, by Stanley F. Horn, published by The Bobbs-Merrill Company, 1949; Dr. White's Messages of the Governors of Tennessee, 1857-1869, Vol. V, Tennessee Historical Commission, 1959; "First With the Most" Forrest, by Robert Selph Henry, McCowat-Mercer Press, Jackson, Tenn.; Official Records of the War of the Rebellion, Washington; and "The Attitude of Tennesseans Toward the Union, 1847-1861," by Mary Emily Robertson Campbell, Vantage Press, 1961. Mrs. Campbell, a native of Robertson County, began her book as a master's thesis at Vanderbilt University.

Like acknowledgement is made, in gratitude, to the following published works: Lincoln Takes Command, by John Shipley Tilley, University of North Carolina Press, Chapel Hill, 1941; Braxton Bragg, General of the Confederacy, by Don C. Seitz, Columbia, S.C., 1924; A History of Tennessee and Tennesseans, by Will T. Hale and Dixon L. Merritt, Lewis Publishing Co., Chicago, 1913 (eight volumes); Co. "Aytch"—First Tennessee Regiment, by Samuel R. Watkins, Nashville, 1882; Life of Albert Sidney Johnston, by William Preston Johnston, Appleton, New York, 1878; The Battle of Stone's River, by A. F. Stevenson, Osgood, Boston, 1884; Autobiography of Henry M. Stanley, Houghton Mifflin Co., Boston, 1906; Morgan and His Raiders, by Cecil Fletcher Holland, The Macmillan Company, 1942; The Bold Cavaliers, by Dee Alexander Brown, J. P. Lippincott Company, Philadelphia and New York, 1959; The Rebel Raider, by Howard Swiggett, Garden City Publishing Co., Garden City, N.Y., 1937; History of Morgan's Cavalry, by Basil Duke, Cincinnati, 1867;

The Confederate Veteran, 40 volumes, Nashville, 1893-1932; Southern Bivouac, six volumes, Louisville, 1886-1887, and The Taylor-Trotwood Magazine, Nashville, 1905-1910.

The site had been poorly chosen. If better-situated Fort Heiman had been completed first of all, the story might have been different.

It was too late now.

Gen. Lloyd Tilghman, commanding both Fort Henry and Fort Donelson, decided to yield Fort Henry but not his men. Under Col. Adolphus Heiman, German-born able soldier and Nashville architect, they would march to reinforce Fort Donelson. To cover retreat, less than 70 men would stay behind and man the guns of falling Fort Henry.

The gunboats returned at dawn. Bombardment resumed. Gen. Tilghman himself had remained. He manned a gun, one of four that still boomed from the fort, against 34 on the gunboats. Beyond the smoke, his men were hurrying on to Fort Donelson.

Hurrying, too, were Grant and his men, floundering through the bottoms toward Fort Henry. They didn't arrive until afternoon, after Fort Henry's surrender to Flag Officer Foote.

The first battle in Tennessee, between Federals and Confederates, had been lost.

Nashville began to have chills and fevers. With Fort Henry on the Tennessee gone, she suddenly saw Fort Donelson, far down the Cumberland, as the gate to her own front yard. If Fort Donelson fell, both Bowling Green and Columbus, Ky., would fall too. Down might roll Buell, out of Kentucky. But if Grant could be smashed, Buell would have to fall back to protect the Ohio!

Reinforcements were rushed to Fort Donelson. Gen. Simon B. Buckner arrived, and Gen. Gideon J. Pillow, who took charge. The unknown Col. Forrest was there. Gen. John B. Floyd soon assumed technical command.

On Feb. 12, through bright sunshine, Grant began his march upon the fort. His forces would be increased eventually to 27,000. The day was balmy. Some soldiers cast aside their heavy clothing. That night they began to deploy about the fort. Its garrison had been increased to around 15,000.

The weather changed. On the afternoon of the 13th a cold drizzle began. It turned to sleety rain. The temperature dropped to 10 degrees. An icy gale roared in with sleet and snow, across a cruel terrain of ridges and creeks aflood with backwater. Artillery roared and musketry crackled. Sharpshooters were busy. The men could make no fires. Lights would draw death.

Earlier, artillery had ignited the woods. Many of the prostrate wounded died horribly. No one could aid them, lest the ridges spew bullets again. The long night seemed endless.

Meanwhile, miles away, in the same terrible weather, 14,000 men were stringing out from Bowling Green toward Nashville. Some were afoot, some astride the finest horses in the land. Bowling Green was being evacuated. Gen. Johnston dared not leave his main army there, with both flanks being rolled up and Gen. Buell eyeing him from the North. Pull out!

The movement had begun days before in better weather, a march of desperation. Many a man would slump by the road as the shivering host trudged south. As it moved through the awful night, a little black mare came along with it, sure-footedly picking her way over the frozen ruts on "hooves almost as small as a clenched fist."

One of Fort Henry's attackers, from a photograph.

A 42-pound gun explodes inside Fort Henry during bombardment.

THE MARE'S name was Black Bess, her coat like black satin and her muzzle was "small enough to drink from a goblet." Astride her rode Capt. Morgan, and Bess seemed to understand almost every word he said.

They were destined for fame, mare and rider. Each seemed made for the other. Together they represented the South's great treasure. Its cavalry. The North could never touch it. Black Bess was part of the reason, a fast fine cavalry horse — the one war material the South would have plenty of, for the first two years.

Around Bess men were swearing. When would they fight? Morgan didn't know. There was rumor they might get a battle. Enemy forces were reported hellbent for Nashville to head off the Confederate Army at the Nashville suspension bridge. Would there be a fight at Woodland Street and the river?

If Fort Donelson fell, what a race! Who'd get to the bridge first? What a stampede, with everybody heading that way! As Morgan stroked the sleet from the mane of Black Bess, he found the moisture turning to snow. Many a man, he knew, would never see the sunrise. Many a man would freeze to death before this night had passed.

At Fort Donelson on the morning of the 14th, two inches of snow had made the world white. A white world spotted with blood. Both sides were numb with cold. The fighting had quieted but not on the riverfront.

The whole flotilla was there, expecting another triumph. Gunboats steamed to within 150 yards of the batteries. Confederates ripped off their armor like "bark from the trees," scoring 180 hits in 370 shots.

Flag Officer Foote was aboard the St. Louis. The Rebels ripped it with 57 hits. Her pilot wheel was swept away. Foote was twice wounded. Every vessel was damaged. The flotilla retired with 54 dead and wounded. In the Confederate batteries not a man had been killed.

Grant's army had now grown to 27,000. The three Confederate brigadiers felt they were being squeezed into a trap against the river. They sent their left flank to strike the Federals' right which reeled back against the center. This opened the escape road to Nashville. Here was a chance to march out. The Confederates didn't take it.

Why? Perhaps it was a failure in command, perhaps a poorly coordinated battle plan. Perhaps as always, "Too many cooks spoil the broth." In the final hours her commanders were Floyd, Pillow and Buckner.

Grant, returning from a visit to the wounded Foote, struck the weakened Confederate right wing and took a part of the breastworks. The Confederates were frosted and hungry. Could another battle extricate them?

The night of the 15th the three Confederate generals wrangled at the Dover tavern. Give up or not?

Somebody sent for the obscure Col. Forrest whose cavalry had been aiding. Upon arrival the swarthy man from Memphis heard them discussing surrender. He was amazed. He urged Floyd to march his men out. He guaranteed no Yankee cavalry would bother the infantry's rear.

His protests were swept aside. The generals believed the roads closed, under three feet of water. Those lights on the hills, aren't they enemy campfires, overlapping the roads? No, Forrest said, not all are campfires. The winds have whipped up old embers.

Gunboat attack on Fort Donelson. Her guns reply. Her flag still flies.

EXPLOSION of a gun aboard the gunboat Carondelet during the attack on Fort Donelson.

STORMING of Fort Donelson's outworks, by the Illinois Volunteers, Feb. 13, 1862.

ONE OF FORREST'S aides came in, cold from reconnaissance and gobbling hot bacon. He stood at attention.

"These people," Forrest said, "are talking about surrendering. And I'm going out of this place before they do if I have to bust hell wide open!"

The aide gulped. The bacon went down. He rushed out and began to wake Forrest's men. Get outa here!

Forrest led his cavalrymen out through the icy backwaters, and behind nearly every horseman clung a gleeful infantryman. Many others simply walked off, including Gen. Bushrod R. Johnson who made his way unchallenged through enemy lines.

Perhaps 3,000 escaped by steamboats. At dawn a steamer arrived with 400 men as reinforcements. They were just in time to be surrendered. Floyd commandeered the boat. It ferried him and his Virginians to safety. Pillow and his staff escaped by using an old scow.

Buckner penned a note to Grant, asking to discuss surrender terms.

They were old friends from West Point days. Six years before, when Grant had needed money to pay his hotel bill, he had appealed to Buckner, in New York. Buckner had restored Grant's credit, effecting release of his baggage. Would Grant remember?

Grant's answer: *"No terms, except unconditional surrender, can be accepted. I propose to move immediately upon your works."*

Buckner submitted. Soon, at the Dover tavern (now often called "Surrender House") about 11,000 Confederates stacked their arms. Dejectedly they waited for transports which would take them to Northern prisons.

They had successfully carried out every battle mission given them. They had even tried to hold back the bugler as he went forward with his flag of truce. Yet they were being surrendered. It seemed incredible.

Did they wish the cavalry colonel had been their commander? Instead of the fancy-talk, wrangling generals?

Hd. Qrs, Army in the Field Camp near Donelson, Feby 16th 1862.

Gen. S. B. Buckner, Confed. Army,

Sir, Yours of this date proposing Armistice, and appointment of Commissioners to settle terms of Capitulation is just received No terms except an unconditional and immediate surrender can be accepted.

I propose to move immediately upon your works. I am sir, very respectfully Your obt. svt. U. S. Grant Brig. Genl.

—Original in the Historical Society of Pennsylvania

—Forrest pictures: From **That Devil Forrest**, by John A. Wyeth, Harper & Brothers

GRANT demands "unconditional and immediate surrender" (above) of Gen. Simon B. Buckner. But Forrest didn't surrender. Through blowing snow and icy backwater, left and below, Forrest led his own men to safety.

About This Book . . .

Four supplements, published by The Nashville Banner in recognition of the Civil War Centennial years, have been combined to make this book.

It is especially hoped that the illustrations may prove helpful to Middle Tennessee teachers in presenting Tennessee's vital role in the Civil War. More than 800 encounters occurred on Tennessee soil.

For permission to reproduce two paintings, "Leaving Home" and "Tidings from the Front," The Banner is grateful to John E. Meyer. The originals, by Gilbert Gaul, are in Mr. Meyer's notable Gaul collection which may be seen at the State Museum in the War Memorial Building at Nashville.

Part I of this series was first published Dec. 16, 1961; Part II, Feb. 9, 1963; Part III, Feb. 22, 1964, and Part IV, Nov. 14, 1964.

THE CIVIL WAR IN

About the Cover . . .

"Forrest at Spring Hill," on the front cover, is by versatile Jack Knox, Nashville Banner cartoonist, artist, writer and horseman, whose prose poem, "The General's Mount," concludes Part I. The painting, the poem, and their accompanying illustrations first appeared in The Nashville Banner of March 5, 1956.

"The Battle of Franklin—Last Moments of General Adams," on the back cover, is by Dave Wright, former Newspaper Printing Corporation artist, now wading through battle-smoke himself—in Viet Nam. Into the casein painting went hours of museum research and the use of live models. It originally adorned the front of Part III.

ST. LOUIS

ILLINOIS

Fort Donelson falls—Feb. 16, 1862

KENTUC

MISSOURI   PADUCAH

BOWLIN

Federals occupy Nash Feb. 25, 1

Fort Henry captured Feb. 6, 1862

NASHVI

Forrest take Murfreesbo July 13, 18

ARK.   TENNESSEE

Battle o Murfreesbo Dec. 31,1862–Jan

MEMPHIS   SHILOH

Battle of Shiloh April 6-7, 1862

Gen. John scores May

ALABA

MISSISSIPPI

—Map design by Newspaper Printing Corporation artist Jim

DDLE TENNESSEE

PART I
1861-1862

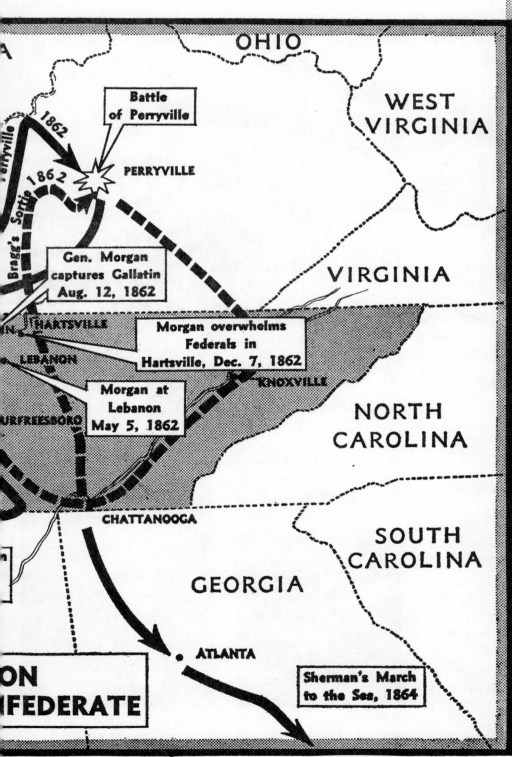

Battle of Perryville

1862

PERRYVILLE

Bragg's Sortie 1862

Gen. Morgan captures Gallatin Aug. 12, 1862

HARTSVILLE

Morgan overwhelms Federals in Hartsville, Dec. 7, 1862

LEBANON

Morgan at Lebanon May 5, 1862

KNOXVILLE

URFREESBORO

OHIO

WEST VIRGINIA

VIRGINIA

NORTH CAROLINA

CHATTANOOGA

SOUTH CAROLINA

GEORGIA

ATLANTA

Sherman's March to the Sea, 1864

ON

FEDERATE

Big Days of the Civil War
for
Middle Tennesseans
(1861-1862)

- Feb. 9, 1861, Tennessee votes pro-Union

- April 14, 1861, Fort Sumter falls.

- April 17, 1861, Tennessee's Gov. Isham G. Harris refuses troops to Union for purposes of "coercion."

- June 8, 1861, Tennessee has changed her mind. She votes for secession.

- June 17, 1861, American Flag is lowered on Capitol Hill and replaced by "Stars and Bars."

- September, 1861. Line of Cumberland (Confederate defensive) established.

- Jan. 19, 1862, right wing of line breaks.

- Feb. 6, 1862, Fort Henry captured.

- Feb. 11, 1862, Confederates begin evacuation of Bowling Green, Ky. The 14,000 troops stream toward Nashville.

- Feb. 16, 1862, Fort Donelson falls.

- Feb. 23, 1862, Nashville evacuated.

- Feb. 25, 1862, Federals occupy Nashville.

- April 6-7, 1862, Battle of Shiloh.

- May 1, 1862, Gen. John Hunt Morgan scores at Pulaski.

- May 5, 1862, Morgan at Lebanon. Famous race to Rome Ferry.

- July 13, 1862, Forrest takes Murfreesboro.

- Aug. 12, 1862, Gen. Morgan captures Gallatin. Wrecks railroad tunnel north of town.

- Dec. 7, 1862, Morgan overwhelms Federals in Hartsville.

- Dec. 31, 1862-Jan. 2, 1863, Battle of Murfreesboro.

SURRENDER of Fort Donelson. Why? Why? asked the enlisted Rebs, and they tried to hold back the flag of truce.

GEN. SIMON BOLIVAR BUCKNER
Fort Donelson's defender

GENERAL GRANT, after his triumph at Fort Donelson. This idealized picture appeared on the cover of *Harper's*, March 8, 1862.

—The Century War Book, 1861-1865

DOVER TAVERN, Buckner's headquarters and scene of the surrender. The house still stands. (Drawn from a photograph taken about 1884.)

FROM THIS HOUR forward a name would rise, starlike in the long dark night of war: Nathan Bedford Forrest.

Another name, too, would begin to glow, Ulysses S. Grant.

(The Federal loss in killed and wounded at Fort Donelson has been given as 2,331; the Confederate as 15,067, including prisoners; the Confederate killed and wounded, 1,420, the latter perhaps an excessive figure — plus 3,000 horses and 20,000 blankets.)

There they go, Buckner and Grant. Old schoolmates. And what is Grant saying to his prisoner? Perhaps the soldiers didn't hear it but Grant is offering to lend Buckner money if he needs it. Buckner is courteously declining.

(Years later, however, when Grant, as a former President, was being carried to his tomb, Buckner would be one of the pallbearers. Grant himself had chosen him.)

It is Sunday morning, Feb. 16. The bitter wind is sweeping across the bloodied snow.

Far up the Cumberland, it is whining between the wires of the Nashville suspension bridge. Gen. Johnston is crossing. He has just received the surrender news at his headquarters in Edgefield (now East Nashville). Daylight is showing. He is on his way to tell Gov. Harris the truth. Fort Donelson has fallen. The news will leak out.

—From Men and Things I Saw in the Civil War, by James F. Rustling

GEN. GEORGE H. THOMAS

—The Century War Book, 1861-1865

GEN. ALBERT SIDNEY JOHNSTON

NASHVILLE, scene of the "Great Panic," 1862. And across the suspension bridge, into the falling city, came Black Bess and her master, in the retreat from Bowling Green.

—Harper's Weekly

IT WILL be a busy bridge today. Within a few hours the retreating vanguard will arrive from Bowling Green.

No longer will it be an army of 14,000. Dying, frozen, frostbitten men— 5,400 of them—will have been scattered along the way from Bowling Green to Nashville, in the homes of friendly people or ready to be placed under medical care on arrival.

Wild rumors are spreading: Buell is within 25 miles of Nashville with 35,000 men. The city will be bombarded by both the army and gunboats at 3 p.m. It isn't true, but many believe.

Some are suggesting that the city be burned to the ground; that Buell find only ashes. Church congregations are being dismissed. Crowds roam the streets. They're getting disorderly, wild.

By noon the streets were almost clogged with fleeing vehicles. The price of anything on wheels climbed to $25 an hour. Trains departed with men hanging onto the outside in the rain. In the afternoon Gov. Harris left for Memphis with the state archives. (He would join the staff of Gen. Johnston on the field of battle.)

Mayor Cheatham spoke on the Public Square. He tried to calm the crowds. He promised to meet the Federals and surrender the city in peace. Gen. Johnston had agreed to that.

Crowds were milling about the Square. The day was nearly done. Nobody paid much attention to little hooves that went clattering over the bridge. Black Bess and her master were crossing into the city.

The tall Van-Dyked man on Bess looked down at the Cumberland. A rabble was plundering boats, pitching slabs of bacon ashore. Some of the slabs missed and hit the water. Black Bess reached the Square. Mobs were ransacking buildings. Her squadron rode on in, enroute to encampment on the Murfreesboro Pike.

The dark night of despair was settling. The tragic news was spreading.

At 8:10 p.m. in Lebanon the door of the Presbyterian Church burst open. In strode a booted man. He gave a note to the pastor who read it aloud:

"Fort Donelson has fallen. The remainder of Crittenden's army is retreating toward Lebanon. Bowling Green forces are retreating toward Nashville."

Yes, from East and West they were coming. Retreating men were pouring into Middle Tennessee from both broken wings of the Line of the Cumberland. Next morning in the steady rain a miserable little band straggled into Lebanon. With it came Crittenden, now hated, abused, drenched to the skin.

In Nashville Morgan's cavalry was assigned to police duty. He was joined on Tuesday by Forrest. They patrolled the streets, restoring order. They commandeered all vehicles to salvage as much as possible of army stores. This included 250,000 pounds of bacon.

Into one stubborn mass of Nashville looters, Forrest rode with his cavalry, batting down leaders with the flat of his saber.

On the Square the mob held fast. Forrest drenched it with a fire hose. The water came from the Cumberland, icy and muddy. The mob calmed down.

Wednesday morning at 4 o'clock, two lines of flame, high in the air, appeared above the Cumberland. Crossties of the railroad bridge and the flooring of the suspension bridge were burning. Cables of the suspension bridge were cut.

Citizens howled at the inconvenience. But military and civic men had conferred. The army was thinking of Buell. Any minute he might show up.

Then it is Sunday, Feb. 23. The week of the "Great Panic" has ended. For days, Confederates have been retreating toward Murfreesboro. Hundreds of sick and wounded are rolling toward Chattanooga in boxcars.

As the day fades, the cavalry falls into line. Now it is forming fours. Black Bess is turning her delicate muzzle toward Rutherford County.

Her Van-Dyked rider looks back. Darkness is settling over the fallen city. He sees a little band of Bluecoats marching in.

Tuesday morning a gunboat and transports steamed up the river. Soldiers poured ashore. Bands blared "Yankee Doodle." They paraded to Capitol Hill and hoisted the Stars and Stripes.

Nashville was a captive city.

Soon there were howls for Gen. Johnston's removal. *"If Sidney Johnston is not a general, then we had better give up the war,"* said President Davis. He stood loyally behind the commander.

—The Century War Book, 1861-1865

GEN. DON CARLOS BUELL
Leave him ashes?

—Harper's Pictorial History of the Civil War

The railroad bridge across the Cumberland River at Nashville. Notice the armed guards.

GEN. JOHN HUNT MORGAN
A battle by the river?

The burning of Nashville's bridges, at 4 o'clock in the morning, doubtless resembled this sketch of a flaming bayou bridge.

JOHNSTON was silent, planning. He would assemble his biggest force at Corinth, Miss., before Grant's forces could be joined by Buell's. On Feb. 28, Johnston began his march through Shelbyville and Fayetteville to Corinth.

As he went, Lincoln, on March 3, appointed Andrew Johnson military governor of Tennessee—the first time such a thing had ever happened to an American state.

From 1853 to 1855, Johnson had served Tennessee as her duly elected governor. The story was different now. A U. S. senator from pro-Union East Tennessee, Johnson was one Southern leader who had not "gone with the South." To most West and Middle Tennesseans he was now a "traitor." Threats upon his life would be frequent. He assumed his duties in Nashville March 12, advisedly "without display." (The level-headed advice came from the Union commander, Gen. Buell.)

Within two weeks Johnson jailed Nashville's Mayor Cheatham upon his refusal to take an oath of allegiance to the United States. The City Council also refused. A new council was appointed, including Union men. An ordinance was passed requiring all attorneys practicing before City Court to take the oath. The same demand was made upon school teachers, upon pain of losing their jobs.

Johnson suppressed four Nashville newspapers, jailed the editor of one and brought in a rabble-rouser to start an administration journal. He shut down printing presses of the Methodist and Baptist churches. Then he moved on to the pulpit, sending six ministers to Camp Chase.

Little wonder, then, that when the State Capitol, months later, was stockaded and fortified, Nashvillians would scornfully call it "Fort Johnson." Its master had a flair for despotism.

In the meantime, Gen. Polk had evacuated Columbus under protest. He did it with such secrecy the watching enemy didn't know it until he was gone. The bishop-general took along every one of his 140 guns.

Downriver went the heaviest, to Island No. 10 on the Mississippi. Nearly 10,000 of Polk's men went with him to Humboldt. From there they might be shifted to Memphis or Corinth if needed. Something grim was shaping up. (Yes, the bishop would be there, at Shiloh, as a mighty good soldier.)

The head of Johnston's column was in Corinth by March 18. Federals were concentrating 22 miles away at Pittsburg Landing. There Grant had about 40,000 men and was daily expecting Buell from Savannah, nine miles away, with 25,000 more. Then Grant would strike Johnston.

Johnston didn't wait to be struck. On the evening of April 5 he drew up close to Grant's line, so close the Rebels could hear the music of the Union bands. Not until daybreak did the Federals know they had an army on their front.

It is a balmy Sunday morning, April 6. Spring sunlight is falling in fragrance upon little Shiloh Church. Dogwood and peachtrees are blooming. Johnston is telling his men. *"The eyes and hopes of 8,000,000 people rest upon you."*

In the stillness a Confederate captain says, *"Aim low, men."* (A wounded man can give more trouble to the enemy than the dead.)

Soon nearly 80,000 muskets and 200 big guns were roaring. What they did to one another would sicken the civilized world.

Johnston's 38,800 men had struck with such skill and dash that the 39,900 Federals were driven back at every point. They rallied and were thrown back again.

The Rebels struck the "Hornets' Nest" about midafternoon. This was an old sunken road, abandoned, thick with blackberry bushes and other growth. The Federals used it as a trench and poured out death.

The Confederates reeled back shouting, *"It's a hornets' nest!"* Thus came the name to history as one brigade after another was thrown against it.

When they seemed hesitant about another lunge, Gen. Johnson galloped ahead. He led them and stuck by until their first foothold was welded to the ridge. Then he rode on to the rear, laughing about the sole of his boot. A Minie ball had cut it in two.

The battle seemed nearly won, before Buell could reach Grant. Then came a loss which may have changed the course of the Civil War. A stray shot struck Johnston in the back of the right thigh, cutting an artery a few inches above the knee.

Gov. Harris rode up. *"General, are you wounded?"*

Johnston was alone, white-faced. He was swaying in the saddle. *"Yes, and I fear seriously."* His words were calm. The reins slipped from his hands.

Harris put one arm around him, held the reins of both horses in one hand, and guided them behind the lines. Johnston was unconscious.

The Confederate governor of Tennessee lifted him to the ground, tore open his shirt. He searched for a wound and found none. Then Harris saw a boot full of blood. It was 2:30 p.m. The great general was dead.

Beauregard, next in command, ordered the news kept from the men. (Southern legend, told to many of us since childhood, says change of command lost the battle. But did it?) The fighting went on till 6 p.m. The Federals fell back steadily toward the river. It was after Johnston's death that the "Hornets' Nest" was taken, with aid of massed artillery.

—Drawn from a photograph by Mathew Brady

ANDREW JOHNSON, a future President, became Tennessee's military governor.

The Confederates had won—as of Sunday night. Beauregard slept in the captured tent of Gen. William T. Sherman near the church. Big factors were ahead, unrelated to the death of Gen. Johnston. Did a swarthy cavalryman sense danger?

That night Forrest dressed 12 of his men in captured bluecoats and sent them out. Learn what you can! They came back with bad news. Heavy Federal reinforcements were landing.

Not only was Buell's host of 25,000 arriving. So was Gen. Lew Wallace with 5,000 men. Thirty thousand!

Next day, the Confederates were compelled to fall back toward Corinth. The fruit of victory, which Johnston had shaken to the ground, could not be gathered.

Who won at Shiloh? Both sides claimed the victory. In the two days of fighting 108,700 men had struggled. When the guns fell silent, 23,746 were dead, wounded or missing.

The Confederates had lost 10,699. Their dead, 1,728; wounded, 8,012; missing, 959. The Federals lost 13,047, including 1,754 killed, 8,408 wounded and 2,885 missing.

Gen. Polk, in a letter to his wife, seems fair in summing up: *"The enemy was badly whipped the first day and we ought to have captured his whole force. We would have done so if we had had one more hour of daylight. The battle of the (next) day . . . was a drawn fight. We left them and they did not follow us."*

Sherman did make a gesture of pursuit. Two streaks of Confederate cavalry, Forrest and Morgan, came jabbing out at him.

Sherman wrote, *"Our troops being fagged out . . . I ordered them back . . ."*

FORREST, THE SOLDIER

GEN. PIERRE G. T. BEAUREGARD

SETTING UP ARMY TELEGRAPH wires during an action. The wire unreels as soldiers run. From a sketch by A. R. Waud.

A T CORINTH, Beauregard learned that Island No. 10 had fallen with 7,000 men. Another link gone in river defenses—more men, more muskets.

In the darkness of his thoughts, two bright sparks flickered. At Shiloh he'd seen two able men. One was Morgan, the Kentucky sport, an aristocrat, from a house designed by Latrobe. The other was Forrest, the cabin-born Tennessean, an unlettered former slaver. Neither was a West Pointer.

To Beauregard's immortal credit, his judgment was serene. Each had shining talent. He would use it.

He'd make the man from Memphis a brigadier, the Kentuckian a colonel. He'd make Morgan's battalion into a regiment or brigade, give him a war bag of $15,000 and send him off to harass the enemy in Middle Tennessee and Kentucky. That little mare of Morgan's, sired by Drennon, was going to be mighty busy in the months ahead. And Forrest would have many a horse shot from under him.

By mid-spring of '62 Morgan and Forrest, working separately as partisan raiders, would become galloping nightmares to the Federals.

Many a bridge would be gone when the Yankees arrived to cross it. And the railroad trestles—burned, too! The crossties, torn up. The rails twisted around trees! The telegraph, cut!

Dawn of May 1 found Morgan and Bess between Lawrenceburg and Pulaski. About midday, nearing Pulaski, he received news. An estimated 400 Federals had just passed on the road to Columbia. Morgan and his men whirled after them.

They found the Federals stringing a telegraph line which was to carry messages to Gen. O. M. Mitchell's headquarters in Huntsville, Ala. *"Charge!"* said Morgan. It didn't take long to capture 268.

Then began a triumphal parade into Pulaski which old-timers long remembered. Morgan rode ahead on Bess. She seemed to know it was their moment. She pranced and tossed her head, shaking the jaunty feather on the big cocked hat of her master. Strung out in the center of the column were the Yankee prisoners, then more of Morgan's men.

Many a Giles County man seemed to "go wild" with enthusiasm at the sight. Pulaski women wept for joy. They wanted to touch Bess. "Just let me stroke her coat!" Soon they had the chance. Morgan stopped her at the hotel's hitching rail.

Admirers crowded close. Pulaski women gave Bess an abundance of the dainties she liked. Some caressed her, begging for a strand of her mane. Bess was Queen of the Day—until late arrivals appeared with scissors, to snip off souvenirs. Then Morgan sent Bess to a stable lest she be too closely shorn.

He soon headed north, crossed Stone's River, and reached Lebanon as darkness fell May 4.

It's a rainy night in the college town. Set up drinks for Morgan's men! All bars are crowded. So is the hotel. Homes open their doors. Share our best!

The rain has turned to a downpour. On the outskirts of town, the pickets are drenched. They go back and forth to friendly farm homes to dry. Farmers offer bottles. Many a cavalryman is sleeping in tents on the campus and about the town. Their horses jam the stables.

MORGAN, the high-spirited cavalier, looks out upon us from this revealing sketch—sharply in contrast to the less friendly drawing on the next page.

Suddenly down the pike there is a noise like thunder. Hundreds of Bluecoats come pounding through the gray dawn of May 5. How many? At least 600. (Some say 2,000.) They have ridden past the drinking pickets. Morgan has no warning.

AS PRO-UNION *Harper's* portrayed Morgan and his men. Drawings such as this helped persuade the North that Morgan led a band of "cutthroat horsethieves."

ONE PICKET is Pleasant Whitlow. He sees his fault. He'll undo it "or die." He jumps astride a fast mare and rides past a column. Suddenly he is galloping, heading for the Square and bellowing a warning.

He was shot dead (some say almost at Morgan's feet as the colonel ran from the hotel). Bugles were screaming "Boots and Saddles." Rebels jumped from everywhere but the Bluecoats were among them, riding them down before they could reach their horses. Others fled upstairs to the windows of houses and poured out a fire as the Federals dashed by in fours. Some barricaded a building and steadily fired from there. Death poured from upper windows of the Odd Fellows Hall. By this time others had got to their horses.

There was hard fighting in the center of town in a wet turmoil of gunsmoke and dung and slick leather. In the first confusion the Confederates couldn't form. Then there was Morgan among them on Bess.

He is rallying Company A long enough to cover men who are forming behind him. Despite the surprise he is calm. The company is holding its fire until the charging Union horses are almost upon them. Now it blazes and the fire seems frightfully red in the dampness. The Federals recoil, fall back. They are charging again.

Men are dying. In the spring rain men are struggling and slashing in little knots of smoking fury, all around the square.

Somehow in one of the first brushes a Federal chaplain has been captured. *"I rode up to pray for the wounded,"* he says. May he rejoin his regiment?

"The hell you say!" says a Morgan man. *"You think Morgan's men don't need praying for—?"*

HOPEMONT, the Morgan home in Lexington, Ky. From here Morgan rode away to war on Black Bess, one of the finest mares of the Southland.

Morgan has ordered retreat. Maybe 100 men are with him as Black Bess tears away toward the Rome-and-Carthage Road. After them goes the Federal cavalry of a Kentucky general, Ebenezer Dumont. They too ride fine Kentucky horses. This is no one-sided race.

"A rattling hurricane," one man has called it who was there. *"Sometimes we jumped over fallen horses, and sometimes a horse would shy around a man on hands and knees, struggling to escape from the road—"*

Pistols were barking. Morgan's men were galloping and firing, turning forward to reload, twisting backward to shoot. And see? Over there! It's Dumont's flanking company closing in and charging at the rear with sabers out.

Did Black Bess see the flashing blades? She has broken her bridle. She's turning into a "tornado" and two or three men can't hold her. She's going and gone, away and away, with her master safely astride her and no man on earth can halt her. The best they can do is keep up, and Morgan has to send orders by courier for all men who have lost their horses to take to the woods. (Many would escape in this way.)

Yet, the Federals were gaining on the mass of shattered Rebels. Close to Rome the Bluecoats thundered up to within 100 yards yelling: *"Halt!"*

Three words flapped back through hoofbeats as the Rebs twisted and fired again: *"Go to hell!"*

Black Bess was racing on through the village of Rome, not stopping until she came to the unbridged Cumberland. The ferry was waiting but too small for all men and horses. It would have to be poled across. All would be under fire any minute.

Morgan was trying to save his men. If time permitted he would send back for the horses. Tom Quirk, brave cavalryman, knew Morgan's heart was breaking. Bess stood on the shore, saddle empty.

Black Bess, from an illustration in the old *Confederate Veteran Magazine.* Legends of her heroic race from Lebanon still lend an aura of magic to the Rome ferry in Smith County.

THEIR HOPES WERE HIGH IN '62. This composite picture of Confederate heroes adorned many a Middle Tennessee home in the 1880s. Its title: "Southern Commanders." Foremost are Gen. Robert E. Lee, white-haired, and President Jefferson Davis, seated, left. Others, left to right are Adm. Raphael Semmes (hand in coat), Gen. John Bell Hood, Gen. J. E. B. (Jeb) Stuart, Gen. T. J. (Stonewall) Jackson, Gen. Nathan Bedford Forrest, Gen. Joseph E. Johnston and Gen. P. G. T. Beauregard. On the wall is a portrait of Gen. Albert Sidney Johnston, who perished in the Battle of Shiloh.

—Library of Congress

THEY REACHED the yon bank and looked back. Bess was running along the shore, head high and mane flying.

"*She was the most perfect beauty I ever beheld,*" one man wrote later. "*. . . Broad tilted loins and thighs—all muscle, her head as beautiful as a poet's dream . . . Wide between the eyes, it tapered down until her muzzle was small enough to have picked a lady's pocket.*"

Quirk leaped into a canoe and started rowing, meaning to swim her back. Federals appeared. They riddled his canoe with shots. Quirk was unhurt. Bess had to be left with the Yankees.

And for 100 years, little Smith County boys whose families knew the story have stood by the ferry at Rome and looked across, and dreamed, as little boys can, that they could see Black Bess streaking along the yellow shore, head up and mane flying, neighing wildly for her master.

She disappeared then and there on the river bank from the pages of history. What became of her? There are many stories: That Gen. Dumont used her for a while, then sold her to a civilian who showed her about the country for 25 cents a look. ("*Hope she kicked the brute's brains out,*" old-time Smith Countians used to say.)

After the war, advertisements were published by her original owner, Warren Viley. He offered large sums for information as to her whereabouts, in vain. And in the town of Liberty years ago, in the early childhood of an aged generation just slipped away, a fine black mare used to appear on Saturday afternoons. There were whispers she was Bess, in her old age. Was she?

Morgan had crossed the Cumberland with 15 or 20 men, some say, and five more seem to have reached him that night. Stragglers joined him at Sparta. What had his losses been at the "Lebanon Races"? One account says 65 were captured, 17 killed and 26 wounded. It lists Federal casualties as 79 killed and 64 wounded.

Morgan carried on. It's said that by May 11 he had 300 men (probably including recruits). On that day he left for Bowling Green.

As they moved north th *y* could hear conchshells being blown from hilltops. Yankee sympathizers were spreading the alarm. Two or three days later he reached Cave City, Ky.

His telegraphic wizard, George Ellsworth, went to work tapping the wires. This was one of their favorite means of learning enemy movements. A freight train came along (or was already on the siding)—with 48 cars, one writer says. A passenger train was due. They filled a cowgap with crossties to stop it and, when it rolled toward the gap, blocked all retreat.

Morgan's great hope was that some of his men captured at Lebanon were aboard, enroute to prison. They weren't, but 20 Federal soldiers were. Several were officers with their wives. One officer came off shooting and was disarmed. A woman begged for her husband's life. "*Don't shoot him!*"

Morgan bowed. "*He is no longer my prisoner. He is yours.*"

He searched the passenger train and found $3,000 in Federal greenbacks.

It became the loot of war. The freight he burned. He placed guards aboard the passenger, took his men to the hotel for a sumptuous feast, invited a captured Yankee major along as guest, and paid the bill from the $3,000.

Morgan begged the ladies to accept the locomotive as a "token." He ordered the engineer to take the wives and the paroled prisoners back to Louisville. When the train was out of sight Morgan and his men headed back toward the Cumberland.

Their chins are up again. The cavalcade goes wending through the hills towards Burksville. Soon they will be in Chattanooga, rallying ground for the new Army of Tennessee under Gen. Braxton Bragg, who will never understand either Morgan or Forrest.

By now Morgan has won the bitter enmity of despotic Gov. Johnson. The military governor doesn't want Morgan's men treated as soldiers. He wants them treated as criminals and is pulling strings in that direction.

On May 18 Johnson writes a Federal congressman: "*Morgan and his marauding gang should not be admitted to the rules of civilized warfare. That portion of his forces taken at Lebanon should not be held as prisoners of war . . .*"

The weeks rolled off like drumbeats. They brought misfortune to Morgan and Forrest's good friend, Gen. Beauregard, now ill. He had become the "scapegoat of Shiloh." He was blamed by many for loss of the battle. Later he was superseded by Gen. Bragg, strict disciplinarian and West Pointer.

Bragg assumed command June 27. Many historians think it was an unlucky day for the South. Some even think the South lost the war "in the West" that day— not by Beauregard's removal but by the promotion of Bragg to lead the Army of Tennessee.

Space here forbids whys and wherefores. Bits will portray a part of what happened while battle blood poured over the soil of Middle Tennessee and adjoining areas as Bragg led his army back and forth. The South had howled for Albert Sidney Johnston's head; she howled for Beauregard's head. Now she got Bragg, and with him she would be stuck for a heartbreak time to come.

Bragg was dedicated to the South — and also to the drill books, something Forrest and Morgan knew little about. They cared less.

Luckily, one of Beauregard's last official acts had been to recommend Forrest for promotion to brigadier general. Beauregard wanted Forrest back in Middle Tennessee, commanding regiments, organizing them into a brigade. To Forrest, it meant leaving the troops he had equipped, trained and led. The parting hurt.

GEN. BRAXTON BRAGG

31

ON JULY 6, from Chattanooga, Forrest headed over the mountains with 1,000 men. Passing Beersheba Springs July 11, he stopped at McMinnville and was reinforced by 400 more. He soon learned Buell had collected 1,750 Federals at Murfreesboro with which to occupy McMinnville as a vital spot between Chattanooga and Nashville. Forrest headed for Murfreesboro.

At 11 p.m. Saturday, July 12, he reached Woodbury. Despite the late hour women were up, astir and weeping. Their menfolks had just been carried off to jail in Murfreesboro by the Federals, on obscure charges of aiding the Rebels. Also in the jail were five or six men under sentence of death, to be hanged at dawn Monday.

Forrest tried to quiet the women. He offered reassurance. They tried to dry their tears. Then they served him and his men their best pies and cakes, the things they'd fixed for their own Sunday dinner.

A few hours before, in Kentucky, a coincidence had begun to happen. Morgan's telegrapher, Ellsworth, had tinkered with the telegraph again. This time, in addition to milking it for Yankee news, he also jokingly sent, at Morgan's order, a fake wire. It said Forrest had taken Murfreesboro. The statement came true next day. (Ellsworth himself deserves a full book.)

Forrest left Woodbury at midnight and hit Murfreesboro at 4:30 a.m. Sunday—his 41st birthday. It's said the sound of his cavalry, pouring into the town, was like the "roar of an approaching storm."

The courthouse and jail were stormed. A fleeing guard set the jail afire. Quick work with axes and crowbars saved the prisoners from roasting to death.

The Yankees fought bravely. Outside the town their resistance continued behind a fence, baggage wagons and baled hay. It was nearly noon. Forrest sent a note, as blunt as Grant's at Fort Donelson:

*"I must demand an unconditional surrender
of your force . . . or I will have every man put
to the sword . . . This demand is made to
prevent the effusion of blood . . ."*

By 6 o'clock it was all over. Forrest had captured the entire force, (including Gen. T. L. Crittenden, nearly 1,200 men, more than 40 wagons, 600 head of horses and mules, four pieces of artillery and 1,200 stands of arms). What stores he couldn't move he destroyed. The day's work had cost the Federals $1,000,000. Nobody was hanged Monday morning.

Federal nerves were jangling. In the week that followed Forrest would cause the concentration, in Middle Tennessee, of more than 10,000 men in his pursuit. Thereby he would gain time for Bragg's arrival in Chattanooga from Mississippi—if that's where the wavering Bragg meant to go.

By the time Forrest clattered into McMinnville, local Federal garrisons were being rushed to protect Nashville. Buell sent Gen. William Nelson panting from Northern Alabama to retake Murfreesboro and McMinnville. Forrest learned the Lebanon garrison, recently yanked to Nashville, had returned to Wilson County.

He set forth, reaching Lebanon at sunrise, Sunday, July 20. He hoped to repeat his Murfreesboro strike of a week before. But the garrison had fled in the night.

Lebanon offered solace. Out came the choicest hams of Wilson County, tender roast pig and poultry, all the good things they could offer. Lebanon not only filled Rebel bellies; it loaded Forrest and his men with enough rich provisions to last three days.

He rode away Monday morning. Enemy wires sizzled. Where's he going? He let them sweat in frenzy.

For one long peaceful hour at noon he rested his men and horses in the tranquil shade of Andrew Jackson's Hermitage. Soldiers strolled its grounds, in happy relaxation behind the enemy's lines. There were pretty girls here, with soft smiles, and gentle people to talk to. For today was the anniversary of the Battle of Bull Run and Confederate hearts had come out to the Hermitage to celebrate. They had brought picnic lunches, and shared them. Then, come boys—

They rattled away toward Nashville. They could see the Capitol's tower. (Yankee sympathizers in Nashville nearly had fits.) The telegraph wires now were just about to melt, so hot were the questions. Where's Forrest? ". . . He will move on Gallatin or Nashville . . ."

Panic seized Gov. Johnson. Don't let Forrest take Nashville! Fortify the city! A heavy column was sent in pursuit.

Forrest swung around the city, toward the Chattanooga railroad. He drove the pickets in, captured some, smashed stockades, burned bridges they guarded and cut the quivering wires.

In Gallatin, the Federals acted. They burned all the ferries from Hartsville

The courthouse at Murfreesboro, 1862, with Union troops encamped. Forrest captured 1,200 of them on July 13, his 41st birthday, in a day's work that cost the Yankees an estimated $1,000,000.

to town and waited at the courthouse for Forrest. The river rose. They believed it saved them.

(Johnson's outcries had effect. Fortifications began next month.)

But where was Forrest on that July night? He'd simply disappeared. To where? The Chicken Pike. He camped there, in earshot of the searching Federals.

Two other things had happened that day. Forrest was commissioned a brigadier general, and Bragg at last decided to move his main western army of the Confederacy from Tupelo, Miss., to Chattanooga.

"Our cavalry is paving the way for us in Middle Tennessee," Bragg wrote exiled Beauregard about this time.

—From **That Devil Forrest**, by Wyeth, Harper & Brothers

Forrest capturing artillery at Murfreesboro. Do you recognize his characteristic chin-beard on the horseman nearest the cannon?

—Courtesy Library of Congress

Civil War "locomotives" in the railroad yards at Nashville. At lower left there's another engine, wrecked or dismantled. Uphill, toward the Capitol, there were many trees in those days.

MORGAN "WITH HIS GUERRILLAS bivouacking in the courthouse square, Paris, Bourbon County, Kentucky, after levying contributions on its inhabitants." The quotation is from *Harper's*.

MORGAN was raiding again in Kentucky. Starting from Knoxville with 800 men, he had crossed the Cumberland at Celina July 8, whipped a battalion at Tompkinsville, Ky., and swung on to Glasgow. Boldly he bivouacked on the Federal communication line between Nashville and Louisville.

Alarm spread through sentiment-split Kentucky and on to Cincinnati. Uneasy telegrams poured into the White House.

"*They are having a panic in Kentucky,*" President Lincoln wired Halleck at Corinth July 13. "*Please look to it.*"

Morgan's cavalry was clattering out its challenge to Harrodsburg and on to the edge of Lexington and Frankfort. He was shattering railroads, burning bridges, and Ellsworth kept tapping the wires. Now and then he'd create another Union nightmare by sending another fake telegram, just for kicks.

In 24 days, Morgan covered 1,000 miles, captured 1,200 men and was back in Tennessee by Aug. 1. He had lost about 90 in killed and wounded.

All this hubbub by Morgan and Forrest was slowing Buell's efforts to reach Chattanooga. Washington sent Buell an impatient wire: "*There is great dissatisfaction here with the slowness of your movements . . .*" Buell replied that he'd had to "*fortify every bridge over more than 300 miles of roads.*"

At retaken Murfreesboro, Federal Gen. Nelson had also been run ragged by Confederate cavalry. "*To chase Morgan and Forrest, they mounted on race horses, in this hot weather,*" he wrote Buell, "*is a hopeless task . . . Neither troops nor officers have had a change of clothing in more than two weeks.*" ("*You could smell 'em a mile,*" old timers used to say of Civil War brigades, both Federal and Confederate.) Within a few weeks Forrest would be running Nelson weary once more between McMinnville and Sparta.

Ripples from the Confederate cavalry were turning into a wave. Why not ride upon it—roll across Kentucky and invade Cincinnati? The audacious Rebel idea came from Gen. E. Kirby Smith, seasoned and gallant commander then up around Cumberland Gap.

It was a Big Idea. Before it ran its course, Cincinnati business houses would close. Martial law would be declared in the city. Smith, armed with Morgan's triumphant reports, outlined his plan to unimaginative Bragg whose ears must have pricked up (although at first Bragg seems to have bought only a part of the idea, the retaking of Tennessee). Bragg wanted to move north from Chattanooga and take captive Nashville free. They would start in August.

This should force Grant out of Mississippi. And Buell, if kept busy around Nashville, would have to give up any notion of advancing into East Tennessee.

Morgan's part would be to move north of Nashville, to around Gallatin, and cut Buell's railroad supply line from Louisville, his primary base. (Nashville was Buell's secondary base.) To do this, Morgan must surprise the Federal garrison at Gallatin and cut the twin railroad tunnels north of town.

It's Aug. 11. The sun is not up. Morgan's riders are leaving Sparta. They cross the Cumberland near Carthage and reach Dixon Springs before dark. Just before midnight they sweep through Hartsville. At 4 a.m., near Gallatin, they swing away from the main pike.

Morgan and Capt. Joseph Desha creep through a cornfield to a street. Moving through the dawn, they ease into the hotel and capture the commandant, a colonel, in his bedroom. He is finally persuaded to order the officer of the day to surrender the garrison without firing a shot.

The Federals soon will strike back, but meanwhile Morgan is busy. He orders destruction of the twin tunnels. Their timbered linings are set afire. Bridges are burned, tracks ripped up.

Ellsworth was at it again at the telegraph office. Rebels looted the freight cars, tossing off whatever they needed. They gave portions to citizens, burned what was left.

One account says a train engine was run at high speed into the burning tunnel where it wrecked itself on heaped crossties. Another says freight cars were run in.

It would burn for days while rock tumbled from overhead. For months it would be blocked, forcing Federals to rely upon the Cumberland for supplies. Not until December would they get the tunnels in good working order again.

Morgan marched back to Hartsville, while news of the tunnel blockade threw Buell's headquarters into bedlam. What was Bragg up to? Something was up! What? Buell rushed a force towards Hartsville. Drive Morgan out of Tennessee!

There were brushes around Gallatin for a week, one side and then the other winning. On Aug. 19 the Federals retreated toward Nashville, taking along Gallatin's male population over 12 on charges of aiding Morgan's men in the tunnel burning.

A scout sped the news to Morgan in Hartsville. He roared back into Gallatin. It was morning, Aug. 20. Storming on down the road toward Nashville in the wake of the enemy, he dispersed the Yanks long enough to free the civilians. He chased on into Edgefield where the fire from a 12-foot stockade raked his lines, killing two officers and three men.

Retreating to Gallatin with their dead across the saddles, the cavalry came upon a string of buggies and wagons. It was the women of Gallatin. They had driven out to bring back their husbands and sons. That night there was great rejoicing in Sumner County.

Before sunup a scout wakened Morgan. A strong cavalry column was moving from Hartsville, under Gen. R. W. Johnson, West Pointer. Furthermore, Johnson, eating at a Hartsville hotel the day before, had boasted he would "*bring Morgan back in a bandbox.*" He had ordered in advance that an evening meal be cooked for his return.

Morgan rode out to meet him. Forces were about evenly matched. Fighting went on for around two hours. By 8 a.m., Johnson had been driven back four miles. He asked for a truce to bury the dead, which Morgan rejected. Fighting resumed. Johnson and his staff were soon surrounded and surrendered.

Part of the encounter had been in an open meadow. This may account for the statement, in one description, that more than 200 horses may have perished in the fight. Many Federals escaped through high corn toward the river.

It is said that Johnson recalled his Hartsville boast and asked to be spared having to face the people there. Morgan, a generous victor, granted the request. (But it is also said that Morgan went back to Hartsville and ate the dinner Johnson had ordered.)

About midnight, Aug. 22, a messenger reached Morgan. He was to meet Gen. Smith in Lexington in early September.

The race for Kentucky was on! Morgan headed north. Their hearts were high and it was during this fulltide of fortune that Basil Duke, Morgan's brother-in-law and second in command (later a general), wrote the "Song of the Squadron":

"Then ho for the Bluegrass
And welcome the chance
Whatever the danger
That bids us advance."

"A CAVALRY CHARGE," from the *Army Sketch Book*. Up the slope in the distance charges a six-horse artillery unit which the superb Civil War artist, Edwin Forbes, always delighted in drawing.

GEN. SMITH had left Knoxville Aug. 14, Kentucky bound. In a few days both Bragg and Buell's armies would be moving too, uncertainly.

There was nothing uncertain about Smith. He knew where he was going. His mind was made up. And soon after Aug. 28, Bragg was rolling through the Sequatchie Valley, on through Pikeville to Sparta, Carthage, Gainesboro. As he came, Gen. Smith urged him to come on into Kentucky and join him.

Buell still wasn't sure what it was all about. He kept his Federals moving north and ordered concentration at Murfreesboro. He had a notion Nashville was going to be attacked. When he reached Murfreesboro bad news met him, but it didn't concern Nashville. The Confederates under Smith had won a smashing victory Aug. 30 at Richmond, Ky., capturing 4,300 Federals.

On the same day Lee in Virginia had delivered a bitter defeat to the Union Army at Second Manassas. Dismay was shaking Washington. Could the Union be saved after all? Was somebody batty, trying to run the South, when the South was about to come swarming through the windows?

In Kentucky, Smith was sweeping on to Lexington. Central Kentucky was under his thumb. He would raid as far as Covington, just across the Ohio from Cincinnati. Already there was panic in Cincinnati streets.

Buell marched on to Nashville. Would Bragg swing back and try to take the city?

In Nashville, Gov. Johnson was clamoring again for fortifications. This time he would get them. A cedar stockade rose around the Capitol. Cotton bales made breastworks. Cannon bristled. And, from behind it all, Johnson loudly declared that he would not be taken out alive.

The stockaded Capitol, with tents of Yankee soldiers just beyond. In center background are towers of Downtown Presbyterian Church.

A close-up of the cedar stockade, looking toward North Nashville. Both pictures are from the Library of Congress.

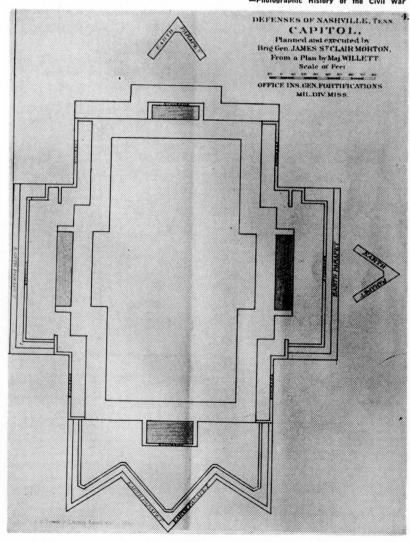

GEN. JAMES S. NEGLEY, upper left, and a sketch of the Federal fort named for him, which overlooked Nashville. The photograph shows a part of the works which included casements, covered with railroad iron and earth. At lower right is a plan of the defenses on Capitol Hill—earthwork parapets before each portico, backed up by a cedar stockade.

BRAGG HAD finally made up his mind. He headed for Glasgow. This time Buell got the drift of his thinking. Louisville! So that's it! Buell set out in pursuit.

He left Gen. Thomas to hold Nashville, then sent word for Thomas to follow him. This left just 6,000 Federals to hold the city, under Gen. James S. Negley. He would build Fort Negley. This would offer the skimpy force something to fall back to. It also would help pacify Johnson who was still loudly asserting that the state must be held by the Union at all cost. Construction of the fort took three months. (It would be completed by Dec. 7.)

Forrest had joined Bragg in Sparta Sept. 3. Confederate hopes were high. Forrest was ordered to ride far to the left of Bragg's column, cover it and hang onto Buell's flank and rear. Slow Buell down!

Forrest did. But meanwhile, two weeks earlier, the first hint of friction had occurred between Forrest and Bragg, the drill book disciplinarian. Back around McMinnville, Bragg had sent Forrest an order in the form of a question. Forrest thought it left him choice of action. He sent an answer and then handled the problem his own way, without waiting for a reply. Actually, he had set his judgment over that of his commander. It drew a curt answer, indicating Bragg's suggestions as well as his orders were to be obeyed.

By this time, Bragg's unpleasant reputation among his men was well under way. "He was a merciless tyrant," a Tennessee private later wrote. "The soldiers were scantily fed . . . He loved to crush the spirit of his men. The more of a hangdog look they had about them the better was Gen. Bragg pleased . . ."

An order issued before Morgan's raid into Kentucky in the summer of 1862.

—Reproductions from **Morgan and His Raiders**, by Cecil Fletcher Holland

There's a warning in the final sentence: "**If any of our men are fired upon . . .**"

ONE OF 12 CHILDREN—and neither the eldest nor youngest—Bragg with power had become the "great autocrat" (with a frequent sick headache). Could he endure an unlettered subordinate, with a greater talent than his own?

Glasgow would remember the "autocrat." Bragg, hoping to conciliate Kentucky in behalf of the South, gave strict orders that no property was to be taken without payment. A farmer reported that two soldiers had climbed a fence and stolen a few apples. Bragg ordered a courtmartial and had one shot. The farmer was horrified. So was all Kentucky.

Bragg had hoped for Kentucky volunteers. He got hardly any. Nearly a brigade enlisted under Gen. Smith.

Strategically, things were going Bragg's way. Fortune was about to beam upon him for all she was worth. She was about to give him a wondrous chance.

Buell's army began arriving in Bowling Green Sept. 14. He hoped to move quickly to Munfordville, 50 miles north, where 4,000 Federals held a garrison at the end of a railroad bridge on the south side of Green River. But Confederate cavalry checked him north of Bowling Green—and Bragg, not Buell, ordered his whole army to Munfordville.

Southern forces blocked both sides, and Forrest threw his cavalry across the rear, pinning the Federal garrison in the town. It surrendered Sept. 17 with all artillery, stores, and 5,000 stands of small arms.

How bright the outlook for the Confederacy in that third week of September, 1862!

Now strike, Bragg! Strike at Buell! Confederate hopes were soaring. Bragg was at the enemy's rear. Elation was everywhere among the Southerners. Bragg was squarely across Buell's line of communications, squarely between Buell and Louisville. Turn on Buell and crush him!

Here was the chance for which Bragg had come 600 miles. He had 30,000 men, Buell maybe 38,000. What of the difference? Since when had Confederates fought even numbers? It would be the first battle of Bragg's independent command.

There was every reason for immediate attack. Bragg's own officers expected it. Did he attack?

No. Some strange irresolution gripped him (and this would happen time and again in the future). He stood aside to Bardstown and let Buell pass on to Louisville.

"*In a negative way, Gen. Bragg's failure to fight . . . was one of the great crises of the Civil War—probably its greatest moral crisis.*" That is the opinion of Stanley Horn, noted Nashville historian, in his book, *The Army of Tennessee.*

Deeper gloom settled over captive Nashville. How bitter the pill of lost chances! In Kentucky, many a Southern officer bit his lips and said nothing. Not Forrest! He swore, long, loud and profanely.

Jefferson Davis as the King of Evil. This bitter caricature of his inauguration appeared in *Harper's*, March 15, 1862.

Sources Of Illustrations, Part I

Most of the sketches and photographs used here were obtained through the courtesy of the Tennessee State Library and Archives Division, the Tennessee Historical Society, the Nashville Public Library, the University of Kentucky Library and the Library of Congress.

The Banner is especially grateful to Walter King Hoover of Smyrna, inveterate collector of Civil War memorabilia, for access to all his Civil War material, particularly a rare and complete set of *Leslie's Weekly*, and to Cecil Fletcher Holland, for use of illustrations from his book, *Morgan and His Raiders*, published by The Macmillan Company.

Many of the illustrations first appeared in *Harper's Weekly*, Frank Leslie's *Illustrated Weekly*, *Battles and Leaders of the Civil War*, and the *Photographic History of the Civil War*, the latter published by the old *Review of Reviews*, its copyright holder. Others came from the Official Records, Army and Navy.

Map-designs are by Newspaper Printing Corporation artist Jim Young, in part from the National Geographic Society's map, *Battlefields of the Civil War*.

The fortified railroad bridge across the Cumberland at Nashville.

A close-up of the ominous "pillboxes" and a rigid sentinel.

DOUBTLESS Forrest's criticism reached Bragg's ears. He summoned Forrest to Bardstown. There he relieved the cavalry genius of further Kentucky duty and sent him back to Middle Tennessee—in effect, as a recruiting officer!

Go back. Raise four regiments of infantry, two of cavalry and, with whatever you can muster, operate against the enemy.

Once more, Forrest must take leave of his brigade; of the fighting men he'd made. *"On partisan service,"* Bragg wrote.

Was he still unable to see Forrest except through the drill book pages?

(A more tragic thing for the Confederacy was this: Bragg seemed to have a strange grip upon the mind of Jefferson Davis. Almost until the end of the war Davis would see Forrest through Bragg's eyes.)

Forrest came back to Tennessee. Soon Bragg and

Buell's armies more or less blundered into each other at the bloodily indecisive battle of Perryville, Ky. This was on Oct. 8, the day Forrest reached Murfreesboro.

Back both armies surged, into Middle Tennessee. By Oct. 28 Bragg's army was showing up at Murfreesboro, about where it had started 60 days before, with nothing much to show for its 1,000 mile march except a new reputation for Gen. Bragg: *"Iron Hand, iron heart and wooden head."*

Buell's army was back in Nashville. Buell wasn't with it. He had been criticized for not pressing Bragg harder. And Buell had never hit it off well with President Lincoln and Gov. Johnson. After the random blood-letting at Perryville, Buell was relieved of command by Gen. William S. Rosecrans, Oct. 30.

Forrest now had nearly 3,500 men. In the next few days he upset Federals in Nashville by making a demonstration against the city. At daylight Nov. 5,

his cavalry advanced along all seven roads toward Nashville. At the same time Gen. Morgan struck Edgefield. Whatever was originally intended, the Nashville episode was never consummated as a serious attack.

GEN. WILLIAM S. ROSECRANS
Buell's successor

THIRTY MILES — the distance between Nashville and Murfreesboro — is mighty close proximity for two great armies. Soon they would clash, but not yet. Meanwhile, Bragg made good use of his two great cavalry leaders.

A Union brigade was encamped at Hartsville. Morgan was sent to wreck it.

He is at Baird's Mill in Wilson County, 30 miles away. It is a bitterly cold day, Dec. 6. Snow covers the ground. A biting wind whines through the cedars.

Morgan sets forth at 11 a.m., passing through Lebanon. It is late afternoon and snowing hard. Big flakes are sticking to the feather in his big cocked hat. With him are 1,300 men, cavalry and infantry. And with him go the prayers of a Murfreesboro girl, Miss Martha (Mattie) Ready, his fiancee. They are to be married next Sunday.

The Cumberland River is up. There are only two small ferries to move his men across. They wait for hours, swearing softly in the freezing darkness as the boats take over a few, and a few more. Horses leap from a four-foot ledge and swim across.

It is past midnight when all are over. Dawn is breaking as they approach Hartsville. Bluecoats form a line in front of the town. Morgan sends a brigade to right and left. Get at them from behind! His cavalry is at the left, infantry at center, a battery on right. His men are cold, wet, hungry. They charge with Rebel yells. They are swarming over Federal lines. The furious fighting is over in an hour.

In the early sunlight, 264 Federals lie dead or wounded. More than 1,800 have been captured. Morgan lost 139 in all.

There is wild cheering as Morgan comes back through Lebanon with his prisoners. Even Bragg will be thrilled. Soon, Morgan will be made a brigadier general. . . .

MARTHA READY MORGAN

A FAR MORE difficult and dangerous assignment awaited Forrest. It related to far-away Vicksburg. There, on the heights above the river. Rebels still manned their guns, despite the fact that the Federal squadron of Adm. David Glasgow Farragut, Tennessee-born, had passed and repassed them after taking New Orleans, June 28. Grant, in West Tennessee, wanted to march through Northern Mississippi and clear the guns out. He hoped this would thoroughly open the Mississippi.

Bragg wanted to prevent it. He ordered Forrest, with his green troops, to raid Grant's rear in West Tennessee. Check Grant's advance through upper Mississippi!

(If a psychologist studied the record, would an unkind thought arise? "Misery loves company." Bragg, are you sick of the Forrest successes? If someone must sample defeat, would you like for it to be this cavalry wizard?)

Forrest would have to lead poorly armed men over dirt roads in the dead of winter, get across the wide Tennessee which Federal gunboats patrolled, raid in enemy territory and somehow escape by the same route, with an aroused enemy in massed pursuit.

Forrest protested. Half his force of 2,100 was armed with outmoded guns. Many had no arms at all. There was not even an adequate supply of flints or caps.

His protest did no good. On Dec. 10, he received final orders to ride just as he was, and he went.

Alarm went before him. By the morning of Dec. 17, he managed to get all across the Tennessee at Clifton, 70 miles west of Columbia. (He had flatboats built and sank them after crossing.) The telegraph spread news of his advance. Grant ordered troops concentrated at Jackson.

Soon Forrest took Lexington and 150 Federals (including a colonel), 300 Sharp rifles and two three-inch guns. These were rifled steel Rodman guns and would be his pride for the remainder of the war.

He whirled on, was driven off at Jackson, and dashed north, taking Trenton, Humboldt, Union City, ripping up railways. He was cutting Grant's northward communications. He was circling through West Tennessee. The chase was on. They were after him. At Parker's Cross Roads, near Huntingdon, capture seemed certain. He was caught between two battle lines. An officer rode up. *"General, what shall we do? What shall we do?"*

"Charge them both ways," Forrest is said to have replied. The legend is recounted in Robert Selph Henry's superb biography, *"First With the Most" Forrest* (McCowat-Mercer Press).

Soon back at the Tennessee River, Forrest had the sunken flatboats raised. It was New Year's Day, 1863. By midnight he had crossed again, eastward now. Fifteen days had passed since he headed west.

For 15 days he had kept more than 10 times his number of the enemy busy. He had destroyed supplies worth millions of dollars.

Yes, he had lost about 500 men. But others had joined. He was taking back more than he led out. And all were soldiers.

Now he was coming back. His men were all well armed. They had new blankets, new saddles, new bridles, 10 guns, 10,000 rifles and 1,000,000 cartridges. He had killed or captured more than 2,500 Federals.

The Confederate Congress would offer official congratulations. Even Bragg would commend him. Meanwhile, much had happened in Forrest's absence.

Gen. and Mrs. John Hunt Morgan, about the time of their wedding . . . Did Murfreesboro ever have a bigger social event? (From *The Bold Cavaliers* by Dee Alexander Brown, published by J. B. Lippincott Co. Courtesy the University of Kentucky Libraries.)

—From *"First With the Most" Forrest,* by Henry, McCowat-Mercer Press

War-worn Forrest. This picture may have been made in 1864. Compare it with his picture as a civilian, made about 1861.

Murfreesboro, crowded with gallant Confederate officers, was having a great social season. The military wedding of Morgan was a highlight.

President Davis visited Murfreesboro. He brought along Morgan's commission as a brigadier general. Gen. Polk was there. He performed the ceremony. Bragg and his staff attended. The South, in the winter of her Golden Age, was still abloom with belles. Mattie Ready was one of them. The wedding was at her home.

A great ball was planned for the day after Christmas. The bridegroom couldn't attend. He must strike northward again. Leaving Alexandria, Dec. 21, he dashed through Glasgow, on to Bardstown, and back through Campbellsville and Burkesville, Ky., to Smithville in Tennessee. He wrecked miles of railroad to within 18 miles of Louisville.

In the raid Morgan inflicted $2,000,000 damage, captured 1,887, and lost only two men killed and 24 wounded. He would not return until Jan. 5.

Both Morgan and Forrest were away on the fateful day set for the ball. Rosecrans saw his chance. The Union camps began to stir.

Early on Dec. 26, scouts rushed to Bragg's quarters. Rosecrans is moving on us! A great battle was shaping up. The Yankee army was advancing along many roads, by way of Franklin Road, Brentwood, Nolensville and the Murfreesboro Pike. (Many Northerners would call it the Battle of Stone's River. Many Southerners would call it the Battle of Murfreesboro.) Bragg sent word not to oppose the advance too much. "Let them come on."

About The Author

Ed Huddleston, author of The Banner's Civil War supplements, sold his first short stories at 18. He joined the Banner staff in 1941 as a police reporter. During World War II he served in the China-Burma-India theater, compiling mission accounts for Gen. C. L. Chennault's "Flying Tigers."

Later, on duty with OWI from the Army's new Psychological Warfare Branch, he wrote leaflets to the Chinese, Japanese and Annamese. Meanwhile, briefly hospitalized, he found time to jot down the first notes of a novel, "The Claybrooks," published by The Macmillan Company, 1951. (An Anglicized edition has since been published in Australia.)

Long a Banner feature writer, he has written many a historical series, including "The Land Between the Rivers" (the Cumberland and the Tennessee) and "Big Wheels and Little Wagons" (about old North Nashville), both available in booklet. Since "The Land Between the Rivers" appeared in The Banner, the area has been designated a national park.

He was "brought up" on stories of the Civil War. As a boy he heard stirring tales at the knees of a great-uncle veteran, Pleasant (Plez) Hall of Brush Creek, Tenn. A great-grandfather, Capt. Claibourn West, of Difficult, Tenn., fought at Shiloh.

The Battle of Murfreesboro, from a Kurz & Allison print.

BAYONET CHARGE of the 78th Pennsylvanians and the 21st Ohioans across a cornfield at the Battle of Murfreesboro. Not until a bayonet was thrust through his arm did the color-bearer of the 26th Tennessee Regiment drop his standard.

—From Leslie's Weekly

THE CHARGE OF GEN. NEGLEY'S DIVISION across Stone's River, Jan. 2, 1862. **Notice the merciful shooting of a wounded horse.**

Night burial of gallant Col. Julius Peter Garesche, adjutant general to Gen. Rosecrans. Garesche's head was swept away Dec. 31 by a cannon ball as he rode over the field at Stone's River with his commander. Comrades cover the body with evergreens before the grave is filled. Can you almost feel the stirring night wind? Many an artist considers this an outstanding drawing of the Civil War.

BRAGG'S cavalry slowed the advance. Not until the night of Dec. 30 was Rosecrans' army arrayed on a line before Stone's River, two miles west of Murfreesboro. Gen. Joe Wheeler led Confederate cavalry around the flank and rear of Rosecrans' entire army, burning 300 wagons at Lavergne. (They were loaded with stores worth $1,000,000.)

All that day the armies kept settling into position. By wintry dusk they lay within bugle call of one another. The Yankees played "Yankee Doodle" and the Rebels played "Dixie." One band began the music of "Home Sweet Home." And soon, amazingly, through the cold, still night, both sides were singing together. For many, it would be the last song.

The Federals planned to attack at 7 o'clock next day. But the Confederates struck first, at dawn. They moved in a great right wheel, shattering the plans of Rosecrans. For another odd coincidence had happened: each had planned assault by the left wing upon the enemy's right.

By noon Bragg's first aim was achieved: the Federal line had been bent back on a four or five mile sweep to the Nashville Pike. It was now somewhat like a V, at right angle with the first line of battle.

In the center of the angle stood a four-acre clump of trees. The "Round Forest" officers called it. To the privates it was "Hell's Half Acre." Here Rosecrans assembled every brigade not in action. It became a red-hot spearhead of death-dealing gunfire, hurling back every brigade Bragg could throw against it. The Confederate advance had been stopped. The "Round Forest" was holding.

But the Federals had been pushed back, on their right, four or five miles. As the bloody day ended, the Confederates held the field.

It is evening, Dec. 31. A red sun is dropping behind the cedars. Darkness comes. The fighting ceases. Bragg's scouts hear wagons rumbling away toward Nashville. They mistakenly think it's Rosecrans' retreating.

Unwisely Bragg wires Richmond, the Confederate Capital, *"The enemy . . . is falling back. God has granted us a Happy New Year."*

"With Fate Against Them."

—From The Century War Book, 1861-1865

This magnificent battle scene is by Gilbert Gaul, the same artist who painted the color pictures, "Leaving Home" and "Tidings From The Front."

ROSECRANS hadn't fallen back. The long wagon trains, rumbling away, had merely been taking the Federal wounded toward Nashville. Rosecrans was still there at sunup New Year's Day, 1863.

That day neither commander showed any mood to fight. As usual, a moment of opportunity found Bragg at a loss. He now seemed to have no certain plan. He had thought Rosecrans would pull back. During the night the Federals had withdrawn from the "Round Forest." Polk saw and occupied it with his men.

Bragg was holding the field. The dead were buried, the wounded attended. He didn't even trouble to take the high ground east of the river. Instead, Rosecrans ordered Gen. Horatio P. Van Cleve's division to occupy it.

Then at last Bragg decided that Gen. John C. Breckenridge should cross the river and take the ridge from Van Cleve! Breckenridge protested. The effort would be disastrous. Why, Federal guns could rake his men from high across the river!

Polk, too, advised against it. Bragg brushed their opinions aside. His orders stood. Take the ridge! It was afternoon, Jan. 2.

Breckenridge rode over to Gen. William Preston. *"General,"* he said solemnly, *". . . If I be among the killed, I want you to do justice to my memory and tell the people I believed this attack to be very unwise and advised against it."*

It was 4:30 p.m. Breckenridge obeyed the fatal order. The Confederates surged toward the river and across, pushing the Federals before them to the other bank. So far so good. Then the 4,800 Rebels swarmed over the ridge and into range.

From the west bank of McFadden's Ford, 58 guns blazed away at them point blank, with at least 100 shots a minute. Within a few minutes 1,700 Confederates were lost, including 300 officers. Breckenridge survived, but Gen. R. W. Hanson was mortally wounded. The remainder were in swift retreat.

The battle had turned. Bragg's officers had lost all confidence in his judgment. He had lost 28 per cent of his army, or a total of 10,306 men. The Union loss was higher, 13,230 men, or 31.5 per cent of Rosecrans' force.

Rosecrans felt a lot better next morning when he awoke and found Bragg's army gone. Bragg's staff had persuaded him to retreat. The men were bitter. Win or lose, it's always fall back or step aside! Just like Munfordville! Would there ever be anything Bragg wouldn't mess up?

Through rain and sleet Bragg moved his headquarters to Winchester, Hardee's Corps to Tullahoma, Polk's to Shelbyville. When Bragg learned Rosecrans wasn't in pursuit, he moved his headquarters to Tullahoma.

For about six months the two armies would be quiescent in Middle Tennessee. Then, for the Rebels, would come the worst years. . . .

Lotta killin', lotta willin',
    Till the pore old pop-eyed sun
Musta wondered why they didn't
    Tuck their ragged tails and run.

But the story wasn't ended,
    It was only halfway run.
They would take a lot of stompin'
    'Fore their fightin' days was done.

Where they got it, wish you'd tell me,
    For it sure did see 'em through,
For the thing was just beginnin'
    At the end of '62.

Hadn't been to Chickamauga,
    That would come in '63,
Then they'd crawfish into Georgia
    And break back for Tennessee.

Hood, he led 'em, something fed 'em,
    Lord knows how they got along,
But they stepped along like men, sir,
    And they gave their land a song.

So we crept along at Spring Hill,
    On a midnight, '64,
So close up to their noses
    You could hear them Rebels snore.

They came chasin' us to Franklin,
  Maddest men I ever saw,
Six thousand Yanks and Rebs would fall,
  And hell, it was a draw.

I can see 'em comin' at us,
  Yellin' "Whooo-oo-pee! Git 'em, boys!"
Made me wish I was a baby, home,
  With Mama and my toys.

Then I met him in an orchard
  Out on Nashville's southern rim,
He's at me with his bayonet,
  My gun is aimed at him—
Hardly know right clear what happened next,
  Peachtrees began to swim.

But I'm tellin' you they had it.
  You could feed a Minie ball—
I'd almost swear he spat it back
  Before I saw him fall.
And I see their banners flyin',
  I can hear their closer drum,
And if that's an angel comin'—
  Hey, there, Rebel, be my chum!

For wherever we're a-goin'
  There's a place for mighty men,
And I'd like you for a brother
  Where both of us will win.

—Verse from "Hey, Rebel," copyright 1961, Nashville Banner and Ed Huddleston

END OF 1862

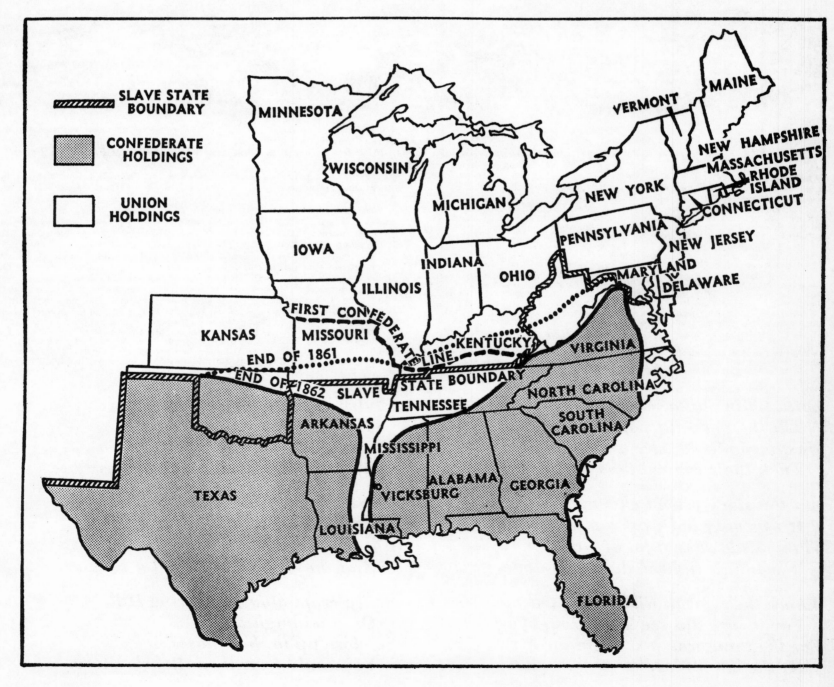

The General's Mount

By JACK KNOX

THE BLOOD from deep inside
  Began to color flecks of foam about the bit.
And pink the moisture in his heavy breath.
And yet the pain,
Sharp and searing hot,
Appeared to make no difference in his stride.
For this great chestnut gelding,
Dark with sweat,
Was all a war horse;
In his pace
And in his sinew,
Bone and blood
. . . and in his heart.

THE towering General, light-reined horseman—
  Light in saddle, too—
His mind and eyes intent upon the fight
Felt the shot
That hit the horse beneath him.

      There is
      Some indescribable communion
      Between a man and horse
      Who've shared the roughest roads,
      The longest hours,
      The hardest battles;
      A singleness of spirit, faith unflagging.

The General felt the pain
As though the gelding's wound was in himself;
It tightened muscles in his jaws and throat.

AND then the second shot
  Struck hard the chestnut's side.
And then the third.
Stunning.
Staggering.

His powerful and easy stride
Became a labored lunge,
Steadied only by the General's balanced weight
And sure hand.
The war horse gathered—
With every ounce of courage in his heart—
To carry on,
To fight the mission through.
Calmingly,
The General reined him in.
And stepping down
He loosed the girth
And lightly slipped the saddle to the ground.

THE GENERAL'S young lieutenant,
  Aide de camp—
His son—
Reined up,
Dismounted;
Took the General's horse and gave his own.
Scarcely a word was passed,
No orders given—
None had to be—
As the General,
With one backward glance, rode on.
And Willie led
The wounded war horse from the field
And to the rear.
Away from powder smoke
And battle strain.
Into the chill of early March,
Into the quieter countryside
In Tennessee.
To the horse holders beyond the second hill.

AND in the cutting chill
  The war horse ached,
Ached under his drying sweat
And drying blood.
A once alert,
Clearheaded "General's mount,"
Stunned and trembling
From the shock and pain.
Jaded.
Limping to the holders
In the rear.
No bugles
And no drumbeats here,
Only fading sounds across the field.

THE HOLDERS slipped the bridle
  From his lowered head,
Wiped the sweat marks
From his cheeks and neck,
Bathed the blood-red foam
From mouth and nostrils,
Sponged his wounds,
Applied a stinging ointment.
They washed his knees
And hocks
And pasterns.
"It's Roderick! The General's mount!
Bring the water bucket to him."

Roderick,
The General's mount.
Trained in his master's ways.
Trained to jump
A fence or wall or gulley,
To back and wheel,
To follow where the General went,
To follow closely,
Ready for an instant need.
And he followed him
From training,
But he followed, too,
From love.

THE stinging ointment touched a spark of feeling.
The water gave refreshment
To his spirit.
He raised his head a little,
Cocked an ear,
And listened . . .
In the distance
There was shooting
And it echoed in the hills.
The General always rode
To the shooting.

HE TURNED to face the sound.
  His ears were up and pointing.
His head was clearing now.
He moved a little,
Toward the sound.
The holders started to him.

Shouting "whoa."
He moved a little faster,
Stiff and aching,
Toward the shooting.
"WHOA" they shouted,
"Head 'im!"
He broke into a trot.
To a painful, labored gallop
To the General.

THE GALLOP warmed his blood,
  Loosened stiff and aching muscles.
Ahead,
A fence,
He cleared it
With a mighty surge of effort.
He was warm
And he was running,
A painful, awkward stride,
But running hard
To the General.

THE next fence—
  Up and over—

He almost lost his footing;
But he could smell the powder now.
The General smelled of powder.

NOW he could see the men and horses,
  Nervous horses,
Ready for the charge.
Now he could see the General.
One last fence before him
And the field.
He cleared it as the bugles blasted "CHARGE!"

HE was racing with the shouting horsemen now.
  He was straining hard
To reach the General's side,
Five good strides ahead.

Bleeding.
Straining hard.
Three good strides . . .
When the killing bullet hit him in the chest.

THE keen ear of the General caught a sound;
  Inaudible, almost, against the din.
Half a plaintive nicker,
Half a choking scream;
Like the scream of horses "bad hit" on the field.
Amid the shouting and the shrieking and the fire
The General heard it.
He stiffened,
Half turning in his saddle.
And there behind him
In the charge,
Stumbling, plunging, dying,
His war horse

—On his feet, but dying
In the charge.

THE feared
  And fearless,
Battle-hardened General
Spurred ahead;
To fight more awesome battles for his cause.
But the man—the horseman—
Underneath his honored uniform
—Bedford Forrest—
Died a little there
On the field near Spring Hill,
March the fifth,
1863.

"TIDINGS FROM THE FRONT" By Gilbert Gaul

—Courtesy of the Virginia Historical Society

LEE AND HIS GENERALS, from the mural by Charles Hoffbauer, in Battle Abbey, Richmond. The generals with Lee (7) are: (1) Wade Hampton; (2) Richard S. Ewell; (3) John Brown Gordon; (4) Thomas J. (Stonewall) Jackson; (5) Fitzhugh Lee; (6) A. P. Hill; (8) James Longstreet; (9) Joseph E. Johnston; (10) George E. Pickett; (11) Pierre G. T. Beauregard and (12) James E. Brown (Jeb) Stuart.

LOADING THE WOUNDED at Seven Pines (Fair Oaks). Gen. Joseph E. Johnston was among the wounded.

GEN. JOSEPH E. JOHNSTON
His suggestions were brushed aside in Richmond.

CAPITOL HILL FORTIFIED—Andrew Johnson, military governor (and future President), thundered defiance from behind its
Yankee stockade.

—Library of Congress

The CIVIL WAR In
MIDDLE TENNESSEE

Part II—1863

IT HAPPENED at sunset.

A Yankee musketball came hissing through the Virginia twilight toward a great-nephew of Patrick Henry. He was Gen. Joseph Eggleston Johnston, sitting his horse in drifting wisps of battle smoke. Behind the bullet came a shell fragment.

Suddenly Johnston went rigid, gripping his bridle. The musketball had struck his right shoulder. The wound was slight. He stuck to his saddle. Then the shell fragment hit his chest. He was unhorsed.

It was May 31, 1862, at the Battle of Fair Oaks (also called Seven Pines). Many an 1863 event of the Civil War in Middle Tennessee would hinge from this hour. Because of his wound, Gen. Johnston would lose his command on the eve of great events in the East.

Upon recovery, he would be placed in supreme command of Confederate forces in the West, beyond the Alleghenies. He would come to Tennessee, and Tennesseans would take him lovingly to their hearts as "Old Joe."

Gen. Robert E. Lee would become the new commander of the Army of Northern Virginia.

The less fortunate Johnston would reach Middle Tennessee a few weeks before the fateful New Year of 1863. On that day the Emancipation Proclamation of the American President Abraham Lincoln would free the slaves across most of the Confederacy, and Federal steamboats would be moored beam to beam at Nashville wharves, disgorging tons of cargo for the push against the second-rate Rebel general, Braxton Bragg, at Murfreesboro.

"THE SANCTUARY"—so Edwin Forbes, superb Civil War artist, entitled his dramatic drawing of slaves welcoming Union forces.

THESE developments were seven months away when Gen. Johnston slumped in his saddle at Fair Oaks.

Two aides helped him from the line of fire. Consciousness faded, but not for long. Johnston's bearing was so gallant that a cheer went up from Rebels streaming by. They were Middle Tennesseans.

It seems almost prophetic that the cheer for the unhorsed leader rose from the throats of men from Wilson, Smith, Sumner and DeKalb counties. Their land would be his in the days ahead. Johnston lifted his hat in response.

Gen. Robert (Bob) Hatton of Lebanon was leading them on Ball, his bay. It was the last hour of life for many.

"*Attention!*" Hatton called, above the roar. "*Quickstep! March—*"

Toward the sound of heaviest firing they went, and it has been written that Jefferson Davis, President of the Confederacy, was looking on as Hatton and his Middle Tennesseans surged forward. Heavy smoke engulfed them.

"*The last time I saw him,*" wrote a Richmond Dispatch correspondent of Hatton, "*he was in the charge, waving his hat . . .*"

Three days before, Hatton had written his wife, "*If we meet again, we'll smile. If not, this parting has been well—*" They would not meet again.

Hatton vanished in the rolling smoke. And how far was this hour from an April day a year before when, as a non-sectional, conservative congressman, he had stood stoutly for preservation of the Union—and had been burned in effigy a quarter-mile from the Lebanon Square. When war came, he had gone loyally with the South, as the heroic colonel of the Seventh Tennessee Regiment.

He was charging on, astride Ball. The bay was hit and collapsed. Hatton tore himself free. He strode on foot about 30 yards. A Minie ball pierced him. Just ahead were the enemy's works. The Rebels couldn't hold them. Back they staggered, "thinned and bleeding," bearing Hatton's body with them. (Today his likeness may be seen on a monument on the Public Square at Lebanon, not far from the spot where smoke from his effigy rose in the Wilson County sky.)

President Davis reached the side of the wounded Johnston. They shook hands. Officers looked on with poker faces. Here was irony. It was well known that the President and Gen. Johnston did not care for each other. Herein, too, would be grievous trouble for the South.

There is a story that, as West Pointers, Davis and Johnston had a fist fight over a girl (a vaporous legend which seems to have no contemporary proof). Whatever the wellspring of their trouble, the gentlemen were zealous, each willing to lay down his life for the Confederacy. They hid their feelings.

Davis offered to take Johnston to the Presidential residence in Richmond. Johnston thanked him but declined. For his convalescence, his staff found him a house in the city's suburbs. Mrs. Johnston joined him.

She was greatly distressed, and not only because of her husband's wounds.

Could anything except misfortune for the South come of the unfortunate relationship between the President and her husband?

She had sensed this even before Johnston, in the spring of '61, had offered his services to the South. Justifiably or not, she had warned her husband, "*He hates you. He has power, and he will ruin you—*"

"*He can't, I don't care, it's my country,*" Johnston had replied.

—Photo by Julian Vannerson, Cook Collection, Valentine Museum, Richmond, Va.

GEN. ROBERT E. LEE

His great chance came when Johnston was wounded.

UNION SUPPLY STEAMERS at the Nashville wharf, Dec. 18, 1862. Thirteen days later Rosecrans struck at Bragg. The Battle of Murfreesboro was on. River-borne supplies mightily strengthened the Federal stand in Middle Tennessee.

MRS. JOHNSTON'S views may have been too strong. (But there are many students of history who feel that, had the two men been friends, Confederate Tennessee would have fared better in the coming year of '63 and Georgia in 1864.)

"You must cure him soon," Gen. Lee wrote Mrs. Johnston June 1. *"In the meantime the President has thought it necessary that I should take his place. I wish I was able or that his mantle had fallen on an abler man—"*

Lee's own great name was yet to be made. (In that springtime, he was just beginning to permit the beard to grow that would become so familiar in history books.) As he took command of the Army of Northern Virginia, he obviously considered himself a substitute until Johnston could resume command. They were old friends, Virginians, classmates, and comrades of West Point days.

"Then my wound was fortunate," Johnston said later, upon learning reinforcements had begun to reach his recent command, now under Lee. *"Lee has made them do for him what they would not do for me."* He knew Lee had a facility for getting along with Davis which he, Johnston, didn't have.

Johnston had an acute sense of strategy. But he liked to keep his plans to himself, and he felt there were too many military leaks from Richmond. The news of his wounding was withheld until June 4. It caused alarm.

"He is the only commander on either side," said the *Richmond Examiner*, *"that has yet proven, beyond all question, a capacity to maneuver a large army in the presence of one yet larger; to march it, fight it or not fight it, at will, and, while so doing, to baffle the plans of the ablest opponents in every instance."*

The *Examiner* also saw Johnston as a general who could *"hold out with the solidity of a rock against all foolish projects formed for him by others."* Was this a potshot at Davis, who had wanted to be a general himself? Davis had been shocked and disappointed when made President instead.

The change in the Confederate high command made big news from the Virginia front. It reached Tennessee about the time peonies were blooming around country porticoes and spring cuttings were popping up cheerfully in sunlit boxes around the doorsteps. In the same sunlight sat many a wounded Rebel, cheerfully recovering to fight again, as Johnston was.

It was the tense springtime in which the Federals would come so near Richmond they could hear the church bells in the Confederate capital . . . But they would come no closer, for three long years . . .

Lee would hold them. He would raise the siege of Richmond and drive back the Federal general, George B. McClellan, with heavy losses.

Under Lee's guidance, the Rebels would ride a winning tide in the East, at the Seven Days Battle, the Second Battle of Bull Run (Manassas), at Chancellorsville and in the Shenandoah Valley, until the spring of 1863.

Lee's fame was dawning. He was on his way to immortality as one of the noblest and purest military leaders of all time.

Johnston was about to step into reverses not of his making—some of which might have been avoided had his advice been taken. He was about to step into the area of old failures, where neither Gen. Albert Sidney Johnston, nor Gen. Pierre G. T. Beauregard, nor the drill book stickler, Bragg, had been able to check the Federal surge. He was coming to Tennessee.

—From an engraving by Samuel Sartain.

GEN. ROBERT (BOB) HATTON OF LEBANON

—Drawn from a photo in the Brady-Handy Collection, Library of Congress.

PRESIDENT JEFFERSON DAVIS, CSA

—An engraving by H. B. Hall Jr., from **The Army of Tennessee**, by Stanley F. Horn, Bobbs-Merrill Co.

GEN. BRAXTON BRAGG

The White House of the Confederacy in Richmond. Here lived Jefferson Davis.

—Reproduced by permission of PUNCH

In this London cartoon on Jan. 10, 1863, the ghost of George III chides the ghost of George Washington, "How about that fine republic of yours now, eh? Eh?"

—Brady-Handy Collection, Library of Congress.

The most famous of all the Lincoln pictures (reproduced on $5 bills). Here you see it unretouched.

On March 17, 1862, pro-Union *Harper's Weekly* cartooned Richmond as a "rotten egg"—soon to be easily punctured. (But three more years would pass before Richmond fell.)

IT WAS November, 1862, when Johnston reported back to the War Office in Richmond for active duty. Bragg was back in Murfreesboro after defeat in Kentucky. There were howls for his removal, but Davis just couldn't believe his old West Point buddy was so incompetent as critics claimed.

Bragg had the Presidential ear. Bragg had already suggested that Johnston be given the whole southwest command, with plenary powers (a suggestion which Davis would eventually follow). This would include the far-flung areas of Tennessee, Mississippi and Arkansas. (Was somebody searching for a scapegoat, just in case things went wrong again?)

Davis didn't remove Bragg. He chose a middle course. He put Johnston over him Nov. 24, by placing Johnston in charge of all western Confederate forces.

What? All the West? Johnston was upset. He would soon ask, in vain, to be relieved of such a sprawling command.

Within a few hours, Johnston offered a plan: Why not bring the men of Gen. John C. Pemberton from Mississippi to Tennessee, combine them with Bragg's at Murfreesboro, and, with the united 100,000 men, fall upon Gen. William S. Rosecrans at Nashville? Drive him out of Tennessee. Then roll on toward the Ohio. Don't wait. Now is the time.

Such action, Johnston thought, should cause the aggressive Union general, U. S. Grant, then eying Vicksburg, to give up any idea of penetrating Mississippi.

Why not bring to Mississippi, Johnston asked, the 30,000 Rebel soldiers now doing nothing in Arkansas? This should help hold Grant at bay. The Rebels could still get across the big river. A little stretch remained unconquered, from Port Hudson to Vicksburg. Act!

Davis was not pleased. Johnston was on the spot. He saw his predicament as "sort of a supervisory command" over forces "too far apart to help each other" and each "too weak to help itself." In effect Johnston said: We're spread too far, too thinly. Tighten up into fewer and mightier fighting units!

Aptly Johnston called Tennessee the "Shield of the South." The prospect of losing the state especially disturbed him. He foresaw that, should all Tennessee fall, the Federal way would be open to Virginia and Georgia, as the enemy chose. He bluntly predicted that an effort to hold both Tennessee and Mississippi at the same time would result in the loss of both.

Johnston's suggestions were scarcely noticed. President Davis did not approve. Through the long struggle, the President would not be too eager for advice. (Did he ever forget his deep-seated desire to be a general?)

Troubled in heart, the Johnstons prepared to leave Richmond. They must go to the failure zone where Bragg, now often called "Woodenhead," had stumbled and fumbled for months, with a chronic disinclination to follow up any rare success that came his way. They must go without new ideas . . .

Johnston attended a farewell breakfast in his honor. Confederate Sen. William A. Yancey proposed a toast: *"Gentlemen, let us drink to the man who can save the Confederacy, Gen. Joseph E. Johnston!"*

"Mr. Yancey," Johnston responded, *"the man you describe is now in the field, in the person of Gen. Robert E. Lee. I will drink to his health."* (Lee was then busy with the Fredericksburg campaign, which would give the South a hopeful Christmas.)

On Dec. 5, the Johnstons reached Chattanooga, his future headquarters. A telegram awaited. Pemberton had fallen back under Federal pressure. The trouble foreseen had begun. Johnston hurried to Murfreesboro. He began an appraisal.

ARRIVAL OF THE NEWSBOY, from Forbes' book, *30 Years After*. The vender, arriving horseback, finds avid readers.

JOHNSTON wrote Sen. Louis T. Wigfall, Dec. 4, *"If Rosecrans had disposed our troops himself, their disposition could not have been more unfavorable to us . . ."*

He still wanted to tighten up the scattered forces. Davis preferred holding big areas, and he arrived in Chattanooga Dec. 10.

With dismay, Gen. Johnston learned that Davis wanted to take 9,000 men from Murfreesboro and send them to Pemberton in Mississippi. Johnston thought it dangerous. He said so. He again suggested that the army of Gen. Theophilus H. Holmes in Arkansas be brought to Pemberton's aid. Don't weaken Bragg at Murfreesboro! There's Rosecrans, waiting, just 30 miles away in Nashville!

This time, for once, Bragg disagreed with the President. He sided with Johnston.

Davis overrode both and directed Johnston to send a large detachment to Mississippi. Away they went, 9,000 from Bragg's army.

"This has blown away some castles in the air," Johnston wrote Sen. Wigfall frankly on Dec. 15. *"I had dreamed of crushing Grant with Holmes and Pemberton's troops, and with the latter, Bragg and Kirby Smith, marching to the Ohio . . ."*

On Dec. 26, just 11 days after the letter was written, Rosecrans marched out of Nashville to attack Bragg. The two-day Battle of Murfreesboro followed, Dec. 31, 1862, and Jan. 2, 1863, with a day's lull in between.

"The enemy is in full retreat," Rosecrans wired superiors Jan. 4. *"They left last night . . ."* He was much relieved.

Johnston was proving himself a prophet.

"Davis will not willingly let the world know," Sen. Wigfall later wrote Johnston, *"that the troops were removed from Bragg before the Battle of Murfreesboro against your advice and by his order and that your advice was not followed as to the union of Holmes and Pemberton."* (Date of letter, Oct. 16, 1863.)

Bragg evacuated Murfreesboro and moved southward to the rich Duck River Valley. There he began to set up a new line with headquarters at Tullahoma. It must serve as a barrier against any farther advance by Rosecrans upon Chattanooga. The city of Chattanooga was the door to the Deep South, just as Fort Donelson had been the gate to Nashville's front yard. The door must not be opened. But the Yankees, moving into Murfreesboro behind Bragg, were 30 miles nearer . . .

Rosecrans didn't go storming after the retreating Rebels. He'd had quite enough of it at the battle. In Murfreesboro he paused, perhaps congratulating himself that Bragg had gone. (After the first day of battle, Rosecrans had been in a mood to retreat himself!)

Both sides had lost about a third of their fighting power. They began replenishing their strength, fortifying their new positions. Rosecrans found in Murfreesboro a forest of crudely built chimneys which had warmed the huts of Rebel soldiers. He also found an example of Southern loyalty which didn't lift his morale

"The place is almost entirely deserted of its former inhabitants," Harper's Weekly would soon report. *". . . Not a store is open . . . No citizens were upon the streets, not a woman or child visible . . ."*

Murfreesboro wasn't playing footsie with the conquerors.

As late as Jan. 6, Gen. Johnston, in Chattanooga, had no direct word from Bragg as to the outcome of the battle. Only indirectly did he first learn that Bragg had fallen back. This he cited to Davis as illustrating the difficulty of directing affairs in both Tennessee and Mississippi.

"The difficulty . . . is realized, but cannot be avoided," replied Davis, harassed by and perhaps preoccupied with economic and diplomatic fronts.

The Emancipation Proclamation, promulgated by Lincoln in the previous autumn, had become formally effective Jan. 1. It declared forever free all slaves in Confederate states not occupied by Union armies—an estimated 3,120,000 Negroes.

What Shall We Do? Go—or stay and be certain of food? Many a slave, suddenly freed, sadly considered the question. Forbes entitled this drawing, "Waiting for Dinner."

A Slave on Emancipation Day: "Know what day dis is, Massa?" *Harper's* carried this gibing cartoon nine days afterwards, Jan. 10, 1863.

BRAGG'S ABANDONED CAMP at Murfreesboro (top). Only chimneys remain where once stood the huts of the Army of Tennessee. The lower drawing shows deserted Murfreesboro. Citizens have gone. The conquerors have come. Both drawings are from *Harper's Weekly*, Jan. 31, 1863.

THE proclamation widened a slowly opening crack in the South's reservoir of cheap labor. It delivered a massive psychological blow to the Southern cause abroad by rallying the moral sense of British and French masses to the side of the North.

Many a man abroad would now forget the issue of coercion which had set off the war. With the cry of "shackles broken," the North acquired a new grandeur as the champion of freedom.

The proclamation DIDN'T free Tennessee slaves. (They would be freed in February, 1865, by an amendment to the State Constitution.)

Why were Tennessee slaves exempted? Why not freed by the proclamation? Because it applied only to slaves within Confederate lines, and most of Tennessee was now inside Federal lines. Tennessee's Capitol was a Federal fortress. The North chose to consider her back in the Union fold. So Tennessee slaves would remain slave for two more years.

Strange? Yes. Many Tennesseans would call the proclamation a "farce." (So would many thoughtful Northerners, for the proclamation had retained slavery within the lines of the Union, which called itself fighting for freedom.)

However, nearly two years later, in 1864, Tennessee's military governor, Andrew Johnson, a Yankee-minded future President from East Tennessee, would issue a "proclamation" of his own, on Nashville's Capitol Hill.

This would come on an October night of uproar, political harangue and surging Negro crowds, just a few weeks before the Union's re-election of Lincoln would sweep Gov. Johnson into the vice presidency as Lincoln's running-mate.

"*I do hereby proclaim freedom . . . to every man in Tennessee,*" Gov. Johnson would shout to a multitude of 3,000 jubilant, torch-bearing Negroes.

They would shout back from old Cedar Street and the southeast corner of Capitol Hill, "*You are our Moses!*"

After Lincoln's proclamation, the South's hope for foreign intervention dwindled fast. But England didn't change her mind overnight. *Punch*, the urbane British magazine, derisively chortled, "*When all those Negroes walk, clothed in the dignity of freedom, what we want to know is who is going to feed 'em?*"

Punch cartooned the ghost of George III chiding George Washington about the war-torn mess of his "fine republic now." It showed a Negro, proclamation in hand, merrily willing to "beat" his former master. It cartooned another as Caesar's ghost, telling Lincoln, "*I am dy ebil genius, Mr. Linking. Dis child am awful inimpressional.*"

The utterly honest Lincoln was doing his best: "*If all earthly powers were given me, I should not know what to do with the slaves.*"

He also said: "*If I could preserve the Union without freeing any slaves, I would do it. If I could preserve the Union by freeing all the slaves, I would do it. What I do about the colored race I do because it helps preserve the Union.*"

Many slaves had long been gathering their meager belongings and swarming upon the nearest Union encampment, creating great problems. Thousands welcomed freedom. Some stayed where they were because they feared starvation elsewhere. Some left and came back, disillusioned.

Some stayed because they chose, and worked on. Others followed burned-out, former owners into the woods, hovering near their tents, comforting and protecting them as best they could in a world distraught. This was to become one of America's sublimest stories of innate nobility, the like of which the world has rarely seen. In the darkest hour for many whites, the Negro cast his whitest light, against the agonies ahead.

BRUTUS AND CÆSAR.

"I am dy ebil genius, Mr. Linking," says Caesar's ghost (a freedman) to a troubled Lincoln, caricatured as Brutus.

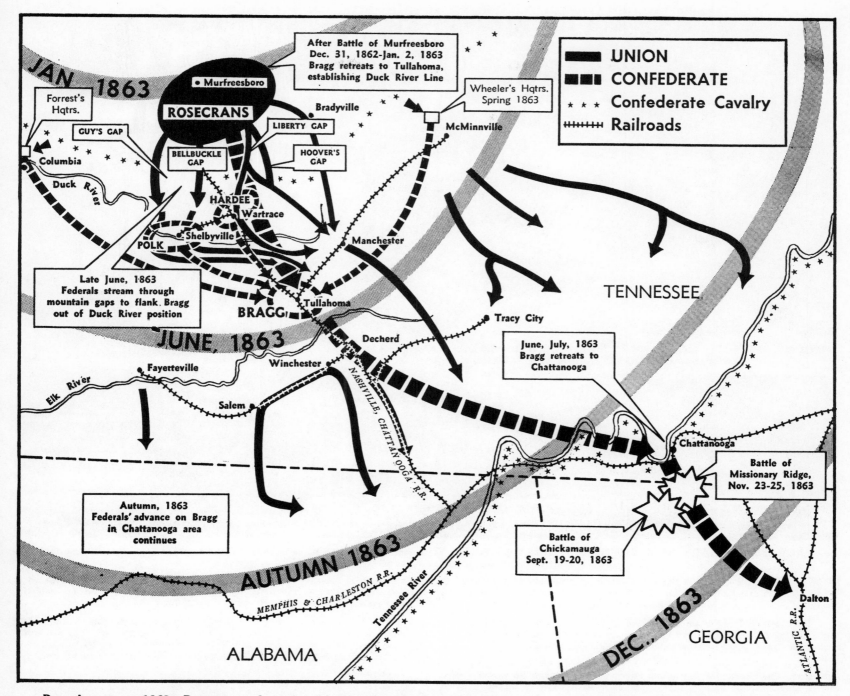

Bragg's retreat, 1863. Bragg moved southward, after the Battle of Murfreesboro, and established a new line along the Duck River Valley. Forced out at last, he moved to Chattanooga. Rosecrans took his time in following. Close of the tragic year found Bragg in Dalton, Ga.

OUT OF this crumbling, near-feudal economy would rise a thing accursed, with its promise of survival—the system of tenant farming. By it, the plow would come again to the fallow fields of penniless masters who had only land to offer. Upon the handles of the plow would go the hands of penniless freedmen and landless whites, now competing, both with only labor to offer. Therein would lie new bondage, for nearly a hundred years, with no man his brother's keeper.

The coming century had its prelude in the wintry nights of January, 1863, when pelting rain and sleet drummed out the dirge of an era upon the roofs of the master's big house and the cabins of his slaves. Under both roofs were whispers and sometimes a shouting voice, with words almost the same: *"What shall we do?"*

The die was being cast and no man could read the future. The present was a puzzle, grim as the tread of Rebel soldiers trudging southward toward the Duck, and ghostly as another sound in the night, that of a slave departing for Nashville.

And who could see the city's face? Did she wear a mask—of painted lips or widow's weeds? There was still fine furniture in big double parlors, but the parlors were empty. The music was gone. There was music down the street in cheaper houses, but the songs were too loud. So were many of the people. So Nashville wore her mask, bereft of native sons and crowded with strangers, Union soldiers, sons of fortune, Union officials and shadowy male and female adventurers.

It has been said that barely a score of hale young native men remained within her limits. Nearly all were with the armies. Rare was the home untouched by grief.

It had become a city in which a man could sell his soul in a second— for contraband coffee or tea, or sugar or muskets, or the right kind of shady service or information.

Some sold once and regretted. Some sold once and forgot it. Some never sold at all. And some sold daily and made fast money. (A year hence a pound of tea would bring around $500.)

One of the latter was a slave-owning double-dealer who lived on the Big Harpeth River in a cabin near Confederate lines, close to both sides. He dealt with both. He had taken the Oath of Allegiance to the Union, which was convenient. Daily he broke his vow, which was also convenient. He smuggled goods, beat his slaves, and made a point of saying a prayer before he broke his bread.

He ran the lines with hard-to-get goods, perhaps with slaves now and then, and certainly with people wishing to go South—if they could cross his palm with silver. Did he think nobody knew? Both sides must have known. Both sides used him. He was convenient to them—which he may not have realized. So he was permitted to function for many months.

No wonder sleuths were needed. They came, efficient Yankees doing their duty. A sickening thing was beginning.

Over the city and out into the midstate, a cold, new fear was spreading . . . dread of the Yankee army's gestapo-like secret police. Its head was Col. William S. Truesdail, ruthless, alert, born for his job. A Missourian as was Grant, he had offices on High Street (now Sixth Avenue) near the Capitol.

After Murfreesboro, Truesdail's activities increased. Scores of spies worked for him, many masquerading as Confederates. Loyal Rebels had to be careful.

Careful of what you say and write! Who's your messenger? Watch your words, even in front of the servants. It may reach Truesdail's office. (Or do you know him through the cotton trade? Shhh! What? Shh-hh! Be quiet. Cotton, man . . . Wake up!)

"GONE OFF WITH THE YANKS," Forbes called this drawing. At right a slave departs, "LOOKING FOR THE YANKEES."

"ACROSS COUNTRY IN A THUNDERSTORM," by Forbes. Through slanting rain, in scenes similar to this, Bragg's army moved southward toward its new stand along the Duck.

IT WAS being whispered that those in Truesdail's good graces were enjoying just about a monopoly in cotton. The whispers would reach the White House. (President Lincoln would hear, from his own military governor.)

Truesdail centered much of his own suspicion upon Confederate women. The Southern Ladies Aid Society became a prime target. Doubtless he had good reason. The hearts of the ladies were in the struggle and not for cotton.

Their menfolk were settling into position along the Duck, getting ready to fight again. Quinine would help them. So would other drugs. So would a good pair of shoes. (Within a year, a good pair of boots would cost several hundred dollars.)

Once a pair of boots fell from the ample skirts of a Nashville woman. Truesdail guessed their intended destination. Not always would he win in his brushes with the ladies.

"Don't trust women!" he preached. (One day he would find a woman to trust, imported from Louisville for a purpose. She would be a Creole actress, and he would send her into the Duck River towns to smile at the men in gray and butternut and try to glean their secrets.) And his maxim, "Don't trust women," kept resounding through the big commandeered mansions near Tennessee's Capitol.

One of these was the spacious old home of deceased George W. Campbell (who had served as an ante-bellum U. S. senator, secretary of the treasury and minister to Russia). It conveniently faced the Capitol's south portico from the proudest block of old Cedar Street. In it lived the Union's jittery Gov. Johnson, close to the reassuring big guns just uphill.

In Johnson's day the house was owned by Campbell's daughter, Mrs. Lizinka Campbell Brown—named for a Russian czarina who had been her mother's friend. She was a great-grandmother of Col. Campbell H. Brown of Franklin, state executive director of the Civil War Centennial Commission.

"Isn't it a shame!" Nashville women said. "That Yankee Johnson, in Lizinka's pretty house! I bet she could tell him a thing or two!" (She would, without saying a word.)

Lizinka was a wealthy widow of strong Confederate sympathies. She had moved away, of course, months ago. She was now in Virginia, nursing her wounded cousin, one of Lee's generals, Robert Stoddert Ewell, who had lost a leg at Second Manassas.

Lizinka was in love with her bachelor cousin. But should she let him know? One day she would write the recovered Ewell a letter . . .

And Tennessee's military governor, an East Tennessee Yankee, would receive the biting news that the woman who owned the roof over his head had become the bride of a Confederate general. (Ewell would lead Lee's Second Corps at Gettysburg. He sleeps in Nashville soil beside Lizinka, at the old City Cemetery.)

Meanwhile, to his credit, even Gov. Johnson had been revolted by Truesdail's methods. "Wholly incompetent, if not corrupt, in the grossest sense of the term," the governor said of Truesdail in a telegram to Lincoln.

Truesdail's encroachments continued. He had strength. He was supported by Gen. Rosecrans. By mid-January, the governor was boiling. He protested to Rosecrans: "I am compelled to say that the provost court and the detective police have greatly impaired the confidence of loyal (Union) men."

Rosecrans felt the governor was getting too big for his britches. (One suggestion would turn up that Johnson be moved to some place "like Gallatin.") Rosecrans, peeved, complained about Johnson to Gen. Henry W. Halleck, supreme Federal commander in the West. Halleck rocked Rosecrans back on his heels.

Lincoln in a characteristic pose, scratching his right ear. This notable drawing, by Albert Hunt, is reproduced from *They Were There*, by Philip Van Doren Stern.

"ARRIVAL OF A FEDERAL COLUMN AT A PLANTER'S HOUSE." *Harper's* reporter wrote, "About all the friends we have in the region" are the Negroes. "Nabobs of the soil," he called the planters.

YOUR business, Halleck replied in effect, is to get along with the military governor and not try to dominate him.

By this time, whispers about Truesdail had extended to Rosecrans. The Federal general heard. He also learned that Gov. Johnson had reported the whispers to Washington. Rosecrans wrote Johnson, demanding vindication for himself.

For two months, Johnson maintained what appeared to have been a contemptuous silence. Finally he replied that he had no information affecting the character of Rosecrans as a citizen or soldier. However, Johnson added, *"I have never believed, and I do not now believe, that you have fully understood the character and extent of the proceedings under Truesdail."*

Whatever Johnson's shortcomings as military governor, he wasn't grabbing for gold. He was standing on principle as he saw it. Was he coming to know men better? (His term as President would show a breadth and depth of character far beyond that which he displayed as military governor of Tennessee.)

To Johnson, Truesdail was *"a base and unmitigated . . . parasite."* The governor declared he had refused to release 50 penitentiary convicts who were better men than Truesdail.

This opinion must have been shared by a mortal foe, Gen. Nathan Bedford Forrest, who said of Truesdail: *"I've given strict orders that, if ever taken, he shall be hung to the nearest tree and brought to me to be embalmed as a curiosity!"* At least, so Forrest has been quoted.

The towering wizard of the saddle, returning from a notably successful raid in West Tennessee, took up his new post at Columbia, on the west wing of the Duck River line, 25 miles from his cabin birthplace at Chapel Hill.

Bragg remained at Tullahoma. From there, Gen. William J. Hardee went on to Wartrace. Gen Leonidas Polk, "the fighting bishop" (Episcopal bishop of Louisiana), took his corps to Shelbyville, 20 miles from Murfreesboro . . . And through the towns the Creole actress soon would be strolling, *"searching for my brother . . . in the Confederate Army . . ."*

Bragg wasn't asleep. Through the same towns a lanky herb-dealer also would be strolling, peddling his wares in Columbia, Franklin, Murfreesboro, Pulaski and nearby places.

To those wanting liniment and tonics, the peddler would be "Dr. E. Coleman." To certain colleagues he would be "Capt. Coleman." Actually he was Capt. H. B. Shaw, CSA, chief of Bragg's scouts. And one day in the coming autumn Shaw would acquire a personable, young, uniformed scout named Sam Davis.

Far to the east, at McMinnville, on the right wing of the 80-mile Con-

federate front, another cavalry leader of song-and-story took his stand. This was newly-wed Gen. John Hunt Morgan, the handsome and dashing raider from Kentucky.

At McMinnville, Morgan was joined by his bride, the former Mattie Ready, to whom he had been married in the gay December of 1862, when the South was having itself a bang-up Christmas, infinitely cheered by Lee's success at Fredericksburg—before the Tennessee clock struck 12 at Murfreesboro.

Mattie remained with her lover in McMinnville, blissfully happy on the rim of danger. *"You think the honeymoon will never end, don't you?"* wrote a sister from occupied Nashville. (Bluecoats were hobnobbing in their Murfreesboro home.)

Mattie replied, *"My life is one joyous dream now, from which I fear to awaken . . . I can correspond almost regularly with you now, Sis. The bearer goes principally on my account."*

—Courtesy Mrs. George Garvin Brown, Prospect, Ky.
MRS. LIZINKA CAMPBELL BROWN
She became the bride of Gen. Ewell.

THE CIVIL WAR IN MII

—Courtesy Library of Congress
Great Seal of the Confederacy.

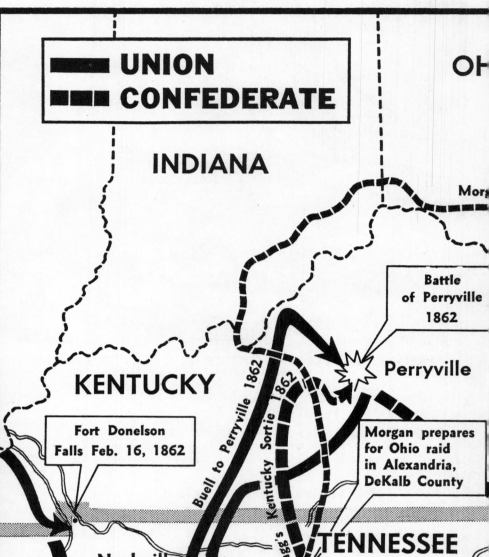

UNION
CONFEDERATE

OH

INDIANA

Morg

Battle
of Perryville
1862

Perryville

KENTUCKY

Fort Donelson
Falls Feb. 16, 1862

Morgan prepares
for Ohio raid
in Alexandria,
DeKalb County

TENNESSEE

Nashville

Alexandria

Kno

Murfreesboro

Battle of
Murfreesboro
Dec. 31, 1862
Jan. 2, 1863

DUCK RIVER LINE

Tullahoma

Chattano

Battle of Shiloh
April 6-7, 1862

Dalton

Bragg
Nov. 28
Joe Jo
takes

Battle of
Chickamauga
Sept. 19-20, 1863

Atlan

ALABAMA

PART II
1863

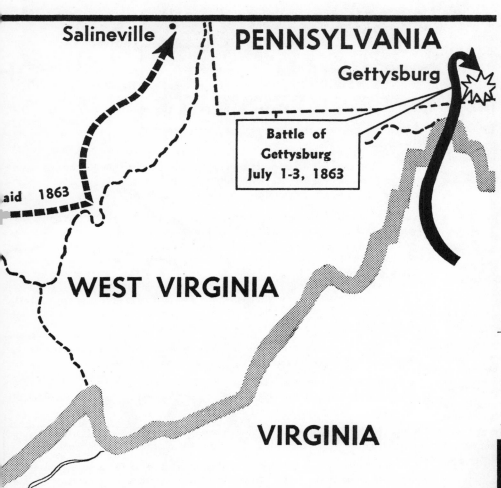

—From an engraving in *Life of Pauline Cushman, the Celebrated Spy of the Cumberland*, by F. L. Sarmiento, published by J. E. Potter, 1865

"Yours Truly," indeed! As the springtime of 1863 came to Middle Tennessee, Pauline Cushman, the Yankee spy, was viewing the scene from the old City Hotel in Nashville. Soon her activities centered along the Duck River Line. In gratitude for her efforts, the Yankees gave her the rank of major.

Battle of Gettysburg July 1-3, 1863

Salineville

PENNSYLVANIA

Gettysburg

Raid 1863

WEST VIRGINIA

VIRGINIA

NORTH CAROLINA

Battle of onary Ridge 23-25, 1863

RGIA

Big Days of the Civil War
for Middle Tennesseans (1863)

- Jan. 1, Emancipation Day. Epochal, but not strictly applicable to Tennessee. See narrative.

- Jan. 2, Battle of Murfreesboro ends. (It had begun Dec. 31, 1862.)

- Jan. 3, Bragg begins withdrawal from Murfreesboro toward Duck River.

- April 10, "Streight's Raid" begins in Nashville with loading of 800 mules onto steamers. Transports sail next day.

- May 3, Forrest captures Streight near Rome, Ga.

- June 11, Gen. John Hunt Morgan leaves Alexandria, en route to his disastrous Ohio raid—and capture. (But the raid will take him, by July 26, to the farthest point North reached by a major body of Confederate troops during entire Civil War.)

- June 24, Rosecrans moves from Murfreesboro against Bragg's Duck River Line.

- June 30, Army of Tennessee, outflanked, quits Tullahoma. Withdraws toward Chattanooga.

- Sept. 8, Bragg evacuates Chattanooga. Moves toward Lafayette, Ga.

- Sept. 19-20, Battle of Chickamauga.

- Nov. 23-25, Battle of Missionary Ridge.

- Nov. 27, Sam Davis hanged by Federals in Pulaski. Around midnight, Morgan escapes Ohio prison.

- Nov. 28, in Dalton, Ga., Bragg resigns command of Army of Tennessee.

- Dec. 27, Gen. Joseph E. Johnston succeeds Bragg.

—By Newspaper Printing Corporation artist Jim Young, after the National Geographic Society's Map, "Battlefields of the Civil War."

Gen. Nathan Bedford Forrest, drawn from a photo by C. C. Giers, Nashville.

Gen. Richard Stoddert Ewell looked much older than his 46 years in 1863.

THE NEW RICH—"One of the Effects of the War." *Harper's* portrays a Northern "contractor's wife." She's ordering "a couple of necklaces, along with them other things."

BRAVE, naive little bride! She didn't know the bearer was a Truesdail spy. She wrote blithely on, of love and fancy dresses: *"I know my liege-lord is devoted to me, and each day I am forced to love him more . . . I have made me an elegant evening dress, a beautiful rose deschaune color, with a black lace flounce around the bottom, a black lace vest and sleeves, and a fall of black lace around the waist . . . It is magnificent."*

The letters would be read in Truesdail's High Street office. One day he would spring the trap. Mattie's sister would be among those jailed.

Both Morgan and Forrest now had a youthful new commander. This was Gen. Joseph (Fighting Joe) Wheeler, just 26. Bragg had made the boyish-looking, pint-sized West Pointer his new chief of cavalry, a promotion for good work in the recently futile Kentucky campaign, which Bragg himself had bungled.

Wheeler was 5-feet-2 and weighed less than 100 pounds. ("War Child," many of his men fondly called him.) He was as brave as the biggest. Doggedly aggressive, he was sometimes perhaps too eager to fight, almost as if for the sake of fighting. The last trait wouldn't exactly appeal to Forrest, who wanted every drop of spilt blood to count.

On Jan. 13, Wheeler made a dash against Federal shipping at Harpeth Shoals on the Cumberland River. He captured four transports and the gunboat Sidell. This shook up Gen. Rosecrans, already uneasy about supply and communications. It also roused the quick concern of Federal Quartermaster-General Montgomery C. Meigs, who warned Rosecrans: Have gunboats convoy your river transports.

Meigs thought it was Forrest, not Wheeler, who was behind the shoals attack and he added, *"Are there any horses left in the country for Forrest to steal?"*

(Forrest had superbly equipped his men in West Tennessee with seizures from the enemy.)

"There are some horses," Rosecrans replied, *"but we mean to steal them ourselves."*

Rosecrans was under pressure. Washington was urging attack upon Bragg to relieve stress upon Grant, who was expected to strike Vicksburg. Rosecrans wasn't in a mood to attack anybody. Not now. No, sir!

He'd had the bigger army at Murfreesboro. The Rebels had retreated, yes. But, before they went, they'd walloped him almost to a draw. He was the victor by the skin of his teeth and he knew it. Before he took them on again, he wanted to be loaded for bear. Whenever he struck, he wanted the stoutest of loaded supply lines.

So he waited, while steamboats at Nashville disgorged more and more. Sometimes people laughed. There were wisecracks that Rosecrans was "waiting for his spring radishes and lettuce to mature" before attacking Bragg.

For six months, the Rebels would be permitted to pause along the Duck, marking time longer than any Confederate army in the entire war.

Here Bragg, the textbook general with a somewhat castiron mind, would be at his best with discipline and drill, organizaion and training, all the folderol of camp.

He would build the "strictest discipline in the Confederacy" while officers and men dreaded the time when he again would lead them in combat.

It was not that they dreaded fighting. They dreaded the outcome of his leadership. Since the retreat from Murfreesboro, clamor for his removal had grown. Get rid of "Woodenhead"! How long must he be endured? Confederate newspaper comment was acid. Bragg read.

On Jan. 11, he wrote his generals: *"I shall retire . . . if I have lost (their) good opinions . . ."* He asked for what they thought and got it. All acquitted him of suggesting retreat at Murfreesboro. (They had suggested it.)

FORREST'S ARTILLERY crossing a stream. From *That Devil Forrest*, by John A. Wyeth, Harper and Brothers.

THE COMMANDEERED CUNNINGHAM HOME (where downtown Cross Keys Restaurant now stands) served as headquarters for the Union Army. Its owner, Maj. George Cunningham, loyal Confederate, was one of Nashville's most prosperous merchants when he built the house in 1858.

"PULLING INTO POSITION," by Forbes. This artist was at his best, and happiest, when drawing six-horse artillery units.

BUT Gen. Hardee wrote Bragg: *"A change in the command of this army is necessary."* Gen. Patrick R. Cleburne replied: *"You do not possess the confidence of the army . . ."* A similar view came from Gen. John C. Breckenridge. Gen. Polk was absent, but he soon wrote President Davis, *"My opinion is he had better be transferred."*

Polk thought the over-all commander, "Old Joe," should take Bragg's place.

By this time Bragg was trying to shut off the opinions and again Davis sent Gen. Johnston to investigate. This time Johnston was in a shakier position than ever. What if he reported unfavorably on Bragg, the friend of Davis? Would Davis interpret it as a bid for personal aggrandizement? A bid to replace the man one criticized?

Gen. Johnston found the men still in a mood to fight. He finally reported that he did not think Bragg should be removed. But he touched one vital aspect: *"Should it appear necessary to remove Gen Bragg, no one in this army or engaged in this investigation should be his successor."* He was extricating himself fast in the last sentence.

President Davis was pleased: *"You shall not be urged by me to any course which would wound your . . . views of professional propriety."* Were two gentlemen leaning over backward when a burst of candor might have better served the Army of Tennessee?

On the surface, things seemed quieter along the Duck.

At Murfreesboro, Rosecrans was just as quiet. Halleck, prodded by Grant, time and again ordered Rosecrans to move on Bragg. Rosecrans stood pat. He said that by holding Bragg in Tennessee he kept him out of Grant's way in Mississippi. And among the Rebels there was more laughter about Rosecrans' "lettuce and radishes."

In the late winter and early springtime of 1863, about the only military thunder in Middle Tennessee came from Bragg's cavalry.

In early February, Gen. Wheeler struck at Fort Donelson, far down the Cumberland. Nearly a year had passed since Federals seized it. The idea was to shut off the flow of supplies to Rosecrans. Whose idea? Nobody is certain. It was poorly conceived. With Wheeler went part of Forrest and Col. John A. Wharton's brigades.

Forrest was not with the command when it started. Bragg broke the news to him: They've already gone, with part of your force.

Forrest must have simmered. When he caught up, after two days hard riding, he found 800 of his men along—with no more than 20 rounds of ammunition each. Artillerymen had less than 50 rounds. Forrest disapproved of the attack upon the garrison-fortifications. He wanted his disapproval made public if he were killed. The decision was made by Wheeler, who said he had "maturely" considered the matter.

The attack proved fruitless. The Federals held. What if they hadn't? Could the small Rebel force have long maintained itself? How, when 100 miles deep within enemy lines?

"It is doubtful if the capture of Fort Donelson could have resulted in a complete blockade of the river, but it would have had a tremendous psychological effect upon the people of the South," says Judge Byrd Douglas in *Steamboatin' on the Cumberland.*

Does the episode illustrate a difference between two incredibly brave and gallant men, Forrest and Wheeler? Did the diminutive Wheeler, his small frame surcharged with catlike energy, feel he had to compete wih the lethal savagery of Forrest? Or with the romantic dash of the handsome Morgan?

It is said that Wheeler participated in 200 engagements and 800 skirmishes before the end of the war. But the older man, the 6-foot Forrest, was always willing to avoid a fight if he saw no chance of winning. Blood was treasure.

M. C. MEIGS
Quartermaster-General, USA

GEN. LEONIDAS POLK
Episcopal Bishop

—From **Confederate Veteran Magazine**
CAPT. H. B. SHAW
The "herb-doctor"

—From a photograph by C. C. Giers, Nashville
GEN. JOHN HUNT MORGAN

—Century Magazine drawing from photograph in Library of Congress
GEN. JOSEPH WHEELER

—From Harper's Weekly
WHEELER'S CAVALRY attacks a Union supply train near Jasper.

AS personalities they were poles apart—this fractious Forrest, brilliant, self-made and cabin-born, unlettered, who could think straight even with tears pouring down his cheeks as he shouted battle orders, and this brave, polite and scholarly "War Child" with the big brown eyes so mild, who seldom smiled.

We find them in a room together, after the futile attack. It is night. They are in a farmhouse at Yellow Creek Furnace. Wheeler begins to dictate a report. It's an account of their defeat. Forrest is lying on the floor before the fireplace, his head propped up on a turned-down chair. He listens. Finally he explodes that he'd rather *"be in my coffin"* than fight under Wheeler again.

He never would. With amazing restraint and self-control for one so young, Wheeler arranged matters so Forrest would no longer have to fight under his immediate command.

Wheeler, with courtly manners, was a model of deportment. He had dignity and a level head but no sense of humor. Some say he *"never laughed."* Why? Had some too-early gloom engulfed his smile?

No one knows and yet, looking back into his early childhood, this fact shows up: In the panic of 1837, which ruined many men of affairs, Wheeler's

Sources Of Illustrations

Most of the Part II map designs are by Newspaper Printing Corporation artist Jim Young. The double page map for 1863 is partly from the National Geographic Society's Map, "Battlefields of the Civil War." The map of Bragg's 1863 retreat is a composite of two maps from *"The West Point Atlas of American Wars," Volume I,* Col. Vincent J. Esposito, chief editor, published by Frederick A. Praeger.

For use of the map, Confederate Breakthrough at Chickamauga, and the picture, Hood in His Prime, both from *The Gallant Hood* by John P. Dyer, gratitude is expressed to the author, to the publisher, Bobbs-Merrill Company, and to Gen. Hood's granddaughter, Mrs. Thomas McClure Peters, owner of the portrait.

Most of the illustrations are credited individually. Some first appeared in *Harper's Weekly, Century Magazine, Punch* and the *Illustrated London News.*

father lost his money—when Wheeler was one year old. Had later discipline been too grim, ambition too determined? Had laughter died forever?

Wheeler also was a favorite of Bragg's, which could not have endeared him to Forrest, who already felt that Bragg was pushing him around.

To the great credit of both Wheeler and Forrest, and to the South's good fortune, the two men tried to hang onto their friendship. Soon, in one of Forrest's dispatches, we find him thanking Wheeler for a helmet the young man had sent him. The next day, Feb. 19, Forrest asked Wheeler's aid in obtaining badly needed arms.

A week later, Feb. 25, a Rebel cavalry corps, commanded by Gen. Earl Van Dorn, established headquarters at Spring Hill in Maury County. In the corps were the divisions of Gen. William Hicks Jackson (later master of Belle Meade plantation) and Gen. William T. Martin, and Forrest's brigade.

At that time, Van Dorn was regarded by some as the ablest cavalry commander in the West. Forrest was out from under "Fighting Joe," (but he'd have hot words with Van Dorn, too).

Three days later, Feb. 28, on the far-off Georgia coast, disaster came to a vessel of which Confederate Tennesseans had long been proud.

This was the cruiser Nashville, which, on Nov. 22, 1861, had become the first Confederate war vessel to fly the Flag of the Confederate States in English waters. She was a swift ocean-going, sidewheel steamer with two masts, and she had a speed of 16½ knots.

Her appearance in South Hampton, three days after sinking the ship Harvey Birch, homeward bound for New York, at the mouth of the English Channel, had created a stir in England. In February, 1862, she had burned the schooner Robert Gilfillan in the Atlantic.

In July, 1862, after running the blockade into Savannah harbor with a cargo of arms for the Confederacy, the Nashville had been bottled up by Federal gunboats. For eight months now, she had been lying in the Great Ogeechee River, watching for a chance to dash out to sea.

Meanwhile, she had been safe under the protective guns of Fort McAllister. Opposite the fort, the river was staked. Above the stakes lay the Nashville, ready to go streaking free at the slightest chance.

At first she had been loaded with cotton, all set for a run to England. The weeks dragged on. The gunboats stayed. The Nashville disappeared up river for a few weeks. When she reappeared, she had a new name, Rattlesnake!

—From Century Magazine
Rebel cavalry raid on a Union baggage train.

Gen. William J. Hardee

Gen. Patrick R. Cleburne

FORREST'S MEN taking a front line fortification.

—From **That Devil Forrest**, by John A. Wyeth, Harper & Brothers

THE Rattlesnake had unloaded her cotton. She was all fitted out as a privateer, with six guns. Freshly painted battleship gray, she lay just out of Yankee reach in the Georgia sunshine. Everybody still called her the Nashville.

Twice in five weeks, the wooden gunboats had tried to take her. They had been joined by an iron-clad monitor, the Montauk. All the Nashville had to do was ease up-river, out of harm's way.

On the night of Feb. 27, a Federal reconnaissance group made an excited report. The Nashville, while trying to slip out to sea, had run hard aground. Whoopee!

A sitting duck! She couldn't get off before morning. Just wait.

It is 7:25 a.m., Feb. 28. The gunboats, a mortar boat and the Montauk are steaming toward her. The monitor approaches to within 1,200 yards, close to the barrier. The fort's guns are blazing. On the ironclad they have little effect. The Montauk is content to pour 11 and 15-inch shells into the Nashville. A fog closes down. The firing continues.

The fog lifts. The Nashville is on fire. It is 9:55 a.m. Her magazines explode. She is blown to bits. The U. S. Navy Department, reporting her destruction, referred to her as the "notorious steamer Nashville."

The Nashville was gone. But she had gone as a Rebel.

A significant development was at hand. The U. S. Navy had begun to play a far more vital role in the war than most people realized. (There are modern writers who give the U. S. Navy more than half the credit for the ultimate Union victory.) By July, when the Battle of Gettysburg would be fought, more than 500 ships would be blocking the Southern coast from Hampton Roads to Galveston.

Back in Tennessee, on March 5, Gen. Van Dorn, with part of his corps, met a Federal task force under Col. John Coburn at Thompson's Station. Forrest, commanding on the right of the line, effected a victory by a wide flanking movement. The bag of prisoners was 1,221 including Coburn and 78 officers.

(It was in this encounter that one of Forrest's favorite war horses, Roderick, wounded and led to the rear, heard the sound of battle and headed back to his master, jumping three fences en route, only to receive a fourth and mortal wound as he reached his master's side.)

Gen. Johnston had gone to Mobile on inspection when, on March 9, he was ordered back to Tullahoma by Secretary of War James A. Seddon. Go back. Relieve Bragg. Assume command of the Army of Tennessee yourself. President Davis at last was getting more worried about his old comrade's ability.

"Old Joe" went. He found Mrs. Bragg desperately ill, presumably at the point of death. She had been proud of her husband's position. "Old Joe" didn't have the heart to tell Bragg of the removal order. He also feared the news would be fatal to Mrs. Bragg. Johnston took over temporarily, allowing Bragg to devote himself to his wife. By the time she recovered, "Old Joe" himself was ill.

Again Bragg had been spared, almost by chance. Both he and Gen. Johnston resumed their former duties.

On the night of March 24, Forrest started after two more prizes. One was an entrenched army camp at Brentwood, surrounded by a quarter-mile belt of felled trees and manned by more than 500 Wisconsin troops.

A mile and a half southward, where the railroad crossed the Little Harpeth River, stood a sturdy stockade manned by nearly 300 Michigan troops.

—From **That Devil Forrest**, by Wyeth, Harper & Brothers
Forrest's horse is killed by a shell.
(More than 20 horses were shot under him.)

The cruiser Nashville destroying a Federal vessel.

—By Forbes, from 30 Years After

A CAVALRY CAMP

—Century Magazine drawing, from a photo

Gen. Earl Van Dorn

FORREST reached Brentwood at daylight. The Federal commander received Forrest's demand for surrender. He sent back word, *"Come and get us!"*

He didn't feel so gay when he found himself surrounded. Two field pieces were being trained upon his position. He surrendered.

Forrest moved on to the stockade. He fired one artillery round and again demanded surrender. (It's said the Rebel who took the demand forward had no white handkerchief. Forrest ordered him to put his shirt on the bayonet instead. The shirt served just as well.) The Michigan Federals became prisoners.

Little more than two weeks later, on the afternoon of April 10, Nashvillians witnessed a spectacle. Hundreds of Yankee mules were plodding toward the wharves.

Down at the landing, 800 quartermaster mules were being loaded aboard eight Federal transports for some unknown purpose. Streight's Raid was beginning—the Yankees sashay into Georgia by Col. Abel D. Streight of Indiana.

(In *Gone With the Wind,* Scarlett and her friends grew apprehensive lest Streight swing on into Atlanta, the "workshop of the South," and destroy

Railroad stockades like this one near Nashville made prime targets for Rebel cavalry units.

factories there. What it would have cost the South if it had not been for Forrest!)

The Federals hoped to do, on a gigantic scale, what Gen. Wheeler had attempted at Fort Donelson— swing around the enemy and cut off his supplies.

It was an ambitious plan, to snap the railroads between Atlanta and Tennessee. Specifically, Streight meant to stop the supplies that were rolling up through Chattanooga to the Rebels waiting on the Duck!

From Nashville Streight planned to descend the Cumberland to Palmyra in Montgomery County, then march westward to meet the transports at Fort Henry on the Tennessee. Then he and his men planned to go up the Tennessee to Eastport, Miss., en route to Georgia. On the backs of the mules, accompanied by cavalry, a portion of the men then planned to strike into Northern Alabama and Georgia. What an elaborate effort!

It would lead Forrest to one of his most spectacular exploits. He heard that 2,000 Federals had landed from transports April 19 at Eastport. Away he went from Columbia. He caught up with Streight at Decatur, Ala.

The hard-riding, hard-fighting race was on, five days of it. On May 3, between Gadsden, Ala., and Rome, Ga., Forrest captured Streight and about 1,800 men with all supplies.

Many of Forrest's men, almost asleep on foot, stood nodding at the heads of their horses as Streight gave up. Rock-bottom endurance, as well as strategy, had paid off.

Forrest took his prisoners to Rome. Ladies rushed out to give him flowers. ("*The pathway of his gallant army was strewn with them.*") Babies were held for him to kiss. He was begged for locks of his hair until he had to say no.

A day or two later came news of Lee's victory at Chancellorsville. Oh, glory! Forrest and Lee! Atlanta went wild. Nashville's celebration was more guarded. Behind closed doors there was laughter and back-slapping. Haw! Oh, the broad-beamed Northern riders! On their commissary mules! And Forrest had made the Feds see double!

(Just before the surrender, Forrest had employed an outworn trick, sending the same two guns around and around an elevation. *"Name of God!"* exclaimed the parleying Streight. *"How many guns have you got?"* Forrest glanced around. *"I reckon,"* he said, *"that's all that has kept up."*)

Forrest reached Shelbyville May 13. Bragg received him with warmth. Forrest's advancement to major general would be recommended. "Old Bedford" declined. Some other officer, he said, might have more capacity for the rank. (Months later he would accept the honor, from other hands than Bragg's.)

The Nashville River Front. Down to the steamers came 800 mules. "Streight's Raid" was beginning.

STREIGHT'S LAST STAND

—From **That Devil Forrest**, by Wyeth, Harper & Brothers

A WEEK before, Gen. Van Dorn had been shot to death at Spring Hill by a private citizen. Forrest assumed command of his corps.

On the Mississippi, Vicksburg was in new danger. Frontal assaults had failed to take the bastion. Grant, on April 30, had begun a bold new move.

He switched his men to the west bank, put them aboard transports, dropped 60 miles downstream and went ashore at Bruinburg on the east bank. He planned to envelop the stronghold from the rear.

Alarm touched Richmond. It would turn to frenzy. Was there sudden remembrance of what "Old Joe" Johnston had said months ago about trying to hold both Mississippi and Tennessee?

On May 9, Johnston was rushed southward from Tullahoma to take command. But on the same day that Forrest was declining a major generalship, Johnston was wiring from Mississippi: ". . . *Communications cut off. I am too late.*"

The siege of Vicksburg was about to begin. Many citizens would live in caves dug out of the hillsides, seeking refuge from the Federal siege guns. Mule meat would become a staple.

The premium on secret military information soared. The gambles for it would produce sublime heroism, treachery and something close to melodrama.

At Vicksburg in May, an exchange of messages was established between Gen. Johnston, in Jackson, Miss., and Gen. Pemberton, whom Johnston kept trying to join with 15,000 men. But their messages—well, they were read in transit, because of a faithless courier.

Back in Tennessee Truesdail would trot out the Creole actress. He would send her through Middle Tennessee.

She was New Orleans-born. To obscure pages of Civil War history, she is known by her stage name, Pauline Cushman, a brave woman of brilliant coloring and a "murky," slumberous type of good looks.

In March she had been playing the role of Plutella in "Seven Sisters" at Wood's Theater in Louisville. The part required portrayal of seven characters, which suggests her virtuosity. In her voice there was something of both the South and of France.

Life had prepared her well. A girlhood in New Orleans had given her an inkling of Old World finesse. Later the family fortune had failed and her father moved up-river to Grand Rapids, Mich., then little more than an Indian trading post. Indians called her "Laughing Breeze." She learned of the out-of-doors.

In Louisville, Southern sympathizers offered her $300 to toast the South from the stage. Her sympathies were with the North.

"*I'd be locked up,*" she protested.

Promising to think it over, she went straight to Provost Marshal Edward Bowers and told him.

"*Do it,*" he said. She didn't understand, and he continued, "*It is for a deeper reason.*" She began to get the idea. Her action might discover secret Rebels.

The plan was to mark her as a friend of the South. She gave the toast: "*Here's to Jeff Davis and the Southern Confederacy! May the South always maintain her honor and her rights!*"

A near-riot broke out in the theater. Yankees were stunned. Some Confederate sympathizers cheered. Men punched one another. There was fighting in the aisles.

Gen. Abel D. Streight
(A colonel when captured by Forrest)

—By Forbes, from **30 Years After**

ARMY MULE TEAM—hard work and scant glory.
For 10 years before the war, Tennessee led the nation in the production of mule colts. And Smith County led the state.

—From the collection of Mrs. Lorraine Dexter and The American Heritage
Picture History of the Civil War
Pauline Cushman in a theatrical pose.

BACKSTAGE the manager grabbed her arm. What did she think she was doing?

"I'd do it again!" Miss Cushman cried. *"I'm not afraid of the whole Yankee crew!"* She was fired.

A crowd gathered. She was publicly told to report to the provost marshal next morning. Bowers cautioned her not to overdo it. She must now talk only *"moderately secesh,"* as if she had been reprimanded.

She was on trial as a secret service agent to the Army of the Cumberland. Her work amounted to counter-espionage. Southern sympathizers soon were sending messages to her boarding house.

She drew up a list of the enemies of the North. She became more intimate with the Southern group and learned about shipments and supplies, guerrilla activities. She learned, for instance, the Southern trick of folding a small message lengthwise, poking it into the craw of a chicken and letting a trustworthy farm woman carry the chicken wherever the message had to go.

Before long Miss Cushman was called to occupied Nashville by a theater manager here. He was just wanting a star. Here was one, unemployed. *"But she will talk secesh,"* the Louisville manager warned him.

Miss Cushman's first appearance on Nashville boards was *"somewhat of a civic event."* She appeared in "The Married Rake."

Nashville Confederates soon considered her their own. Federal soldiers, unaware of what it was all about, *"couldn't help admiring so magnificent a woman, Rebel or not."* On with the show!

On with the espionage, too. Col. Truesdail asked her to visit Bragg's camps. *"It's a rough road,"* she commented, *"along which more hemp grows than corn."* A spy could meet a hemp rope. Bragg was one of the most spy-conscious of generals.

It is May 23. In Truesdail's High Street office Miss Cushman is taking the Oath of Allegiance to the Union, formally entering espionage. She is kissing the American Flag.

Outside the windows, less than a block away, she might have been able to see the spacious house of Lizinka Brown. How far apart their sympathies!

On this very day in Richmond, important news was coming to Lizinka, the sweetheart of Richard (Dick) Ewell. He was to be made lieutenant general, following the death of the great Thomas J. (Stonewall) Jackson, who had died May 10 of complications from injuries received at Chancellorsville.

Today Lizinka was happy, yet deeply troubled, too. When one's beloved is in the thick of fighting, as Dick Ewell had been and would be, who could base all hope on earth's tomorrows? Days ago she had written him:

We shall be together. If not in life, then in another world—

Nor did it matter to Lizinka that Ewell, 46 and one-legged, looked many years older. Rigorous years of army life had taken their toll. Soldiers called him "Old Bald Head." Let them! He had wit, a fighting spirit. He made friends by the hundreds.

In his reply, Ewell admitted his love for her. But could it avail, in this troubled world? Yet, even now, he still hoped for happiness, for both of them. And he said so.

Why wait for another world?

They were soon married, May 24, at St. Paul's Episcopal Church in Richmond. President Davis attended.

A FEW DAYS later in Nashville, Miss Cushman was ready for her biggest act.

In those days there was such a thing as "public expulsion" by which women were removed from the city for too loudly *"talking secesh."* In such an outsweeping southward, Miss Cushman received star billing.

In late May, a carriage carried her three miles out the Harding Pike. A fine bay horse awaited. She mounted and rode to the Big Harpeth. The prayer-saying double-dealer had a new customer.

When she *"paid proper,"* he got her through the lines in a buggy. Cronies took her to Columbia. She met a captain who introduced her to a major.

She was searching for her brother, she said. Establishing herself in a hotel, she decided upon a natty quartermaster captain as a man she might use.

He was just back from Vicksburg and he lectured her about cannon. When she was ready to depart for Shelbyville, he gave her a *"letter of safeguard,"* commending her to the protection of all good Southerners!

Armed with it, she went to the best hotel in Shelbyville and saw scores of well-informed Confederates. Sitting quietly at the table, she noticed that one guest was a tight-lipped young captain of engineers. He was working night and day on fortifications for the area.

She showed him her letter of "safeguard." Yes, ma'm, he'd give her a letter to Bragg himself.

Before the night was over he was called upstairs. She waited, then went up and knocked. So sorry, but she was leaving unexpectedly. Could he give her the letter to Bragg now?

When he went downstairs to a writing desk, Miss Cushman threw caution aside. She helped herself to his documents, including blueprints. This was too much to remember! Away she went.

She didn't get to see Bragg this time in Tullahoma. She was busy meeting young officers. And she had a woman's longing for pretty clothing. Her own were in Nashville. While coquetting, she complained about her lack of a nicer wardrobe. The Federals, she said, had ruthlessly taken hers at the City Hotel when they put her out of town.

One young Rebel thought he knew just the man who might get her dresses back. He'd try. (He was thinking about the smuggler at the Harpeth.)

Oh, wonderful! She was having luck everywhere and learning so much she thought she just had to put it down on paper. She even put information in her extra shoes. Now, get back to Nashville.

She made it to the smuggler's cabin.

So she was going back North, was she? (He'd been to the City Hotel, all right, for that young officer. And he'd learned that Truesdail had her clothes— Truesdail! Head of the secret police!)

He had left the hotel fast.

What was between this woman and the Yankees? Going South was one thing. Turning around and coming back was something else. What if she talked? He found an excuse to leave the cabin.

A Confederate sergeant entered. Your pass, ma'm? He led her away. The documents were soon found, along with her sketches of fortifications. Miss Cushman protested innocence.

She would be taken before Morgan, Forrest and Bragg. Morgan was gallant. He shared refreshments with her and she managed to keep up a gay banter. Outside, soldiers were lustily singing, "Trust to Luck, Alabama!" The song wasn't exactly soothing to the nerves of a young Yankee woman gambling with possible death.

"Been looking for you a long time," Forrest said. *"You're pretty sharp at turning a card, but I think we've got you on this last shuffle."*

She blazed away at him a time or two, admitting nothing.

He came to the point, the documents. *"Should their evidence show you to be . . . a spy, nothing under heaven can save you from a hempen collar."*

He doubtless knew the Confederate armies had never hanged a woman. But why not scare this bold creature soundly? He advised her to *"prepare for the worst"* and sent her to Bragg.

In due time, she was found guilty and sentenced to be hanged. There the gentlemen halted. She was placed in a house with barred windows "near the Duck." Later she was quartered in a Shelbyville home.

As a condemned prisoner, Miss Cushman would become ill. What would the Rebels really do with her? They let her sweat. They had more important things to think about than hanging a woman.

The Yankees were about to strike in more places than one. The Federals in Murfreesboro were feeling optimistic. Had Rosecrans received good news from Vicksburg? Did he think Vicksburg might fall in a week or two? After which, aid might be sent him?

On June 22, Bragg informed Gen. Johnston that all Kentucky had been evacuated for a movement to support Grant at Vicksburg. Here they come! (And as the Yankees left Kentucky, Bragg would send Morgan there to raise tumult in their rear.)

Again Washington was urging Rosecrans at Murfreesboro to move out. Attack Bragg! (*"Old Rosey must like them radishes,"* the Rebels grinned.)

Halleck wasn't grinning. *"Is it your intention to make a movement?"* he demanded. *". . . Answer, yes or no . . ."*

At 2:10 a.m., June 24, Rosecrans telegraphed Washington, *"Army begins to move at 3 o'clock this morning."* The long wait was over.

The push was on. Rosecrans, now with around 70,000 men, was moving against Bragg's 42,000.

It was a master-plan of offensive strategy. Had Bragg never thought of what a flanking attack could do to him? Frontal defenses were strong. But, suddenly, Rosecrans was at his right flank. Bragg realized too late.

—From an engraving in **Annals of the Army of the Cumberland**, by John Fitch, J. B. Lippincott & Co., 1863

William S. Truesdail—the Yankee Terror.

HANG HIM "TO THE NEAREST TREE," Gen. Nathan Bedford Forrest said of this man, head of the Federals' secret police in occupied Nashville. Truesdail directed a far-flung espionage. But he was never captured. For many years, no picture of Truesdail was believed to be in existence in Nashville. This one was found in the course of research for this narrative. In a 102-year-old book, it is now kept under lock and key in the Tennessee Room, Nashville Public Library.

GIANT foothills—the Highland Rim—lay between the armies. The rim had four gaps. Rosecrans used the gaps. (See map.)

One corps forced Hoover's Gap and moved to Manchester. (The Federals were using Spencer's new seven-shot repeating rifles which would cause some Rebels to say, *"You Yankees ain't fightin' fair! You load them guns on Sunday and shoot 'em all week!"* Many a Federal soldier had bought such a gun for himself.)

Another corps, rebuffed at Liberty Gap, sideslipped eastward to Hoover's and also went to Manchester.

A reserve corps, demonstrating through Guy's Gap, was threatening Shelbyville. This caused Polk to withdraw to Tullahoma. A fourth Federal corps marched to Manchester by Bradyville.

All this meant Rosecrans was flanking Bragg out of his Middle Tennessee position, forcing him southward. It meant Union forces were pressing closer to Chattanooga and the gateway to the Lower South.

To Pauline Cushman, it meant surcease from worry as to whether the Rebs would hang a woman. In evacuating Shelbyville, they simply left her behind. Union forces found her wrapped in a blanket, eagerly awaiting them on the balcony of a physician's house.

Through a rainy morning two generals carried her in a chair to a waiting ambulance. It would take her to Nashville. Beside her walked a major, holding an umbrella over her head.

Rosecrans would pay her a visit. Northerners would beg for her autographs. Soon she would be back on the glory road of gaslight and greasepaint.

The curtain was coming down on her grand finale. She would talk of it for years, from the lecture platform . . . a woman of the grand manner, sweeping superbly into hotel lobbies, riding in carriages and victorias, bowing and smiling to a wearying public until, at last, when youth was gone, the Grand Army of the Republic would honor her with rifle fire in a final salute across her grave.

As Miss Cushman rode away toward footlight fanfare, Lee's invasion of Pennsylvania was under way. On July 2, Bragg's army fell back to Cowan and set up a battle line. Both flanks were against the mountain. He was ready to fight. Would Rosecrans come on?

No. Rosecrans halted. The Confederates caught their breath, then retreated over Sewanee Mountain.

To Gen. Polk, perhaps the hour was awesome. As a bishop of the Episcopal Church, this spot meant much. Old, old dreams must have come surging up. For here, in 1860, on a tract of about 10,000 acres, a cornerstone had been laid for the main building of the University of the South, established by the church at Polk's recommendation.

His dream had been that a great educational institution one day should rise here. Was that dream gone . . .? The war had halted everything. Federal soldiers would ruin the cornerstone. (Yet the dream, years later, would be carried on by others.)

Polk is leaving now . . . Oh, great dreamer! March on and on . . . Is he looking back? He will never see this spot again.

Sometimes a chicken had a secret in its craw—a Rebel trick Pauline Cushman had discovered.

The Army of Tennessee is withdrawing toward Chattanooga by way of Sewanee and Monteagle.

Is Bragg too weary to think of all details? Does no one think of destroying the railroad tunnel at Cowan? Apparently not. Had this been done, Sherman's later march into Georgia would have been a much harder struggle.

Bragg went on from Cowan to Chattanooga by train. His report of withdrawal was received by President Davis in Richmond July 4.

It was a tragic day for the South. No other day of the war would be filled with so much bad news.

—Brady-Handy Collection of Negatives, Library of Congress

As a spy against the Rebels, Pauline sadly missed her elegant Yankee attire.

"RESCUE OF THE FAIR SPY" at Shelbyville. So this old drawing is entitled. She wasn't exactly "rescued." The Rebels just left her behind, like excess baggage.

AT VICKSBURG, Gen. Pemberton was giving up with 31,600 men, 172 cannon and 60,000 muskets, the largest body of men ever surrendered on the American continent up to that time.

Pickett's charge at Gettysburg, one of the most gallant efforts in the annals of war, had failed the day before, July 3.

In Pemberton's effort to hold the town commanding the Mississippi, he had lost 9,362 men, killed, wounded or captured. Details of the siege and fall are too complex for inclusion here. President Davis blamed Gen. Johnston and wrote him a 15-page letter of criticism. Yet he retained Johnston in command of the western forces.

"Old Joe" spoke out in self-defense, with spirit and detail. The frying fat wound up in the fire before the Confederate Congress. There was bitter debate, which did the Confederacy no good and brought no better feelings between the President and "Old Joe."

In that early July, Lee at Gettysburg was preparing to fall back across the Potomac River after the three-day battle in which 3,903 Confederates had been killed, 18,725 wounded and 5,425 listed as missing. Union losses were 3,155 killed, 14,529 wounded and 5,365 missing.

Bragg was giving up Tennessee, virtually without a battle. His army was already on the edge of Georgia. By Vicksburg's fall, the Confederacy had been cut in two.

"Old Joe" Johnston was right again. In trying to hold both Tennessee and Mississippi, both were just about lost. And on his desk lay the 15 pages of criticism. Did he think then of Mrs. Johnston's warning, months and months earlier . . .?

The Confederate tide had crested. The turning point of the war had been reached.

Few vessels were now piercing the blockade of Southern ports. Southern factories were running short of machinery and materials. Labor was no longer a simple problem. Lincoln's Emancipation Proclamation was taking its toll. After Gettysburg, what foreign minister wanted to back a failing cause?

Northern factories were roaring full blast. Bumper crops were being exported. Much of the manpower was being restored by immigration. Many a well-educated Southerner, for the first time, was setting to work with his hands.

For the Old South, the ebbtide had begun.

But not to Gen. Morgan! Into the gloomy day, the Kentuckian was injecting a fresh new courage that typified Southern resolve. Even as the bad news came, he was pounding across Kentucky.

He had left in early July. Just two days later, as he thundered North, the terrible news of Gettysburg and Vicksburg had come, and gloom had settled thick as battle smoke upon the entire edifice of Southern hope. Then, suddenly, like a peal of a great pipe organ in a burning church, had come the inspiring word that Morgan was invading the land of the foe.

Oh, can it be? Hooray! Wake me. I'm dreaming. He's in Kentucky! Indiana! Ohio! He's crazy! I'm crazy! Hooray! Hooray! Morgan was on his way to the "Farthest North" point to be reached by Southern troops in the whole war.

It had taken plenty of planning. His orders were to ride far north into Kentucky, thus taking pressure off Bragg. But his orders didn't include crossing the Ohio.

For days before departure, the horses of Morgan and his men had been coming into fine fettle on the lush grass around Liberty and Alexandria. Into the area on May 26 he had ordered concentration of all his regiments. Soon, almost incredibly, wagons loaded with supplies had come rolling up from Chattanooga. Morgan himself, resplendent in a new uniform, had arrived June 10.

Big doings again! The men sensed it. Morale was high. The DeKalb County hills began to ring with a song, "Morgan's Men":

> *"On the Cumberland's bosom*
> *The moonbeams are bright,*
> *And the path of the raid*
> *Is made plain by their light.*
> *And across the wide ripple*
> *And up the steep bank*
> *I see the dark squadron*
> *Move rank after rank."*

It was another song by Morgan's own composer, Basil Duke, who had married Morgan's sister. Duke was Morgan's second in command.

CAVE HUTS AT VICKSBURG. Many a Vicksburg resident dug into the hillside for shelter from Yankee siege guns.

—From Harper's Weely, July 25, 1863

GEN. GRANT, IDEALIZED
He was now the "man of the hour."

"JEFF DAVIS' FACE—" aghast with shock and fear, as
Harper's portrayed him in July, '63, after Gettysburg and
the fall of Vicksburg.

SOON Morgan had started his men toward the Cumberland. He had planned to capture the Federal garrison at Carthage and clear the river-crossing before his drive into Kentucky. But other orders had delayed him, and he started all over again July 2, this time from Burkesville, Ky.

Ride with speed! So "Fighting Joe" Wheeler had urged him. Be back in Tennessee before Rosecrans can learn of your absence. Morgan was on his way, with 2,480 men and two pieces of artillery.

He had no intention of stopping at the Ohio River. He'd had enough of Bragg's timidity.

The raid would prove as spectacular as Morgan himself. By July 8, he had reached the banks of the Ohio. He seized two steamboats to put his men across. Gunboats interfered. He was across, anyway, by the 9th.

Terror went before him. Many a Yankee, for the first time, began to get a little taste of war.

More than 100,000 men would take part in the chase of Morgan's 2,400. Could he elude such numbers? (Back in Tennessee, Bragg would be needing his cavalry.)

On the day Morgan crossed the Ohio, Bragg entered Chattanooga. Hardee took his stand along the railway line to the north, near Ooltewah; Forrest, at Kingston; Wheeler, south and west of Bridgeport, Ala.

There, at the door to the Deep South, the Army of Tennessee would remain inactive for the summer. The soldiers wanted to fight. ("*As sure as you are born, that army is better than its commanders,*" Confederate Sen. G. A. Henry of Tennessee wrote President Davis.)

Even in Richmond, the idea of attack was considered. Bragg was queried: "*If we can reinforce you, can you attack the enemy?*" Bragg replied, "*It would be unsafe.*"

He cited geographic difficulties of getting at the foe. Great mountain ranges and the broad Tennessee River now separated the armies.

About this time, President Davis promoted Gen. D. H. Hill to lieutenant

general and sent him to Chattanooga. Bragg and Wheeler were having some bad moments. They'd been reading dispatches: Morgan in Ohio! Had the man gone mad?

Dashing northeast, Morgan had roared on through the suburbs of Cincinnati at night, with a speed and unpredictability that left the Federals dumbfounded.

Sometimes, when Morgan's men wanted something from a Yankee, they'd simply point a pistol and, with crisp courtesy, order the man to come forward (according to Northern newspapers).

The North was years ahead of the South in looting. Now some of Morgan's men, breaking out of control, began to show the North what looting could be. There's wide variety in the alleged loot at some places, ranging from a stallion and corn to pies, pants, pills, candy, cash and a violin. (Every dog has his day!)

The wild raid failed. Perhaps it was too flamboyant to last.

It is 2 p.m., July 26, on a farm south of Lisbon in Columbiana County, Ohio. Morgan, with a small part of his men, is surrendering. How far away the friendliness of Liberty and Alexandria now! A woman is restrained as she rushes at him with a butcher knife.

The small group of captives is taken to Cincinnati by train. A crowd of 5,000 stares. Shouts go up, "*Hang the cutthroats!*" Bayonets push the crowd back. The prisoners are led through as a band triumphantly blares "Yankee Doodle."

At the jail Morgan turns to a Federal officer. *General, would you consider getting me a drink?* He's unflurried. He bows to reporters and, cigar in mouth, walks away to his cell.

—From The Century War Book, 1861-1865

**Bragg retreated from Duck River through rain. So did
the Rebels from Gettysburg.**

MORGAN'S MEN entering Washington, Ohio. In its news story, *Harper's* called the Kentucky general a "famous bandit."

HE WILL not be treated as a prisoner of war. (Have the letters of Tennessee's military governor had effect? Johnson months ago had asked that any of Morgan's captured men be treated as criminals.) Morgan and a number of his men will be sent to the Ohio state prison at Columbus.

Their beards and heads will be shaved like common criminals. Convicts will be sent in to scrub their bodies with rough brushes.

But in the years ahead, to have been in that raid was many a veteran's

NASHVILLE'S MYSTERY HOUSE. This charming house of Civil War days stood on College Street, now Third Avenue (according to the street sign). Whose house? Where? Do you know? Writers, artists, architects, librarians—all have tried in vain to find it. (Can you see the parrot in the upstairs window?)

—From a picture in State Library

proudest memory. "*Another day,*" they would say, "*and Morgan would have watered his horses in Lake Erie.*"

A marker stands today on the spot where he was captured:

This Stone Marks the Spot where the Confederate Raider, Gen. John H. Morgan, Surrendered his command to Maj. George W. Rue, July 26, 1863, and is the Farthest Point North Ever Reached by Any Body of Confederate Troops During the Civil War.

Near the Tennessee on Aug. 16, the Federal Army began to move. Suddenly again, the Confederate government in Richmond saw the urgent need of strengthening Bragg. It decided to send Gen. James Longstreet with the division of Gen. John B. Hood and Gen. Lafayette McLaws from Virginia.

They would go by rail to Augusta, Ga., on to Atlanta and north to Chattanooga. It would be Sept. 9, however, before the first trainloads departed, a stupendous operation for its day, in wobbly cars over jumping, outworn rails.

Hood was on sick leave when the orders came through. His arm, badly wounded at Gettysburg, still hung limp in a sling. That didn't matter. His men should not go without him. When he heard of the transfer, he took the first train to join them.

In Virginia, Longstreet goes to Lee's tent to say goodbye. As Longstreet leaves, Lee walks with him to his horse. "*Now, general,*" Lee says, "*I want you to beat those people in the West—*"

"*If I live,*" Longstreet promises. He knows what Lee wants, should the Chattanooga effort succeed. Push them north! "*—Vigorous pursuit, even to the Ohio,*" Lee says.

By late August, Rosecrans was crossing the Tennessee. Bragg faced a grim choice. If he permitted Rosecrans to cross North Georgia, breaking the Confederate link with Atlanta, his own Army of Tennessee would be bottled up in Chattanooga, like Pemberton's at Vicksburg.

Bragg must evacuate Chattanooga. He did this Sept. 8, moving to Lafayette, Ga. There he was convenient to a railroad. There he could make contact with Longstreet's corps coming from Virginia. Bragg would strike Rosecrans as the Yanks filed out of the mountain gorges.

A crisis is near. Information is growing more precious by the hour. Bragg is needing more scouts to keep him informed of enemy movements. We see one of them, a capable youngster, riding through the river mists toward Nashville . . . on a horse that is fresh from his home stable in Smyrna.

In Sam's pocket is a pass, dated Sept. 12:

Sam Davis has permission to pass on scouting duty anywhere in Middle Tennessee . . . he may think proper. By order of Gen. Bragg.

E. Coleman
Commanding Scouts

In setting his trap for Rosecrans, Bragg "propagandized" his own retreat in a manner which would have done credit to modern warfare. He sent "deserters" through Federal lines to spread cooked-up stories. They were to say Bragg was in headlong retreat to Rome, Ga. (This was far from the truth.)

"All Aboard! Off for the Front."

—By Forbes, from 30 Years After

Gen. Lafayette McLaws

IT IS easy to believe what we want to believe. Rosecrans fell for it. He decided to give chase, and it was not until Sept. 13, after days of fumbling through mountain passes, that he realized the enemy was still about in large numbers.

Instead of a merry pursuit, it now became a deadly game of hide and seek, until Rosecrans almost abruptly met the foe 12 miles south of Chattanooga, on the banks of Chickamauga Creek.

And Chickamauga, in the Indian tongue, is said to mean River of Death. Death was waiting for her harvest.

It was morning, Sept. 19. The biggest battle of the western theater of war had begun, on a five-mile front. One unit after another went to it. Forrest's cavalry dismounted and fought as infantry on the Confederate right flank. About 120,000 men were to lock deadly horns before the two-day battle ended. This time, because of various reinforcements, there would be about 60,000 men on each side, one of the rare occasions when the Confederacy would be able to match the foe in number.

The gallant Hood had arrived. A shout of welcome had gone up the day before when he rode out on the field, his arm still in a sling. Spirits rose as some of the men beheld him for the first time, sitting majestically astride his charger as if the arm in a sling didn't matter.

Tall, blue-eyed and only 32, Hood had eyes that always seemed "fiercely burning." Beneath them was a vast amount of "tawny" beard (although in most pictures it appears dark). He was a fighter, rash and impetuous, but a fighter, and the men knew it. Many months later, in December, 1864, Hood's own story and that of Nashville would be conjoined.

On the 19th, Hood shoved the Federals back a mile on the Confederate left. By sunset, Rosecrans was battered. But his army had given little ground. It still held most of its positions.

Darkness fell over the broken and wooded terrain. Guns and rifles still flashed. All either side could see were the bursts of light.

Soon Bragg was sleeping. So far, his men had done well. Neither side had put its full strength into the field that day. So high-spirited had been the

Rebel attack that Rosecrans over-estimated their number. (In his official report he said he faced "superior numbers." Actually, official records show he put 45,000 men into the field. They met 30,400 Confederates—22,000 under Polk on the right and Hood's 8,400 on the left.)

At 11 p.m., Bragg was awakened by good news. Longstreet had arrived with about 5,000 men. They conferred for an hour. Bragg gave him command of the entire left wing for the next day's battle.

Rumors of Longstreet's arrival reached Rosecrans. He thought Longstreet had brought 15,000 to 20,000! Before morning, Rosecrans decided he faced a force of more than 110,000! Through the night he worked for a stronger defense against the imaginary host.

Doubtless his fears transformed the next day's battle into an even more dreadful ordeal than it was. The Rebels struck at dawn. Disaster hit the Federal right wing about 10:30 a.m.

Because of incorrect information, Rosecrans gave an order which caused a big hole in the blue line. Into it Longstreet sent Hood. The man with his arm in a sling went rip-roaring through with eight Confederate brigades in three solid lines!

Seeing his chance, Longstreet hurled aside the orders of the day to bear to the left. He swung his main force right, took the enemy in reverse, and his men went howling through the Federal lines, overrunning Rosecrans' own headquarters.

The tumult of battle was drowning out orders. The wildly yelling Rebels were roaring on.

SCENE FROM THE AMERICAN "TEMPEST."

—Reproduced by permission of PUNCH

A former slave, as Caliban, receives the Proclamation from Lincoln, while a sullen planter looks on. Slave to Lincoln: "You've beat him enough. Very soon I'll beat him, too!"

—Courtesy of Mrs. Thomas McClure Peters. From The Gallant Hood by John P. Dyer, Bobbs-Merrill, Inc.

Hood in his prime.

The Wounding of Gen. Hood, Battle of Chickamauga.

THE panic even seized bold Gen. Phillip H. Sheridan, who departed at a gallop. The entire Union right wing was in flight.

At 4 p.m., Rosecrans rode up to the adjutant general's office in Chattanooga. His face was pale. He was faint and ill. He had to be helped from his horse.

All seemed lost for his army, with one exception. Gen. George H. Thomas was still holding out on Horseshoe Ridge. Other Federal units which had escaped the breakthrough joined him. Sixteen Confederate charges failed to dislodge the courageous Yankees. Thomas and his men kept throwing the Rebels back. He was also earning himself a new name, "The Rock of Chickamauga."

Then, about 5 p.m., the seventeenth charge drove Thomas down the hill. By holding out, he had bought badly needed time. Rosecrans' entire army was in retreat.

Again the sun was setting. Chattanooga was filling up with defeated Yanks. Behind them, 34,350 men were either dead, wounded or missing. Of these, 17,800 were Confederates and 16,550 were Federals.

Shadows were deepening on Horseshoe Ridge when a courier came to Longstreet from Gen. William Preston. He's asking permission to pursue in the moonlight.

Longstreet does not order pursuit. Has he forgotten the words of Lee, "... *Even to the Ohio*"? Or is he remembering an interview with Bragg that afternoon following the beginning of the breakthrough?

About 3 p.m., Longstreet had suggested that the Confederate right wing briefly take a defensive postion while he led detachments in pursuit. Such a thing, Longstreet said, might even wreck Rosecrans' whole army. It would upset brigades retreating to Chattanooga and also put the Confederates behind Thomas.

Bragg had been in no mood for such ideas. *"Not a man left in the right wing has any fight left in him,"* he unfairly said of Polk's brave men, who were to fight on and on. *"If anything happens, communicate with me."* Bragg turned and walked off.

For the remainder of the afternoon, Bragg had taken small part in the battle. It has been written that he "sulked in his tent." Was one of his frequent sick headaches troubling him more than usual?

Longstreet had hurried back to the fray. Left largely to his own devices, he and Polk directed what amounted to separate battles against different Yankee positions. As the sun went down, victory was theirs.

Is it any wonder that Longstreet, standing on Horseshoe Ridge as darkness came, didn't order Preston to pursue?

Later that night the bishop-general, Polk, was summoned to Bragg's tent. Vainly Polk urged chase. It was no use. Bragg couldn't believe he'd won a victory!

"The moon was as bright to guide us in pursuit as (it was to guide) the enemy in flight," Polk wrote President Davis on Oct. 6. *"Gen. Bragg . . . allowed the fruits of the great but sanguinary victory to pass from him by the most criminal negligence, or rather incapacity . . . By that victory and its heavy expenditure of the lifeblood of the Confederacy, we bought and paid for the whole State of Tennessee to the Mississippi River at the very least; and all that was wanted was to have gone forward and taken possession of it."*

As Polk pleaded, Forrest's men were bivouacked on sloping ground near the windows of a hospital-house. Inside, surgeons worked under flickering lamps which cast a glow upon a grisly pile outside in the frost. It was a pile 20 feet wide and 12 feet high, of arms and legs amputated during the two-day battle.

Among the severely wounded had been Gen. Hood, not long after his breakthrough. A leg had to be amputated on the field. But the man with the burning eyes would not give up. Months hence he would return to fight for the Southern cause—strapped to the saddle.

Gen. George H. Thomas
"Rock of Chickamauga"

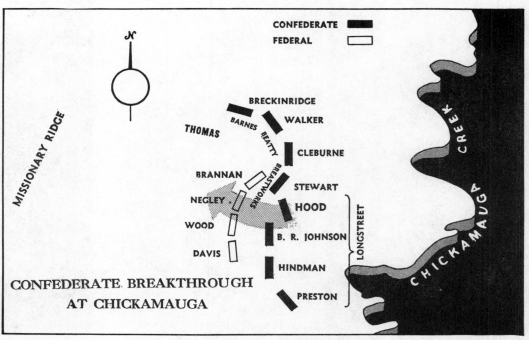

The Confederate Breakthrough, Chickamauga.

Rebel attack on Federal wagon train at Anderson's Gap.

POLK was right. The price of Chickamauga had been high. For the first and last time in major combat a clear-cut triumph had come to the hard-fighting Army of Tennessee. And her commander couldn't see it. Was defeat in his heart?

Rosecrans saw. He wired Halleck, *". . . Serious disaster . . . Enemy overwhelmed us . . ."*

Next day Rosecrans wired Lincoln, *"After two days of the fiercest fighting I ever witnessed, our left and center were beaten . . . We have no certainty of holding our position here."*

What damage might pursuit have wrought? Would Lee have known his dream of Federals fleeing across Tennessee and Kentucky, even to the Ohio?

Four days later Bragg wrote Richmond, *". . . Vigorous pursuit followed . . ."* What was he talking about?

It's not difficult to find historians who think the only "vigorous pursuit" came from Forrest. Around 4 p.m., Sept. 21, with 400 troops, he jumped a Federal rearguard and drove it into Chattanooga. (This was the storied ride on which a Minie ball severed an artery in the neck of Forrest's horse. He stuck a finger in the hole, checking the flow of blood until the chase had ended.)

Forrest fully expected pursuit. None came. "Why DON'T we follow?" his men kept asking. When night fell, Forrest could stand the delay no longer.

If delay continued, Rosecrans could fortify himself in Chattanooga, using what the Rebels themselves had built. To Forrest, the time to whip the enemy was when he was running! And that pitiful pile of arms and legs—should they have bought nothing?

Oh, Lee in Virginia! O, God, make Gen. Bragg listen! Somebody, somebody make him understand—

Suddenly Forrest is walking out into the autumn night. He is mounting a charger and riding to the tent of Gen. Bragg.

Bragg is sleeping. Forrest orders him roused. He urges Bragg to attack. Now! And captures will be certain.

Bragg asks: How can we move this army without supplies?

Take them from the foe, Forrest replies—from the Yanks in Chattanooga. That was the way Forrest had supplied himself many times . . . Bragg did not answer.

Forrest steps back. He says nothing. He is bending his gaunt and powerful body under the flap of the tent. His mood is black.

He springs to his horse, forces him to a gallop, and a terrible stream of profanity pours forth. Why plead with Gen. Bragg? What was the use? After a while he checks himself, muttering furiously, *"What does he fight battles for?"*

Even then Forrest doesn't give up. Next day he rides to Gen. McLaws and suggests: Let's take matters in our own hands and attack anyway!

It was too salty a dish for McLaws. He was unwilling to become responsible.

The cock of challenge has crowed thrice. Three generals have begged Bragg to pursue. Again, as at Munfordville, he has failed to gather the full harvest of victory.

Later, when Chattanooga could not be taken except by bitter contest, Bragg spread his army in a six-mile semi-circle from Chattanooga Creek to Missionary Ridge. His left extended to the foot of Lookout Mountain, thus cutting Rosecrans off from railroad facilities to Nashville.

Bragg meant to starve the Federals out of Chattanooga. Soon their supplies would have to be hauled up through Jasper over 60 miles of rutted roads, across Sequatchie Valley and Walden's Ridge. Very well, he'd cut that line too!

He'd send Gen. Wheeler roaring up through the valley to smash the wagon trains. Then on into Middle Tennessee! This decision seems to have been made Sept. 28.

Wheeler roars through Sequatchie Valley, lighting the skies with flames from Federal wagons.

An Army Forge.

—By Forbes, from **30 Years After**

The Maxwell House during the Civil War.

THAT day orders went to Forrest from Bragg's headquarters on Missionary Ridge. Turn over "the troops under your command" to Gen. Wheeler. This was to strengthen Wheeler for his raid on Rosecrans' rear. But no explanation was given Forrest.

He received the message while on the road near Athens. Give up his men again? The brave men he'd trained from raw recruits? Men he'd equipped with battle-bought arms? Fury rose again.

Personal injustice was one thing. Mistreatment of men and horses was another. Whatever Bragg had in mind, they were in no condition for long new effort. After the busy week and the hard fighting just before it, Forrest's men and horses were worn out.

Forrest sat down and wrote Bragg a blistering protest. He promised to follow it up with a personal visit. He would say it all to Bragg's face.

No copy of the letter seems to have survived the years. But there would be a witness to the personal visit. Forrest would take a witness along.

Meanwhile he obeyed the order. He gave up his men. They begged and pleaded against the transfer. There was "fearful discontent" and almost open mutiny.

It was early in October when Forrest went to see Bragg. Uncertainty exists as to the exact date. (One historian thinks it was Oct. 1.) Forrest summoned his surgeon, Dr. J. B. Cowan, to ride with him.

They reach Bragg's tent. Forrest tosses his reins to an orderly and strides on without acknowledging salutes, in contrast to his usual courtesy.

Inside, Bragg offers his hand. Forrest lets it hang in air.

"I am not here to pass civilities or compliments with you, but on other business," Forrest says.

He pulls himself to his full height. He crosses his arms like a proud Indian.

Bragg's hand falls. He walks to the back of his tent and sits down at a small field desk. In his face not a muscle moves. Forrest begins to speak: *"You commenced your cowardly and contemptible persecution of me soon after the Battle of Shiloh, and you have kept it up ever since. You did it because I reported to Richmond facts, while you reported damned lies.*

"You robbed me of my command in Kentucky, and gave it to one of your favorites—men I had armed and equipped from the enemies of our country. In a spirit of revenge and spite—because I would not fawn upon you as the others did—you drove me into West Tennessee in the winter of 1862, with a second brigade I had organized—with improper arms, and without sufficient ammunition, although I had made repeated application for the same. You did it to ruin me!"

Maybe Forrest's voice rose as he went on, *"When, in spite of all this, I returned with my command, well equipped by captures, you began again your work of spite and persecution. And you have kept it up! And now this second brigade, organized and equipped without thanks to you or to the government—a brigade which has won a reputation for successful fighting second to none in the army—Taking advantage of your position as commanding general in order to further humiliate me, you have taken these men from me!"*

Forrest began to shake his finger in Bragg's face. *"I have stood your meanness as long as I intend to! You have played the part of a damned scoundrel, and are a coward, and if you were any part of a man I would slap your jaws and force you to resent it!"*

He was roaring now: *"You may as well not issue any more orders to me, for I will not obey them! And I will hold you responsible for any further indignities you try to inflict upon me.*

JEFF DAVIS'S LAST APPEAL TO ARMS.

A bitter cartoon against Davis. "Victory is within your grasp," he says to maimed veterans, one of whom grasps with a claw.

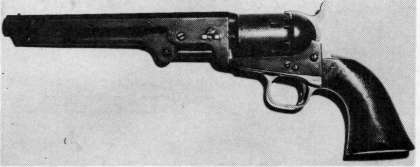
—Staff Photo by Don Foster

Forrest's Pistol. You may see it at the State Museum, where it is on loan to the Tennessee Historical Society from Winston Rutledge, Lewisburg, Tenn.

"A CAUTIOUS HALT." Yankees spot their foe. (Notice the big bones of their horses. After the war, such mounts would leave their mark upon the more finely boned Tennessee horses.)

—By Forbes, from *30 Years After*

"*YOU HAVE threatened to arrest me for not obeying your orders promptly. I dare you to do it! And I say to you if you ever again interfere with me or cross my path, it will be at the peril of your life!*"

Forrest dropped his long finger and abruptly walked out. Soon he would take his problems with Bragg directly to President Davis. Meanwhile, he would turn to the person who understood him best—gentle and patient Mary Ann Montgomery Forrest, his wife.

Eighteen months had passed since he last saw her, in Memphis, while recovering from his Shiloh wound. He received a 10-day leave in which to visit her at LaGrange, Ga. (Afterwards she would follow his command, living just behind the lines, close to her husband—always his "best friend," his solace and his greatest comforter.)

About this time a dreadful accident occurred in Nashville—perhaps the worst in the city's history. It happened at breakfast time on the hot, dry morning of Sept. 29, at the incomplete Maxwell House.

Sam Davis' home at Smyrna, before restoration.

There 400 captive Confederates were confined, many from the Battle of Chickamauga. They were crowding down from the fifth floor on a temporary stairway, toward food, when a guard briefly halted the line at the bottom. During the pause, more men crowded onto the flimsy structure from the top.

Under the weight, the stairway broke. It fell with more than 100 Confederates. The head of one soldier was crushed "flat as a board" and 90-odd were injured. Four perished in the fall. Four more died within minutes. Death eventually came to an additional 37 from their injuries. These figures are a rough composite of various accounts.

One newspaper said 200 men dropped from the fifth to the second floor. One survivor said the fall was to the first floor with 126 men. Another said 104 men. Federal masters of the city cared for no wide publicity on such a disaster. News accounts were brief.

Buggies and carriages sped to the Maxwell House. Weeping Nashville women pressed at its doors, bandages in hand, begging to aid. Federal bayonets held them back.

The Federals did their best to aid. The medical director rushed surgeons and ambulances. At least 92 survivors were sent to hospitals.

As the injured lay abed, news leaked in which made them smile. Wheeler's raid had broken loose Oct. 1. With 4,000 cavalry, he had come sweeping up through the Sequatchie Valley, hitting at the Federal rear. Capturing a 10-mile train of 800 wagons, he burned the vehicles, killed the mules and stormed on to McMinnville, capturing it and setting its stores ablaze.

He swept on to Murfreesboro, nearly to Nashville, then down through Middle Tennessee to Pulaski and across the Tennessee River at Decatur, Ala., on Oct. 8.

He was back with Bragg by Oct. 17. Despite all the damage done, some writers have said the raid resulted in "more loss than gain" to the Confederacy as it had no substantial effect on Rosecrans' plans for the operation of his main army in Chattanooga. It also left Wheeler's own force (and the men taken from Forrest) disorganized and spent. They were long in getting back in fighting shape.

It had NOT been the Forrest type of foray. Not willingly would he have undertaken such an effort with his command in such condition. Forrest was a masterly quartermaster. He liked ready rations and shelled corn on the saddle, although he knew how to survive—for a while—without either.

He was a blacksmith's son. He knew the horses taken from him and used on the raid were badly in need of shoeing. He knew an improperly shod horse could cost the life of man and mount, or cause the capture of both. The wanton waste of resources on this raid must have left him sickened and infuriated.

NOR WAS his the only anger on Missionary Ridge just then. General uproar among Bragg's officers had begun. More than ever, they wanted him removed. And for several days Bragg had been looking about for someone to blame for his own mismanagement at Chickamauga.

He chose three of his generals, Polk, Hill and Thomas G. Hindman. He sacked all three and preferred charges against Polk.

President Davis suggested that the order be countermanded in the case of Polk, who was later restored to his command. But Polk refused to serve any longer under Bragg and was transferred to Mississippi. Bragg later restored Hindman.

Longstreet wrote Richmond, *"Nothing but the hand of God can save us as long as we have our present commander."* He advocated replacing Bragg with Gen. Robert E. Lee. *"We need such a mind as Lee's . . ."*

Bragg's chief of staff, Gen. W. W. Mackall, wrote to his wife in a similar vein. Couldn't President Davis *see?* If only Davis would send Gen. Johnston to this troubled spot! Johnston, Mackall thought, would be invaluable. Instead, as Mackall saw it, Davis was indulging his likes and dislikes in an almost childish way. (Johnston had his hands full, then, with military affairs in Alabama and Mississippi.)

Polk also spoke out as to Bragg's inability to gain the full benefits of Chickamauga. And about this time, a "round-robin" hit Richmond, signed by high-ranking officers. It sought Bragg's removal on the diplomatically-stated assertion that *"his health . . . unfits him for command."*

In the midst of all this, on Oct. 9, President Davis arrived at Missionary Ridge and began trying to quiet things down. Soon Forrest went to Davis and told of his long trials with Bragg.

The President had now become more aware of Forrest's talents. Their talk would result in the early transfer of Forrest to West Tennessee. He would have an independent cavalry command.

Once more, Forrest would have to start all over, and once more he would distinguish himself. More than a year would pass before the Army of Tennessee would again have the fire of his genius to aid it. But he would return . . . and save its shattered remnants from being hacked to pieces in retreat . . .

On Oct. 14, Davis left for Richmond, leaving the problem of angry generals largely unsolved except for saying "cordial" cooperation was not always essential among high officers. Bragg was retained.

Longstreet eventually went back to Virginia, perhaps rejoicing to be back under Lee.

In the meantime, the Federal generals also had a ruckus. Quick action cut short their bickering. Rosecrans preferred charges against three of his generals, Thomas L. Crittenden, McCook and Negley. After a hearing in Nashville, all three were exonerated.

On Oct. 19, Rosecrans was removed. Thomas took his place. Grant , now very much the "man of the hour," was sent to Chattanooga. He arrived Oct. 23. This meant big trouble was ahead for Bragg. What would Grant do? What reinforcements would he get? From where?

Bragg's scouts were kept busy informing him of Federal movements. On a hurried and dangerous mission a scout detachment moved quietly into the Midstate. They were to learn what troops were on their way to reinforce Grant at Chattanooga. The scouts started in November, working under the "herb-doctor."

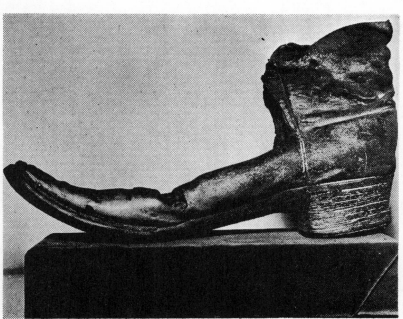

—Staff Photo by Bill Goodman

Sam Davis' boot. You may see it today, ripped open by the searching Yankees, in the State Museum, a cherished possession of the Tennessee Historical Society.

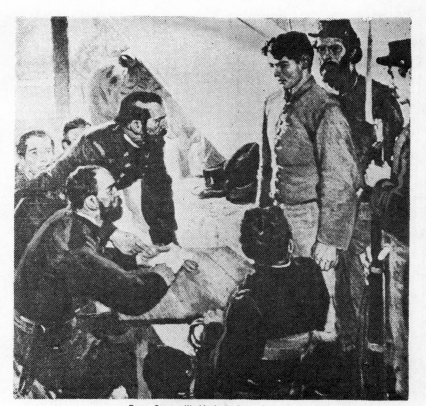

—From **George Washington's Sons of Israel and Other Forgotten Heroes,** by Charles Spencer Hart, J. B. Lippincott Co.
Sam Davis Before Gen. Dodge.
The original of this painting, by Paul Von Schmidt, is owned by Dr. Joe King of Murfreesboro.

In Appreciation

FOR VALUED AID in preparing Part II and assembling its illustrations, The Banner expresses its gratitude to Col. Campbell H. Brown, state executive director, Civil War Centennial Commission; Dr. Robert H. White, state historian; Walter L. Jordan, state archivist; Robert T. Quarles Jr., former state archivist, retired; Mrs. Gertrude Parsley, Mrs. Hermione Embry and Miss Kendall Cram, State Library; to the Joint University Libraries, the Nashville Public Library, the Library of Congress, and to Mrs. Frank Owsley, senior archivist, manuscript section, State Library and Archives, who provided photographs of Gen. Nathan Bedford Forrest and Gen. John Hunt Morgan, by Nashville's own C. C. Giers.

Published works frequently consulted include *The Army of Tennessee,* by Stanley F. Horn, published by The Bobbs-Merrill Company, 1949; Dr. White's *Messages of the Governors of Tennessee, 1857-1869, Vol. V,* Tennessee Historical Commission, 1959; *"First With the Most" Forrest,* by Robert Selph Henry, McCowat-Mercer Press, Jackson, Tenn.; *A Different Valor,* By Gilbert E. Govan and James W. Livingood, Bobbs-Merrill, 1956; *Official Records of the War of the Rebellion,* Washington;

Morgan and His Raiders, by Cecil Fletcher Holland, The Macmillan Company, 1942; *The Bold Cavaliers,* by Dee Alexander Brown, J. P. Lippincott Company, Philadelphia and New York, 1959; *The Rebel Raider,* by Howard Swiggett, Garden City Publishing Co., Garden City, N. Y., 1937;

Life of Gen. Robert Hatton, by James Vaulx Drake, Marshall and Bruce, Nashville, 1867; *The Gallant Hood,* by John P. Dyer, Bobbs-Merrill, 1950; *Fightin' Joe Wheeler,* also by Dyer, Louisiana State University Press, Baton Rouge, 1941; *General Joseph Wheeler and the Army of Tennessee,* by J. W. DuBose, Neale Publishing Co., New York, 1912; *General Johnston,* by R. M. Hughes, D. Appleton and Company, New York, 1897;

Life of Pauline Cushman by Ferdinand L. Sarmiento, published by John E. Potter, Philadelphia, 1865; *Spies of the Blue and Gray,* by Hartnett T. Kane, Hanover House, Garden City, N.Y., 1954; *Secret Service,* A. D. Richardson, Hartford, 1865;

Lee and His Lieutenants, by E. A. Pollard, E. B. Treat and Co., New York, 1867; *From Manassas to Appomattox,* by James Longstreet, Lippincott, Philadelphia, 1865; *Belles, Beaux and Brains of the 60s,* by T. C. DeLeon, G. W. Dillingham Co., New York, 1907; *Recollections of a Virginian in the Mexican, Indian and Civil Wars,* by Maj. Gen. Dabney H. Maury, Charles Scribner's Sons, New York, 1894, and *Whip and Spur,* by Col. George E. Waring Jr., Boston, 1875.

To Mr. Govan and Mr. Livingood, authors of *A Different Valor,* and to The Bobbs-Merrill Co., publishers, The Banner is grateful, in particular, for permission to quote the 1861 warning to Gen. Joseph E. Johnston from his wife, and Gen. Johnston's reply.

To the same authors and publishers, The Banner expresses its gratitude for permission to quote three letters of the Gen. Johnston-Sen. Wigfall correspondence, all from *A Different Valor.* Appreciation is also expressed to the Henry E. Huntington Library and Art Gallery, San Marino, Calif., (repository for much of the correspondence) for permission to quote one of the letters, of Oct. 16, 1863; and gratitude for quotations is also tendered the Library of Congress, repository of the letter of Dec. 15, 1862.

For generous permission to quote the letters of Mattie Ready Morgan and a sister, from *Morgan and His Raiders,* The Banner is deeply grateful to Cecil Fletcher Holland, the author, and to The Macmillan Company, publishers. Much of Holland's research was done in Middle Tennessee.

And often consulted, concerning Gen. Morgan, was the *Confederate Veteran Magazine,* Nashville, 1883-1932 (40 volumes).

Gen. Hooker's Column Storming Lookout Mountain.

—From Harper's Weekly

SAM DAVIS is along—chosen because of his coolness, his courage, his engaging personality and endurance. There's a chill in the air. But Sam has a captured Yankee overcoat at home, waiting for him—if he just has a chance to go by and pick it up. He had left it there, at his Smyrna home, for his mother to dye a butternut brown. And shoes—his father will have his extra shoes mended. Sam had left them, too, his last time at home. Now, if luck will just take him close to Smyrna . . .

At the same time, hundreds of miles to the North, in the Ohio prison at Columbus, Morgan and his men were working on an escape plan.

They had learned that an air-chamber was beneath the six-inch concrete floor of their cell. Using a table knife, they had been scraping away. Over the slowly deepening hole they set a black bag.

Into a stove went the powdering concrete; into a mattress the larger pieces. Later they had to pierce a brick wall and dig a tunnel toward the courtyard. They smuggled in a shovel from the yard.

One day the lookout called a halt. A woman's footsteps were sounding in the corridor. Over the hole went the bag. Strolling toward Morgan was a beautifully dressed woman. She was singing, ever so softly, "Trust to Luck, Alabama . . ."

"Pauline!" he exclaimed. It was Miss Cushman, now toasted in the North as the "Spy of the Cumberland."

She smiled. "The shoe is on the other foot now."

Morgan laughed. "It's not difficult to tell now where you belong."

"But you must own up, you were deceived nicely."

Maybe he smiled at the black bag. He let her have her moment. "Those eyes," he said, "would deceive the devil himself."

They chatted briefly and Miss Cushman rose to go. She hoped he'd be comfortable in prison.

"Oh, I'm just staying a few days," he said lightly. "And I shall go down South again shortly."

Was there derision in her soft laughter? She'd had her moment—she thought. The moment was his. When she departed, the scraping resumed. But there was more to it than just digging. Around the courtyard ran a high wall. Watchdogs prowled within it. Eventually, the wall would have to be scaled.

From strips of bedsheets they plaited a rope. The stove's poker they bent into a hook and tied to the rope. When all was just so, they would try to catch the hook on the wall and climb over, if the dogs were silent—

This meant the Rebel prisoners would have to wait for a night of rain, when the dogs would retire to their kennels. By late November, all Morgan needed was a downpour.

Back in Tennessee, Sam Davis and the other scouts were ready to return to Bragg's headquarters. They knew the Sixth Corps of the Union Army, under Gen. G. M. Dodge, was near Pulaski, en route from Corinth, on its way to join Grant.

A CIVIL WAR REPORTER, with news of the battle. Notice the jouncing binoculars with which he's been watching the battle.

In pursuit of Forrest, through darkness and across streams, came the Federal horde, in scenes similar to this drawing of a Federal advance in Mississippi.

Gen. William T. Sherman

SAM'S assignment was nearly completed. He had even picked up, in Nashville, three cakes of soap and three toothbrushes for Gen. Bragg (things hard to come by in the troubled Confederacy). The final hours of his scouting took him near Smyrna.

It is late at night. He moves through the shadows toward the white-porticoed farmhouse. Home! Gently he taps on the windowpane. His mother hastens toward the sound.

"*Shh!*" she whispers and lets him in. They must be quiet, lest the younger children or the servants hear. Any chance word might bring danger. They have a few precious minutes together.

Sam wants to see the other children. He tiptoes into their bedroom. A moment he stands looking at their closed eyelids and peaceful faces. He kisses each one, then prepares to leave. He must pick up some important papers somewhere, but he'll be back.

He is not in disguise. Soon he returns with the papers. He must go now. He takes the coat which his mother had dyed and the shoes his father has had repaired. He embraces his mother. His father is squeezing his hand.

The scattered scouts set out for Chattanooga Nov. 19. In Sam's boot is his captain's letter to Bragg with ample detail on Federal troops. Sewn into his saddle is a map of unusual accuracy, describing Nashville fortifications.

Sam's luck didn't hold. He was on his way back when arrested on Lamb's Ferry Road in Giles County ("on or about Nov. 20," according to Federal records). The astonishing things he carried were soon found.

He was charged as a spy. But he wore a Confederate uniform and was a member of the First Tennessee Regiment. Did he tattle? No. The sentence was death.

Gen. Dodge felt sure, from the accuracy of the documents, that they came from someone on or near his staff. Who, boy? Who is it?

The Federals had the right man in jail, but they didn't know it—the herb doctor. The youth in uniform and the wandering peddler had been picked up at different places. No link was suspected.

Sam Davis told nothing. He wrote a letter:

Pulaski, Giles County
Nov. 26, 1863
Dear Mother—Oh, how painful it is to write to you! I have got to die tomorrow morning—to be hanged by the Federals. Mother, do not grieve for me. I must bid you goodbye forevermore. Mother, I do not fear to die. Give my love to all.

Your son, Samuel Davis

During the night a song was sung, "I Am Bound For the Promised Land." It is around 10 a.m., Nov. 27. There is a ruffle of drums. A regiment is marching to the Pulaski jail. Up to the door of the jail pulls a wagon with a wooden coffin on it.

The provost marshal comes out of the jail with his prisoner. Sam sits down on his coffin. He had hoped that, if he must die, they would shoot him.

The wagon rolls off toward a hill on the edge of town where a gallows has been built. Sam is allowed to sit briefly under a tree. He asks a captain: How long?

"*Fifteen minutes.*"

Soon a captain arrives. Gen. Dodge has sent him. He hurries to Davis. Speak, boy! Speak and go free. Who gave you those documents?

"*If I had a thousand lives,*" Sam said, "*I would lose them all here before I would betray my friends or the confidence of my informer.*"

A few minutes later Sam turned to the chaplain. "*I am ready.*"

He ascended the scaffold. The hangman's white mask was placed about his head. He stepped into eternity and into the hearts of every Southerner.

(Later, Capt. Shaw, en route to a Northern prison, would leap from a train near Louisville and escape.)

Today the Sam Davis home is a cherished shrine. He is buried in the garden. You may see his statue on Capitol Hill.

Many a Yankee conqueror, strolling on Fourth Avenue, whirled about and squealed with pain—shocked by a mysterious attack. It came from slingshots of the Stockell boys behind Venetian blinds in the tower of this house, at 119 Fourth. They were never discovered. (Built by William Stockell about 1848, the house had two bathtubs, said to have been the first in Nashville.)

SAM DAVIS' HOME after restoration.

AS THE sun set that first night on the fresh grave of Sam Davis, Morgan and his men were studying the Ohio sky for any sign of rain. All had been ready since Nov. 24.

As the sun went down the sky was clear. Before midnight a drizzle began. The dogs went into their kennels. It was around 10 minutes past midnight when Morgan and six of his men moved the carpetbag and slid downward.

They are in the shadows of the courtyard. Over the wall goes the hook. It catches. They're up and over. They're free and hurrying for the southbound train. They'd timed their escape to catch it.

As prisoners they had worn civilian clothing. It attracts no attention. Morgan sits down beside a Yankee major. Cecil Fletcher Holland, in *Morgan and His Raiders,* tells of an ironic conversation as the train rushes past the prison.

"Over there," says the friendly major, *"is where they put the Rebel general, Morgan, for safekeeping."*

"I hope he stays as safe as he is now," Morgan replied. Soon he's safe with Kentucky friends.

"Hurray!" writes a Louisville woman. *"I feel that I want to go somewhere and scream as loud as I can. I think I will go to the cellar and then no Yankee will hear me . . . Hurrah! For John Morgan!"* This, too, Holland records.

The North would have itself a near-conniption. It would yell for hearings. It would yell bribery, and much else. But all it would ever be able to prove in that direction was that Morgan had paid a guard—how much? a dollar or so?—for a newspaper. From it he had learned train schedules.

News of his escape created a sensation in Nashville. (There is a story that the occupying Yankees received a tip to rush to a certain house: *"John Morgan's there!"* They rushed, all right, and found a newborn Rebel baby—freshly named John Morgan.)

The real John Morgan would soon be on his way to his Mattie, in Columbia, S.C. What a reunion there'd be, and the news that he'd be hearing! So much had happened in the past few days.

Under Grant, Gen. Joseph Hooker's forces had taken Lookout Mountain Nov. 24, in the so-called "Battle Above the Clouds." (It was fought in rising mists from the Tennessee River.) Gen. Thomas and Gen. William T. Sherman had taken Missionary Ridge the next day.

With Chattanooga a base for Federal operations, the way was open for a Federal sweep into the Lower South. There would be a lull in operations until the spring of 1864. Bragg retreated to Dalton, Ga.

He had often blamed his generals. Now he blamed his troops. *"No excuse could be given,"* he fumed after Missionary Ridge, *"for the shameful conduct of the troops on the left—"*

Trying to halt the rout, he had ridden in among them, shouting, *"Here's your commander!"* Did it thrill a soul? No, according to Stanley F. Horn, in *The Army of Tennessee.*

"Here's your mule!" they shouted back and ran right on. (The "mule" gibe was a favorite inanity of Rebel soldiers, good for a laugh, somewhat like "Kilroy was here" in World War II.)

The South was about ready to stop up its ears at Bragg's excuses. Clamor for his removal had turned into a roar. There were rumors the Confederate cabinet would split on the question. It didn't.

On the night of Nov. 28, in Dalton, Bragg at last took up his pen and wrote, *"I deem it due to the cause and to myself to ask relief from my command."*

He got it. Bragg stepped down Dec. 1. Thousands of Southerners sighed with relief. "Old Joe" Johnston took his place. He received the news around Dec. 18 in Mississippi and hurried to North Georgia.

Johnston gave a pardon to all absent without leave who would return to ranks. Johnston instituted a furlough system by which every man could go home for a visit. Johnston went to work to make the Army of Tennessee an effective fighting unit. (A private wrote, *"He is loved, respected—yea, even worshipped by his troops."*)

What happened to Bragg? (Hold onto your chair.) He was kicked upstairs as military adviser to the President! (In the months ahead, Gen. Johnston would have to take many an order from him!)

"This happy announcement," snapped the Richmond Examiner, *"should enliven confidence . . . among the people like a bucket of water on a newly kindled grate."*

As Gen. Johnston headed for his new post, a wagon was moving along the road from Smyrna, toward Pulaski. Pulling it were two mules, Sam Davis' old friends. In the wagon rode a younger brother and a friend, on their way to bring Sam's body home.

It is Christmas Eve when they return. The mules are pulling the wagon up to the back porch. Behind it comes a little group of friends and neighbors, the men bareheaded in the cold, holding their hats in their hands. The casket is borne into the farmhouse parlor. Sam has come home, an obscure enlisted man, unknown to the fame that is echoing across the South in the wake of romantic Morgan.

In Danville, S.C., Morgan pauses and sends a lover's wire to his Mattie. He's happily on his way there. They will have Christmas dinner together.

To Forrest and his men, a desperate Christmas is coming, hundreds of miles away in West Tennessee. Danger hovers in the cold darkness, near the icy Hatchie River.

Three Yankee columns—nearly 15,000 men—are in pursuit of his recently recruited 3,500, only 1,000 of whom are armed. It is a danger he had foreseen.

On Dec. 2, he had entered the area through Hardeman County with 450 men—and two pieces of artillery. To have come west with such a small force had been "rash." Before departure he had said as much to his new department commander, "Old Joe," who even then didn't guess Forrest's full abilities. But Forrest had come, and nobody paid much attention—just then.

"A Plantation Christmas, 'Fo De Wah"

—From a drawing by W. T. Smedley in The Confederate Museum, Richmond

"**F**ORREST *may cavort about the country as much as he pleases,*" sniffed the Union general, Sherman, when informed Forrest was going west. (Sherman would change his mind.)

A day would come, too, when Gen. Johnston would call Forrest *"the greatest soldier the war produced, second not even to Lee and Jackson."*

In West Tennessee's thick woods and swampy bottoms, Forrest had set up little recruiting "shebangs." These were seven-by-four-foot strips of oilcloth hung over poles and forked sticks. Under their shelter, 50 to 100 men had been enlisting daily.

Soon Forrest had more than 3,000 men. Fighting men must eat. He was looking out for that, too. He had been gathering great herds of cattle and livestock, 200 beef cattle and 300 hogs. But his men were poorly armed, unequal to the three Federal columns, each larger than his own command, which were now closing in upon him from all sides.

It is Christmas Eve. The Federals are closer. Forrest is trying to escape, to withdraw across the Hatchie River and take all those hogs and cattle with him. He has no intention of giving them up. The Hatchie is swollen, its bottoms flooded.

He is spreading a line of troopers 10 or more paces apart. In this way 60 men can form a quarter-mile line. Each junior officer and sergeant is told to pick up and repeat orders as if commanding a company in brigade drill. The command is roared, "Brigade—charge!"

Along the line it rings, echoing on in the frosty night, *"Brigade—charge! Brigade—charge!"* The little band creates enormous uproar as it attacks through still-standing cornstalks. The nearest Union commander, suspecting well-armed superior numbers, moves away in the moonlight, 10 miles westward . . .

—Staff Photo by Bob Ray

The grave of Sam Davis, in the garden of his Smyrna home.

—Courtesy Sam Davis Memorial Association

Parlor of the Sam Davis home. Into this room his Confederate neighbors came, on Christmas morning, 1863, to pay their final respect to the boy whose statue now stands on Capitol Hill.

FORREST goes back to the river crossing. Driftwood fires cast feeble light.

Cattle are bawling, pigs squealing, all terrified by the surging waters, the masses of men, the babel of voices. There is one small ferry. It capsizes. Into the stream pitch a wagon and team.

Forrest plunges in after them, armpit deep. He is trying to cut the mules from the harness. On the bank, stomping around, is a loud-mouthed conscript, grumbling. Get into that cold water? Not me. *"Not for anybody!"*

Forrest is climbing out. He hears. Is the whole world lost? Is every standard going by the board? Is there nothing left for weakling men—and brave ones too—except the taste of ashes?

He grabs the conscript by the seat-of-the-pants and hurls him into the flood. (One day the recruit will make a pretty good soldier.)

Work resumes in the half light. Several hours hence, all will be safely across, men, cattle and hogs. Forrest will have a Christmas present, the rank of major general. (It had become effective Dec. 3.) This time he will accept. Christmas Day is coming.

But how different from the Christmases of yesteryear, when he'd had a self-made million dollars, a warm plantation house, and Mary Ann had stood beside him, in his fancy weskit, on the snowy porch at Christmas morning, greeting the slaves as they filed by . . .

He squeezes the half-frozen moisture from his beard. Carry on! Cross over. It is morning by the icy river.

It is morning back in Smyrna.

In the clear, pale sunlight of Christmas Day, a casket is being carried down the garden walk. The white mask of the hangman has been removed from Sam Davis' face, by those who love him. Sam never had a million, nor a big plantation house. The military minds of Europe would never study his maneuvers.. But he'd given all he had. In the nearby barn, his stall is empty. The Yankees have his horse, too.

It's Christmas, '63, in Middle Tennessee.

—By Forbes, 30 Years After

Forrest and his men, crossing the freezing Big Hatchie, may have looked much like this drawing which Forbes called "Through the Ice."

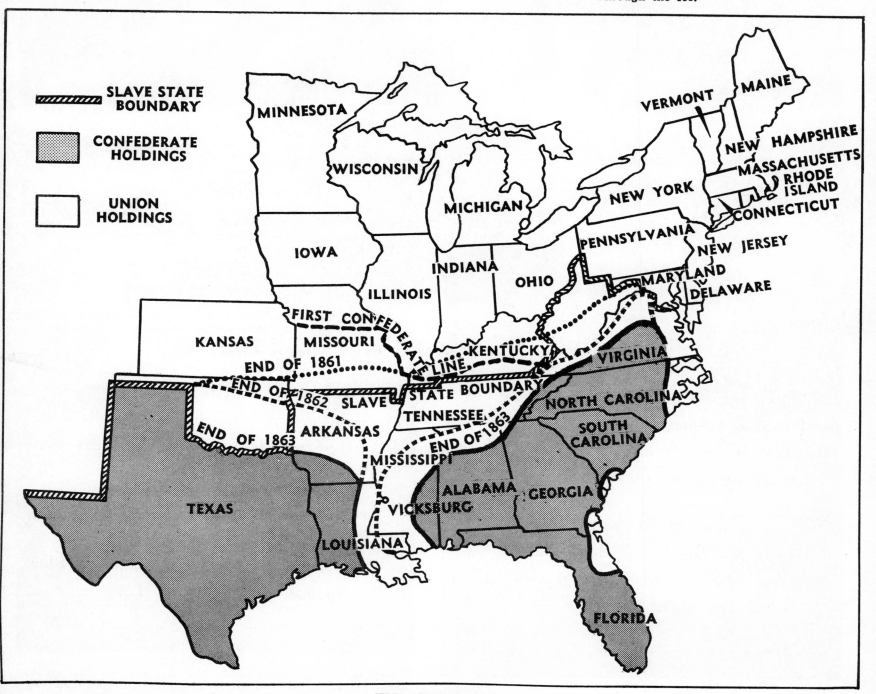

END OF 1863

The Sam Davis Statue on Capitol Hill

. . . When the Lord calls up earth's heroes
  To stand before his face,
Oh, many a name unknown to fame
  Shall ring from that high place.

Then out of a grave in the Southland,
  At the just God's call and beck,
Shall one man rise with fearless eyes
  And a rope about his neck.

He would not sell his manhood
  To purchase priceless hope;
Where kings drag down a name and crown
  He dignified a rope.

Oh, grave, where was thy triumph?
  Oh, death, where was thy sting?
He showed you how a man could bow
  To doom, and stay a king . . .
—By Ella Wheeler Wilcox from inscription on the Davis Monument on Capitol Hill

The battlefield of Franklin, looking north across the peaceful meadows from Gen. B. F. Cheatham's headquarters.

From Century War Book, 1861-1865

The CIVIL WAR In MIDDLE TENNESSEE

PART III—1864—JAN. 1-NOV. 30

"The years creep slowly by, Lorena,
  The snow is on the grass again.
The sun's low down the sky, Lorena . . .

"There is a future, oh, thank God!
  Of life this is so small a part—
'Tis dust to dust beneath the sod,
  But there, up there, 'tis heart to heart."

THERE was a loneliness and a sadness in the song the soldiers were singing now, in the closing days of 1863. How long ago since first they'd heard the quick bright beat of "Dixie." How long ago Fort Sumter, in the confident springtime of '61! How long since high-hearted Middle Tennesseans first went forth to war which many Northerners had predicted would last just 90 days . . .

In the North it was a prosperous sadness. A whole new crop of millionaires was being spawned. In the South the times were lean. Oranges, in Richmond, cost $5 each.

One lionized Southern hero was getting his share. This was Gen. John Bell Hood, convalescing in Richmond from the loss of his right leg at Chickamauga. Patriotic ladies showered the handsome bachelor with oranges and all the other delicacies they could find.

Eleven months hence, on an amber autumn afternoon, Hood's gallant name would become forever linked with the bloodiest two hours Middle Tennessee has ever known—the Battle of Franklin, Nov. 30, 1864.

Three days later, Nashvillians would see his ragged survivors pouring into the Brentwood hills and digging desperately into the earth of Davidson County, earth that to thousands was the soil of their native state.

In the fateful weeks that followed, the city's Confederate hopes would rest upon him—and his dream of freeing the captive city would be shattered on her Southern hills.

Could he envision that now? Not Hood!

Buzzards Roost Pass, Federals in foreground. In the distance may be seen the smoke of the Rebel encampment.

A DAUNTLESS GIANT, 6-foot-2, with a luxurious "tawny" beard and sad blue eyes that sometimes "burned," he was having a gay winter while his stump healed, very close to the body. Richmond society adored him. He was swamped with invitations to fashionable parties and he went.

After all, he was only 32. His patriarchal beard made him look much older. Vast beards were high fashion, and Hood was moving in high fashion in this last effulgent social season Richmond would know for many years.

The White House of the Confederacy was open to Hood. His friendship with President Jefferson Davis was growing. And Hood was in love with the serenely beautiful Sara (Sally) Preston, a niece of Gen. Wade Hampton who, before the war, was probably the wealthiest planter in the South.

Hood would still be in love with Sally—an unrequited love—on the lazy Indian Summer day when he would stand under a linn tree on Franklin's Winstead Hill and hurl the Army of Tennessee, without preparation, across two miles of open meadow, into the roaring guns of an enemy well-entrenched behind ditch, parapet and headlogs.

Pickett's charge at Gettysburg, the nearest thing to it, covered only a mile. Pickett's charge was against an enemy which had been battered by 100 guns for more than two hours, with only a stone wall for cover.

Hood would bring what remained of Confederate hope, and bring it with knightly courage, into the darkest and most awesome final weeks of the Civil War in Middle Tennessee. No man could have been braver. Ache of body and unease of heart may have been among his many burdens in that autumn of 1864—when he would come marching his high-hearted, tattered veterans back into the Middle Tennessee from which they had been driven in 1863. The odds would be against him then, even as now in his love for Sally.

Her suitors were many, rich and handsome. Sally was amply endowed with brains, including common sense. Had she ever really loved any man as yet? Perhaps she wasn't sure. Impetuous Hood, incredibly brave and somewhat rash, in love as well as war, meant to make her sure.

He was sure of himself. While in Richmond, he said, he meant to be *"as happy a fool as a one-legged man can be."*

What did it matter that a leg was gone? Or that his left arm hung nearly limp in a sling, from another wound, received at Gettysburg? Good soldiers don't worry.

All Hood's men knew he was a fighter, a superb combat officer. His admiring Texas brigade, after Chickamauga, had passed the hat and raised nearly $5,000 with which to buy him an artificial leg. It was coming.

SALLY (BUCK) PRESTON

Gen. Wade Hampton
Sally's Uncle

A few weeks ago, in September, 1863, when his staff surgeon, Dr. John Darby, had departed for Paris on a medicine-buying trip, Hood had given him a memorandum which said, *"Three cork legs and a diamond ring."*

This was Hood. This was the stout-hearted fighter.

Of what he did and didn't do men since have asked: Why? What drove him? What manner of man was he? Perhaps no one knows the full answer.

Behind Hood the general stands Hood the youth, the cadet, the lover, the Rebel hero of Chickamauga who had lain there on the ground, his blood gushing, and shouted to his Texans, *"Go ahead—keep ahead of everything!"*

To see the general better we need a glimpse of his early life, and more than a passing glance at his days in Richmond. For it was in Richmond, in the slowly sifting snows of '63-'64, that the story of the Battle of Franklin and the Battle of Nashville may have had their beginning.

Hood meant to return to the struggle; to help regain lost Tennessee or stem the Yankee drive into Georgia. Whatever the Richmond decision, action was Hood's forte. Attack!

Hood meant to win the woman of his choice before leaving for Dalton, Ga., where the weary Army of Tennessee—pushed southeast from the state whose name it bore—now hopefully awaited the coming of brilliant Gen. Joseph E. Johnston, to replace inept Gen. Braxton Bragg. Even now, Gen. Johnston was on his way to the little North Georgia town in which the Army of Tennessee, outnumbered more than two to one, stood behind Rocky Face Ridge, near Buzzards Roost Gap.

Back in Middle Tennessee, Coleman's Scouts—the *"big eyes"* of the Rebels—still prowled behind the Federal lines, risking their lives to gather vital news on what the Yankees did or planned to do.

Secret patriots helped them. From under many a Midstate rock, and from many a Midstate hollow tree, the scouts relayed messages in cypher toward the Roost and on to Dalton. Now and then, to the cypher writers in Middle Tennessee, a special messenger would bring, verbally, a new key-word which, in those days, was never put in print. The stakes were too high. They would go higher.

Near the Roost the railroad to Atlanta passed through a tunnel. Here, seven miles northwest of Dalton, the Rebels had an outpost. Hold the railroad!

Its northward hub was already gone. This was Chattanooga, now a Federal stronghold.

The Rebels had railroad communication as far north as Ringgold, Ga. By wagon road this was only 18 miles from Chattanooga.

How near the foe! How vital to the Rebels at Dalton was their line of rails, stretching behind them to Atlanta. And how vital to the Yankees their railroad at Chattanooga, reaching northward across Middle Tennessee to the Ohio River.

If the supply line of either were cut, retreat or surrender must follow.

The best rail-wrecker for the Confederacy was Gen. Nathan Bedford Forrest, unlettered wizard of the cavalry, then in Mississippi, who had been sent West (with a faintly soothing promotion to major general from President Davis) but sent without an army and told to raise one.

Forrest had raised one. Within weeks it would be used against the shrewd Federal planning of Gen. William Tecumseh (Cump) Sherman, who was also back in Mississippi.

Months hence, when the last Confederate blue chips were down, Forrest would be summoned, post-haste, back to the Army of Tennessee as it headed back to Midstate. The desperate call, from Hood, would come too late to reap the full benefit of Forrest's natural genius.

Meanwhile, the Yankees in Chattanooga were wintering quietly (*"not in condition to assail us for some weeks,"* Bragg wrote Davis Dec. 2, '63). His scouts made certain of that.

Richmond was breathing easier, too. The Army of the Potomac, under Gen. George G. Meade, had backed up northward and crossed the Rapidan River, after being checked at Mine Run by Gen. Robert E. Lee in late November. Lee held the south bank.

Now in winter quarters, Meade's army licked its wounds along the Hazel River, in the vicinity of Brandy Station, where deserters were being shot almost every Friday.

Many people in the North were weary of the war. The North had fought and fought. It had won and won. Still the South wasn't whipped. Who said 90 days? It was still fighting after three years. Northerners who vigorously opposed the war were called Copperheads. The word would find a political use.

"Running the Gauntlet." By Forbes, in *30 Years After.*

Snap the enemy's railroad—and he's ruined. So both sides reasoned in Georgia.

THIS WOULD be a year of politics, and President Abraham Lincoln's generals had better come up with solid victories if he were to be re-elected in November. He would have strong opposition. In the North, the Democrats were favoring peace.

Actually the South was exhausted. Conscription had caused direst poverty in many homes. Womenfolk and children carried on, with zeal and ingenuity. (At the siege of Knoxville, in late November and December, the Yankees had thrown dead mules in the river. Downstream, Rebels had dragged them out, to get the horseshoes.) The South's will to fight lived on.

In the North, if a man were conscripted, he could buy legal exemption for $300. In the past August, conscription had set off bloody draft riots. In New York there had been murder and pillage for two days.

The whole Broadway block which housed the draft office was burned, the mayor's house sacked. Fire engines were halted, telegraph wires cut, streetcars overturned. Negroes were mobbed and murdered, presumably for association with the Republican Party and its "Black Republican War."

About 20 Negroes perished the first day, many more the second. Several were beaten, stoned to death and hanged to lamp posts. A Negro cartman's body was set afire and burned. The total of killed and injured, white and black, was estimated at 1,000, and property damage at $1,500,000.

This was ominous writing on Lincoln's political wall. In it, the South began to see a ray of hope. A strange thing was happening.

Ironically, in the last 15 months of war, when the South was weakening and weakest, her best chance of separation would come. A chance at independence. It would come politically, not militarily, because of the South's unwillingness to give up.

It would be a political chance because, if Lincoln's generals didn't win a great victory soon, Lincoln might be defeated in the November elections. His successor might make peace. Lincoln knew this and the Confederate War Office knew it.

Why say "calfrope" now? Richmond wasn't merely thinking of keeping Yankees out of Georgia and Richmond. Reclaim Middle Tennessee!

The Midstate's secret heart stayed Rebel. And many an average-looking person went to such places as the Squire Schuler house and the Tom English house at Campbellsville in Giles County on a quiet gamble with death. Both places served as headquarters for Coleman's Scouts. Retake this loyal land!

On Dec. 2, 1863, the very day after relinquishing command of the Army of Tennessee, Gen. Bragg wrote President Davis:

"Let us concentrate all available men and, with our greatest and best leader at its head, yourself if practicable, march the whole upon the enemy and crush him. I trust I may be allowed to participate in the struggle which may restore to us . . . the country we have just lost." This was Middle Tennessee.

Had Bragg indulged in a little flattery? Soon Hood would use similar words: *"Mr. President, why don't you come and lead us yourself? I would follow you to the death."*

Both men must have known that Davis longed to be a general. Hood's words we learn from the justly famous diary of Mrs. Mary Boykin Chesnut, published as *A Diary from Dixie.*

Both Bragg and Hood would fare well at the President's hands. The thoughts of the three were converging: Strike the enemy! And meanwhile the scouts were counting the enemy's men and horses, his guns and freight cars . . .

Hood's hour would come. In the critical summer ahead, he would be chosen to lead in the grapple for Atlanta, and thereafter for Middle Tennessee. His hour was not yet. It was Johnston's.

First, and soon, upon Johnston's shoulders would fall the burden of Richmond's plans. He would be expected to reclaim the area which Bragg had been unable to hold. Bragg would join in the expectations. Davis would elevate the unsuccessful Bragg, his old friend, to a rank similar to that of Commander-in-Chief.

Bragg will have power. (*"Bragg now seems to rank the Secretary of War,"* Rebel war clerk J. B. Jones would write April 21, in *A Rebel War Clerk's Diary.*)

Gen. Johnston, rolling toward Dalton by train, will become in effect *The Dissenter,* defense-minded. Personal antipathy, long smoldering between Johnston and the President, will not improve matters.

In Richmond, Hood's friendship with the President was blooming. On fair days Hood took long carriage rides, often with the President. A part of the Civil War history of Tennessee may have been in the making as the horses clopped along. What were Hood and Davis talking about?

"If we knew," Nashville's historian Stanley F. Horn has written, *"we might know more about the inner history of the Army of Tennessee."*

Hood later wrote that he *"cheerfully acquiesced"* to Davis' views with the clear understanding: There would be an *"aggressive campaign."*

Hood often rode with Sally beside him, elegant in black velvet and ermine, with a pheasant's feather in her English hat which had come through the blockade months before. *"They say,"* Hood told her banteringly, *"that I am engaged to four young ladies."*

GEN. NATHAN BEDFORD FORREST

GEN. JOSEPH E. JOHNSTON

Secret Cypher System Of The Confederacy

```
A B C D E F G H I J K L M N O P Q R S T U V W X Y Z
B C D E F G H I J K L M N O P Q R S T U V W X Y Z A
C D E F G H I J K L M N O P Q R S T U V W X Y Z A B
D E F G H I J K L M N O P Q R S T U V W X Y Z A B C
E F G H I J K L M N O P Q R S T U V W X Y Z A B C D
F G H I J K L M N O P Q R S T U V W X Y Z A B C D E
G H I J K L M N O P Q R S T U V W X Y Z A B C D E F
H I J K L M N O P Q R S T U V W X Y Z A B C D E F G
I J K L M N O P Q R S T U V W X Y Z A B C D E F G H
J K L M N O P Q R S T U V W X Y Z A B C D E F G H I
K L M N O P Q R S T U V W X Y Z A B C D E F G H I J
L M N O P Q R S T U V W X Y Z A B C D E F G H I J K
M N O P Q R S T U V W X Y Z A B C D E F G H I J K L
N O P Q R S T U V W X Y Z A B C D E F G H I J K L M
O P Q R S T U V W X Y Z A B C D E F G H I J K L M N
P Q R S T U V W X Y Z A B C D E F G H I J K L M N O
Q R S T U V W X Y Z A B C D E F G H I J K L M N O P
R S T U V W X Y Z A B C D E F G H I J K L M N O P Q
S T U V W X Y Z A B C D E F G H I J K L M N O P Q R
T U V W X Y Z A B C D E F G H I J K L M N O P Q R S
U V W X Y Z A B C D E F G H I J K L M N O P Q R S T
V W X Y Z A B C D E F G H I J K L M N O P Q R S T U
W X Y Z A B C D E F G H I J K L M N O P Q R S T U V
X Y Z A B C D E F G H I J K L M N O P Q R S T U V W
Y Z A B C D E F G H I J K L M N O P Q R S T U V W X
Z A B C D E F G H I J K L M N O P Q R S T U V W X Y
```

—From "The Coleman Scouts," a thesis by Mabel Baxter (Mrs. Homer Peyton) Pittard, presented to the Graduate School of Middle Tennessee State Teachers College, August, 1953. Reprinted by special permission.

Using Manchester Bluff as key word, suppose you want to write in cypher: SHAW CAPTURED NEAR PULASKI. First, find M, the first keyword letter, in horizontal column. Find S (first letter of message) in vertical column. Then, at the intersection of the columns, find the letter E. This begins the cypher. Now find horizontal A, vertical H, and intersectional A, second cypher. You have EA. Proceed. Full code message: EANY-JEHMYIFO-HJFD-AHNHWCB. ("Dr. E. Coleman," scout head, was Capt. H. B. Shaw. Manchester Bluff is an authentic key word. It was much used.)

SHE DIDN'T bat an eye. Rumor, she said, had her engaged to two young men. *"I think I'll set a mousetrap,"* Hood replied, *"and break some of those young fellows' legs."*

Does his armor crack with the words? And show a glimpse of a tortured man within? Or is it merely the remark of a startled lover, newly come to the repartee of Richmond?

Where did he come from, this amazing man under whose command the war in Middle Tennessee would reach crescendo? Hood was no Texan, despite the song which says, *"The gallant Hood of Texas played hell in Tennessee."*

Hood was a Kentuckian by birth and blood, from a prosperous Bluegrass family, born in Owingsville, Bath County, and reared in Montgomery County. His father was a doctor who offered Hood an education in Europe if Hood would follow medicine.

The youth preferred an Army career. His uncle, Judge Richard French, was a congressman. Appointment to the United States Military Academy at West Point came easily. Could Hood conform to regulations? As a youngster in the Bluegrass, with more than enough money to spend, Hood had been somewhat rambunctious.

As he departed for the Point, his father had cautioned, *"If you can't behave, don't come home. Go to the nearest gatepost and butt your brains out."*

What a dashing cadet Hood had made, with good looks, 6-foot-2, in a cap seven inches tall, with an eight-inch black plume! He wasn't too studious. Records show that during his four years at West Point he checked out two books for reading, Scott's *Rob Roy* and Jane Porter's *Scottish Chiefs.* In a class of 55, he was graduated as 44th in general merit.

Hood saw action in the Indian troubles of the Old West. He served a while in Texas.

When the Civil War broke out, Kentucky was divided. What did Kentucky mean to do? There was no doubt about Texas.

Hood adopted Texas as his own, volunteering his services while in Montgomery, Ala. This, plus assignment to the Texas brigade, gave rise to the popular notion that he was a Texan.

The song was unheard of in that Christmas time of 1863, when a lionized Hood sat down to a feast with Sally's family.

Holiday provisions had arrived from the Prestons' South Carolina plantations. There was boned turkey, ham, mutton, wild duck, partridge, plum pudding and four wines—sauterne, madeira, burgundy and sherry.

Few in Richmond knew such bounty. For the average man, supplies were scarce. Hood was glum at the feast. For the second time, Sally had turned down his proposal of marriage.

"Good heavens, how I wish the man were gone!" she said to Mrs. Chesnut after dinner. But Sally must have found something to admire in the wounded giant whose voice was boomingly musical, and whose blue eyes, *"normally sad and fawn-like,"* would suddenly blaze whenever he spoke of returning to the war in Tennessee. She called Hood *"Sam,"* as had his classmates at West Point. For some obscure reason, he called her *"Buck."* The courtship continued.

Two days after Christmas, Gen. Johnston reached Dalton. Dispirited soldiers rejoiced. A band went marching to Johnston's house. Gen. B. F. Cheatham, coming to the door beside him, patted Johnston's bald head and said, *"Boys, this is Old Joe."*

They roared. "Old Joe" he would remain, beloved and trusted, for as long as any of them should live.

"Old Joe" took over. Morale soared. Thousands who had gone home in disgust, after the disaster of Missionary Ridge under Bragg, would now come surging back.

Gen. Johnston found the Army of Tennessee without enough rifles, shoes or horses. Many men were barefoot *"in every regiment."* As late as February, the horses would be too weak to pull guns to battle or away in case of retreat.

Two letters awaited "Old Joe" at Dalton. One was from James A. Seddon, Secretary of War. Seddon wanted *"an offensive . . . as soon as conditions"* would permit. But Johnston must not expect any reinforcements.

The other letter, from President Davis, took an even rosier view of the army's plight. Davis hoped Gen. Johnston would *"move against the enemy,"* and *"soon."*

Johnston was irked. *"To assume the offensive from this point,"* he wrote Davis, *"we must move into Middle or East Tennessee. To the first the obstacles are: Chattanooga now a fortress, the Tennessee River, the rugged desert of the Cumberland Mountains, and an army outnumbering ours two to one."* Two to one. Remember.

Supplies would have to come from Atlanta by rail. Georgia owned the railroads. Her governor, Joe Brown, had not got along with Bragg.

"Old Joe" made friends with Gov. Brown. Boxcars of food rumbled toward Dalton. A blockade runner moored at Nassau. Aboard were 10,000 pairs of shoes. "Old Joe" learned and made certain that many of his barefoot men were shod.

What a pity for Georgia and Middle Tennessee that Gen. Johnston would never handle President Davis as smoothly as he handled the governor! What a pity that more ships couldn't run the blockade!

How? When Federal men-o-war stood off-shore at Southern ports, with guns trained on the harbor mouths?

A man born in Middle Tennessee had been doggedly trying to find the answer. His name was Horace L. Hunley, born in Sumner County in the 1820s. His plan was startling: a submarine!

Yankee spies were nearly as busy as Coleman's Scouts. They had wind of Hunley's contraption, made from a big boiler. At first they thought it a Confederate brainstorm. Their view would change.

The strange craft had fins, screws, cranks and ballast tanks, all powered by the muscles of a crowded nine-man crew. Inside, in the choking stench of perspiration, it was lighted only by a single candle because of the scarcity of oxygen. But it was a true submarine, capable of submerging, and silent.

First built in 1863, it had been designed by Hunley, James R. McClintock and Baxter Watson. Hunley led the group. The other two were marine engineers.

Right now it was in Charleston, a crude and dangerous little craft. A propeller shaft ran its full length. Eight men turned the cranks which were geared to the shaft. The ninth man, commanding, stood near the forward hatch and steered by dead reckoning when submerged. He controlled the fins which tilted the ship up or down and from side to side.

Could it dive beneath the warships that blocked Charleston harbor? And pull a floating torpedo, at the end of a long line, against an enemy hull?

The Confederacy doubted, after the first model had sunk in Mobile Bay. It failed to appropriate money for a second try. But Hunley still believed.

He became the financier. He persuaded friends to aid him. A second craft was built. This was the one in Charleston. In naval history it bears Hunley's gallant name—the H. L. Hunley, a stirring word which the admirals know, far out on today's seas, but almost forgotten in the Middle Tennessee of Hunley's birth.

In 1863 Hunley's craft had been dubbed, with sad derision, the *"Peripatetic Coffin,"* because of its habit of drowning the bold volunteers who manned it. Crew after crew had perished, and Hunley feared it was not being properly operated.

He went to Charleston and took command. On Oct. 15 (a month after Hood's leg was amputated) Hunley gave orders for another dive. He stood at the rudder.

Air bubbles rose. The Hunley failed to rise. A note was entered in the journal of operations:

> . . . *It is supposed the hole in the top of the boat by which the men entered had not been properly closed. The water was some nine fathoms deep.*

The craft was pulled ashore. They found Hunley's body near the hatch, the candle clutched in his hand.

The dream of the Sumner County man lived on. The humble little craft stood waiting in disgrace in Charleston as the 1864 New Year came. Before springtime another man would try.

As the New Year came to Richmond, gala affairs honored Gen. John Hunt Morgan, the famed Kentucky raider who had escaped an Ohio prison shortly before.

His name still made Southern magic, despite the 1863 midsummer madness of his plunge into Ohio. Danville citizens sent him silver spurs. And a 10-gallon punchbowl flowed at the Ballard House, in tribute to the debonair hero who was to die in a Tennessee garden before the year was out.

It is Jan. 7, off Charleston. Aboard a Union warship an officer sits writing a report about the Hunley. He's just talked to a deserter who said the Hunley had been *"brought on two flatcars to Charleston."*

The deserter has seen her *"dive under"* a big ship, *"about 250 feet from her and come up about 300 feet beyond."*

The officer issues a warning. An attack may be expected, *"on the first night when the water is suitable."* This means a still night when waves will not lap into the Hunley's hatches as they are opened for air.

It also means the blockading ships must stand farther out to sea. His advice is heeded, and a week later he writes, *"It was an ugly, rainy night, but I found all on the alert,"*—alert for a dead man's dream.

In Washington, weeks before, Lincoln had decided that conquered Tennessee was ready for *"reinaugurating a loyal state government."* He wrote his military governor in Nashville, Andrew Johnson, *"Not a moment should be lost."*

Unionists met in Nashville Jan. 21. Gov. Johnson spoke for two hours. He said secession leaders *"ought to be hung. Treason must be made odious. Traitors must be punished and impoverished—"*

"How the Copperheads Obtain Their Votes"—*From Harper's Weekly, November 12, 1864.*

LOCAL UNITS, said the Yankee-minded governor from East Tennessee, should start the new civil government. He set March 9 for the election of county officials.

Who could vote? Well, if you'd once been a Rebel you'd have to swear to a lot of things. The great-hearted Lincoln proposed a full pardon to all who swore loyalty—the "amnesty" oath. Then Gov. Johnson stepped in and required an oath more severe. This was called the "damnesty" oath.

Hatred of Gov. Johnson grew.

By mid-February, Hood was able to ride a horse again. Often he rode with Davis. Soon, at church, he was sitting in the President's pew.

"Every manjack who was a general while he was a colonel says he's going up too fast," Mrs. Chesnut wrote.

Hood's star was not rising so swiftly with Sally. One night as Hood entered a carriage, his body servant, Cy, almost caused him to fall from his crutches. Hood stormed, in Sally's presence.

In the carriage Sally blazed, "I hate a man who speaks angrily to those who cannot resent it."

Nor did her parents favor the match, although they admired the brave officer whose advancement to lieutenant general was confirmed by the Confederate Congress Feb. 4. And as things looked, Hood was not going to leave for Tennessee with personal peace in his heart.

His hours with Sally were drawing short. As their carriage rolled along, Hood held out his hand.

"Don't do that," Sally pleaded. "Let it stand as it is. You know I like you. But you want to spoil it all."

"Say yes or no," Hood commanded. "I will not be satisfied with less. Which is it?"

Cy was looking on. Sally didn't want to embarrass the general before his servant. (So she told Mrs. Chesnut.) She put her hand in Hood's.

"Heavens, what a change came over his face," she told Mrs. Chesnut. "The practical wretch said at once, 'Now I will speak to your father.'" Then Sally asked Mrs. Chesnut, "Do you believe I like him now?"

"No!" Mrs. Chesnut replied.

A day or two later Mrs. Chesnut saw Hood's carriage halt. He couldn't come in, but could Sally come out? Mrs. Chesnut records: "Sally flew down and stood 10 minutes in the snow, Cy holding the carriage door open while the general kissed her hands and proclaimed his love."

In Tennessee, a new anger was rising, against an imported Yankee from Massachusetts. He was Horace Maynard, Tennessee's attorney general under Gov. Johnson.

Maynard had just ruled that no former Rebel should vote in the election unless "amnestied" six months before—and the election was nearly at hand! The suddenly-set time element slammed the door on some who had finally decided to take the "damnesty" oath. It was too late.

In far-off Charleston harbor, the sea is still. Night has fallen. There is no moon. Something is moving just above the dark waters. The Hunley is heading toward the Yankee blockaders. It is Feb. 17.

Ever so quietly, a hatch is being opened. Fresh air rushes in. A man looks out, Lt. George E. Dixon, stout-hearted Alabama infantryman. He sees the Union frigate Housatonic, ducks below and aims straight at her.

Perhaps he hissed, "Full speed ahead!"

Eight men bent to their cranks with blistered hands. Already they had come about four miles. Blood trickled from their fingers. The Hunley surged ahead. This time it towed no torpedo. It pushed one, on a long spar attached to the nose.

It was 8:45 aboard the Housatonic when one of her officers saw what appeared to be a floating barrel. He leaned over the rail. It was coming toward him, fast.

He shouted an alarm. Cables were slipped. Engines backed. Drums rolled. Sailors tumbled from bunks and went running toward their posts.

The Hunley's torpedo struck on a line with the Housatonic's magazine. Flames shot toward the sky, lighting the topmost spars. It has been written that half the Housatonic's men were blown into the rigging, the other half into the sea.

The dream of the Sumner Countian had found its mark. The 1,264-ton Housatonic was sinking stern foremost with 13 guns, heeling to port as she went down, "in three minutes." Many of her crew would be rescued by sister ships.

Hanging a Negro. Tragic toll of the New York draft riots.

"The Hunley"—a mural by J. Augustus Walker in the City Hall of Mobile.

FOR THE first time in the history of warfare, a submarine had sunk a warship in combat.

Did the Hunley survive the blast? No one knows. Signals had been agreed upon, in case the submarine wanted a return light exposed. Such signals from the Hunley were *"observed and answered,"* (according to a letter of Feb. 19 from Col. C. M. Danzler to Gen. P. G. T. Beauregard).

On March 10 an entry was made at Confederate Headquarters in Charleston:

> Nothing has since been heard
> of Lt. Dixon. . . . It is therefore
> feared that gallant officer and his
> brave companions have perished.

Something had gone wrong. In all, 36 men had died in proving the point of the man from Sumner. But proved it had been. Fifty years later, in World War I, a world would find that Hunley had opened the door to a new era in war at sea.

The day after the Housatonic sank, Gen. Johnston wired from Dalton, "Lt. Gen. Hood is much needed here."

Hood's diamond from Paris had not arrived. He left Sally the diamond-studded star from his hat.

As he went, this seems sure: Ambition was flaming in his brain.

". . . *Fame and a beautiful wife. This obviously was Hood's dream,*" says John P. Dyer in his book, *The Gallant Hood.*

A rocking little train sped Hood toward Buzzard's Roost. a tall, gaunt native of Middle Tennessee was riding hard through the wintry night of Mississippi on a desperate mission. Gen. Forrest was rushing his 3,500 recruits toward their first big fight, against 7,500 well-equipped Yankees under Gen. William Sooy Smith.

Smith was sweeping down from Collierville, near Memphis, to join Gen. Sherman, who was advancing from Vicksburg with more than 20,000 infantrymen. They meant to meet at Meridian, destroying railways as they went, and presumably go *"eastward to Selma,"* where cannon were cast.

The plan came from Sherman, red-bearded and peppery-voiced, a man so thorough that, as a boy, he is said to have hanged a cat nine times to be sure he got all its nine lives. Sherman was one Yankee commander with a dawning comprehension of the deadliness of Forrest.

As Smith advanced, about 3,000 Negroes deserted plantations and followed him, encumbering his march. For two days *"the sky was red with flames of burning corn and cotton."* Negroes, driven wild by invasion excitement, *"set the torch to mansion houses, stables, cotton gins and quarters, and came en masse to join our column, leaving only fire and destruction behind them,"* according to Col. George E. Waring, U.S.A., (in *Whip and Spur*).

Smith tried to stop the excesses. But some of the burnings were authorized. Forrest saw the rising smoke.

Smith, sensing a trap, finally turned around, Feb. 21, near West Point, Miss. Forrest jumped him. Yankee blood began to spill on the ashes they had made.

Sherman had reached Meridian Feb. 14. He would wait in vain. Smith would never join him there. Gen. Smith's 7,500 were headed back toward Memphis with 3,500 Rebels nipping flank and rear.

Next day, seven miles northwest of Okolona, the Federals manned a hogback ridge. The Rebels charged. Forrest saw his youngest brother fall, a bullet through his neck.

Forrest is dismounting. *"Jeffrey!"* he says, over and over, lifting him gently. The best-loved of his five Confederate brothers is dying.

Forrest is covering Jeffrey's face and charging back into the fray, saber and pistol going. Three Yankees are dying at his hands.

Gen. Smith's men are yielding their fifth position of the day. The last part of their return to Memphis will become a *"60-mile fight."*

In Meridian, smoke is rising from ruins. Sherman, chattering in disgust and tired of waiting, has burned the town. He is marching back to Vicksburg, burning as he goes. He will blame Smith for the collapse of his plans.

For a while, Selma is safe.

It is Feb. 25. Hood, in Georgia, is back with the Army of Tennessee. Into the night he and Johnston discuss the Richmond plan for moving back into Tennessee, with reinforcements from Gen. James Longstreet in East Tennessee and Gen. Leonidas Polk in Mississippi.

Hood's all for it. Johnston is eager for the reinforcements. But he's cool to the plan.

Hood, disappointed, is uninclined to think of whys and wherefores, of terrain and forage and ammunition and blankets. Does Johnston think of these things too much? Therein lies their great difference—Hood the fire-eater, Johnston the cautious strategist.

(Johnston's retreats, however brilliant, will lead to his removal. And on a frosty night at Spring Hill, in Maury County, after Johnston is replaced, Hood will have the enemy at virtual gunpoint, only to discover that he's left the ammunition wagons behind at Columbia!)

Just now "Old Joe" is assigning Hood to a corps of 17,084 men, with three major generals. Perhaps the ablest is Alexander P. Stewart, brave, trustworthy and steady, on an old roan horse.

Stewart had resigned his West Point commission before the war to teach at Cumberland University in Lebanon and at the old University of Nashville. "Old Straight," he's called, because of his erect carriage.

"Old Straight" and Forrest will be among the clear-headed on that mysterious night at Spring Hill when, encountering each other in the darkness, they will guess that something is wrong. They'll ride together to Hood to try to get it straightened out.

But these things were months ahead, and Hood, newly come to lonely Buzzards Roost, chafed with the willies of If-I-Were-King. He thought he could run the Army of Tennessee better than Johnston. At least, so his letters to Richmond would indicate.

How different the Georgia dreariness from war-time Richmond where Mrs. Chesnut, looking out her window Feb. 24, recorded a sight of which Hood may have been dreaming:

"... Buck (Sally) on Fairfax, the most beautiful horse in Richmond, his brown coat looking like satin, his proud neck arched, moving slowly, gracefully, calmly. ... There sat Buck, tall and fair, managing her horse with exquisite ease, her English riding habit plainly showing the exquisite proportions of her figure. ..."

In the critical months ahead, would such visions add to Hood's discomfort and to his ferocious, headlong drive?

Hood had been with Johnston less than two weeks when, on March 7, he began his series of letters to Richmond. (Had Johnston known, he might well have asked, Who's running this army, Hood or I?)

Hood's letters are pertinent because of the old argument: Were Johnston's ideas right or wrong? (Eventually Hood would take Johnston's place; Atlanta would fall; Sherman would march to the sea, and Hood would head for disaster in Middle Tennessee.)

"We should move to the front as soon as possible," Hood says in his first letter to President Davis. With Polk and Longstreet's men, (Hood says) Gen. Johnston should have nearly 70,000 men, enough to *"defeat and destroy all the Federals on this side of the Ohio River."*

Hood's letters have caused many persons to believe he was serving as a confidential observer for Davis. Had such insubordinate letters been unwelcome, would not a reprimand have been in order?

The conclusion seems to be: His letters were expected, by a Confederate president who had wanted to be a general.

In Washington, Lincoln worried about an opposite situation—Gen. U. S. Grant, a general who just might want to be president. Grant, commanding in Nashville, was the North's great hero; he would make a strong opponent, and Lincoln's popularity was at low ebb.

Lincoln was tagged with the failure of many of his generals. But Grant, the big exception, had racked up glory after glory, at Chattanooga, Missionary Ridge, Vicksburg and—much earlier—Fort Donelson. Was he setting his sights on the White House?

Lincoln wanted to know. He sent for a mutual friend, from Galena, Ill., where Grant had lived. Find out!

Not long afterwards Grant wrote a relative: *"All I want is to be left alone to fight this war out."* Someday he would like to be mayor of Galena—long enough to *"build a sidewalk to the railway station."*

The North chuckled, Lincoln sighed with relief, and on March 4 a momentous telegram came to Grant in Nashville.

Lincoln was summoning Grant to Washington, to become the first man since George Washington to bear the rank of full lieutenant general in the U.S. Army. (One other, Winfield Scott, had served as such but only by brevet.)

On March 8, after a White House reception, Grant and Lincoln talked. *"Quickness of action"* was imperative, Grant said. With the Union spending millions daily, there was a *"limit to the resources of the people."*

How well Lincoln knew! And they might vote for somebody else in November, unless—

Grant's query: What service is expected of me?

Lincoln: Take Richmond.

Grant: If given the troops.

Lincoln promised. Next day Mrs. Lincoln wanted Grant as an honor guest at the White House.

"Time is precious now," Grant told Lincoln. *"And really, Mr. President, I've had enough of this show business."* He must *"get back to Tennessee"* and put his trusted friend Sherman in charge at Chattanooga.

In Nashville that day, the *Daily Union* said proudly, *"We now have a responsible military head."* It was election day for local offices.

Few Tennesseans were voting. The results would go unheeded.

Had Johnson not meddled with Lincoln's plan, some people said, state government could have been restored. Others bitterly said Johnson didn't want it restored, because this would end his *"reign"* on Capitol Hill.

The governor retorted that Tennessee wasn't yet ready for civil government. This may have been true.

Most of Middle and West Tennessee still clung to a prayer, that their sons and husbands would come marching back some day, and chase the Yankees *"clean across the Ohio."*

A handful was back, but not boldly marching. These included the Scouts, sometimes clad in gumcoats against the spring rains—and against detection. Often, with Federal bridles and saddles, they would ride along *"side by side with the enemy."* Much information came to them in this way.

—Courtesy of the Confederate Museum, Richmond, Va.

The Hunley ashore, from the painting by Conrad Wise Chapman

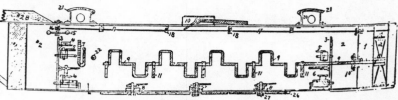

Official U. S. Navy Photograph

A midship section, drawn by W. A. Alexander

Hunley's interior, as a Northern artist imagined it to be (with many inaccuracies). Courtesy the Submarine Library, Electric Boat Division, General Dynamics Corp., Groton, Conn.

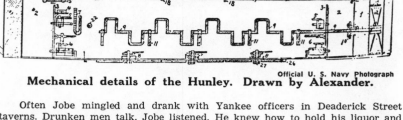

Official U. S. Navy Photograph

Mechanical details of the Hunley. Drawn by Alexander.

ONE OF the boldest of the Scouts was DeWitt (Dee) Smith Jobe, son of a Rutherford County farmer and coffin-maker, Squire Elihu Jobe of old Mechanicsville (now sometimes called Big Spring) between Triune and Overall Creek in western Rutherford.

Jobe was nearing his 24th birthday in that dark springtime of '64. Before autumn leaves settled along old Nolensville Road, he would go down into the valley of the shadow, one unarmed man against 15, to face the worst that men or devils could devise.

Jobe's story is seldom told, perhaps because it is so terrible. Yet it has been written that the whole South, in all the Civil War, produced *"no braver soldier, no greater patriot,"* than Pvt. Dee Jobe, scout, from out Nolensville way, of Company D, 20th Tennessee Regiment, CSA.

In 1861 Jobe had left his father's two-story log home to enlist at College Grove in Williamson County. By the spring of '63 he was a seasoned soldier, with battles, capture and exchange behind him.

Then Gen. W. J. Hardee had assigned Jobe to dangerous work around Shelbyville. Jobe continued his risky efforts for Hardee until Bragg was pushed into Georgia. Soon Jobe was transferred. On an order and account book of Company D, kept by Sgt. James L. Gee, we find four words:

Transferred to Secret Service.

No date is given. Jobe had joined the little band of Scouts, who were headed by Capt. H. B. Shaw (the real name of *"Dr. Coleman,"* who posed as an herb doctor).

Dangerous work? So dangerous that some men, *"brave and fearless as men ever get,"* could not stand its strain. Worse than combat? Well, one man preferred *"10 times over to stand in line of battle."*

Not Pvt. Jobe. He would become one of the *"big eyes"* of the Confederacy, near Nashville and his home.

He will not see the leaves fall.

Details of the Tennessee invasion plan were delivered to Gen. Johnston in Georgia March 18. He was to cross the Tennessee near Kingston. With reinforcements, he was to destroy the railroad between Chattanooga and Nashville. This, said Richmond, should force Federal evacuation of Chattanooga.

Should the enemy *"not offer battle,"* Bragg wrote, *"you might move across the mountains to Sparta...If the entire army could be thrown on Nashville, the enemy would be in a precarious position."*

Gen. Johnston still preferred to stand on present ground, defeat the enemy when he advanced, and then take the offensive.

It is April 13. Hood is writing another letter: *"I have done all in my power to induce Gen. Johnston to move forward. He would not consent...I regret this exceedingly, as my heart was set on regaining Tennessee and Kentucky..."*

However, Hood did recommend that Polk's troops be sent. They would arrive when Sherman was striking. By that time the Richmond plan would have wilted. And *"the opportunity to throw 90,000 Confederate troops—even paper troops—into Tennessee never again presented itself,"* says Horn, in *The Army of Tennessee.*

Grant was evolving a broad plan. It had two big targets: Crush Lee's Army of Northern Virginia and destroy Johnston's Army of Tennessee.

The plan called for simultaneous pressure on all Confederate armies. Crush Lee with Gen. Meade's Army of the Potomac. Let Gen. Benjamin Butler advance with his Army of the James to menace Richmond—cut Lee's supply line. Let Sherman destroy Johnston. Send Sherman on a crash through Alabama to Mobile. (This would be changed to the March from Atlanta to the Sea.)

Grant left Nashville and went back to Virginia, making headquarters with Meade. Sherman would be brought from Mississippi to Chattanooga and placed in Federal command in *"the West."*

"Get into the interior of the enemy's country as far as you can," Grant wrote him, *"inflicting all the damage you can."*

Sherman felt confident. His chief concern, for the next four months, would be his supply line, that little stem of railroad 473 miles long, dropping down to him from the Ohio, through Nashville to Chattanooga and Atlanta.

It must furnish supplies to his 100,000 men and his 23,000 mules and horses —an eyedropper to feed a giant.

Sherman came to Nashville. It would become his main supply base, Louisville his main source of supply. Day and night Sherman worked, planning, ordering. Buy this, buy that. Don't quibble. Buy!

Cut me bridges, to a standard pattern! (To replace those which Gen. Johnston would burn.) Get me census and tax reports, on every county in Georgia. (He'd learn what to expect, where and from whom.)

At a quartermaster Sherman bawled, *"If you don't have my army supplied, and keep it supplied, we'll eat your mules up, sir, eat your mules up!"*

Mules meant power. Horses meant speed. Both were precious. They could save life, or become food.

More than one colt was hidden in a Middle Tennessee bedroom, behind a big headboard, in an effort to save treasured bloodlines. Sometimes the try succeeded. Nor were Yankees the only takers. Jobe had taken a few from the Yankees in the summer of '63.

Often Jobe mingled and drank with Yankee officers in Deaderick Street taverns. Drunken men talk. Jobe listened. He knew how to hold his liquor and think. Good horses were hitched outside.

Jobe made sure the owners were drunk. Then he left, mounted one horse and led two. He made his escape with all three, *"between the Nolensville and Franklin Pikes,"* disappearing into *"his hideout in the hills south of Nolensville."*

Under Sherman, Nashville became *"one vast storehouse"* with warehouses covering blocks, *"one a quarter-mile long—stables by the 10 and 20 acres, repair shops by the fieldful."* So Gen. J. F. Rustling described it.

The magnitude of the railroad cargo! What if Forrest interferes?

Forrest will want to. But he won't always have his way with Richmond. Nor will "Old Joe," who will soon suggest that Forrest be rushed to Middle Tennessee for just the purpose of railroad smashing.

Sherman painfully sees what Forrest can do. In late April, when about to leave Nashville for Georgia, Sherman lets fly a batch of warnings.

One will go to Admiral D. D. Porter, in charge of the Federal fleet in Western waters:

> *Keep a bright lookout up the Tennessee, that Forrest doesn't cross and cut my roads while I am in Georgia.*

Sherman also knows the Richmond weakness for wanting to hold large territories—a weakness Gen. Johnston had protested months ago. Sherman will prey on the weakness. He will pour expeditions into Mississippi.

Richmond will fall for the lure. It will send Forrest charging into Mississippi, again and again, thus preoccupying the ablest man who might have snapped the road in Middle Tennessee and perhaps have changed the outcome of the whole Georgia campaign.

On May 4 the fast-talking Sherman moved out of Chattanooga with 103,000 men, toward Gen. Johnston who now had around 45,000.

In Dalton, Johnston wasn't doing much talking. His plan was to *"spare the blood"* of his men; to sidestep and backstroke, awaiting a chance to strike the mightier force only when the Confederates have the advantage.

The Oath of Allegiance

—From *Harper's Weekly*

GEN. HOOD and HIS BETROTHED. A dramatic moment of their engagement is envisioned here by Jim Young, Newspaper Printing Corporation artist.

JOHNSTON will adopt defensive tactics, forcing Sherman to deploy, maneuver. This won't set well with Richmond, which wants decisive action (one thing it has in common with Washington).

Although Sherman will have nearly twice as many men as Johnston (after Johnston is reinforced by Polk), in 74 days Johnston will let him move only 100 miles toward Atlanta.

Even the men in the ranks won't grumble when Johnston orders retreat. Bragg's retreats had set off bitterness and despair. Circumstances are different now. Do the men sense a situation which Grant would put into words?

"Johnston's tactics were right," Grant would write. *"Anything which could have prolonged the war a year beyond the time it did finally close would probably have exhausted the North to such an extent that they might have abandoned the contest and agreed to a separation."*

Sherman didn't go crashing down the highway into Johnston's high-spirited 45,000. He moved with caution. Not until May 8 did Sherman reach the western side of Rocky Face Ridge which Johnston occupied.

"Old Joe" couldn't risk a big battle at Dalton. In case of defeat—well, 100 undefended miles lay between him and fortified Atlanta. And if "Old Joe" won? Sherman could find quick shelter; he could easily withdraw into the nearby safety of fortified Chattanooga. Far better for Johnston to make the big risk deeper in Georgia, when Sherman would be farther from his base.

The Rebels withdrew swiftly to Resaca. When Sherman arrived the Army of Tennessee awaited him behind breastworks. These would become, for both sides, a characteristic of the last campaigns. Trench warfare had begun.

Meanwhile, the arrival of Polk's 10,000 infantrymen (plus his cavalry) had made Johnston 14,000 stronger. Hood met Polk, the sturdy old soldier-churchman (Episcopal bishop of Louisiana) and together they rode back to Hood's headquarters where, in the light of a tallow candle, the aging bishop, using a dishpan as font, administered the rite of baptism to Hood.

Did the grievously maimed young general, standing wet-haired in the shadowy tent, perhaps think of himself as the consecrated fiance of Sally Preston? Was she thinking only of him?

Hardly. Hood might have been startled had he seen the entry Mrs. Chesnut had made in her diary less than a week before:

Annie (a maid) reports that R. L. has arrived and she believes he is the only man Buck really cares for. Le roi est mort. Vive le roi. (The King is dead. Long live the King.)

Top competition! R. L. almost certainly meant Col. Rollins Lowndes, handsome scion of the Charleston elite. When Lowndes tried to buy some fine Confederate gray, for a uniform, Richmond smiled at what the tailor told him:

"No, my dear, sir, you can't have that. Gen. Hood asked me to keep that for his wedding clothes."

On May 13, two days after Polk's arrival, Sherman came marching out of Snake Creek Gap. The Battle of Resaca was on. Three days they fought, May 13, 14, 15. Sherman struck at Rebel entrenchments and was rolled bloodily back.

He tried a safer way, and the Rebels heard of it as darkness fell on the third day: A part of Sherman's army had swept several miles to Johnston's left and rear. It was crossing the Oostanaula River on pontoons.

Who was keeping Johnston and his cavalry so well-informed? The scouts. (They were also smelling some good Yankee bacon, on the wind from Sherman's mess tents.)

To protect his rear, Johnston fell back at midnight, crossed the Oostanaula, destroyed the railroad bridge behind him, and hurried on across a great exposed valley. Sherman was close behind.

So it went, with Sherman flanking, reaching around for the railroad; Johnston retreating to protect his rear—through Adairsville, Cassville, and on into the rugged heights of Allatoona.

"You-uns," said a captured Rebel, *"swings around on your ends like a gate."*

Near Cartersville, below Cassville, one of Sherman's wagon trains camped a little too long. Gen. Joe Wheeler swept in and drove out 100 wagons loaded with bacon and coffee. Was it one of the last big meals for many a Reb?

Soon it is morning, May 25. In a booming thunderstorm the armies collide, at the Battle of New Hope Church. Lightning flares as cannon roar. Rain pours.

The struggle lasts four days, May 25, 26, 27, 28—skirmish, charge and countercharge. Each side will lose about 3,000.

This scale model of the Hunley is in the Mariners Museum, Newport News, Va.   The spar on the nose pushed a torpedo.

THERE'S A river of blood in Virginia, too. On May 4 as Sherman moved on Johnston, Grant had crossed the Rapidan and begun his struggle with Lee in the Wilderness. The sixth drive to take Richmond had begun at dawn.

Lincoln had kept his promise.

Grant has the troops, 118,000 men against more than 60,000 under Lee. Grant also has 4,000 wagons occupying 65 miles of roads.

A pushover for Grant, with all that? No.

By sunup, May 7, more than 2,200 Yanks were dead in the Wilderness and 13,000 were wounded. *"On this line,"* Grant said four days later, *"I propose to fight it out if it takes all summer."*

This was while he moved on Spottsylvania where 3,000 more Yanks would be killed, 15,000 wounded and more than 2,000 captured.

At Spottsylvania, Lee would lose less than half as many. The North would grow sick with the slaughter. Grant would stick to his plan.

"He is not distracted by 1,000 side issues," Mrs. Chesnut wrote. *"He . . . sees only in a straight line."*

In a pouring Georgia rain June 4, Johnston threw his right across Kennesaw Mountain, his left across Lost Mountain and his center onto Pine Mountain. Thus the railroad and wagon roads to Atlanta were blocked, just when the Republicans up North were gathering to nominate a presidential candidate.

Little single-track railroad, down through Tennessee, you'd better not fail Sherman now! He has a President on his back!

It was *"taxed to the utmost to supply our daily needs,"* Sherman wrote Ellen, his wife, on June 12. He hoped an expedition *"from Memphis"* would give Forrest *"full employment . . ."* in Mississippi. Keep Forrest away from Middle Tennessee!

As Sherman wrote, 8,000 Yankees under Gen. Samuel D. Sturgis were pounding out of Mississippi, toward the safety of Memphis. Forrest's smaller force had whipped them to a frazzle June 10 at Brice's Cross Roads.

Sherman really yelled this time: *" . . . Go out and follow Forrest to the death if it costs 10,000 lives and breaks the Treasury. There will never be peace in Tennessee until Forrest is dead . . ."*

But Sturgis' raid had served its purpose. It had caused Forrest to be pulled back from a proposed expedition into Tennessee. The Yankee line remained intact, at a time when a break might have been critical.

In Virginia, Grant still was having no luck against Richmond. He could see Richmond's church spires, but what of it? So had Gen. George B. McClellan two years before, when McClellan was *"the young Napoleon"* of the early war years and the North was seeking, in vain, its *"coming man,"* a hero.

But Lincoln had said McClellan had *"the slows."* (What in the name of goodness does Grant have?) Many thought Lincoln had treated McClellan shabbily.

Grant had spoken too soon about *"this line,"* upon which he would stand if it took *"all summer."* After the bloody repulse at Cold Harbor, he had to change his line. And summer wasn't half gone.

Who's got the *"slows"* now? Anybody see a Yankee flag over Richmond? Anybody see a Yankee flag over Atlanta?

"If we lose Atlanta, the game is up," Mrs. Chesnut wrote. If the Rebels held Atlanta, the game might be up with Mr. Lincoln who must have Atlanta by election time.

The Republican convention had begun in Baltimore June 7. It re-nominated Lincoln for the presidency. Tennessee's military governor, Johnson, was named as his running mate for the vice-presidency.

Gov. Johnson received the news in Nashville. Knowing his name was poison to the mass of Tennessee's gentry, he gave them eloquent scorn in words attuned for humbler voters.

"Slavery is dead," he said. *"In trying to save slavery you killed it, and lost your freedom . . . As MacBeth said to Banquo's ghost,*

" 'Never shake those gory locks at me,
Thou canst not say I did it.'

"I am for emancipation," continued the military governor, a former tailor, *"because, in the emancipation of the slaves, we can break down an odious and dangerous aristocracy. I think we're freeing more whites than blacks in Tennessee . . ."*

Meanwhile, near Kennesaw Mountain, both sides were readying lines. Rebel spirits were high, despite all the falling back. Let the big fight come!

About this time Gen. Polk wrote his wife, *"Gen. Johnston seems to be managing things very prudently."* It was one of Polk's last letters.

On June 14 Sherman saw Confederates eyeing him through spy-glasses from Pine Mountain, 2,400 feet up the slope. Polk was among them, but Sherman didn't know.

"How saucy they are," said Sherman. *"Fire three volleys into 'em."* He rode away, the gunner fired, and a cannonball crashed through Polk's chest.

"Old Joe" knelt beside the dying warrior-bishop and wept, *"I'd rather anything than this."* To the men he said, *"His mantle rests upon you."*

Had Polk lived 13 days longer he would have witnessed the Confederate triumph at Kennesaw Mountain, June 27. Here, four miles from Marietta, Sherman tried a direct assault against the Rebels who were waiting in prepared positions.

A WINTRY MARCH.

From 30 Years After

The desperate advance of Gen. Forrest, through bitter February cold, must have been much like this grim scene by Forbes.

From **That Devil Forrest** by John A. Wyeth, Harper & Brothers

A Charge of Forrest's Artillery.

WITH ALMOST incredible valor the Federals storm up the heights *"like wooden men."* They head into withering fire, toward a summit wrapped in smoke. Up! They're scaling rocky slopes, through underbrush and fallen timbers, with the temperature 100 degrees in the shade.

The brush is blazing. Flame rolls toward the wounded, the dying and the dead, piled in front of the breastworks. No one can survive that hail of lead to pull them back. Must they burn?

Atop a parapet leaps a Rebel, Col. W. H. Martin of Gen. Patrick R. Cleburne's division.

"Get those men away from the fire!" he shouts, waving a handkerchief on a ramrod. *"We won't fire a gun till you do. Be quick!"*

Rebels rush from behind the logs. They help drag the foe from the fire. Then they dash back to their guns.

In the very midst of it are the 1st and 27th Tennessee Regiments, of the brigade of a Nashville attorney, Gen. George Maney, Cheatham's division, a native of Franklin.

By 11:30 a.m. the nightmare is over. The worst had lasted 45 minutes. The Rebel loss: around 800, by Johnston's admission; Sherman's overall loss, nearly 2,500. The Rebel line had not budged.

Sherman is deep in enemy land. How doubly vital the railroad now!

Clearly Johnston sees this. So does his friend, Gen. Howell Cobb who wrote that, if the line could be *"cut for 10 days,"* Sherman's army would *"be destroyed."*

Quickly, on the first day after Kennesaw, Gen. Johnston sends for Sen. Benjamin H. Hill of Georgia. Senator, go to President Davis. Beseech him to throw the cavalry of Forrest and Morgan on Sherman's line.

Hill hurried to Richmond. Others concurred, including Gen. Lee. Big-hearted Wheeler offered to waive his rank as cavalry chief to let Forrest lead such an attack.

Richmond said no. Why? Forrest was needed in Mississippi again. And Morgan hadn't done so well in a recent Tennessee-Kentucky swing.

Richmond was doing what Sherman hoped for. Had Sherman heard, he might have chuckled.

Sherman was seeing what others would someday see. The preponderance of Confederate brilliance was in her generals, not her statesmen. And all were trying to do their utmost best.

Sherman pushed on, changing back to a warfare of maneuver in another far-flung flanking move. *"Sherman'll never go to hell,"* a Rebel said. *"He'll flank the devil."*

By July 2 Sherman's right was nearer Atlanta than Johnston's left. A Yankee taunted a Rebel picket, *"Well, Johnny, how far now?"* Atlanta was beyond the Chattahoochee.

"So far you'll never get there!"

"Oh, yes, we will, and have a big dance with your sister!"

Lead flew, and the Yank took cover. The river was just ahead. When would Johnston turn and fight?

His retreats had been masterly, agile, *"clean,"* with nothing left behind. Some people called them the *"masterpiece"* of his career. But retreats are retreats. Alarm was rising in Richmond. Could Atlanta be saved?

A number of Georgia officials were urging Johnston's removal. So were members of Davis' cabinet. The President was uneasy.

For weeks, Davis had been trying to learn Johnston's plans. For weeks, Johnston's replies had been cryptic, politely unrevealing.

"Johnston's greatest mistakes . . . were not of a military nature," says Dyer. They *"had to do with his relations with Davis. He (Johnston) never seemed to realize that he might have confided in the President at times, even though he thoroughly disliked him."*

Soon Sherman was just outside Atlanta, but still north of the Chattahoochee.

From a hill, he could see the city's spires . . . just as Grant now looked upon the spires of Richmond, and as "Little Mac" had looked upon them two years ago. Now "Little Mac" might become president. And Richmond was still Rebel.

So was Atlanta, with nerves tense. "Old Joe's" soldiers were calm. Many Southerners shared their confidence in "Old Joe." One was War Clerk Jones in Richmond.

As late as July 8, Jones wrote, *"The news of the falling back of Gen. Johnston causes no uneasiness, for the destruction of Sherman's army is deemed more certain the farther he advances."*

As Jones wrote, Sherman was flanking once more. Ten miles up-river, early on July 8, Gen. John M. Schofield made the first Federal crossing of the Chattahoochee.

By July 9, Sherman's main army was following on pontoons, leaving Johnston unattacked in his fortified lines on the north side.

To meet the new threat, Johnston also crossed the Chattahoochee, on the night of July 9, to the mouth of Peachtree Creek, six miles from city limits. Then, on July 11, Johnston recommended to Richmond that Federal prisoners be removed from Andersonville, south of Atlanta.

Davis was dismayed. Did this mean Johnston wouldn't defend the city? *"There are strong indications he will abandon Atlanta,"* Davis wrote Lee. *"Who should succeed him?"* Hood?

A bad time, Lee replied, to change commanders. *"We may lose Atlanta and the Army too. Hood is a bold fighter. I am doubtful as to the other qualities."*

Davis rushed Bragg to Atlanta. But Bragg told Johnston the visit was unofficial, and "Old Joe" confided little. Then Hood wrote another letter, which he handed to Bragg July 14.

"Several chances" to attack had been passed up, Hood said. *"I have so often urged . . . battle as to almost be regarded as reckless by the officers of high rank, since their views have been so directly opposite . . . "*

In Richmond, Sen. Hill had failed to change Davis' mind about the cavalry. *"You must do it with your present force,"* Hill wired Johnston, also on July 14. *"For God's sake do it."*

Again Davis asked to know Johnston's plans, *"specifically."* And again Johnston replied they must depend *"upon the enemy."*

"A reply," says Robert Selph Henry in *The Story of the Confederacy,* *"that President Davis considered evasive—as it was."*

Johnston's army was at Peachtree Creek when word came that the enemy was crossing the stream.

"The time has come!" Johnston exclaimed, electrified.

The time? To attack! He meant to strike while the enemy was divided in crossing.

But time for Johnston has run out in Richmond. Davis' patience has ended.

Why did Johnston plan to attack just here? Because, he would write, should a Confederate attack succeed at this point, Sherman would be *"driven against the Chattahoochee where there are no fords . . ."*

"If only," Horn says in *The Army of Tennessee,* Johnston *"had said as much to President Davis and Secretary Seddon."*

That night the Richmond lightning struck. "Old Joe" received a telegram stripping him of command: *"As you have failed to arrest the advance of the enemy to within the vicinity of Atlanta . . . and express no confidence you can defeat or repel him, you are hereby relieved of your command . . . which you will immediately turn over to Gen. Hood."*

Johnston yielded at once. In reply he threw a verbal punch, *"Confident language in a military commander is not usually regarded as evidence of competency."*

Gen. Hardee and "Old Straight" Stewart came hurrying to Johnston's tent. The Battle of Atlanta was near. Stay, Johnston, till it's over!

On a barrel a tallow candle flickers, casting its light upon the fateful telegram . . . which, as one of its indirect results, would help send the Army of Tennessee marching northward, to Columbia, Tenn., and on to Franklin and Nashville.

Hood urged Johnston, *"Pocket that dispatch"* until after the battle. (So Hood wrote, years later.)

Johnston said he couldn't, unless the order were countermanded. The three others framed a telegram to Davis. It did no good.

Hood took over, the eighth and last full Confederate general.

Gallant Hood, brave and rash—one arm limp and one leg gone, strapped to his saddle to sit a horse—would now lead the Army of Tennessee. Who could ever doubt the sublimity of that courage?

GEN. A. P. STEWART
"Old Straight"

JEFFREY FORREST
Favorite Brother

GEN. U. S. GRANT
U.S.A.

GEN. LEONIDAS POLK
C.S.A.

WOULD courage suffice? Secretary Seddon wired, *"Be wary no less than bold. God be with you."*

The shake-up brought furor. President Davis was commended and criticized. Some people blamed it all on his dislike of Johnston. The charge seems unfair.

To the Confederate cabinet, *"strategic retreat"* was not the dish. Its anti-Johnston members now included Seddon who had favored Johnston as Bragg's successor.

"The President," one newspaper said, *"was reduced to retaining Johnston and losing Atlanta, or losing Johnston and the possibility of saving Atlanta."*

Said another, *"Hood's abilities may be equal to the task. But the case does not admit of experiment. Too much is at stake."* It called Hood an *"untried general, made for the occasion..."*

"Poor Sam," cried Sally, in South Carolina. *"They have saved Johnston from the responsibility of his own blunders, and put Sam in!"*

"Why Buck," said her sister Mary, *"I thought you would be proud of it."*

"No," Sally said. *"I have prayed God, as I have never prayed before, ever since I heard this. And I went to the convent and asked the nuns to pray for him, too."*

In Nashville, Federal officers told a reporter they had seen Hood, in Texas, borrow $600 when broke, put it on one faro card, and win. Once, they said, he'd put $1,000 on one card and won.

"This is the man," the reporter wrote for the *New York Times, "who has charge of the Rebel Army of Tennessee, consisting of nearly 40,000 men. His whole character is one of utter recklessness."* The reporter's story is cited in Dyer's *The Gallant Hood,* from which it appears here.

A freight car is rolling toward Atlanta. In it are Gen. and Mrs. Johnston. "Old Joe" is stepping out of the picture. (Seven months hence, as the Confederacy sinks to its knees, Johnston will be called back to leadership by his old friend, Gen. Lee.)

The news of "Old Joe's" removal made many a Rebel soldier weep. On the Chattahoochee, a whole picket guard deserted. One man wrote, *"I saw thousands of men cry like babies."*

"Old Straight" Stewart shared the feelings of his weeping men. Gen. Josiah Gorgas wrote in his journal, *"The general judgment is that Hood has not the capacity for such a command."*

"I confess I was pleased," Sherman would write. He knew what the change meant. The Confederacy was tired of defensive tactics.

He braced for Hood's impetuous attacks. Maybe they'd be easier to handle. They would be.

Hood struck three times before the month was out, at Peachtree Creek, the Battle of Atlanta and the Battle of Ezra Church. Each time he was beaten back with heavy casualties he could ill-afford.

Hood's losses at Peachtree Creek, July 20, may have totaled 5,000, including the captured. The Yanks lost half as many. Hood's move two days later, July 22, has been termed *"very bold and brilliant...very near being successful."*

Usually called the Battle of Atlanta, it cost Hood around 7,000 in killed and wounded. Sherman lost 2,000, including Gen. James B. McPherson, Hood's old friend of happier days who had helped him with his studies at West Point.

On July 28 Hood swung westward down Lick Skillet Road to the bloody encounter at Ezra Church. This came as Sherman spread his lines westward, hoping for a southeast curve toward Rebel railways. Out of their trenches the Rebels poured.

"Just what I wanted, just what I wanted," Sherman chattered. *"They'll beat their brains out, beat their brains out."* Again Hood was repulsed.

Richmond had wanted action. It had got it. By now, more than one Rebel soldier out of five was dead or wounded.

"Well, Johnny, how many you got left?" a Yankee picket shouted.

"Oh, 'bout enough for another killing," a Johnny Reb replied.

Hood's reputation as a fighter may have grown. His striking power was shrinking. Can glory be written in smoke? What good the bright name if men die in vain?

Back east, Sally Preston was weeping bitterly. Her brother Willie had been killed in the defense of Atlanta, *"his heart literally shot out."*

Richmond changed its tune. Davis cautioned Hood to avoid frontal assaults. After the Battle of Ezra Church, the siege of Atlanta began. It would last a month. Shells screamed over Rebel lines and dropped within the city. The biggest Federal gun could fire a shell every five minutes. *"There goes the Atlanta Express,"* Sherman's men would say as it zoomed over.

Atlanta's spirit did not break. The Army of Tennessee was with her. It would *"charge hell with a cornstalk."*

Sherman stood on dangerous ground before the city, unable fully to invest it. Behind him flowed the Chattahoochee. The strip on which he stood became the runway of his cavalry, pounding southwest, then southeast, hitting around Hood at his railroads.

A big raid began July 27. Gen. Wheeler's cavalry would cut it to pieces. Of the Yankee horsemen who rode southward, 1,500 would be captured.

About this time Hood set promotion afoot for two able officers who were to meet disaster in December, in the Battle of Nashville.

One was Col. Thomas Benton Smith of Jobe's village, Mechanicsville. The other was Lt. Col. William M. Shy, who had been living on a farm near Franklin, Tenn., at the beginning of the war. Both were of the 20th Tennessee.

Col. Smith, Hood wrote, *"is strongly recommended by all his commanders to be a brigadier general."* Richmond would approve.

Shy, gentle and kind, will succeed Smith as colonel and perish on a Nashville hilltop to which he will leave his heroic name.

A few days later, Sherman received a message which said Forrest had *"died some days ago of lockjaw."* Dated Aug. 2, it came from Gen. C. C. Washburn in Memphis.

"Is Forrest surely dead?" Sherman replied, warily.

Forrest was alive and going, a wounded foot propped up over the dashboard of a swiftly moving buggy. (Some say he had been shot in the big toe.) It had happened in mid-July, in a Mississippi creek-bottom fight.

Early August has come. In Mobile Bay, the Confederate ram Tennessee is about to take on the whole Federal fleet. The Union is assembling the most powerful fleet ever then brought together for a single action. In gun-weight, it equaled the combined British, French and Spanish fleets at Trafalgar (where Napoleon's sea power was destroyed).

Ironically, the Federal commander was Adm. David Glasgow Farragut, Tennessee-born, a native of Knox County, greatest of all the Yankee naval commanders.

Up the channel from the sea, on Aug. 5, through a storm of shot and shell, came the Federal fleet. In front steamed four mighty monitors.

Next came seven steam-powered sloops-of-war, each with a gunboat lashed to its portside. If one were rendered helpless, the other could pull it.

Orders were to go east of a red buoy. One monitor, the Tecumseh, went west. She struck a torpedo, (homemade, from beer kegs and glass demijohns). Her stern rose so high in the air that her propeller could be seen whirling. She rolled over and sank.

The others paused, ripely bunched for Confederate guns. Farragut bawled an order which gave America an immortal phrase, often quoted as, *"Damn the torpedoes! Go ahead!"*

For three-and-a-half blazing hours, he bombarded the defending forts and engaged the little Confederate squadron within the bay. Part of the time he was lashed high up in the mast—tied there, so that if wounded he would not fall off—in order to see above the smoke.

The Tennessee was 209 feet long and covered with 25 inches of yellow pine and oak, topped with five to six inches of iron plating.

(What engine pulled such weight? It had been taken from a Mississippi river steamboat and adapted to a propeller!) With the Tennessee, however, were only three small paddlewheel gunboats—22 Confederate guns and 427 men, against nearly 200 guns and 2,700 Yankees. The rickety Rebel gunboats were soon forced from the fight.

From Harper's Pictorial History of the Civil War

GRANT'S BRIGHT HOUR. Arriving in Washington from Nashville, Grant receives his commission as lieutenant general from President Lincoln. Cabinet members look on.

GEN. WILLIAM TECUMSEH SHERMAN
"Cump"
Georgia's Nemesis

THE Tennessee didn't back off. One historian has written of that famous day, *"Singlehandedly, she came on the whole Union fleet."* This consisted now of three monitors and 10 wooden vessels.

The lone Tennessee steamed into their midst, shelling at will. She was taking on everything Yankee afloat. She became the target of the entire fleet. She was rammed. She was hammered and pounded. She pounded back. She even raked the foe with rifle fire.

For a few minutes she lay so near the Lackawanna that the crews swore at one another. They grabbed what would come loose and threw it through the gun ports.

The Tennessee's smokestack was shot away. Shot entered her port until not a gun could be fired. Her rudder chain was severed. She surrendered only after she could no longer answer her helm.

The Rebel loss: 10 killed, 16 wounded, and casualties inside the forts. Adm. Franklin Buchanan, the Confederate commander, lost a leg. The Yankee loss: 52 dead, 170 wounded, 113 drowned. Not a bad showing against such odds.

The Confederate forts surrendered a few days later.

Gone was the lair of many a blockade runner. The Union now had command of all Southern ports except Wilmington, N. C. The blockade was beginning to strangle like a noose. But it wasn't enough.

In Washington, Lincoln was more troubled than ever. The month of August, 1864, for the Union, would be called by some people, the *"darkest month of the war."*

Lincoln's two great armies were balked—Grant in Virginia, paralyzed by Lee's resistance, and Sherman fretting before Atlanta.

Lincoln must look to Sherman. Sherman must save him. Or Lincoln's successor would make peace and the South, so nearly whipped, might go free. In effect, the North would have lost the war!

The irony of it! When the South, draining of her blood and treasure, had her back to the wall, fighting for time . . . time for Lincoln's rival to win.

This was Gen. McClellan of whom Lincoln had said, during the Peninsular campaign, *"I would hold McClellan's horse if it would bring us victory."* McClellan almost certainly would be nominated by the Northern Democrats.

Pvt. Dee Jobe, who had just turned 24 in June, was near Nashville, probing for information, speeding it southward. With him had come Tom Joplin and other Coleman Scouts. They were operating around College Grove, Triune and Nolensville. Danger didn't matter. They knew what had happened to their fellow-scout, Sam Davis.

In Atlanta, young Hood, unimpressed by Sherman's cavalry, thought he saw another chance to strike. Hood sent young Wheeler galloping north—rip up tracks toward Nashville!

Up came 35 miles of tracks near Marietta. Wheeler kept going. Hood received fragmentary reports. His optimism rose, too high.

A wild goose chase, Sherman called Wheeler's raid. (*"I have abundant supplies for 10 days,"* he wrote on Aug. 11.) Then, in Wheeler's absence, Sherman again sent his cavalry against Hood's railroads.

Don't fight, Sherman told his cavalry. Work. Heat and twist rails.

Off they went, into South Georgia, as Wheeler plunged on into Tennessee. Wheeler would demonstrate against Chattanooga and veer east to Strawberry Plains, in East Tennessee. (". . . *Good place for him to break down his horses, and a poor place to steal new ones,"* Sherman snorted.)

Rain fell. Westward, the Yanks of Gen. A. J. Smith bogged down near Oxford while trying to move eastward—13,000 infantrymen, 3,000 Negroes and 4,000 cavalrymen, waterlogged in the continuing try to preoccupy Forrest. In addition, they meant to join Sherman by pushing east through Alabama.

With Smith away from Memphis, Forrest's men stormed north into the city on a quiet Sunday morning, Aug. 21. Through a door of the Gayoso Hotel rode Capt. Bill Forrest, the general's brother, looking for the Federal commander. Gen. Washburn was spending the night away. Col. Jesse Forrest, another brother, pursued. Washburn escaped in his nightshirt. The Rebels captured 600 and left the city in tumult.

"They removed me from command," said Yankee Gen. Stephen A. Hurlburt, *"because I couldn't keep Forrest out of West Tennessee. Now Washburn can't keep Forrest out of his bedroom!"* (From *"First With the Most"* Forrest.)

Splattering back toward Memphis came Smith, Georgia and Alabama out of his mind. Out of Nashville, Chattanooga and Atlanta Federal troops were rushing, after Wheeler and Forrest. Wheeler was still wrecking railroads, including tracks of the Nashville & Chattanooga west of McMinnville. He would swing near Franklin, destroying tracks of the Nashville-and-Decatur line.

Four miles south of Franklin, Sept. 2, a Yankee cavalry force from Nashville would encounter the division of Gen. John Herbert Kelly of Wheeler's corps. The gallant Kelly, only 23, would fall mortally wounded. Then the Rebels would head southward, much to the relief of the Yanks who that day reported, from Franklin, that they were out of ammunition.

About the time Yankee nightshirts were snapping in the Memphis morning, Hood's Georgia railroads were being ripped up behind him again, by Sherman's horsemen. Back clattered the riders, boasting to Sherman. A 10 days' break! Watch Atlanta get hungry!

Sherman watched. A day passed. He listened. It's Aug. 23.

Toot, toot! Maybe Sherman stared.

Into Atlanta, loaded with supplies, little Rebel trains came rolling, even as Federal shells continued to drop into the city. Only two days had passed.

Did Sherman swear? Was he facing a courage that would not die? A people who wouldn't give up? Well, if his cavalry couldn't break a railroad, his infantry could!

That day in the White House, Lincoln sat in gloom.

There was no good news. The only news was of how madly the Rebels were riding; how firmly standing and fighting in their rags. Grant, with 80,000 dead, was not as close to Richmond as "Little Mac" had been in '62. And had Lincoln heard that Grant's horde of well-fed, well-clad, well-armed men had been cheering for "Little Mac"?

That day Lincoln wrote:

"This morning, and for some days past, it seems exceedingly probable that this administration will not be re-elected. Then it will be my duty to cooperate with the new President-elect as to save the Union between the election and the inauguration, as he will have secured his election on such grounds that he cannot possibly save it afterwards."

In other words, Lincoln thought McClellan would win, make peace, and cleave the Union.

Two days later, Sherman sent word to Washington: *"Give currency to the idea that I am to remain quiet until events transpire in other quarters . . ."* Let it leak to Richmond.

He is taking cavalrymen off horses, putting them in trenches, to free infantrymen for railroad-wrecking.

Night comes. Sherman is sending his sick and wounded back to the Chattahoochee bridge. Gen. Henry W. Slocum will remain and cover it.

Under cover of skirmish firing, Sherman's entire army is coming out of the trenches, with 10 days rations.

Spies told Hood. The Yanks are moving out! An old woman, brought to headquarters, said the Yankees had refused her food.

Hood rejoiced. He jumped to a conclusion: The Yanks are hungry, leaving—because Wheeler has cut their line! Wishful thinking? (It has been written that Georgia ladies arrived in Atlanta by train, expecting a victory ball.)

Hood was wrong. Many scouts were away with Wheeler. Hood was short of information.

A future master of Nashville's Belle Meade plantation was there, Gen. William H. Jackson. He tried to convince Hood that Sherman was not on the run. Hood stuck to his notion.

Belle Meade's future master was right. Sherman was not retreating. He was beginning a great wheeling swing westward, then southeastward. Chief target: Jonesboro, in Hood's rear, on the Macon line, 25 miles south of Atlanta.

The Montgomery line went first. By Aug. 28 Sherman was astride it at Fairburn, southwest of Atlanta. Hood was not alarmed. He sent Gen. Hardee and Gen. Stephen D. Lee, with five brigades, down the railroad toward Jonesboro, to repel any *"raids."*

It was a balmy Sunday morning. Young and old were strolling again on Peachtree Street. The siege is lifted! Laughter was returning to Atlanta.

Monday comes, Aug. 29. West of Atlanta, Sherman is tearing up 13 miles of the Montgomery line. In Chicago, the Democrats are nominating McClellan, with bright prospects of victory. Near Nolensville, the luck of Jobe is running out.

A former Tennessee governor, William B. Campbell, addressed the Democrats in Chicago, urging peace, amnesty for Southerners, restoration of rights and property. He blasted Gov. Johnson as a despot.

Between Nolensville and Triune, Jobe was in grave danger. He had an important message on his person and Yankees from Murfreesboro were scouting nearby.

The father of two Rebel soldiers had given Jobe breakfast. The house might be searched. Jobe hurried away on his horse.

It is said that, as he rode on, a telescope lifted on a farm not far away. It searched the hills to the west. Did a Yankee see a horseman going along a fencerow, uphill, in a cornfield? Jobe had been spotted. Soon the horse was being tracked, perhaps as Jobe lay sleeping.

BATTLE OF RESACA—"Old Joe" wasn't caught napping.

DID JOBE hear corn leaves rattling? Was that when he yanked out his message and tore it up? He started chewing and swallowing.

Too late! The Yankees grabbed him—a patrol of 15 men, under the command of a sergeant of the 115th Ohio Regiment. They grabbed the scraps of paper. What remained could not be made out. The nearness of their miss must have been maddening.

They tied Jobe up. Now talk! What did the message say? Where'd you get it? What's your meeting place with other scouts, and when?

Jobe didn't talk. They put a bridle rein around his throat and hung him up a few times, then let him down. They knocked out some of his teeth with a pistol butt.

Bound and disarmed, helpless and bleeding, Jobe revealed nothing. They were dealing with a man in gray who held the welfare of the Confederacy above his life.

The torture went on. The Yanks were whooping now, yelling so loudly that they could be heard at a distant farmhouse.

They put out Jobe's eyes. Perhaps then it was that Jobe heaped epithets upon them. How much courage did it take to do what they did then? They cut out Jobe's tongue.

Enough? They're at him again. Tell, and we'll let you live. Did they want him to write out a few words? This, Jobe, is your last chance.

They're tieing something to a horse's tail. The reins, or a leather strap? The other end—Jobe, it's about your throat. (Did you think for a moment of your friend Sam Davis, who was hanged . . .? Ah, but they let him die in dignity, compared to this.)

The horse is struck. It gallops away. Jobe's agony is ending.

Some of the Yanks, when they reached the Nolensville Road, had the grace to say that Jobe was the bravest man they'd ever seen.

A woman friend rode by, dismounted, and placed a handkerchief over Jobe's face, to keep off the hot August sun. Word of the crime was spreading.

For years afterwards, an aura of evil would seem to linger there, and passersby would shudder.

> *Many good men who passed the spot*
> *Would think of Jobe and the deal he got,*
> *Or cross themselves like nuns.*
> *And say, on nights when the dark clouds toss,*
> *Can you hear the clatter of a runnin' hoss?*
> *Oh, Lawdy! What's the matter? But nobody talks.*
> *The clatter stops and the ghost hoss walks.*
> *It's the Yankees teachin' Dee Jobe who's boss*
> *At the point of 15 guns.*

Days hence, the news would reach DeWitt Smith, Jobe's cousin and friend, of the 45th Tennessee Regiment. They had been close companions and may have been namesakes.

Smith's mind would become *"unhinged"* when he heard it. He would break away from Hood's army and *"run up the black flag."* That is, he would vow to take no prisoners; to kill every Yankee he met.

Smith would come riding back into Middle Tennessee as the avenger. Many a Yankee would die in the night, his throat quietly slit with a butcherknife.

The August sun is sinking. A spring wagon is creaking through the shadows. Old Frank, the Negro slave who had tended Jobe as a child, is driving. His cheeks are wet as he lifts his young master's body, places it in the wagon, and heads back to the big log house where Jobe was born, June 4, 1840.

Today a roadside marker speaks of Jobe, on U. S. Highway 31A in Williamson County between Triune and Nolensville:

"DeWitt Smith Jobe, a member of Coleman's Scouts, CSA, was captured in a cornfield about 1½ miles west, Aug. 29, 1864, by a patrol from the 115th Ohio Cavalry. Swallowing his dispatches, he was mutilated and tortured to make him reveal the contents. Refusing, he was dragged to death behind a galloping horse. He is buried in the family cemetery six miles northeast."

No granite shaft stands tall today to mark the spot of the Middle Tennessean who wouldn't be brain-washed. On a lonely little knoll he sleeps, where visitors seldom go, near the site where he was born. There is no inscription on the stone. The night of oblivion has almost closed in. Ask anyone, who was Dee Jobe? And the answer may be, *"I don't know what you're talking about."*

Next day in Georgia, by 6 p.m., Sherman was within three miles of the Macon railroad. That night Hardee rode a locomotive into Atlanta and conferred with Hood. Go straight to Jonesboro, you and Lee, Hood ordered. Attack!

They struck next day at the oncoming host which had thrown up breastworks to receive them. *"Only 1,400 men were killed,"* Hood would report. *"A disgraceful effort,"* he would wire Bragg. How much slaughter would have been enough?

Hood appears to have thought the swing at Jonesboro was to cover a bigger push on Atlanta. He ordered Lee back to the city (before learning, however, of the afternoon repulse at Jonesboro. Wires to Atlanta were down.)

Hardee, left alone, protested to Richmond. (Wires to Richmond still functioned.)

"The enemy movement is to gain Atlanta," President Davis replied. The foe, he said, is divided.

Divided? No. Almost all Sherman's army was closing in on Hardee at Jonesboro, six corps against one. They smashed at Hardee next day at midafternoon, Sept. 1. He was partly enveloped.

But a portion of his line stood firm. That night, with what was left of his corps, Hardee managed to slip seven miles away to Lovejoy.

Hood's last supply line had been cut—Jonesboro was lost. Atlanta must fall.

In the darkness, Sherman paces before a Jonesboro campfire. He hears low rumbles, like thunder, from the direction of Atlanta, 20 miles away.

Hood is blowing up 81 cars of ordnance and six locomotives. At 5 p.m., Sept. 1, Hood marches out, southeast, by Sherman's flank, to join Hardee at Jonesboro.

Sherman wired Lincoln, *"Atlanta is ours . . ."*

Rejoicing rocked Northern cities. Horses galloped down country lanes with riders shouting the news, *"Atlanta has fallen!"*

ABOUT THE SIZE OF IT.

GENERAL GRANT. "Well, and what if it *should* come to a Kilkenny fight? I guess Our Cat has got the longest tail!"

... but the long-tailed cat will yield.

LINCOLN cheered up. His Secretary of State William H. Seward aptly said, "*Sherman and Farragut have knocked the bottom out of the Chicago platform.*" It was true.

"*I had pleased Mr. Lincoln,*" Sherman would write. "*But Hood's army, the chief objective, had escaped.*"

Hood, at Lovejoy, has a heavy heart. His army is weakened. He has wrought no wonders. He will be further depressed by news from the east, within the month. Sally's sister Mary will be married to Hood's good friend, Dr. Darby. Will it make Hood even more eager to get the war over and get back to Sally?

The fall of Atlanta brought fresh despair to the South. Nor would the gallant Kentucky raider, Gen. Morgan, this time be able to spark the gloom with incredible hope as he had done with his Ohio raid, after the fall of Vicksburg.

It is Sept. 3 in Greeneville, Tenn., a night of stormy rain and lightning. Silhouetted in the flashes of light is a tall man, with a Van Dyke beard, standing on the gallery of the largest house in town. Gen. Morgan is about to retire for the night.

Morgan stands peering into the dark. Are his sentinels alert? Is he thinking of another night of rain, and a surprise attack, back in Lebanon in '62, and a race to the Cumberland River at Rome, when he'd had to leave his beloved little mare, Black Bess, to the Yanks?

The lightning flashes again. It shows masses of roses clambering about the porch. Again the flare. It lights Morgan's face. The old careless dash is gone. He looks worried and gaunt. Tomorrow he will leave for Bull's Gap.

Rain drips from the eaves. The fragrance of roses hovers close beneath the roof. All is well. It will be a good night.

Rain was falling when Morgan was awakened at 7 a.m. At first all seemed quiet. Then he heard it, gunfire, suddenly, through the rain. Federals, a surprise attack! He leaped up and dashed out, not fully clothed. Some of his sentinels were dying.

What happened next? There are different versions. It may have been like this:

Morgan, with two companions, is running into the garden. Get to the horses! How close are the Yanks? For a moment Morgan is sheltered, at least from the eye, by a high board fence which runs around the garden. Within the enclosure are flowers, grapevines, gooseberry bushes.

The three head for a stable across the street. They're too late. Bluecoats come galloping. The three wheel and race back. They dart into a small church at the end of the garden and fasten the door, just in time. Fists and gunbutts hit it. They've been seen.

They hesitate. More hoofbeats sound. The three are far outnumbered. Shall they break across the garden for the house?

No, Morgan says. "*They've sworn never to take me alive.*" He steps out into the garden from behind the vines. Which way did he mean to go? Did he think the fence would conceal him? Beyond were Yankees on horseback.

From astride his horse an alert Yankee private saw over the fence. He fired over the boards.

"*Oh, God,*" Morgan said and threw up his hands.

He fell on his face in the gooseberry bushes, in the fragrant, dripping garden . . . and perhaps it is only kind to hope, if one is unafraid of sentiment, that in his fading mind he heard again, as his world went slipping away, the distant clatter of little hooves, hammering nearer and nearer, until at last, close up to his ears, there is a delighted little whinny as a small black mare, Black Bess, comes prancing down to meet him on the shores of Over Yonder.

Morgan is dead in the garden, leaves are a-glitter with raindrops, and a Yankee is yelling in glee, "*I've killed the damned horsethief!*"

He's proud of his bag. He'll prove what he's done. He throws the body across a horse and takes it to show his commander, Gen. Alvin C. Gillem,

who gives him a scolding for such treatment of the body. (However, promotion will come to the private.)

Perhaps, we say, it happened thus. Is any man really sure? Details of the different versions may be easily found in many libraries.

Next day a one-horse wagon pulled away from Greeneville. On it rested a walnut coffin, en route to temporary burial in Abingdon, Va.

As the wagon jolted along the lonely road, Morgan's fellow-cavalryman, Gen. Forrest, was wiring President Davis from Meridian, Miss.:

"*If permitted, I believe I can proceed to Middle Tennessee, destroy the enemy's communications or cripple it . . .*"

Did Forrest know Atlanta had fallen three days before? No one seems positive. In the long view, his strike at Sherman's supply line was coming late. But it was something Forrest had been favoring all summer.

Now, before he can leave, Hood is urgently wiring, on Sept. 11, "*Hasten Forrest upon Sherman's communications. It is all-important.*"

How important!

Sherman's supply trains were running again between Nashville and Atlanta, and Wheeler's command, back from the Tennessee raid, was scattered and shaken—more damaged by the effort than was Sherman.

A blow struck by Forrest, north of the Tennessee, could take some pressure off Hood who meant to swing around Sherman. Hood meant to hit Federal communications in North Georgia.

But when he moved, would Sherman follow? The situation in Georgia was confused. The Rebels didn't know Sherman's yen was to break free of Hood and march to the sea. Nor did Sherman know how eagerly, back in the spring, Hood had looked forward to reclaiming Middle Tennessee.

For a moment in that militarily scrambled autumn we see Forrest, chin down, lost in thought, perhaps planning his move into Middle Tennessee.

He's walking around and around the little railway station at West Point, Miss. His hands are clasped behind his back, under the tails of his coat, and a luckless someone keeps trying to interrupt him about a trifle.

Almost without looking up, Forrest lets his fist pop out. It strikes the interrupting man, knocking him unconscious, and Forrest keeps on walking, stepping over the limp form as he comes around again. There's fire in his thoughts, for somewhere, and it's likely for Yankees in Tennessee!

A few days passed. It's daybreak, Sept. 21, at the Tennessee River. Forrest is crossing.

Freed of the repeated strippings under Bragg, given his own command, Forrest is ready to make war in style.

Eight horses are pulling his caissons. Six mules are pulling his artillery pieces. Four horses are pulling his ambulances. He has supplies, blankets, guns, ammunition—and every piece is stamped "U. S." (So an observer said.) Forrest is loaded for bear, and his load has been taken, as usual, from the foe.

He is now riding King Philip, his famous mount which will survive the war. (This is the horse which is said to have learned to hate men uniformed in blue. King Philip learned to identify Union soldiers to the extent that he sometimes bit at them after the war.)

Nightfall found Forrest encamped north of the Tennessee, five miles west of Florence, Ala.

As Forrest crossed, Hood had been shifting his Army of Tennessee from Lovejoy to Palmetto, about 25 miles west of Atlanta, on the Montgomery railroad. Here Hood must reorganize his disspirited army.

Big names of the Confederacy arrived at Palmetto Sept. 25. One was President Davis. Also present was Isham G. Harris, Tennessee's stalwart Confederate governor.

As the President of the Confederacy rides along the weary lines with Hood, a startling cry arises. "*We want Johnston! Give us back Gen. Johnston!*" Davis didn't turn a hair. To Hood it must have been shocking.

The soldiers heard stirring speeches. One came from Harris, who watched his words. Davis spoke less discreetly.

To Cheatham's division of Tennesseans he said, "*Be of good cheer, for within a short while your faces will be turned homeward and your feet pressing Tennessee soil.*"

Applause thundered. Home! Freedom or death. Set Tennessee free—at last!

(Later Davis would deny he gave a hint of the Tennessee plan. But more than one newspaper quoted similar statements. So did many persons who heard. Did Davis forget what he'd said?)

Sherman read the papers and commented, "*He gave us the first full key to his future designs.*"

It's Sept. 26. Forrest is entering Middle Tennessee, heading for Pulaski. Soon he's raiding as far north as Spring Hill, within 30 miles of Nashville, capturing blockhouses, taking prisoners, tearing up tracks of the Nashville & Decatur Railway.

Sherman is shouting from Georgia, "*The whole resources of Tennessee and Kentucky must be turned against Forrest until he is disposed of.*"

To take charge of the grim effort, Sherman on Sept. 29 sent his gallant second-in-command, Gen. George H. Thomas, the "*Rock of Chickamauga.*" Thomas was to offset the chance that Hood might head for Tennessee. Reorganize Federal defenses in Middle Tennessee! Thomas left for Nashville and Chattanooga with two divisions.

The day before, Sept. 28, Hood had crossed the Chattahoochee, heading into North Georgia. Soon he would be striking at Sherman's precious railroad, ripping up more tracks.

Was it about this time, as Hood moved north, that Dee Smith learned what the Yankees had done to Jobe? Legend says: Smith was near Chattanooga when he slipped away from his regiment in the night.

Several miles from Hood's army, Smith obtained a horse at a farmhouse. How long he rode and hid we don't know. Night had fallen when he reached the outskirts of Tullahoma. He found a small company of Yankees sleeping, eight men to a tent.

Smith evaded pickets and slipped into camp. He needed a noiseless weapon. Crawling around in the darkness, he reached the mess tent and found a large butcherknife.

From the "Valentine," published by the Western & Atlantic Railroad
CONFEDERATES DRAGGING GUNS up Kennesaw Mountain.
By a noted Civil War artist, A. R. Waud.

P RESENTLY he's inside a tent and quietly slitting the throats of eight men. He moves on to the second tent and is finishing off the seventh man when the eighth awakes, shrieking at what he beholds.

Pandemonium rose. Smith panicked, too. In trying to get back to his horse he roused the pickets. Lead started singing, but Smith found his horse and hammered away, out the Manchester Road.

It has been written that, as he rode away, he still clutched the butcherknife and that he turned and waved its bloody length in the moonlight, as if in promise of its further use.

Pursuit failed, somewhere past Manchester.

Not much later Smith was back in his native Rutherford, hiding in the woods near where Jobe had been killed. Good Rebels smuggled him food. For a while they provided him with a place to sleep.

Was he mad or half-insane? Or was he merely doing what many others had wanted to do when they had looked upon Jobe's butchered face?

Later Smith surprised two Yankees on *"the Road between the Charles King home and the Franklin Road bridge."* He had *"two braces of pistols"* but no ammunition. The Yankees didn't know. Jobe made them hold his horse while a farmer's wife fixed his breakfast.

While she cooked, Smith molded bullets. Then he marched his prisoners a half-mile and shot each in the back of the head. On each corpse he left a note, *"Part of the debt for my murdered friend, Dee Jobe."*

With each slaying, the search for Smith grew hotter. Yankees came to dread his name.

There is a story that Smith once carried six pistols and a musket. He was armed in this manner when he stopped for tobacco at *"Mr. Snell's store on the Franklin Road."*

Just after Smith left a small company of Yankees came by, inquiring for him. Yes, he's just gone. Armed? Yes. (The arms were described, perhaps with secret glee.)

The pursuers drew off and conferred. Then they turned and hurried back toward Murfreesboro at a gallop.

Smith was crossing Stone's River when a lone Negro corporal drew abreast and demanded that he halt. A shot sounded from Smith's small cap and ball derringer. The corporal slid from his horse and out of sight beneath the waters. Smith was still free.

So was Forrest, and swinging southward. In pursuit are 13,000 men, in three columns. They are aided by two gunboats.

On Oct. 4 (the day Thomas reached Nashville) Forrest crossed into Alabama. He's passing south of Lawrenceburg, trying to escape. He reaches the Tennessee again, near Florence, Oct. 5. It's a mile wide, swollen with rain, choppy from high wind. An enemy column is approaching.

Rebel troops are sent to hold off the column. Again Forrest must get his main body of men across. There's frantic work once more, on skiffs and rafts. One more river to cross!

For two days and nights they row and pole. The men mount horses and swim them to an island. Behind it, the ferrying goes on for two days.

Forrest is standing in a boat, poling furiously. He spies an idle lieutenant. Why isn't he helping?

Because, says the lieutenant, there are plenty of privates. Forrest slaps him out of the boat. As the young man climbs back, Forrest storms, *"Now damn you, get hold of the oars! If I knock you out of the boat again, I'll let you drown!"*

They made it.

"Forrest has escaped us," reads a Federal message of Oct. 7, *"much to the chagrin of Gen. Thomas. . ."*

Very shortly Forrest, safely over the river, is reporting the result of his raid: 2,360 officers and men captured and nearly 1,000 killed or wounded. Also captured: 800 horses, seven guns, 2,000 stands of small arms, dozens of wagons and ambulances, and a huge quantity of saddles, other ordnances and precious medical supplies.

"How fortunate," a Union officer wrote, *"that Forrest's raid did not happen before the capture of Atlanta, when no troops could be spared . . ."*

They were being spared now, and fast. Grant wired Sherman Sept. 28, *"I have directed all recruits . . . from all the Western States be sent to Nashville, to receive their future orders from you."* Was Hood heading that way?

Sherman wasn't sure. He wired Grant: *"If he goes the Selma-Talladega Road (through Alabama into Tennessee) why will it not do to leave Tennessee to Thomas and the reserves soon to come to Nashville, and for me to . . . march across Georgia?"*

There's the dream, out in the open, in full bloom. Sherman is itching to march to the sea. Salt water! Fire and salt . . .

It had to wait. Within a few hours Hood was threatening Sherman's railroad between Marietta and Allatoona—on the very day when Thomas was marching into Nashville and Forrest was barreling south into Alabama, with the 13,000 chasing.

Sherman turned heavily, with 65,000 men, to slap Hood away. One reason: behind Allatoona's forts were 9,000 head of Yankee cattle and a million hardtack rations.

"I'll follow Hood wherever he goes," Sherman declared. But he'd follow only a while. Hood's light little army was shifting this way, that way.

"I cannot guess his movements," Sherman wrote, *"as I could those of Johnston, who was a sensible man and did only sensible things."*

Hood was luring Sherman back toward springtime battlefields. Sherman was furious. What good to the Union?

Impatiently he wired Grant: *"It would be a physical impossibility to protect the roads, now that Hood, Forrest and Wheeler and the whole batch of devils are turned loose without home or habitation."* (Back comes the Dream.) *"I propose we break up the railroad from Chattanooga . . . and strike out with wagons . . . for Savannah. I can make the march, and make Georgia howl."*

On Oct. 10, Hood crossed the Coosa River west of Rome. To Sherman the move was *"inexplicable to any common-sense theory."* Was Hood really heading for Tennessee? Sherman wired Thomas in Nashville to *"be prepared for anything."*

Then Sherman wired Grant: *". . . Hood may turn into Tennessee and Kentucky, but I believe he will be forced to follow me . . . Answer quick . . ."*

Grant was restive. *"If you have a way of getting at Hood's army, I would prefer that . . ."* But he changed his mind next day and saw more eye-to-eye with Sherman.

Hood soon encamped a few miles south of Lafayette. Sherman, in full force, came to Snake Creek Gap, just 15 miles away. Could there not have been a pitched battle, had either side wanted it?

Did each general think he saw something brighter—Hood, the invasion of Tennessee; Sherman, the Big March?

Hood's is the smaller army; he has the smaller choice. Does it, too, include a dream? Perhaps.

It is night, Oct. 16. Hood has made up his mind.

Middle Tennessee, here I come . . . ! I, Hood, will set you free.

Does courage seems to glow from his tent, into the darkness that wraps the Georgia pines?

Can free Nashville? Grow stronger with victory, and move northward? Establish a line, eventually, in Kentucky? Threaten Cincinnati? How proud Sally would be!

A man can dream, can't he? Of what he might do? That he might even be able, with victory and new enlistments, to send aid to Lee in Virginia? Or, if Sherman goes to the sea, and then North—that he, Hood, can swing over the mountains to join Lee before Sherman can join Grant?

What other choice? None.

March! Ah, Middle Tennessee . . . I'll free you! Lift up your head!

Almost suddenly, Hood found himself commanding a happy army, homeward bound. Laughing, jesting. Swinging along with a song, as in the early days:

> *". . . early on one frosty mornin',*
> *Look away! Look Away!*
> *Look away—Dixie Land!"*

In such a mood Hood's army left Gadsden, Oct. 22, heading for a crossing at Guntersville, 70 miles west. There Hood meant to cross. Forrest was to meet them. They'd need his cavalry north of the Tennessee.

Where did the idea originate, of that tragic—and sublime?—surge back into Middle Tennessee? The answer is obscure. Years later, President Davis would write that he did not approve. But he did not object, when he could have. This we know, Hood manfully accepted the whole burden, and never ran from the blame.

In Gadsden, Hood met Beauregard, newly placed in command of the region. Beauregard approved the plan, apparently with misgivings as to its execution. But, Beauregard specified, Wheeler was to be left in Georgia to watch Sherman. Hood was to have Forrest instead.

"Jeff Davis's breakfast spoilt by a shot from Baltimore"
"The Hardest Shell Yet"

Jefferson Davis, shaken by Lincoln's renomination—as wishfully portrayed by *Harper's.*

SHERMAN STILL followed. By Oct. 26 he was at Gaylesville, about 25 miles southeast of Gadsden. There Sherman tarried until Oct. 28, puzzling over Hood's plans. He learned Hood had gone on to Decatur.

"Damn him, Sherman said. *"If he will go to the Ohio River, I'll give him rations...! Let him go North, my business is Down South."* Anyway, where would Hood's army get the shoes?

Who needs shoes when you're marching home?

Then and there, in Gaylesville, Sherman made a decision vital to both Tennessee and Georgia. He'd pursue Hood no farther. He'd reinforce Thomas —on the chance that Hood might really invade Tennessee.

With Thomas secure in Nashville, Sherman then could go marching through Georgia. He'd return to Atlanta, make plans for his march. To heck with shattered railroads! Sherman would break for the coast. Let Washington send new supplies by sea, to meet him there. Once more, Federal control of the Southern coast was about to pay off.

Up North, torchlight parades are winding through the night. Election day is near. The wind has changed for Lincoln. Victories are filling his sails.

The Shenandoah Valley of Virginia, which has so largely supplied Lee, is being laid waste by Gen. Philip H. Sheridan until *"a crow flying over it would have to carry its own rations."*

In Tennessee many a good Union man, disenchanted with both Lincoln and Gov. Johnson, would like to vote for McClellan. Gov. Johnson fears this trend. He doesn't want his ticket to be defeated in his own state.

So another oath is required for prospective voters, even more restrictive than

In Appreciation (Part III)

FOR ASSISTANCE IN COMPILING Part III and assembling illustrations, The Banner expressed its gratitude to Col. Campbell H. Brown, state executive director, Civil War Centennial Commission, and Thomas A. Wiggington, assistant director; to Mrs. Gertrude Parsley, Mrs. Hermione Embry and Miss Kendall Cram, State Library; Miss Bettye Bell of the Tennessee Room, Nashville Public Library; Miss Catherine Clark, Andrew L. Todd Library, Middle Tennessee State College; Dr. Robert H. White, state historian; Walter L. Jordan, state archivist; Robert T. Quarles Jr., state archivist, retired; the Joint University Libraries and the Library of Congress.

The Banner is deeply grateful for material used and permission to quote from:

The Gallant Hood by John P. Dyer, Bobbs-Merrill Company, Inc., especially concerning Hood's youth and background and, in particular, the advice of his father on Hood's departure for West Point;

A Diary from Dixie by Mrs. Mary Boykin Chesnut (Ben Ames Williams, ed.) Houghton Mifflin Co., 1949, especially concerning Hood's Richmond convalescence, his romance with Sally Preston and his friendship with Jefferson Davis;

The Army of Tennessee by Stanley F. Horn, Bobbs-Merrill; *The Decisive Battle of Nashville,* also by Mr. Horn, Louisiana State University Press; *"First With the Most" Forrest,* by Robert Selph Henry, McCowat-Mercer Press; *The Story of the Confederacy,* also by Mr. Henry, Bobbs-Merrill; *Messages of the Governors of Tennessee,* 1857-69, Vol. V, by Dr. White, published by the Tennessee Historical Society, and a *Rebel War Clerk's Diary* by J. B. Jones, J. B. Lippincott Co. All were frequently consulted.

GEN. ROBERT E. LEE
President Davis Sought His Advice.

the *"damnesty oath."* By the new oath, all voters must voice opposition to *"all . . . negotiations for peace."* This is aimed at eliminating votes for McClellan.

(*"Andy will let us vote,"* said the *Nashville Daily News, "If we promise to vote for him—not otherwise.")*

There were reputable Union men in Tennessee who thought this unfair. They went to Lincoln and protested.

How long, Lincoln asked, did it take the Tennessee delegation and the New York politicians to put this protest together? The Tennesseans replied that they alone had prepared the protest—not New Yorkers.

Lincoln then said, coolly, *"I expect to let the friends of George B. McClellan manage their side of this contest in their own way, and I will manage my side."*

Did memory wake for the Middle Tennesseans? Did they think then of Nashville's brilliant John Bell, patiently trusting, who had tarried too long with Lincoln before Fort Sumter?

The Tennesseans came home, disillusioned. A few days later they announced withdrawal of the McClellan ticket in the state. Gov. Johnson's crowd was now in full control. Another election farce was coming up.

This may have been about the time of another incident in the legend of Dee Smith. He encountered an elderly resident of Franklin Road who had sworn allegiance to the Union.

"Got your (loyalty) papers?" Smith asked.

The man produced them. Perhaps his hands trembled as Smith placed a *"horsepistol"* against his temple.

"Eat them!" Smith commanded.

The man ate. Then he asked, *"Dee, why did you do this to me?"*

"Because," Smith replied, *"you wouldn't let me run rabbits in your pasture when I was a little boy."* Smith spared the man's life.

While the campaign raged, Forrest was about to go unforgettably amphibious on the Tennessee River with gunboats he would capture from the Federals. He was about to light up the skies with a multi-million-dollar fire of Federal stores at Johnsonville.

Forrest marched on Paris Landing Oct. 24 from Jackson, Tenn. The division of Gen. Abraham Buford led. Gen. James R. Chalmers followed, a day behind.

Under Buford's direction, artillery was emplaced five miles apart on the west bank. Into the fallen Confederate works of Fort Heiman, now deserted, Buford moved two new 20-pound rifled Parrott guns and part of his horse artillery.

A few hundred yards downstream, a section of Capt. John W. Morton's battery was stationed. Five miles upstream, Bell's Tennesseans took their stand. With them was the other section of Morton's artillery.

It is morning, Oct. 29. The steamer Mazeppa rounds the bend, into the five-mile trap. She's new and shining, out of Cincinnati, towing a barge. Suddenly three rounds blast her from the long-silent fort. She shivers from stem to stern, disabled, and drifts to the east bank, into mud and bushes. Her crew is scrambling ashore.

Toward her swims a naked Rebel, a pistol strapped to his back. He captures the brass-braided Yankee captain. The Mazeppa is roped and warped to the west bank.

Rebels swarm aboard. The Mazeppa is emptied and burned. Any of Forrest's men who needed shoes had plenty before the sun went down, for the Mazeppa's cargo was largely footgear—9,000 pairs. Plus blankets, warm winter clothing, hardtack and a demijohn of French brandy.

"Just enough for the general, boys!" Gen. Buford shouted, upping the jug.

Federal gunboats came and were greeted by Forrest's guns. They retired. Next day the steamer Anna appeared, downstream bound. She ran up the white flag and her pilot promised to round to at the lower landing. Then she heeled and ran, full speed. The lower batteries walloped her but she got away, reaching Paducah *"badly damaged."*

Author, Artists

Ed Huddleston

Jim Young

Dave Wright

Bill Zeigler

Working together in producing "The Civil War in Middle Tennessee" have been Ed Huddleston, member of the Banner staff since 1941, who wrote the narrative, and Newspaper Printing Corporation artists Jim Young, Dave Wright and Bill Zeigler.

Young, from Murfreesboro, drew many of the map designs and illustrations, including "Hood and His Betrothed" (Part III).

In the color picture, "Battle of Franklin—Last Moments of Gen. Adams," The Banner has presented the first major work of a young Nashville artist, Dave Wright, for whom a brilliant future is being predicted. (See back cover.)

Wright, at 21, also drew the dauntless "Johnny Reb" (beside the 1864 double-page map, Part III). He is now in the U.S. Army, assigned to South Viet Nam with the Military Assistance Command.

Zeigler, from Pulaski, did much of the lettering for all four parts. He also drew the area-attrition map for 1865 (Part IV). Young and Zeigler were classmates at the Art Institute of Pittsburg and have worked together since. (Zeigler died July 1, 1965.)

Morgan, Cushman and Sherman Sources

In addition to the Official Records of the War of the Rebellion, hundreds of sources have been consulted in the writing of this narrative.

Here is a partial list, to which The Banner wishes to acknowledge special gratitude as having been most helpful, particularly concerning Gen. John Hunt Morgan, Pauline Cushman, and Gen. W. T. Sherman:

A History of Morgan's Cavalry, by Basil W. Duke, Cincinnati, 1867; *The Rebel Raider,* by Howard Swiggett, Bobbs-Merrill Co., 1934, and The Garden City Publishing Co., Inc., 1937; *The Bold Cavaliers,* by Dee Alexander Brown, J. B. Lippincott Co., 1959; *Morgan and His Raiders,* by Cecil Fletcher Holland, The Macmillan Company, 1942; *Morgan and His Captors,* by the Rev. F. Senour, C. F. Vent & Co., 1864; *History of the Thirteenth Regiment, Tennessee Volunteer Cavalry, USA,* by Samuel W. Scott and Samuel P. Angel, P. W. Ziegler & Co., 1903; *Secret Service,* by A. D. Richardson, Hartford, 1865; *Spies of the Blue and Gray,* by Hartnett T. Kane, Hanover House, 1954; *Life of Pauline Cushman,* by F. L. Sarmiento, published by J. E. Potter, 1865.

Memoirs of Gen. W. T. Sherman, C. L. Webster & Co., 1891; *Sherman, Fighting Prophet,* by Lloyd Lewis. Harcourt, Brace & Co., 1932, and *Sherman: Soldier, Realist, American,* by Basil Henry Liddell Hart, Dodd, Mead & Co., 1929; and Praeger, 1958; *The Confederate Veteran, Southern Bivouac, Taylor-Trotwood Magazine,* and many old newspapers.

Old *Banner* copies were also consulted, including the issue of June 11, 1904, which carried "The Story of Gen. Morgan's Escape from Prison," by Jacob Bennett.

NEXT CAME the gunboat Undine and the transport Venus, then the steamer J. W. Cheeseman, twenty minutes later. The gunboat fought 55 minutes. Guns of the horsemen ripped her. She was run to the east bank and abandoned. The Venus and Cheeseman surrendered.

The Cheeseman was crippled. Forrest burned her. The Venus and Undine he manned with cavalrymen. Aboard the Venus went the Parrott guns.

Washington was astounded. If Forrest and Hood got together, then what? Grant wired Sherman, uneasily, *"If you see a chance of destroying Hood's army, attend to that first, and make your other move secondary . . ."*

Sherman replied, *"If I turn back now, the whole effect of my campaign will be lost—"*

Grant yielded again: *". . . Go on as you propose . . ."*

Next day Sherman was adding, *"He (Hood) proposes to invade Middle Tennessee, for the purpose of making me let go of Georgia . . . I detached the 15,000 strong IV Corps (Gen. David S. Stanley) and subsequently the XXIII Corps (Schofield) 10,000, which is now on the cars moving to Nashville . . ."*

Meanwhile, for three days Forrest had a navy. He cruised the river, trying to divert attention from other parts of his command. He called it his "horse marines."

Forrest's nautical luck wouldn't hold. By Nov. 2 the Venus was run aground and captured. The Undine was burned to prevent capture.

The Yanks thought Forrest had retired. He was merely out of sight. The curtain was about to go up on one of the biggest shows of his career.

Behind the bushes across the river from Johnsonville, Forrest had been working like mad. Since Nov. 3 his men had been emplacing 12 artillery pieces, aimed at Johnsonville. Through Nov. 4 the work went on, along the big bottoms across from the hilly depot.

Johnsonville!

This was his main target—with stores worth millions, brought south by steamer; ready for trains that would take them by Nashville and Chattanooga to Sherman's Atlanta.

In a natural levee on the west bank the Rebels dug gun pits. Here they set up artillery, 20 feet lower than the east bank. Here the Rebels could never be reached by the 50 guns in the Yankee fort high above the town across the river.

The 50 guns would boom in vain, too high. Gunboats would have a similar problem. Their shells would go shrieking overhead.

At 2 p.m., Nov. 4, the bushes were parted by Rebel thunder. At the Johnsonville wharves were three gunboats, 11 transport steamers, 18 barges, two freight trains and broad acres of stores piled 10 feet high.

Against all this 10 Rebel guns cut loose with a 40-minute roar. Johnsonville became an eruption of consternation and flame. Boilers burst. Screams rose. Vessels drifted, igniting more. The Union commander, wanting no vessel captured, set the others afire. The whole fleet burned to the water's edge. (As late as 1925 their wreckage could be seen at low water.)

High on a hill above the town, a warehouse held hundreds of barrels of liquors. A shell hit. The barrels burst. All went. Alcohol quivered downhill in a vast sheet of blue flame. The air was filled with the smell of burning brandy, coffee and sugar. The Rebels sniffed and swore. It couldn't be theirs. But neither would the Yankees get a dab!

By 4 p.m. a one-mile stretch of fire was leaping skyward. The whole place was aflame. Ash was raining . . . from supplies that would never ride the rails to Nashville and Atlanta.

—From *Harper's Weekly*

HOSPITAL TRAIN TO NASHVILLE. This one brought wounded Yankees from Chattanooga. (Sketched by Theodore R. Davis.)

From *Harper's Weekly*

THE SPIRES OF ATLANTA . . . still out of reach to the Federal officers who are watching from a signal station. (Sketched by Theodore R. Davis.)

THE HARTFORD AND THE TENNESSEE, in thunderous combat, side by side.

THAT NIGHT Forrest headed south. The great news had reached him. Join Hood. Quickly, in Florence, Ala., at the crossing of the Tennessee. The struggle for Nashville and Middle Tennessee was beginning.

Whoooo-peeee!

A six-mile glare lit Forrest's path as his horsemen moved away through the smoky night. He was thinking, estimating the damage done. His own figure was $6,700,000. (A conservative Federal estimate, of $2,200,000, presumably didn't include four gunboats and artillery.)

Rain poured again. The river rose. Roads became quagmires. The big guns had to move, but how? The mud was too deep for even 16 horses to a gun. Oxen were brought in. Four, six, and finally eight yoke were required. The big guns rolled at last, down the west side of the Tennessee. Meet Hood. Then on to Nashville!

Forrest was taking the road back, to the land where he was born. Nearly a year he'd been away. And what a name he'd made for himself, on his own!

As Forrest struggled with the oxen through the mud, he didn't know the black magic of his name was scrambling nerves in one of America's biggest cities.

An Illinois story was flying that he was about to "sack Chicago"! A Federal general would pay serious heed to the hokum.

On Nov. 7, author Robert Selph Henry says, a telegram was sent from Danville, Ill., by the provost marshal, Capt. W. Fithian. It went to Gen. Joseph Hooker, commander of the Northern Department of Cincinnati and said:

"Forrest has been in disguise alternately in Chicago, Michigan City and Canada for two months. Has 14,000 men. On Nov. 7, midnight, will seize telegraph and rail at Chicago, release prisoners there, arm them, sack city, shoot down all Federal soldiers, and urge concert of action with Southern sympathizers."

Hooker scoffed. "All stuff!" But the telegram must have got under his skin. (After all, next day was Federal election day. And a pretty sight for election day, if Forrest sacked Chicago!)

Hooker ordered troops from Springfield to Chicago. The governor of Illinois called out the militia. Hooker thought again, then sent 500 more troops from Indianapolis and a regiment from St. Louis. Finally, he went to Chicago himself! (From "First With the Most" Forrest.)

It's Nov. 8. The election is on. Lincoln wins—2,216,067 popular votes, against 1,808,725 for McClellan. Did not the great Lincoln have a closer brush in the popular voting than we might guess today?

A TORPEDO sinks the Tecumseh.

LASHED TO THE RIGGING, Admiral Farragut sees the ram Tennessee give battle to his entire fleet.

GEN. WILLIAM H. JACKSON, whose astute warning Hood brushed aside in Atlanta, was married Dec. 15, 1868, to Selene Harding, daughter of Gen. William G. Harding of Belle Meade plantation. Under Gen. Jackson's direction, Belle Meade became one of the foremost horse-breeding establishments in America. Jackson became master of the famed estate in 1888, following the death of his father-in-law.

HOWEVER, he carried every "Northern" state except three, Kentucky, Delaware and New Jersey. He would receive 212 electoral votes; "Little Mac," only 21.

In Tennessee, it's a farce again. The state's total popular vote for the Lincoln-Johnson ticket cannot be determined. In Nashville, Lincoln received 1,317 votes; McClellan, 25. In Shelby County, Lincoln won 1,579; McClellan, 24.

In the long run, the Tennessee showing did Gov. Johnson little good. The U. S. Congress, by joint resolution, later threw out Tennessee's whole vote as invalid.

As Lincoln triumphed, and Forrest inched along, Gen. Schofield, rocking by rail for Pulaski, was re-shuffled from Nashville to the fire-blackened spot by the river.

He needn't have been. Johnsonville wouldn't be of much importance to either side for the remainder of the war. But who knew? Schofield left two brigades there, then turned the oncoming trainloads of troops to Pulaski and joined them, in command of 23,000 men, his own and Gen. Stanley's.

Schofield didn't guess it at first . . . but positions for a desperate and deadly game were being taken. Himself at Pulaski. Forrest rushing to join Hood. Hood at Florence, arriving Nov. 13. Thomas, in Nashville, wondering . . . will Hood break for the Ohio, or what?

In Washington, Grant is dreading the same possibility. Lincoln's cabinet is getting jumpy with the thought. Watch Hood!

It's midnight, Nov. 11. Sherman wires Thomas: If Hood attacks Nashville, *"you will whip him out of his boots."* Thomas has no fear. Next day he boldly wires Sherman, *" . . . If he attempts to follow you, I will follow him . . ."*

That afternoon Sherman ordered the cutting of wires to the North. At last he was on his own, ready to plunge toward the sea!

Ahead were big days. Big and terrible days, for Georgia and Middle Tennessee. In Tennessee, there would be days of resurgent hope which would come echoing down a century in the stories of Middle Tennessee families. The suspense of their soldier-men for Columbia, when both Hood and Schofield would race for the town; the mystery of Spring Hill to everyone; then the meadows of blood at Franklin and, finally, collapse of a dream at Nashville.

On Nov. 14 Forrest joined Hood. Bedlam broke loose; Forrest was serenaded.

On the morning of Nov. 16, Forrest began putting his arriving men across the Tennessee on pontoons leading to Florence. The day before, he had been assigned to the command of all the Confederate cavalry of Middle Tennessee. Yes, recognition from the Confederate high command was coming, at last.

How late the hour!

On the same morning, from the outskirts of Atlanta, Gen. Sherman looks back at a rising pall of smoke. Atlanta is burning. With about 62,000 men, he is starting on his way to Savannah. He will cut a swath of desolation 60 miles wide.

All is ready. Sherman's men will be in clover. Georgia's crops are harvested. Corn is in the crib. Hogs and cattle are fat for the slaughter. Yankees marching through Georgia will be feasting on Irish and sweet potatoes, pigs and chickens and chestnuts. Their mules will eat down the cornfields.

Ashes and desolation, to Sherman, were a way to hasten the end, and a song rose as his army, too, marched along, another happy army:

> *"Mine eyes have seen the glory*
> *Of the coming of the Lord;*
> *He is tramping out the vintage*
> *Where the grapes of wrath are stored."*

As Sherman goes, he is marching out of the story of the Civil War so far as it immediately concerns Middle Tennessee.

The Tennessee story is now in the hands of Hood, waiting at Florence—for the rains have begun again, and a lack of supplies, delaying him once more, day after day; and it is also in the hands of Thomas, making ready in Nashville and glad, glad of the rains. They have given him more time to prepare. But before the two collide on Nashville's snowy outskirts, Schofield will rush for the city, and Hood will meet him at Franklin.

The end was coming, too, about this time, for Dee Smith the avenger—locked tight in a Murfreesboro jail. He had been captured in Williamson County, mortally wounded, and brought to Murfreesboro to be hanged.

Smith had killed, according to tradition, about 50 Yankees, within 60 days. The figure may be a slight exaggeration, but there seems little doubt that he killed a large number. Now, at last, were the Yankees to have the last laugh? Smith on the scaffold . . .

Not if Smith's friends could help it. They visited him on the night before the scheduled execution. Legend says they *"gave him a drug."* Smith died before the hour set for his execution.

SURRENDER OF THE TENNESSEE. It's over. Courage has been no match for Federal might.

From *Century War Book*, 1861-1865

By Edwin Forbes, from *30 Years After*

"A TOUGH PULL." In the full maturity of his powers, long after the war, Forbes developed this from earlier sketches.

BY NOV. 21, the Alabama rains have slackened. Hood's army is entering Tennessee from north of Florence. It is moving in three columns, churning three roads to quagmire, toward Columbia, Tenn., 75 miles northeast.

Schofield at Pulaski received the startling news next day. Alarm gripped him, understandably. Why, they meant to cut him off from Nashville! To separate him from Thomas!

If Hood beat Schofield to Columbia, between Pulaski and Nashville, Schofield's 23,000 men and 800 wagons would be isolated. And Columbia was 30 miles north of Pulaski—

Schofield pulled out of Pulaski as fast as he could go. March! For your lives! His 800 wagons hit the road, with 23,000 men at double-quick. It was Nov. 22. He must get to Thomas, before Hood can block the way at Columbia. Or Hood will attack Schofield singly, then go for Thomas at Nashville—with a very good chance of winning.

And at Columbia, on the Duck, Forrest will grab the fords and bridges, blocking the way of withdrawal, unless Schofield gets there first. March!

Hood's three columns are making time, too, through rain, snow, sleet and icy winds. On, Hood! Burn the icy wind!

"*If Hood could prevent Schofield from joining Thomas,*" says Dyer, "*complete victory would be in Confederate hands and Hood's dazzling dream of marching to the Ohio, and then joining forces with Lee, would have come true. Such a victory would completely neutralize Sherman in Georgia and compel him to abandon the state . . . That was Hood's plan.*" (In *The Gallant Hood.*)

His Middle Tennesseans are homeward bound—ah, forget the pink on the snow!

One column is that of "Old Straight" Stewart, from Lebanon. He's moving by Lawrenceburg. The second is Gen. Stephen D. Lee's. He is advancing by country roads 10 miles west of Lawrenceburg. The third is Gen. Cheatham's, coming by Waynesboro. All told, they're about 29,000.

Forrest's cavalry, 6,000 to 8,000, had left Florence two days before the others. He's operating out ahead. He's pushing the enemy cavalry from "*one position to another.*" They are under Gen. Edward Hatch and Gen. John T. Croxton.

The Rebel horsemen, in two columns, are screening Hood's march. Gen. James R. Chalmers is on the west. He is moving toward Columbia by Henryville and Mt. Pleasant. Forrest, with the east column, moves through Lawrenceburg.

Schofield is marching his army day and night. Stanley is leading. And they were a few miles nearer Columbia when the race began.

Schofield won. Stanley reached Columbia Nov. 24, just in time to keep Forrest from seizing the Duck River bridge. This would have cut off Schofield's retreat toward Spring Hill, Franklin and Nashville.

Forrest arrived the same day. The Yankees were entrenching. For three days Forrest kept up a fire, until Hood's infantry began to pull in three days later, on the morning of Nov. 27.

Forrest then was sent to picket the river. Scout for crossings!

Schofield had thrown up stout works. Hood made no effort to storm them. Leave Schofield unattacked, Hood reasoned, and he'll cross to the north of the Duck. Well, let him! (Schofield won't go far, if plans work out!)

That night Forrest was called to a conference at Beechlawn, Hood's headquarters. This was the home of Confederate Maj. Amos W. Warfield, three miles south of Columbia on the Pulaski Pike.

That night, too, Hood permitted Schofield to cross the Duck. Gen. Lee remained on the south side to demonstrate on Schofield's front.

Schofield burned his bridges and took up the expected position. Thomas, from Nashville, had directed him to hold Hood until concentration at Nashville was farther along. Schofield was obeying.

Courtesy of Tennessee Historical Society

ISHAM G. HARRIS
Tennessee's Confederate Governor

"CLEARING THE WAY," by Forbes, from *30 Years After.*

A BITTER POLITICAL BLAST at the Northern Democrats' "peace party" convening in Chicago. If it triumphed, would Northern soldiers have died in vain? The broken dagger on the grave is labeled "Northern Power."

AT BEECHLAWN the Rebels were making sound plans. If carried out, they would provide an excellent chance for Confederate victory in the Tennessee campaign. Under cover of Lee's demonstration on the south bank, Hood meant to lead his main force by country roads to a deadly position behind Schofield at Spring Hill—between Schofield and his escape route. They'd box Schofield in.

The village was a vital crossroads, 11 miles northeast of Columbia. Within it, the Columbia-to-Nashville pike was intersected by several other roads. Confederates controlling the crossroads would have Schofield at their mercy.

Forrest was to cross the Duck (above and to the east of Columbia) and put down pontoons for the infantry. In the crossing he would meet, for the first time, the able opposition of young Federal Gen. James H. Wilson, the new cavalry commander in the West. Forrest pushed him back.

By dusk Forrest was crowding Wilson north and east, away from the river and Columbia. Before nightfall of Nov. 28, Forrest had three of his own columns across. By daylight, the last column, Buford's, was over.

Before daylight, however, Wilson sent a warning to Schofield. It went from Hurt's Crossroads, on the turnpike from Lewisburg to Franklin. On the back of the message Wilson wrote, *"Important, Trot!!!"* It was 1 a.m.

Wilson was saying: Not only is Forrest across. He's putting down pontoons for the infantry. *"Get to Franklin without delay."* Hours would pass before Schofield received it.

Before then, dawn would bring the tread of Rebel feet. Hood's infantry had begun its move for Spring Hill, the intended cut-off point. He crossed by pontoons at Davis' Ford, then moved along dirt roads between the Lewisburg-Franklin turnpike and the Columbia-Spring Hill-Franklin turnpike.

TWO YANKEES DIE at DeWitt Smith's hands. Their capture may have been like this old drawing, "Guerrilla Depredations."

A BRITISH BANTLING.

JOHN BULL. "Now, then, my friend JONATHAN, there is a child I want you to adopt."
JONATHAN. "Looks a kinder sickly—got Peace on the Brain, ain't he? Guess ye better take keer of yer own children. I don't wish ye to interdooce any of yer rickety stock inter my family."

Harper's ridicules the "Chicago platform" of the "peace party."

"NO BRAVER SOLDIER, NO GREATER PATRIOT." Dee Jobe's body, in the hot August sun, may have looked much like this drawing, "A Dead Rebel," from *Harper's Weekly*.

NOTHING, IT SEEMED, could save Schofield, who wasn't yet sure Hood had crossed the Duck in force. Back in Columbia, two divisions of Lee's corps were spouting uproar, in an effort to conceal from Schofield that the bulk of Hood's army had gone; and Schofield had to keep part of his army in line, facing Lee—unaware that two-thirds of the Rebel army was swinging around the Federal flank.

Forrest was taking good care of Wilson, pushing him northward five miles, along the Lewisburg Pike to Mount Carmel Church. Wilson then marched the remainder of the day to get across the Big Harpeth. Forrest, Wilson thought, was headed for Nashville.

Instead, with Wilson out of the way, Forrest left a brigade to worry Wilson and marched back west for Spring Hill.

At 7:30 a.m. on the Duck, Schofield received Wilson's message. Schofield got moving. He sent his wagons, most of his artillery and two divisions of infantry scurrying out the macadamized pike toward Spring Hill and Franklin.

Reproduced by Permission of Punch

"FEDERAL PHOENIX" — As London's pro-Confederacy *Punch* saw Lincoln's re-election.

Photos from The Journal of B. L. Ridley

DEWITT (DEE) JOBE
Forgotten Hero

DEWITT (DEE) SMITH
His Avenger

Forrest, riding west at noon, met Schofield's eastbound vanguard. Forrest's column was about two miles outside Spring Hill when it ran into the enemy skirmishers. Behind them, a Federal division was coming into Spring Hill at double-quick. The wagon train stretched all the way back to Columbia.

Forrest didn't have his whole force. He was still waiting for them to come up from such places as Mount Carmel. But he had reached Spring Hill in time to halt the escape-march of Schofield's column.

Forrest couldn't straddle the pike; but he made more than one attack while waiting for his own men and the infantry. He prevented Schofield's northeastward advance beyond Spring Hill. But enemy guns kept rumbling into position on an elevation to the southwest; and the endless line of wagons, on and on, kept creaking into a little park west of town, until far in the afternoon.

Hood sent Forrest word: Hold! At all hazards.

Forrest held. Hood was arriving, Cheatham's corps in front, led by Cleburne's division. From the south came the muted sound of Lee's guns, still holding Schofield himself at Columbia.

"Rarely in the whole war was a commander to have such an opportunity as was Hood's that November afternoon, with his troops in position to close and bar the way to Schofield and to crush or capture his divisions as they came marching northward . . . The opportunity was lost. How it was lost, and whose was the responsibility, became the subject of long and bitter controversy . . ."
This is the view of Robert Self Henry, in "First With the Most" Forrest.

It was then, as Cleburne began to reform his line to seize the pike, that a puzzling sequence of orders began. Some were contradictory. Confusion spread. It would become one of the most written-about enigmas of the Civil War in Tennessee.

Jobe and Hunley Sources

THIS IS CERTAIN of DeWitt Jobe: he died in agony, telling nothing. No account precisely agrees with another in every detail.

For aid in assembling the story and legends, The Banner expresses its gratitude to Mr. and Mrs. Homer Peyton Pittard of Murfreesboro for permission to quote from their theses: "The Coleman Scouts," by Mrs. Pittard, presented to the Graduate School of Tennessee State Teachers College in 1953, and "Legends and Stories of Civil War Rutherford County," by Mr. Pittard, submitted to the Graduate School of Education of George Peabody College for Teachers, in 1940.

For additional aid, The Banner is grateful to Miss Adeline King, author of "Son of This House," the Sam Davis pageant at Smyrna, who cited us to the forgotten hero; to Hughey King of Murfreesboro for access to unpublished family documents, including a manuscript by the late Col. John Jordan of Triune; to Mrs. Frank Owsley, senior archivist, manuscript section, State Library and Archives, who made available the account book of Sgt. James L. Gee, Co. D, 20th Tennessee Regiment.

Also consulted were the *Journal of Bromfield L. Ridley* of Murfreesboro, *History of the 20th Tennessee Regiment*, by W. J. McMurray, and his article, "Heroes and Martyrs," in the *Confederate Veteran Magazine*.

Much remains to be learned concerning Hunley. The U.S. Navy is understandably interested.

For assistance on his story, The Banner expresses its appreciation to Winston DeVille, head of special collections, Mobile Public Library; Mrs. Dorothy Whittemore, Tulane University Library; Robert H. Burgess, Mariners Museum, Newport News, Va.; Miss Dorothy Cason, *Mobile Press-Register*, and to Eustace Williams, Van Nuys, Calif., whose *Dawn of Modern Warfare* may find a publisher soon.

Published works often consulted were *The Story of Mobile* by Caldwell Delaney, and *The Peripatetic Coffin* by Robert Walker in the *South Atlantic Quarterly*.

THINK HARD, SHERMAN! Think fast! The next presidency may hinge on what you're thinking.—Sherman, just outside Atlanta.

JUST BEFORE sunset an officer from Cheatham's staff arrives. He has a directive. Make no attack until further orders.

None came. Night fell. Cleburne went into bivouac. His line of battle faced the pike—the pike he had been ordered to take. Odd? Indeed.

What happened and why? Even the principals contradict one another. Morning showed this fact: Schofield's army had escaped down the road toward Franklin.

One of the greatest opportunities of the Confederacy—from all the bloody years of warfare—had been lost. For nearly 100 years, Tennesseans have been hearing it said, "Hood let the whole Yankee army slip by him at Spring Hill."

That is what it amounts to.

When writing of the great lost chance a few years later, Hood tried to put much of the blame on Cheatham. Hood wrote:

". . . I led the main body of the army to within about two miles and in full view of the pike from Columbia to Spring Hill and Franklin. I here halted about 3 p.m. and requested Gen. Cheatham and Gen. Cleburne to advance to the spot where, sitting upon my horse, I had in sight the enemy's wagons and men passing at double-quick along the Franklin Pike."

Cheatham read the above statement. His comment: "There is not a word of truth in the entire paragraph."

Hood also wrote that he rode up at twilight and demanded of Cheatham, "General, why in God's name have you not . . . taken possession of that pike?"

GEN. JOHN H. MORGAN
End of the Trail

GEN. GEORGE H. THOMAS
Hold Middle Tennessee

Cheatham read that, too. No such conversation transpired, he declared, except in the "imagination of Gen. Hood."

Much more is involved in the controversy, too voluminous for this limited space. In short, it has been said and written that during the afternoon, Hood easily could have:

● Cut the pike below Spring Hill with Cheatham's corps.

● Cut it above with Stewart's.

● Or he could have attacked Spring Hill directly.

"A single Confederate brigade . . . planted squarely across the pike, either north or south of Spring Hill, would have effectually prevented Schofield's retreat, and daylight would have found his whole force cut off from every avenue of escape . . ." So Col. Henry Stone of Gen. Thomas' staff would say.

Either move might have led to the fulfillment of Hood's bright dream, to free Nashville and roll on to the Ohio, or, perhaps, even to push eastward across the mountains to the relief of Gen. Robert E. Lee, now before Petersburg in Virginia, with his force much reduced by Grant's incessant hammering.

Soon Lee would be forced to spread a 37-mile line before Petersburg. To man it, he would have only 59,000 men, hungry and shivering, to face Grant's 110,000.

And when Sherman reached the Georgia coast, would Sherman not swing north to join Grant? Should this happen, and if no aid came—then would not both Petersburg and Richmond have to be evacuated? But should Hood come——!

Hood, this is your hour. Oh, one-legged fighter, strapped to your horse—grasp this chance. It's yours, and jewel-bright.

It was the witching hour of Hood's destiny, from 4:30 p.m., Nov. 29, till midnight, at the Middle Tennessee crossroads village of Spring Hill, in Maury County.

Is it beyond conjecture that had the road been blocked, Hood might have become the military hero of a new nation? The conqueror of Schofield and Thomas; the savior of Lee?

Luck was trying hard to knight Hood. Opportunity would not go tearing past him, gone in a moment. She would come back to his door and pound and pound, as if loath to pass him by. As if to give him another chance, and another—

Out in the darkness Gen. Stewart is on unfamiliar terrain. He also has received contradictory orders. For one thing, he's in doubt about what his position should be.

He runs across Forrest. (After the infantry came up, Forrest's men had been withdrawn. The horses have been fed.) Their men are in bivouac.

The two clear-headed old friends are puzzled. What strange orders have been coming through! They decide to get it all straightened out. So they ride together back to Hood's headquarters.

DRAGGING ARTILLERY THROUGH THE MUD—so Waud called this sketch, reminiscent of the quagmire trials of Federal Gen. A. J. Smith, as Forrest moved on Memphis.

"Johnny Reb"
by Dave Wright

Map by Jim Young

Nashville

1863

BATTLE of FRANKLIN
Nov. 30, 1864

Lavergne

Franklin

Union & Con... forces battle... Nashville... Chattanooga 1...

Murfreesboro

Spring Hill

BATTLE of MURFREESBORO
Dec. 31, 1862
Jan. 2, 1863

McM...

Columbia

Mt. Pleasant

Lewisburg

Lawrenceburg

Pulaski

Elkton

Fayetteville

Florence

Athens

FORREST'S RAID INTO TENN., SEPT. & OCT., 1864

Tuscumbia

Huntsville

TENNESSEE RIVER

HOOD'S

Decatur

Forrest Joins Hood

Guntersville

ALABAMA

CAMPAIGN, 1864

Gadsden

---- **CONFEDERATE**

—— **UNION**

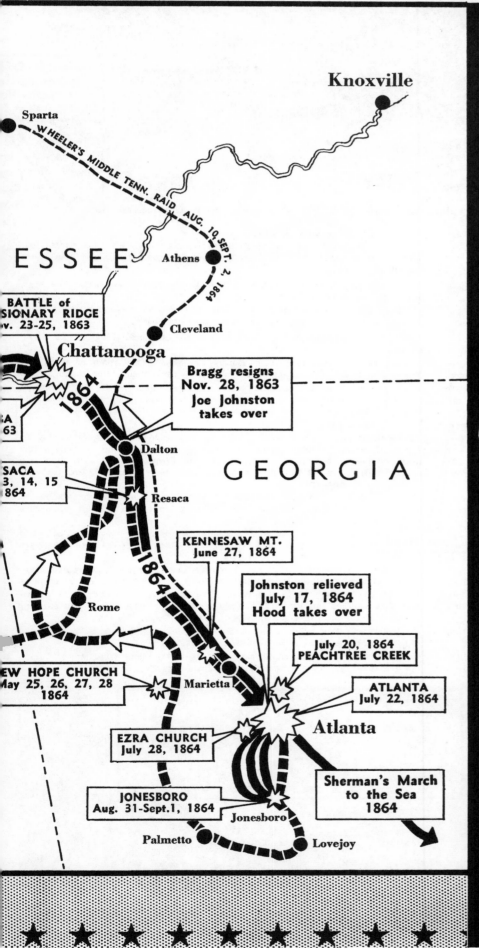

Big Days of the Civil War for Middle Tennesseans (1864)

● Jan. 21, Unionists in Nashville plan new civil government for Tennessee. Set March 9 for county elections. ● Feb. 17, submarine Hunley sinks warship Housatonic. ● March 9, elections a farce. Results unheeded. ● May 4, momentous day. Grant crosses Rapidan as Sherman moves on Johnston. ● May 13, 14, 15, Battle of Resaca. ● May 25 through 28, Battle of New Hope Church. ● June 10, Forrest triumphs at Battle of Brice's Cross Roads. ● June 14, Gen. Polk killed. ● June 27, Battle of Kennesaw Mt. ● July 17, Johnston relieved of command. Succeeded by Hood. ● July 20, 22, 28, Battles of Peachtree Creek, Atlanta and Ezra Church, respectively. ● Aug. 5, ram Tennessee takes on whole Union fleet at Battle of Mobile Bay. ● Aug. 21, Forrest raids Memphis. ● Aug. 29, "Dee" Jobe, scout, tortured to death off Nolensville Road. An almost forgotten hero. ● Sept. 1, Hood evacuates Atlanta. ● Sept. 4, Gen. John Hunt Morgan slain in Greeneville. ● Sept. 26, Forrest heading for Pulaski. ● Oct. 16, Hood decision: invade Tennessee. ● Oct. 29, through Nov. 2, Forrest strikes on Tennessee River. ● Nov. 4, Forrest blows up Johnsonville. Washington astounded. ● Nov. 8, Lincoln re-elected; Andrew Johnson, vice president. ● Nov. 14, Forrest joins Hood's Tennessee campaign. ● Nov. 16, Sherman begins March to Sea. ● Nov. 21, Hood enters Tennessee, Nashville bound. Excitement soars. ● Nov. 21-24, the race for Columbia. ● Nov. 24 through 29, action around Columbia. ● Night of Nov. 29, the mysterious "slip-through" of Federals at Spring Hill. ● Nov. 30, Battle of Franklin.

GIDDAP! Columbia first—or disaster! Schofield's frantic rush was much like this scene from Chancellorsville.

HOOD IS TOLD that, because of the contradictory orders, Stewart also has his men in bivouac. Then Hood remarks (according to Stewart) that it is not material. Let the men rest.

Hood turns to Forrest. Can he block the road with his cavalry? Forrest replies that Buford and Chalmers are *"without a cartridge."* (They've already expended 60 rounds today.)

Poor Hood! His ammunition trains are far in the rear, back with the trains at Columbia. He's stumped. Can the infantry commanders supply Forrest? No!

A half-chance remained. Gen. Jackson had captured some ammunition a few hours before. With that, Forrest promised to do the best he could.

Gen. W. B. Bate came in as they talked. It was between 10 and 12 o'clock. Bate was worried. The Yanks were moving right along the pike he had wanted to block.

"It makes no difference now," Hood replied, according to Gen. Bate. *"Gen. Forrest informs me he holds the turnpike with a position of his forces north of Spring Hill, and will stop the enemy if he tries to pass toward Franklin. And in the morning we will have a surrender without a fight. We can sleep quiet tonight."*

Is Hood sleepy? Exhausted? He has made a remark which is far from what Forrest actually said.

Out in the cold, Rebel campfires are glowing on the hillsides. The encampment stretches four miles along the pike. They're within gunshot of the road. Federals are surging along it with *"their hearts in their throats."*

The Yankees are trying to be quiet. Talk is forbidden. Wagon-wheels are muffled. But Rebel soldiers, in the ranks, see and hear the passing host. Now and then, on his own, a Rebel grabs a Yankee straggler for whatever is in his knapsack.

Down in the middle of the road, the Yanks are marching beside their wagons, now and then bumping into the man ahead; halting, starting again. For more than half the night, Schofield's immense wagon train keeps rolling by, almost under Rebel noses.

History is being made, almost in silence. An enemy army is simply walking away, unmolested, unchallenged, unshot.

Forrest goes to Jackson who provides the bit of ammunition he has. Then, northward down the turnpike, Forrest's men receive the *"handful."*

A *"handful,"* to stop an army . . .

And again opportunity hammers upon Hood's door. This time an excited, barefoot private comes to Hood's rooms out of the frosty night, in a house near the village.

The private knows something is wrong. The enemy is passing, he says, almost in the light of the campfires!

Hood asked his adjutant general, Maj. A. P. Mason, to send a note to Gen. Cheatham: Delay the march. Order your picket line to fire.

(Be sure you remember the note. One of the strangest things of the whole strange night will concern it.)

Tennessee's Confederate Gov. Harris was sharing the room of Hood and Mason. Harris saw the private come in. Twenty-three years later Harris wrote:

". . . Gen. Hood directed Mason to order Gen. Cheatham to move down on the road immediately and attack the enemy. Gen. Hood and myself remained in bed. I went to sleep, and I suppose Gen. Hood did the same."

Did Mason write as ordered?

Schofield had reached Spring Hill. He was wide-awake, reconnoitering in the darkness on his own, as far as Thompson's Station. Had he gone a few miles farther north, he would have run into Forrest's men, with their dab of ammunition. (As it was, Schofield must have been amazed to find the road clear as far as he went.)

Upon return, Schofield ordered his whole command—the remainder—on toward Franklin. Go! Day would be breaking before the last of Schofield's wagons creaked away from Spring Hill.

Thus it came about that only *"a small body of Rebel cavalry* (as Schofield put it) *made a dash"* upon the line of wagons a few miles north of Thompson Station. These were the horsemen of Forrest.

Out of the passing 800 wagons, Forrest's men managed to destroy 39. They stampeded teamsters and wagon guards. The road was blocked for 30 minutes.

Then Schofield swept on toward Franklin, 12 miles north. And as the rear guard pulled out under Gen. George D. Wagner, Gen. Cox was entering Franklin at the head of a column. Light was showing in the sky.

Hot words flew when most of Hood's generals sat down to breakfast at the stately home of Maj. Nat Cheairs.

Hood was *"wrathy as a rattlesnake."* He threw blame right and left, upon his generals and soldiers, sparing few except himself.

GEN. WILLIAM B. BATE

Does this remind you, at least in part, of the slip-through at Spring Hill?

Forrest's men, with their "handful" of ammunition, had done their best. Schofield's wagons were rolling on. Forbes entitled this drawing "Coming Out of the Fight."

THERE WERE ACCUSATIONS, demands for apologies. It is said that swords were drawn.

During the day Hood would bitterly tell Gov. Harris he blamed Cheatham. Maj. Mason may have heard the remark. He soon called Harris aside.

Mason confided to Harris that Cheatham was not to blame. Eh? What's that? I, Maj. Mason confessed, *fell asleep and failed to write the note to Cheatham!*

(This disclosure came four years later, verbally, from Harris, May 5, 1868. The information is on record in an unpublished manuscript account by Maj. Campbell Brown—an incident carefully recounted and footnoted in Horn's *Army of Tennessee.)*

Harris, shocked, advised Mason to inform Hood. Mason promised. There seems no proof, however, that Mason ever told Hood.

Now comes a more puzzling aspect: Cheatham says he received Mason's note; that he acted in accordance with its orders— although Mason says he fell asleep and didn't write it!

So the reader and researcher of today, probing patiently into the far-off, mysterious night, winds up in a dead end.

All this brings the regrettable need to include a legend which has persisted through the years—that Hood was *"drunk"* on the fateful night. Was he?

"It can not now be proved or disproved," Horn says. After all, Hood often was in pain, from his wounded arm and the stump of his leg—a big man, strapped astride his mount for hours of riding. Riding irritated his stump. In addition, he had been ill with rheumatism at Florence.

On that morning nearly 100 years ago, one fact was clear: The enemy was gone. Schofield's army was marching as fast as it could go toward Franklin.

"Hood's Tennessee campaign was lost that night at Spring Hill," says Henry, in *The Story of the Confederacy. "The slaughter at Franklin grew out of the failure at Spring Hill, the disaster at Nashville out of both."*

Schofield's army had marched all night. Hood's had slept. But by *"nearly dawn,"* Hood's men were up and pursuing. They seemed to share his fury. Make fools of us? Well, we'll make you pay! The air seemed filled with Rebel anger. They went streaming toward Franklin along three pikes.

Forrest as usual is out front and on the flanks. The main Confederate column is swinging down the Columbia Pike from Spring Hill.

(As it had passed Ashwood, near Columbia, a few days earlier, Gen. Cleburne saw a beautiful little Episcopal church, St. John's. Beside it was a small cemetery. It would be *"almost worth dying,"* Cleburne said, *"to be buried in such a spot."* He was astride his favorite, Red Pepper. Were some now remembering?)

About 1 p.m. Hood reaches Winstead Hill, about three miles from Franklin. He looks out over the scene with field glasses. The enemy has stopped. It stands at bay, more than 23,000 men. From somewhere comes the tinkle of cowbells.

Schofield is strongly entrenched in old breastworks, made by the Federals in 1862-'63. They've been strengthened. The works stretch across the south side of town, making a neck across the loop of the Big Harpeth River.

Shall Hood storm the works? If so, his army must advance nearly two miles, across an open and beautifully rolling plain. His forward-surging columns would have no shelter from concentrated fire.

His generals wait. Hood continues his survey.

An advance skirmish line has been posted out in front of the works. This is astride the Columbia turnpike, about a half mile out on the plain. (There Gen. Wagner is in command.)

The town, inside the loop of the river, lies well beyond the breastworks. Behind the town is the river, to the north. Fort Granger stands across the river, on an eminence, to the northeast. It commands the whole.

SAVE THE WAGONS! Schofield's train, tearing for Columbia, at its swiftest may have resembled this Virginia scene.

"Building Breastworks"

SCHOFIELD WILL soon be there, inside the fort, atop its parapet, using the fort as headquarters. He will not be upon the field during the holocaust ahead. He will leave Gen. Jacob D. Cox in charge of the line.

Already Schofield has telegraphed Thomas in Nashville: Send help! Thomas can't. Instead, Thomas asks: Can you hold Hood at Franklin three days, while reinforcements tighten at Nashville?

Schofield has his doubts. He knows Hood's impetuosity, the deadliness of Forrest. Shofield's biggest worries are his wagons, and the bridge east of town, across which his wagons must escape at the earliest possible moment.

What if Forrest whips across the river above the town, slashing in between Franklin and Nashville? (This is exactly what Forrest meant to do.)

The hard-pushed Schofield informs Thomas of his fear: Forrest may flank me. *"Wilson is entirely unable to deal with him."*

Bridges, wagons, and a bottle-neck! Schofield was struggling with the problem. He wanted to get away. He wasn't begging for battle.

At best the bridges were makeshift. To the north, the highway and railroad bridges had once crossed the river close together. But the highway bridge has been destroyed. A footbridge had been improvised. Scant help for 800 wagons!

To open the way, Schofield has had planks placed across the crossties of the railroad bridge. It makes an airy path for his wagons. They are rattling across the Harpeth toward Nashville, even as Hood stands watching through his glasses.

Federal troops will follow, if no attack has been made by 6 p.m. The order has been given. Actually, at first, Schofield does not expect a general attack—surely Hood will not be so foolish!

On Winstead Hill, Hood snapped shut the case of his field glasses.

"We will make the fight," he said.

In the shocked silence, did the cowbells tinkle again, as if in gentle warning?

GEN. B. F. CHEATHAM
He warned

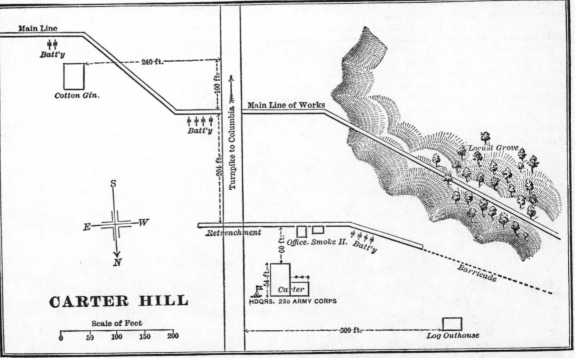

Drawn by Lt. Col. Moscow Branch Carter who leveled the works on the Carter farm after the war. This is from *The Battle of Franklin*, by Gen. Jacob D. Cox, 1897, Charles Scribner's Sons, New York.

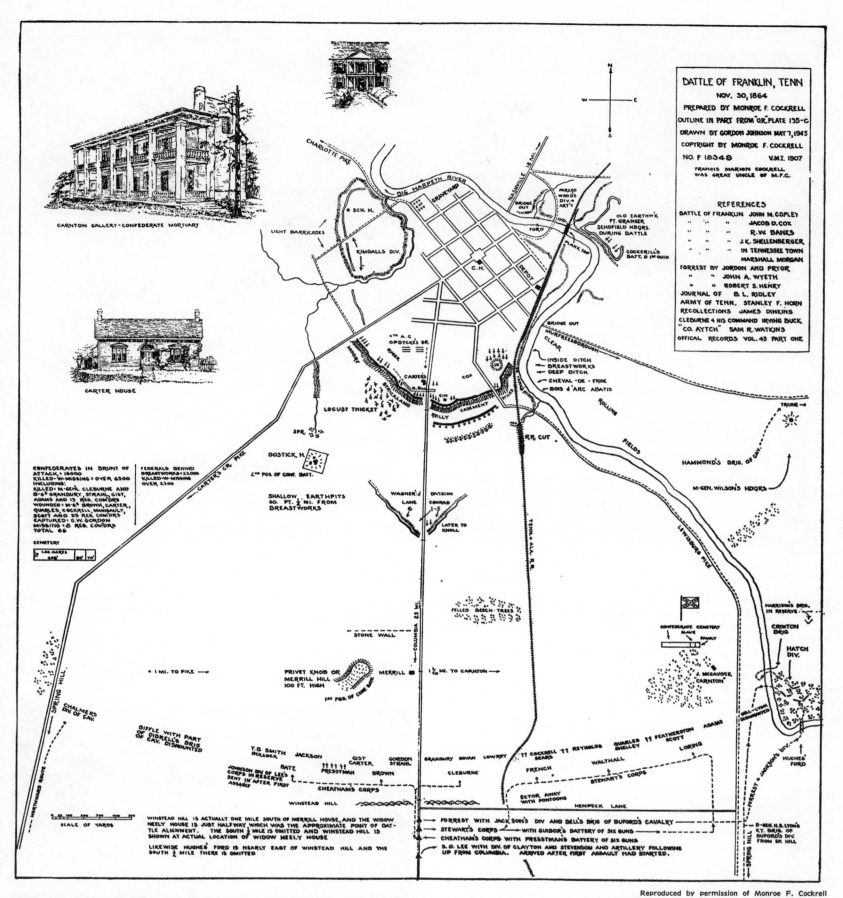

Reproduced by permission of Monroe F. Cockrell

Courtesy Stanley F. Horn

THE GINHOUSE. Cleburne perished almost due south of this building, now razed. In front of it, a withering crossfire raked his men after Stewart was thrown back. The Carter ginhouse stood southeast across the pike from the Carter home.

THE GIN. Fierce fighting raged between it and the house, distant left. In *The Field Book of the Civil War*, this picture is entitled, "A View of the Battlefield of Franklin."

"I DON'T *like the looks of this fight,*" said Gen. Cheatham. "*The enemy has an excellent position and is well-fortified.*"

Hood was brusque. He preferred to fight here, he said, where the Yankees have had only a few hours to prepare; here, rather than "*to strike them at Nashville where they've been strengthening themselves for three years.*"

Forrest, too, spoke out. Don't try frontal assault. Flank 'em. Forrest knows the river can be forded above the town.

"*Give me one strong division of infantry with my cavalry,*" Forrest says, "*and within two hours time I can flank the Federals from their works.*"

Hood is in no mood for flanking. His anger boils. He can't wait. He thinks Schofield is in full retreat behind those works. Forrest's cavalry will be unwisely divided, its impact dissipated, while almost the entire force of Wilson's cavalry, on the north side of the Harpeth, will be used to cover Schofield's flank.

Hood can't wait for his artillery to come up and soften the enemy line. He can't wait for Gen. Lee's divisions. Get ready! For a frontal assault.

The main Confederate column arrived around 2 o'clock by the pike from Spring Hill, Stewart's corps in the lead. It was ordered up along the Lewisburg Pike, near Carnton, the John M. McGavock place. Cheatham's came next, then Lee's. Cheatham went straight forward along the Columbia turnpike, Cleburne to the right, Gen. John C. Brown to his left.

On a powerful gray rides a young Rebel, Capt. Theodorick (Tod) Carter, who must have been having some awesome and uneasy thoughts—not for himself, but for the welfare of his family. He has marched and marched, and fought and fought, with the Army of Tennessee; and now, almost before him, across two miles of familiar countryside, Tod can see his home. Ah, so long he'd been away . . . ! His home, in enemy hands.

There it is, solidly built of brick, with evergreens clustered close—just inside the curving line of the enemy's powerful entrenchments. His home . . . with Yankee tents in the dooryard. The Federal Flag is fluttering.

What's going on inside! Is his family safe? Have they gone? Oh, God, keep them safe!

Capt. Carter couldn't know that Gen. Cox, arriving in the early morning darkness, had ridden up to the house, awakened its occupants and commandeered the place as a command post. Then weary Yankees had dropped upon the floors and snatched a few minutes of desperately needed sleep. Gen. Cox dozed.

After a while, someone had shouted, "Attention!" Schofield had arrived.

"*Gen. Cox,*" Schofield had said, "*the pontoons are not here. The county bridge is gone. The ford is hardly passable. You must take command of the XXIII Corps . . . Hold Hood back at all hazards until we get our trains over . . .*" The Federals might have to fight to save the wagons.

Cox got busy. Build breastworks!

To top them, logs were torn from the Carter barn. The main line of defense was placed south of the house. A salient was the gin, 100 feet farther south. The inner entrenchment was 60 feet south of the house, in line with the smokehouse.

From their home, the Carter family sees the massing of Rebel troops. Oh, Tod! Are you there? My son, my son. So near home. Oh, my brother. Live! God sustain you! The family takes refuge in the basement—perhaps 22 persons, relatives, neighbors, servants.

The bustling ground floor is left to the Yankees. Below them the Carters are praying, for the captain on the gray; for the Cause he fights for. Has the advance been sounded? Is he there?

Is his mind rushing out, to the scenes of his childhood? The old brick smokehouse; the cotton gin, just across the Columbia turnpike—and then, to the east, a hedge of Osage orange, between the gin and the river . . . with the big green sticky balls they used to throw as children . . . and have to scrub their hands. Who ever thought this heaven on earth would come to this?

A moment now, and the lines will move toward the cannon—

It is 4 o'clock, Nov. 30. The November sun is setting in the amber afternoon.

"*Boys,*" says Gen. O. F. Strahl, "*this will be short but desperate.*"

A flag dips.

Hood, gaunt from his wounds, eyes flaming, looks like a patriarch as he hears the Rebel yell. "*Whooooooo-peee! Ee-YOW—whooo! Git 'em, boys, git 'em!*"

There they go!

ADVANCE GUARD. Toward Nashville streaked Schofield after the Battle of Franklin, leaving his wounded behind. Time was still precious. Get to safety!

THE CARTER HOUSE. A close-up of the south end, roughly sketched in the preceding field view.

From Harper's Weekly
GEN. JOHN M. SCHOFIELD

Courtesy the Carter House Association
CAPT. THEODORICK (Tod) CARTER

From Century War Book
GEN JACOB D. COX

"Last Act Of Friendship"
From Forbes, 30 Years After

HAS ALL THE story of American battles ever seen such a sight as this? Eighteen brigades of Confederates go storming across the open fields. Bands are playing. Bayonets glisten. Tattered battle flags are flying as the straight lines move.

The pounding feet disturb the rabbits and they hop up by the hundreds and go running across the fields. Up from the grass whir thousands of quail, circling, trying to settle back, then whirring on.

A rain of canister and shrapnel has begun. Men drop. Ranks close. They surge on. On and on the music plays, now dwindling away in the thunder, then pealing out again. From the enemy's outpost comes a burst of rifle fire. Its men are outnumbered. They have been ordered to stay until Hood might show signs of a major advance. Man, this is major! Run!

They're fleeing, streaking toward uncertain safety in the breastworks, and so great is their terror they won't stop there. They'll run on through the town to the river.

As the foremost Yankees run, their comrades in the entrenchments have to hold their fire to keep from hitting them. The Confederates rush closely up behind the racing men, using them as a screen, and are within a few yards of the works before the Yankee guns can blaze without destroying their own.

"The booming of cannon, the bursting of bombs, the rattling of musketry, the shrieking of shells, the whizzing of bullets, the shouting of the hosts, and the falling of men in their struggle for victory, all made a scene of surpassing terror and awful grandeur." So wrote Gen. George W. Gordon, who commanded a Rebel brigade.

A few minutes pass. The fighting is furious. The Rebels are at the entrenchments. They're up and over. They're behind the breastworks. They're seizing the battery. Is the whole Federal position threatened? It's hand to hand, in the yard of Capt. Carter's home. In the garden. Along the road. Around the gin.

Sources Of Old Pictures

MOST OF THE illustrations in Part III are individually credited. Many first appeared in *Harper's Weekly, Century Magazine* and *Punch.*

The Banner is especially grateful to Walter King Hoover of Smyrna who again has given us full access to his extensive Civil War library. From it came such rarities as the Franklin gin and Farragut in the rigging.

—Courtesy of the Tennessee Historical Society
THE BATTLE OF FRANKLIN, from a Kurz & Allison print. Schofield's fleeing wagons in the distance help capture the frenzy of battle, but the river was behind the Yankees, not before them.

The Carter house cellar, top photo, where 22 took refuge. The back porch, lower photo, where Federal officers rested before the battle.

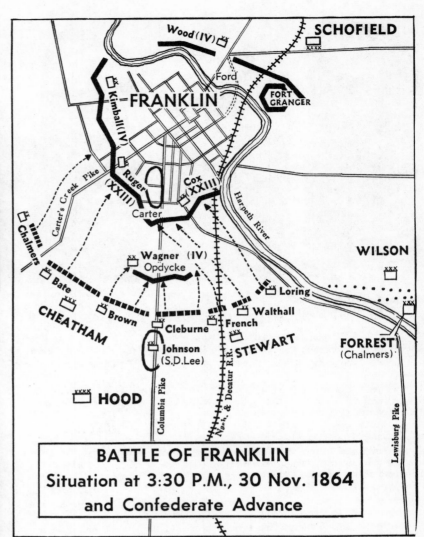

BATTLE OF FRANKLIN
Situation at 3:30 P.M., 30 Nov. 1864 and Confederate Advance

WATCH! From behind the house comes a reserve brigade of Federals. It is Col. Emerson Opdycke's. The Rebels are contesting every step. But they're being pushed back—

Opdycke's men will capture 400, and 19 battle flags. (He "saved the day," Gen. Thomas wrote.)

Cleburne's men are east of the gin. He's in trouble. Stewart, on his right, has been thrown back. Federal crossfire can now rake Cleburne's men. Cleburne's horse drops. Red Pepper has been shot from under him. Another is brought. It too is killed. Cleburne's saber is swinging. He goes on afoot. He's leading his men. He's nearing the works. A bullet hits him—how many bullets? He drops. They'll count 20 wounds.

Through the rolling smoke, Gen. John Adams is riding on. His horse looks almost white. What a target, out front, also leading his men. Look! He's leaping the Federal works. Guns roar at horse and rider. Adams pitches dying in the ditch.

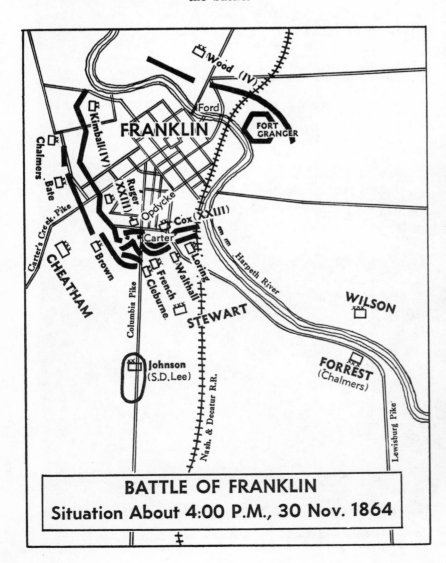

BATTLE OF FRANKLIN
Situation About 4:00 P.M., 30 Nov. 1864

CARNTON, the McGavock house at Franklin. On the back gallery shown here, five Confederate generals lay dead on the day after the battle. For their pictures, see next page.

REVEILLE. Dawn, above the dying. Dawn, above the dead. And on will go the struggle. Ahead is the Battle of Nashville.

"*YOU'RE TOO BRAVE a man to die,*" says a Yankee, putting cotton under his head.

"*Sir,*" said Adams, as life slipped away, "*it is the fate of a soldier to die for his country.*"

Did his magnificent pale horse hang high, kicking violently for an instant, until quickly dispatched? More than one account says so, and that it dropped with forefeet over the palisade.

West of the Columbia turnpike, Gen. John C. Brown's division goes tearing past the Carter house. The wild charge seems inspired. Capt. Carter is home at last, fighting the enemy in his own front yard.

He's near the barn. There's a rain of lead again, hitting horse and rider. Does the rider feel a sting, over one eye? Does the world swim suddenly, and his horse go wobbly? They're sinking . . . into the battle's swirl. It rolls on, and Gen. Gordon, one of Brown's brigade commanders, sweeps so deeply into the rear that he is captured. The Rebels strike more reserves but hold on.

Then slowly, foot by foot, the Rebels are pushed back. Back into the works through which they had battered. There they hold, and hold and hold. Men are dying by the score. Some have no room to fall. Dawn will find some standing in death, wedged upright between dead comrades. At places the bodies will be found seven deep.

Gettysburg saw no fighting as furious as this. Here neither side could budge far. This spot the Confederates will hold till the end of the battle. It forced the Federals to throw up a barricade, right across the Carter garden.

Enemy fire was now drubbing the Confederates from three sides. Gen. States Rights Gist and Gen. Strahl will perish in the ditch. Gen Brown and Gen. John C. Carter are both wounded. Carter's wound will prove mortal.

And Forrest, whose ideas have been swept aside, where is he? Well, a third of his force, with a shred of Forrest's first concept, gave Schofield one of his worst frights of the terrible 120 minutes. As arriving infantry had begun to deploy at the northern edge of Winstead Hill, Forrest had to move Buford and Jackson out to the right. This was to make room for the infantry and also to close the space between its line and the river. Chalmers and Lt. Col. Jacob B. Biffle, coming up Carter's Creek Pike, were assigned to duty on the left.

Schofield's own report of the battle shows that Forrest had the right notion in the first place:

"*A short time before the infantry attack commenced, the enemy's cavalry forced a crossing about three miles above Franklin, and drove back our cavalry, for a time seriously threatening our trains, which were accumulating on the north bank and moving toward Nashville.*"

"*I sent Gen. Wilson orders,*" Schofield continues, "*to drive the enemy back at all hazards . . . and moved a brigade to support him . . .*"

If Forrest had been permitted to strike full-force with his full flanking plan, might not the outcome of the Battle of Franklin have been different?

Meanwhile, on the right, Gen. Samuel G. French had forced some of the breastworks in front of the cotton gin. They couldn't be held. Gen. E. C. Walthall and Gen. William W. Loring's men charged through the bowdock hedge.

They met fire that was like sheet-lightning. It came from the new and deadly repeating rifles. Gen. John S. Casement's division had them. Death was walking. From the artillery came enfilading fire. The loss of life was sickening.

Cheatham and Stewart's men had reformed. They struck in front of the gin. Thrown back, they stormed again and again, into the withering musketry, grappling man to man across the parapet. The corps of Cheatham and Stewart fought the main battle at Franklin.

Some Union officers reported that before the afternoon was done, their lines received "*as many as 13 distinct shocks.*" One desperate charge was made as late as 7 p.m. Over dead and wounded the Rebels stumbled in the darkness and were again repelled.

Do you see that youngster over there, by that corpse-filled entrenchment—half crouched, half flat, hands busy with the guns? Well, he lacks a few days being 21. A few minutes ago he was passing up guns to Gen. Strahl, in that heroic general's last moments. The boy is Bedford County-born.

Years later, as S. A. Cunningham, widely known editor of the *Confederate Veteran Magazine,* he will write:

"*He (Gen. Strahl) said to one man, 'Have you shot any?' To another, 'Have you?' Then he simply pointed toward me. I arose, stepped onto the pile of the dead, resting my foot on the man killed while aiming my gun . . . A strong, large man took position to my right and the two of us fired for a long, long time . . . I became thirsty and as dry in my chest as dust from the street, and my shoulder was black for weeks from the jar of firing so many times.. The enfilade fire from the cotton gin was so severe that our dead were piled upon each other . . . and I said to Gen. Strahl, 'What had we better do?' His reply was instant, 'Keep firing.'*

"*. . . The soldier who had been firing by my side was shot and fell against me with azonizing groans . . . He sank to the pile of comrades back of him and, I presume, was soon dead. At the same instant the soldier was shot, Gen. Strahl was struck; and throwing up both hands above his head, almost to a clasp, he fell limber on his face, and I thought he was dead. Not so, however . . . He crawled away, his sword dangling against dead soldiers,*" in search of his successor in command. "*Members of his staff started to carry him to the rear but two bullets hit him, either one of which, it was said, would have proved fatal.*"

Fitful gunfire stabbed the night until 9 p.m. It would keep flaring until around midnight.

It is 11 p.m. Schofield orders his men to retire. Out they come, from entrenchments they have defended so courageously. Away they rush, across the Harpeth—rattling across the plank-covered railroad bridge Forrest had not been allowed to flank.

They go thundering along the highway toward the safety of fortified Nashville. Schofield is leaving behind his dead and most of his severely wounded. His casualties: about 2,320. Of these, around 1,000 are prisoners.

Schofield will call it a victory. It wasn't. The Battle of Franklin was a bloody draw, the bloodiest America ever saw.

GEN. PATRICK R. CLEBURNE

GEN. HIRAM BRONSON GRANBURY

GEN. O. F. STRAHL

GEN. STATES RIGHTS GIST

GEN. JOHN ADAMS

BETWEEN THE LINES DURING A TRUCE, by Gilbert Gaul.

From Century War Book, 1861-1865, Courtesy Appleton-Century

"THOMAS WANTED *Schofield to hold Hood at Franklin three days—and Schofield held him hardly three hours,*" Horn says in *The Army of Tennessee.* "*...Accurately, it should be classified as a drawn battle, a heartbreaking, murderous, unnecessary battle that settled nothing...*"

Nothing, except the near wrecking of Hood's army and impairment of confidence in Hood.

Confederate casualties, in killed, wounded and captured, were around 6,000. The loss in leadership was staggering. Two major generals, 10 brigadier generals and 53 regimental commanders were killed, wounded, missing or taken prisoner.

Dawn is breaking. Stretcher-bearers are moving across the fields. So are the good citizens of Franklin, trying to aid the injured. Among them are the sisters and the father of Capt. Carter. They carry a lantern.

Word has come that Tod is somewhere out on the field, among the dead and wounded. Near the barn they find him, shot through the head. His gray is dead nearby.

Tod is delirious. Gently they bear him home. The house is crowded with wounded. It has been written that Tod died 48 hours later.

Not far away, on the back gallery of the McGavock house, five generals lie dead, from the group which had sat down to breakfast at the Cheairs home. They are Gens. Cleburne, Gist, Adams, Strahl and Gen. H. B. Granbury. Someone will recall Cleburne's words about the little churchyard at Ashwood. He will be buried there temporarily.

Public and private buildings of Franklin will be crowded with the wounded. The women of Franklin will help tend friend and foe. Food will be scarce. But there will be plenty of soup which, flavored with red pepper, will taste mighty good to men still willing to live. Some, hideously maimed for life, will try to push their soup aside. For them the dream is ended.

But your dream, Hood—what now?

Hood sits his horse in the pale light, looking over the awful scene. Two long trenches are being dug, one for the blue, one for the gray.

The time has come. Straight on to fortified Nashville?

A more prudent man might have chosen to retreat to the Duck River or the Tennessee. Not Hood!

Then where advance? (*"I was never so anxious during the whole war, as at that time,"* Gen. Grant wrote 15 years later.) Grant feared that Hood might break for Louisville or Chicago.

The suggestion is made to Hood. He puts it aside. He will move on to Nashville, set his army down on the city's southern hills, and wait for the reinforced Thomas to come out and meet him, two to one.

Fantastic?

Some modern writers have said so, with benefit of hindsight.

"It cannot be too strongly emphasized, however," says Horn in *The Decisive Battle of Nashville, "that nobody thought it fantastic then."*

Fantastic, Middle Tennessee?
  No! I saw you lift your weary head
  To the windrows of my dead;
    To Hood, the headlong, dead-wrong man—
How mad could I be?
  Well, before you hiss
When you think of me,
  Remember this—
I was trying to set you free.

Fantastic, Nashville?
  No, not then!
When I saw you captive, trembling,
  At the end of Johnson's rope.
For I, Hood, the one-legged man,
  I and my ragged, shoeless men—
  I was your only hope.

Courtesy Minnesota Historical Society

"THE BATTLE OF NASHVILLE," by Howard Pyle. Shy's Hill looms in background. In the key attack are troops of the Fifth, Seventh, Ninth and 10th Minnesota Regiments (commanded by Col. Lucius F. Hubbard of Red Wing). In taking the hill, 302 Minnesotans were killed, wounded, or missing—Minnesota's heaviest loss of any Civil War engagement. The original oil hangs in the Governor's Reception Room at the Minnesota State Capitol, St. Paul.

From the Collections of the Library of Congress

Dramatic but inaccurate, this 1891 Kurz & Allison print, "The Battle of Nashville," shows Union horsemen and Negro infantrymen at the final breakup of Hood's left. But it didn't happen this way. Actually, when the left broke, Negro troops were about two-and-a-half miles away, near "Peach Orchard Hill"—where they had fought and died bravely, against Hood's right. And, when Hood's left lifted, the Union cavalrymen had dismounted and were fighting afoot.

This 1868 view shows the work of two notable architects—Tennessee's Capitol, the Yankee prize, which Hood in '64 hoped to reclaim, designed by William Strickland; and the old First Lutheran Church, one of the earliest buildings credited to Adolphus Heiman. Built about 1837 on Fifth Avenue for the congregation of the First Baptist Church, it was sold to the Lutherans in the 1880s.

The George Campbell house on Charlotte Avenue (old Cedar Street). It faced the Capitol's south portico. The pool is on the Capitol's grounds. In this commandeered house Gov. Andrew Johnson spent much time as Federal master of Tennessee, close to the safety of his stockade across the street. The house was then owned by Campbell's refugee daughter, Mrs. Richard S. Ewell, wife of the Confederate general. Later owners added mansard roof. Date of picture unknown.

—Courtesy Cook Collection, Valentine Museum, Richmond, Va.

John B. Hood
His dream: Set Nashville free!

WARTIME NASHVILLE. West portico of Capitol, showing Federal encampment to northwest (left) in vicinity of what is now Fisk University.

BRIGHT WAS THE DREAM. This picture of a fallen Confederate, perhaps the finest photographic shot of the war, is attributed to Thomas Roche, who once worked for the more famous Mathew Brady.

—Library of Congress

The CIVIL WAR In
MIDDLE TENNESSEE

PART IV—NOV. 30, 1864—APRIL 9, 1865

THE cannon were silent.

The Battle of Franklin was ending. It was night in Middle Tennessee, Nov. 30, 1864. Even nearby Nashville was yet to learn what had happened by the Harpeth River, where cowbells had tinkled in the early afternoon.

On the trampled meadows, moans quavered out of the gloom. Sometimes a man screamed, or prayed. Sometimes a wounded horse threshed, neighed, and lay still. Here and there gunfire still flashed. The bursts of light were coming farther apart.

The artillery of Gen. John B. Hood was arriving in full force . . . after the battle was over. All his guns, at last,

were up. Hood ordered that each should fire 100 rounds in the morning, into the Yankee works, before the Rebels should charge again.

Poor Hood! His guns would fire a few volleys at dawn. There would be no reply. The enemy would be gone, tearing up the road toward Nashville, through the wintry dawn . . . Just now—oh, for an hour of sleep . . . Sleep, Hood, if you can . . . Dream that you are capturing Nashville . . . and pushing on north to the Ohio . . . or that you are surging eastward to Richmond, joining Gen. Robert E. Lee and greeting the woman you love, she of the "angelic beauty," Sally (Buck) Preston, who has promised to marry you . . .

Will she marry you, really? Sally, the niece of Gen. Wade Hampton, who can pick and choose? She's wearing your diamond, yes. You're engaged. But will she marry a military failure, this daughter of Old South wealth? Or will you recoup your glory, Hood—at Nashville?

Gen. George H. Thomas

—National Archives

"Old Slow Trot," a descendant of Virginia's Huguenot Rochelles, found bitter heartbreak when he stuck by the Union. Disowned by his family, belittled by Grant, he was, nevertheless, one Union commander who can be charged with no defeat. Did some of his Yankee critics envy him? This seems certain. In Washington today, his statue faces South . . .

GEN. THOMAS' HEADQUARTERS in Nashville? Identity of this house is now sometimes debated. Nearly 40 years ago, in the 1920s, when The Banner ran this picture, no one seems to have challenged it as the old Cunningham house, where Thomas had his offices (at the present site of Cross Keys Restaurant). Many old timers were then living. Compare this with a later picture, presumably of same house, in Part II. Could remodeling have wrought such a change? Today, some people wonder.

IF SALLY really loved a man, then he might well call himself *"happy . . . even though he lost name, fame, life and limb."* So Mrs. Mary Boykin Chesnut had written only two weeks before in her journal, later published as the matchless *Diary from Dixie.*

Well, Hood, you have one leg left, and one good arm. You'd better succeed at Nashville, where the jittery Yankees are waiting but unready, under sturdy but imperturbable Gen. George H. Thomas, behind a fortified line that swings from the Cumberland River above the town to the Cumberland below it.

How many Yankees behind that line? Not enough, Hood, at this moment. Not enough for their peace of mind. Not crack troops. They're largely quartermaster and garrison troops. And pick-ups from scattered outposts, hoofing it in. Many more are enroute, plenty of them, tougher men. From St. Louis by steamboats. And a hodgepodge, including Negro troops, from Chattanooga by train, under Gen. James B. Steedman.

"Thomas . . . has only to ring the bell and call for more," Mrs. Chesnut wrote: *"Grant can get all he wants, both for himself and Thomas."*

Thomas has been ringing the bell for days, Hood, ever since it became clear that Nashville was your destination. Horses and men! Horses, men and mules! That's what the Thomas bell has been clanging. They will play the decisive role in the Battle of Nashville, and Thomas knows it. He's learned it from the Southerners.

In particular, he has learned it from his archfoe, Gen. Nathan Bedford Forrest, the cavalry wizard son of Middle Tennessee, now with the Army of Tennessee at Franklin.

But it's time, Hood, not men; time, not horses, that is about to run out on the Yanks at Nashville, with you only 18 miles down the road. They don't know you've met disaster at Franklin.

To relieve Thomas, the Yankee veterans of Gen. A. J. Smith are having to come all the way from the Kansas border, all across Missouri, boarding steamboats at St. Louis for Nashville. The question: Will they arrive in time to help Thomas? Will you, Hood, reach Nashville first, and free the city?

It is not yet 9 o'clock in crowded, gas-lit Nashville which, at the beginning of the war, had a population of 30,000. Now it is packed with 100,000. Men and women of every calling, high and low, including a vice president-elect, Andrew Johnson, military governor of the Yankee-held State of Tennessee.

Excitement is high and rising. It is said that Gov. Johnson's nerves are getting edgy again behind his cedar-post stockades on Capitol Hill.

The Capitol itself has become a citadel. Within its massive lower stories thousands of men can maintain themselves against the enemy. So the Yankees think. They've even provided for siege. (*"Cisterns within the building held a bountiful supply of water,"* Col. Henry Stone would write years later, in *The Century Magazine* for August, 1887.)

—Courtesy State Library and Archives

The St. Cloud Hotel (where Harveys now stands), at Fifth Avenue and Church Street. Here Thomas lived.

—Library of Congress

Gen. John M. Schofield

GEN. THOMAS IS worried but calm. All day in Nashville his hat has been pulled down over his bushy-browed, deep blue eyes, as was his habit when troubled. His troubles are many. They may get worse, terribly and suddenly worse. All depends upon how rapidly reinforcements can reach him, and whatever may be happening at Franklin.

Thomas is waiting for news. Telegraphic communication is imperfect. He wanted Gen. John M. Schofield to hold Hood at Franklin three days. Schofield said he couldn't. That was hours ago. Thomas then ordered him to fall back to Nashville.

What if Schofield can't fall back? What if he's cut off at the Harpeth?

And what of Gen. Smith, who had left St. Louis Nov. 24 on transports loaded down with 14,000 men for Nashville? About 5,000 had arrived several hours ago, but not in time to get to Franklin. The remainder, 9,000 more, were somewhere on the Cumberland. But where?

If! If!

Thomas didn't know that the bitterest and bloodiest of all American battles, in terms of time and numbers, had just been fought, and that dead men were lying seven deep in places, in the Middle Tennessee starlight.

He didn't know that the Williamson County earth was dark with the blood of more than 5,000 Rebels and 1,200 Yanks, and that Schofield, with his flowing beard, was even then burning the wind toward Nashville, with nearly 800 wagons thundering behind him, and 20,000 men thumping behind the wagons—all pouring toward what they hoped was the safety of fortified Nashville.

Not all the city worried. Nighttime Nashville, on its tinsel surface, was feeling safe. Live tonight! Theaters and hotels were crowded. A circus was in town. The patrons? A variety indeed.

The city's sons are in the armies. Their families are at home. Many a door is secured. On the streets are many strangers. Some have legitimate business. Many do not.

Speculative talk is not confined to barracks. What will Hood do? Civilians are having their say, sometimes gleefully, at Gov. Johnson's expense.

Nerves sorta jumpy, Guv'nor? About that big state convention you Yankee politicians are gonna hold—for us Tennesseans—in Nashville, on Dec. 19? A real shindig, hmm? With you Yanks re-making the whole state government, just as you would have it?

Well, Guv'nor, hadn't you better postpone that big convention, till you see who's gonna be runnin' this here town on Dec. 19? 'Cause hit might be a peg-legged man named Hood, and not you or Gen. Thomas at all. And Hood mightn't like having Ole Mummy Face around.

"Ole Mummy Face" was "Parson" Brownlow (William Gannaway Brownlow), an East Tennessee Unionist of cadaverous face and fierce hatred for Rebels. (He had never served any church circuit longer than one year.)

As an acid-penned journalist of vivid phrases, Brownlow's cry for vengeance would hit the jackpot of Radical politics. (He will become governor after Johnson goes to Washington to be sworn in as vice president.)

But if Hood comes . . . Guv'nor, reckon you politicians gonna like hot lead, and hit a-flyin'?

Not all laughed. (But the Unionist convention would be postponed until Jan. 8 . . .)

Grim-faced officers hurried in and out of the St. Cloud Hotel where Thomas was staying, at Church and Summer streets (Fifth Avenue, where Harveys now stands). His headquarters, however, were in the commandeered Cunningham mansion (where the downtown Cross Keys Restaurant is located).

The officers were full of questions. Any word of Smith? No. And Schofield? Nothing yet.

The wintry wind, stirring the manes of the waiting horses, wandered on across the street into a stone-cutter's yard at the northeast corner, where tombstones were made. Some of the stones, recently completed, stood tall and ghostly in the gaslight, waiting for somebody's grave.

In far-off Virginia, the wind was stirring through the branches of a stately oak of almost perfect symmetry. It towered above a big white house, in once-prosperous Southampton County where Negroes outnumbered whites almost three to two.

Here lived two maiden sisters, Miss Judith and Miss Fannie Thomas. They were sisters of Gen. Thomas, and they may have been reading a newspaper. If so, the news for the South was grave. Gen. U. S. Grant was still besieging Petersburg, the key to Richmond. The siege had begun in June. Soon Lee would have to spread a 37-mile line before Petersburg. To man it, he would have only 59,000 men, hungry and shivering, to face Grant's 110,000, better fed and warmer. How could the line hold forever?

Gen. William Tecumseh Sherman was somewhere deep in Georgia, with

Andrew Johnson, Vice President-Elect

60,000 Yankees, swinging toward the sea. When he reached it, would he not swing north, to join Grant? If this happened, and no aid reached Lee, then what? Would not both Petersburg and Richmond have to be evacuated? But Hood might come—

And Hood, gallant Hood, he of the dangling arm, the missing leg and dauntless courage—Hood was heading North! Sister, North! Do you hear?

Sister! To Chicago! Or Louisville! Or eastward to join Lee, through Murfreesboro or Nashville—

Nashville . . . a silence fell. The sisters knew their brother was in Nashville, the commanding general. They did not call his name.

They did not want to hear his name called, for he had cast his lot with the Union. A Virginian, their brother—of this house, Thomaston, fighting with the Yankees! Oh, shame!

They had turned his picture to the wall on April 13, 1861—the day after Confederate guns in Charleston Harbor had opened fire on Yankee-held Fort Sumter. That was the day on which Thomas had sent them word of his decision to stick with the Union.

And turned to the wall his picture would remain, 25 years after Appomattox, for the sisters in the big house would never forgive. To them, their brother was dead.

Their house stood in the "Black Belt," so called because of its many Negroes. The "belt" extended across the nearby state line into North Carolina, a fertile land of apple orchards and apple brandy; of cotton and corn and tobacco.

Gov. William G. Brownlow
*His private life seems
to have been flawless.
His public life drew
hatred.*

Corner of Fifth Avenue and Church Street, as it looked in 1868, showing a stone-cutter's yard and to-day's Downtown Presbyterian Church.

HURRY! Yankees rushed Negroes into a hasty strengthening of their lines as Hood approached the city.

ACROSS IT, in 1831, had rolled the Nat Turner Insurrection, when 60 slaves, loaded with brandy mixed with gunpowder, had suddenly used scythes, axes, knives and clubs to slaughter 55 whites, men, women, children and infants.

The sisters had survived it because their mother, warned by faithful slaves, had halted their fleeing carriage and taken through the woods to the safety of the nearest town, Jerusalem (now Courtland).

The sisters remembered. But it hadn't been enough for their brother George who, even afterwards, had continued to teach the Negroes things he'd learned at school and church . . . against his mother's wishes. He was independent, had always been.

He had gone to West Point. He had married a Northern woman (who denied, however, that she influenced his mind). He had been long away—too long, perhaps. Twenty-five years away from Virginia, when the Civil War broke out. In those years, he had spent not more than 18 months at home.

But Thomas remembered his family. Even in war-time his gifts and letters kept coming. "Miss Judith" and "Miss Fannie" returned them unopened. Nor had they written to him since, except to suggest that he change his name.

Gen. Thomas had not changed his name. He had made it famous in 1863 as the "Rock of Chickamauga," for his immortal stand while Gen. William S. Rosecrans fled. Thomas' troops fondly called him "Old Pap." He was steady, thorough, deliberate. Rashness was not in his nature.

Rarely did he urge his horse to a trot, perhaps because of his very nature, and perhaps, too, because of twinges from an old spinal injury. Sometimes he was called "Old Slow Trot."

His belittlers in Washington, including Grant, would be known to say he was "too slow to fight, too brave to run away."

But Thomas had a habit of winning, which couldn't be said of many a Northern general. Middle Tennessee had heard of him long before Sherman, in Atlanta, took the best 60,000 troops available and headed on his March to the Sea, sending Thomas back to Nashville to do the best he could with whatever troops he could scrape together in a hurry-up, catch-as-catch-can fashion.

Middle Tennesseans had first heard of Thomas nearly three years ago, in January, 1862, from Fishing Creek, across the Cumberland in Kentucky, when the Rebels had been thrown back into Tennessee and had come straggling down through Chestnut Mound and Lebanon, from the tragic failure which had cost the life of Nashville's beloved Felix Zollicoffer.

They had heard of Thomas at the Battle of Murfreesboro and resoundingly from Chickamauga whence he had emerged with the golden nickname of "The Rock." It fitted.

Some people said he looked "like a mountain." Others, "a cannon." Through the years many had commented that Thomas "looked like George Washington."

And all had heard of Thomas at Shiloh where Grant, walking off with jolted glory, nevertheless didn't walk off with the approval of Gen. Henry W. Halleck, who, as field commander, for a while thereafter favored Thomas and clipped Grant's wings. This resulted in a "coolness at Corinth" between Grant and Thomas. The "coolness" remained.

President Lincoln, however, saw Grant more brightly. Later, perhaps, Lincoln saw Thomas through the eyes of Grant, Secretary of War Edwin M. Stanton, and others. Once, when discussing promotions, Lincoln is rumored to have said, "Let the Virginian wait."

So Thomas had fought, and fought, ably and with distinction; and yet at Nashville on the night of Nov. 30, he was still a brigadier general of the Regular Army, which he had been since late in 1863.

Prior to that he had been a colonel in the Regular Army until August, '61. Then he had been made a brigadier general of volunteers, which meant a salary of $124 a month—for the two years of bitter fighting in which his deeds had lent luster to the Union cause.

But the rank also entitled him to "12 rations a day, forage for five horses, food and uniform for three servants, $30 for fuel, $80 for quarters, $90 for transportation of baggage and $15 monthly for stationery." (So Francis F. McKinney tells us in his excellent biography of Thomas, Education in Violence.)

Thomas was Regular Army, a field-trained and seasoned cavalryman who had studied under the famous Dennis Hart Mahan at West Point.

Later, as a West Point instructor in artillery and cavalry, Thomas had tried to pass on some of those teaching to his students, including Hood and Schofield.

Both were out there in the night; both in their early 30s, both with flowing beards as was the fashion, and both ambitious—Hood, a blue-eyed Kentucky giant, impetuous and rash, a fighter; Schofield shorter, stocky, round-bodied, shrewd, from Ohio. Both had their eyes on Nashville.

Thomas had taught them in 1853. They had been friends, each with a habit of acquiring demerits. Hood, a "jolly good fellow," had been a mediocre student. Schofield, on graduation, had stood in the forefront of his class in tactics and he thought he understood the mental processes of Hood.

It hadn't looked that way a few hours ago, before the slip-through at Spring Hill, when Schofield had almost blundered into extinction by letting Hood cut him off. Rarest luck had saved Schofield.

No doubt Thomas would feel relieved when Schofield got back to Nashville with his hide intact. (Schofield had a reputation for looking after his hide.)

Soon Thomas would learn that Schofield had stayed on the north side of the Harpeth River during the Battle of Franklin, although in top command of his own XXIII Corps and also the IV Corps. (In contrast, Gen. David S. Stanley, of the IV, had been wounded in the thick of the fray.)

In this troubled hour, Thomas may have recalled Hood as a somewhat rough-and-ready cadet, not intellectual, who nevertheless had developed into a magnificent personality. Thomas also may have guessed that Hood, his foe in war, was perhaps a better friend, at heart, than Schofield the clever ally.

Why? The trouble reached 'way back, to West Point days when Thomas had taught and Schofield had come close to being dismissed.

In fact, dismissal had been ordered, because of some blackboard obscenities Schofield had used in coaching others. However, the case had been reconsidered; Schofield remained and was commissioned. But Thomas had been one of two (out of 13) who had not voted for remission of the sentence.

It's nearly 9 p.m. At last, Schofield's telegram is arriving: Hood has struck. Hood has been thrown back with heavy losses. Nashville now knows of Franklin.

Relief rolled over Thomas' face. His "hat was up" when Col. James F. Rustling (later a general) dropped by from the quartermaster's office where Gen. James L. Donaldson was struggling with the problem of getting more mules.

Thomas shows the telegram to Rustling who is going to a party and forget it all . . . if he can. He will return around midnight.

There's a stir at the St. Cloud's door. Schofield and Gen. Thomas J. Wood have arrived from Franklin.

With no demonstration, Thomas congratulates Schofield. He tells him he has done well. Wood will eventually succeed the wounded Stanley as commander of the IV Corps.

"I did not feel very grateful to him," Schofield wrote of Thomas' greeting. Is there a chip on the younger man's shoulder? After all, it's been a desperate day. No doubt he expected more praise than he got.

Schofield knows the gravity of this hour. He knows the Battle of Nashville must be won—for more reasons than one. He knows that, for the Union, money is about to run out.

Schofield knows the floating of war bonds is no longer easy, that the price of gold is falling. The U. S. Treasury is running low. (Both Schofield and Gen. James H. Wilson would write about it.)

Just now they're keeping their mouths shut. But Schofield has the word from Secretary Stanton, that the United States doesn't have the "financial strength" to make "further military use" of all the soldiers already on the rolls.

Does Rustling know all this? Maybe not. He knows the mules must be obtained. He had written home, "Trust in God, and keep your powder dry . . ."

The party ends. Rustling is on his way back to the St. Cloud. Then he hears it, long, low sounds from the river. Whooo-ooh! Whoooo-oooh! Steamboats! Many steamboats, tooting into Nashville.

—Library of Congress

Looking southwest at Fort Negley on first hill, with Fort Casino nearby, pillbox-like, almost over smokestack (of a large gun factory). The present Children's Museum in left foreground.

Looking southeast from Capitol, 1868. Towers of Downtown (First) Presbyterian Church stand boldly forth near center with old Masonic Theater nearby, left, and the Maxwell House next, toward river. Large, dark spire, right, is old McKendree Church, with cupola of old Christ Church, Episcopal, extreme right. Big building with turret, distant right, near skyline, is old Howard School. Foreground shows intersection of High and Cedar streets (now Sixth and Charlotte avenues).

IT'S SMITH'S veterans! All the way from Missouri! Rustling goes rushing to Thomas: *"Smith's all right—"*

There's rejoicing. In almost no time the door flies open and Gen. Smith comes striding in, a big rugged Westerner.

For Thomas, the tide has turned.

Thomas throws his arms around the grizzled old warrior and hugs him. What a trek, what a voyage—from the Kansas border to Nashville!

Thomas can face Hood now. Schofield safe; Smith arriving; Steedman to come! Hooray! Now for horses, and—Rustling, get me mules! ..

Maps of Nashville are spread on the floor. Down on their knees go the four generals—Thomas, Schofield, Smith and Wood—studying the positions they must take.

Schofield will occupy the left of the outer line, extending his men to the Nolensville Pike. (For the actual battle, Schofield will be pulled from left and used near center.)

Smith's men? Occupy the right, northeast of Harding Road. Wood, now commanding the IV Corps? Take the center, out Belmont way. Steedman, when he arrives? Fill the space between Schofield and the river above the town.

So Rustling leaves them, at the heart of town. It's midnight. Through the edge of town runs a seven-mile fortified line, bristling with 20 batteries, manned by quartermaster troops and encompassing vast supplies and hospitals.

Seasoned men are now at hand to man the bigger line that's being built.

The clock hand moves. It's early morning, Dec. 1, 1864.

Let Hood come.

Dawn is breaking east of Franklin. A tall, gaunt man of iron-gray hair is thrusting his feet into the stirrups of a big iron-gray gelding. Gen. Forrest is mounting his warhorse King Philip, which has learned to hate the color blue.

In the pale winter morn they seem one, big horse and rider, 6-foot-2 and Middle Tennessee born, who one day will be called the greatest leader of mounted troops the English-speaking world has ever known.

Forrest is thinking of the fleeing Yanks, miles up the road toward Nashville. Nearly all night they've been in flight. He gallops away in pursuit, eastward on the Murfreesboro Pike toward Arrington, then across to the Wilson Pike, heading for Brentwood.

Forrest's cavalry has not suffered such shattering losses at Franklin as has the infantry. But the chase will be in vain. Schofield is far ahead, perhaps already entering Nashville. A brave and able young Yankee, only 27—Gen. James H. Wilson, Thomas' new cavalry chief—is fending Forrest off. Wilson's men have Spencer repeating carbines, and they're deadly.

Forrest can do little more than harass the rear guard. That young Wilson (newly come from the Army of the Potomac, by way of Sherman in Georgia) will bear watching!

Before noon, Schofield's men were pouring into the safety of the city. Thomas placed them on the left of his incomplete outer line. They flopped on the ground, thankful to be alive. They will sleep nearly 24 hours. Wilson's men were assigned to the area between Schofield and the river above the town.

It's noon. The now-cheerful Thomas is establishing his big line on the hills in front of the city, under the direction of Gen. Zebulon B. Tower, U.S. Army Engineers.

More reinforcements were arriving, six hours after Schofield and Stanley. This was Steedman, with more than 5,000 from Chattanooga—parts of four corps, plus one or two Negro brigades. Soon, two days hence, Steedman's men will take Wilson's place by the river. Wilson will move over to Edgefield (the present East Nashville). Plenty men now for the big line!

Beginning about where General Hospital now stands, the line swings across eight highways that fan out from town toward Lebanon, Murfreesboro, Nolensville and Franklin, and on across Granny White, Hillsboro, Harding and Charlotte pikes. It ends on a knoll by the Cumberland River (at the present site of A&I University).

Down at the wharves, Smith's doughty men, guarded by gunboats, are pounding ashore. Other troops have arrived from outposts. The garrison at Murfreesboro is the only big one Thomas hasn't called in.

It's heavily fortified. Thomas may use it, should Hood try to swing east, to join Lee. (Does Hood know the Yankee strength of Murfreesboro? He does not.)

By sunset, more shovels were swinging on the long Nashville line. Citizens and slaves had been impressed to help.

"We may expect one of the most decisive battles of the war," the *Nashville Daily Union* was crowing, *"one we trust will make a quietus of this adventurer and his hordes of traitors."*

Dirt is flying. The big Federal line is stretching in a halfmoon from the river on the northeast to the river on the northwest. Its guns will face two creek valleys, Brown's Creek to the south, Richland Creek to the west. The sun is sinking.

On the hills beyond the creeks, Rebel campfires will be twinkling by tomorrow night. Awaiting them, Forrest encamped within sight of the city, from Nolensville Pike on the right to Granny White on the left. Gen. Stephen D. Lee tented farther south.

In the fading light, Forrest can see the Capitol, where the Yankee vice president-elect holds forth as military governor of captive Tennessee; a most uneasy man and next in line for the White House, who has said of Secession leaders: *"They ought to be hung! Treason must be made odious; traitors must be punished and impoverished . . .*

To thunder with Johnson! No wonder he kept such a "bodyguard" of men. He'd better stay behind his stockade!

Dark laboring figures are moving on Nashville's busy hilltops. The forts are there, linked by breastworks, to protect this growing host of well-fed men, soon to number 50,000 to 60,000?

There's Fort Negley on St. Cloud Hill, where Nashvillians in happier days had spread their picnic lunches, under the beautiful oaks. Now the oaks are gone, for Federal firewood, headlogs, stockades. How treeless Nashville is becoming!

There's Fort Morton, high on a hill west of Franklin Road, near South Street, and Fort Houston, deep behind the inner works (where 16th Avenue today intersects Division Street).

These forts are big, dating from the early occupation. The guns of Negley and Morton control a blockhouse. It's called Fort Casino, on Casino Hill (site of the present city reservoir on Eighth Avenue S.). Others are under construction.

In North Nashville there's Hill 210 (where Washington Junior High School stands). It can shelter 15 guns.

North of 210 is Fort Gillem (later called Fort Sill) with 13 guns (on the present site of Fisk University). This is a redoubt 120 feet square with 6-foot walls of stone, named for Gen. Alvin C. Gillem who directed its construction—the same man whose men had shot Gen. John Hunt Morgan in a rainy Greeneville garden. (See Part III.)

—U.S. Signal Corps photo, Brady Collection, National Archives

Gen. D. S. Stanley

—Harper's Pictorial History of the Civil War

Gen. A. J. Smith

—National Archives

Gen. James H. Wilson

—National Archives

Gen. T. J. Wood

Gallant Hood, the Hope of Nashville

NORTH OF GILLEM is Fort Garesche, near Hyde's Ferry on the Cumberland, with 14 guns and three magazines. It's named for Col. Julius Peter Garesche, whose head had been swept away by a cannon ball in the Battle of Murfreesboro, in 1862 (just after he had opened his prayer book, before his first engagement).

Between Forts Garesche and Gillem is Battery Donaldson (later to be called Fort W. D. Whipple). It's now named for Thomas' busy quartermaster, Gen. Donaldson (Rustling's boss) who is trying to find all those mules.

And where are the mules of Tennessee, which used to lead the nation in their production? (Don't be foolish! Where are the mares to foal them? Our mares and horses were taken long ago, for war use, by friend and foe.)

Other Yankee troubles were growing. Their new recruiting system has been pouring riffraff into the army. Some recruits were diseased, depraved, criminal. Kentucky's slaves were being enlisted. Kentucky was furious. The state, always divided by war sentiment, had been placed under martial law by Lincoln.

Kentucky bordered Ohio, and Ohio's borders were nervous. They felt threatened by Kentucky. The north has long been sick of the struggle. Failure at Nashville could well set off the old cry: *Peace! Set the South free . . .*

(Oh, what of tomorrow? Don't think of that. Just keep on breathing.)

It is late in the afternoon just north of Franklin. Shadows are falling upon a marching army of ragged men. Hood is starting his remaining 23,000 on their way to Nashville's outskirts. An army with thousands of barefooted men, but one of the fightingest America has ever known.

Supper? On what? Middle Tennessee has been ravaged for years. Bread, you say? Mills have been burned. Find some corn? All right, parch it. Three ears has sometimes been the ration. Or grate the corn and make some meal. (Sometimes the Rebs had only cornmeal for breakfast.)

Hats? Who needs one? (When there's a Yankee to stomp, in your own wheat field?) Shoes? Well, brother, if you must cover your feet, cut off your coat sleeves, stick your feet inside, tie up the ends to shield your toes, and tie the armholes to your ankles. (If it gives your shoulders a sorta "ball gown look," who gives a hoot?)

No matter. This is the Army of Tennessee, infinitely brave, infinitely adaptable, and often badly led. If anybody fools with it, he's a-gonna *"get his comb cut."*

Somebody was a-gonna *"go up"* (one of the most frequent of Civil War terms). To *"go up"* meant to die, or just to be put out of action, by wounds or capture. (*Where's Johnny? "Gone up."*)

Hood, strapped to his saddle, was riding toward Nashville with his dream *"gone up."* The guns at Franklin had ripped it. Time had run against him. There could be no lunge now toward the Ohio, across cattle-rich Kentucky, unless reinforcements reached him from Texas. He must go it alone, with what he has.

There were some in Charleston who said, *"Hood will be rash enough for you."* The remark also turned up among the ladies, intrigued by his career and romance. Would there be a wedding?

Some said Sally's patrician family objected. No, said others, they are *"meek as mice. But they know he is unfit for his high command, and they are frightened."* To others, Sally would be *"throwing herself away on a maimed man."* The retort: *"Nonsense! She will love and honor him fourfold, for his honorable wounds."* (So Mrs. Chesnut wrote.)

There would be no reinforcements for Hood, in love or war. Didn't he guess? The Confederacy had long since been scraping the bottom for manpower. Hood wasn't a man to retreat.

"I therefore determined to move upon Nashville," he later wrote, *"to accept the chance of reinforcements from Texas, and, even at the risk of an attack . . . by overwhelming numbers,"* to take the chance. He was *"grasping at the last straw,"* as he himself put it.

Was the Confederacy heading for the *"last ditch"*?

Ah, Time! At Tuscumbia on the Tennessee River Hood had lost three weeks. There had been bad weather, a wait for supplies, for Forrest, pontoons, other factors. Finally he had crossed with 38,000 men. This included Forrest's 8,000 horsemen. Suddenly, Hood's march into Middle Tennessee had begun to burn the wind.

On he'd come, after Schofield, and things had looked squally indeed for the Yankees on Nov. 24, when Forrest had stood facing Columbia, almost on Schofield's coattail.

That day, Thomas had wired Grant the raw facts:

"All my cavalry was dismounted to furnish horses . . . which went with Sherman . . . (on the March to the Sea). *Horses* (in replacement) *are arriving slowly . . . The moment I get my cavalry, I will march against Hood."*

Gen. Nathan Bedford Forrest

Gen. U. S. Grant

Gen. William T. Sherman

SO SMITH had been yanked to Nashville, from away out West toward Kansas, and the mad scramble had begun, in hindsight, to get Thomas ready for Hood.

Worse still, Sherman had taken along, on his March to the Sea, Thomas' own elite XIV Corps, over Thomas' protest. *"Too compact and reliable"* to leave behind, said Sherman. He wanted it himself.

Sherman was top commander in the West. He had his way. He was palsy-walsy with Grant. Thomas wasn't. The breach would widen. Sherman didn't help pull Grant and Thomas closer together.

"As fast as Thomas wrote down the specifications for his (Tennessee) campaign, Sherman sought to make an ambiguous settlement between the divergent views of Thomas and Grant." So says McKinney.

Sherman picked the best, in men and horses. He sent Thomas cavalrymen without horses. He sent Thomas what has sometimes been called the "culls."

Not all were such. Sherman had sped Schofield and Stanley toward Nashville as things turned scorching hot, but the near-fatal race had taken an enormous toll in horses. Survivors needed days of rest. Some had been shod with pocketknives. (The best of the horses were now clopping serenely through Georgia, an almost undefended land.)

In taking his pick, Sherman overlooked one ace. This was Wilson. To lead his cavalry from Atlanta to the sea, Sherman had chosen the veteran "Irish madcap," Gen. Judson Kilpatrick. Back to Thomas in Tennessee Sherman sent Wilson.

An accidental blessing for Thomas? Yes, it would last beyond the grave. In Wilson, Thomas found a friend not sunk in apple-polish.

When Grant yowled and·howled at Thomas in the hectic days ahead, the cocky cavalryman from Shawneetown, Ill., would stand on the side of "Old Slow Trot," unawed by the powers that be. (After death claimed Thomas, and highly placed Yankee personages tried to damn him with faint praise, Wilson would snatch up their words, tear them to tatters and throw them back into some famous faces.)

"I have balanced all the figures well," Sherman had contentedly wired Halleck, now Federal chief-of-staff, on Nov. 11, just before heading for the sea. *"I am satisfied that Thomas has in Tennessee a sufficient force for all probabilities."*

Balanced? Horsefeathers! Sherman had taken the best and left Thomas in the lurch.

McKinney, citing the telegram, comments: *"It would hardly seem possible that Sherman was deliberately stirring up trouble between Grant and Thomas but he (Sherman) marched out of the combat zone leaving the distinct impression in Grant's mind that he did not agree with Thomas and in Thomas' mind that he did not agree with Grant."*

Near-panic had come of it. Only in the nick of time had infantry arrived for Thomas. He still needed thousands of horses and mules, saddles, hours of blacksmithing, tons of forage and plenty of time for broken-down horses to munch. Lacking transportation, Thomas hadn't marched anywhere.

It was Hood who had done the marching and who, by morning, would be breathing down Yankees necks at Nashville.

In *Steamboatin' on the Cumberland*, Judge Byrd Douglas says, *"Grant, it is now known, had completely misunderstood Hood's campaign from its inception and so had Sherman, whose obsession was his 'March to the Sea.' Furthermore, Grant, although fully advised, failed to analyze the situation at Nashville after the Battle of Franklin."* Of mules and horses, Douglas says, *"There was not even a (spare) mule to be found in Middle Tennessee, let alone a horse."*

So Washington remained in a sweat. It didn't know how crippling had been the blow to Hood at Franklin. It didn't know his infantry now numbered 23,000 or 24,000. It thought Forrest had a stronger force. It knew that in just 10 days "Peg-leg" Hood had shoved the Yankee line back, from the Tennessee to the Duck River, then to the Cumberland and — would the Ohio be next?

Washington didn't know Hood meant to take his stand and wait. What if he by-passed Nashville? What if he crossed and swung on toward Louisville and Chicago?

That is what Grant would have done. ("If I had been in Hood's place," Grant later wrote, *"I would have gone to Louisville and on North until I came to Chicago."*)

Hood might have done just that, had he been able to cut off Schofield from Nashville. Perhaps nothing then could have stopped Hood short of the Ohio. The hour had passed. Hood had lost the initiative.

The foe was now united. Nashville was becoming the most strongly fortified city in America, with the exceptions of Richmond and Washington. The number of Federals would grow until, on Dec. 10, Thomas' report would show 71,842 equipped for duty. All would not take part in the battle. Not all were in Nashville. Many were unassigned or reserves. On the same day, Hood would report only 23,053.

Hood couldn't attack such numbers. He was arriving too late, too weak. His

—Courtesy Lanier Merritt

The old Tennessee Bank, where the First American Bank now stands, on Union Street. Federals called it their "Pay Department." More than one Yankee general knew that money was running painfully short.

—Courtesy Lanier Merritt
Gen. H. B. Lyon

—U. S. Signal Corps Photo, Brady Collection, National Archives
Gen. Edwin M. McCook

tattered standard would attract few recruits. Only a dribble of supplies could reach him over the little railway from Decatur, Ala.

Thomas had acres of bulging warehouses. Steamers and trains had brought a wealth of supplies. They kept coming. (The North was proud of how well it had fed its soldiers at Thanksgiving.) The Yanks were living high.

Hood hoped to interfere. He hoped to raid the Yank-held railroad leading through Murfreesboro to Chattanooga. He hoped to hit their lines to Kentucky.

Already, from Paris, in West Tennessee, Hood had readied Gen. Hylan B. Lyon for a light and flying cavalry raid toward Clarksville and on into Southern Kentucky.

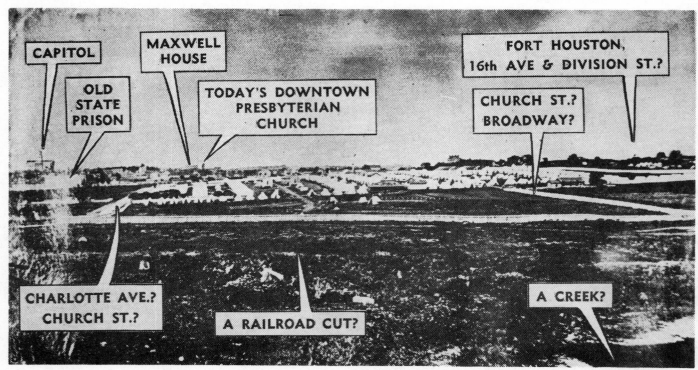

—Courtesy Lanier Merritt

THE ENEMY ENCAMPED. This old picture sets off much argument as to exact locale. The view is due east, so you see only one tower of Downtown Presbyterian Church. Old state prison, left, stood on a large tract between Church Street and Charlotte Avenue, near 16th Avenue. The mansion at skyline, right center? Some ask, is it Rokeby—which stood on today's Grand Avenue?

—From **Old Glory, The True Story**

Old steamboat landing, at the "foot of Broad." Here supplies poured in for Gen. Thomas.

—From **That Devil Forrest** by John A. Wyeth, Harper & Brothers

Col. D. C. Kelley
The "Fightin' Parson"

LYON'S RAID, like Hood's Tennessee campaign, is coming too late. But Lyon will draw 3,000 or more Federal horsemen away from Nashville in pursuit.
"*Move upon him wherever found,*" Thomas will order Gen. E. M. McCook. (Wilson preferred to keep the 3,000 to face Hood, but Wilson wasn't giving the orders.)

Cross the Tennessee and the Cumberland, Hood ordered Lyon. Capture Clarksville, cut rails and telegraph wires. Set idle mills to grinding for the Rebs.

It is a big order for just 700 recruits on horseback and 100 more afoot. They have only two artillery pieces (12-pound howitzers). Most of Lyon's men have been in the army only a few days. His shivering greenhorns won't capture Clarksville, but their raid will be amazingly well-executed.

Lyon's raid will seem, in a way, just a firecracker on a Sunday morning. But news of his raid will go off in Washington like a psychological blockbuster, because it wakes old fears.

It smacks of the massive raid which Grant and Thomas had feared would be made far earlier by Forrest.

Hood, coming up the wintry road, has an additional plan. He means to blockade the Cumberland near Nashville. But cross it? Not now. Gunboats, including ironclads, are patrolling the river—the Carondolet, Brilliant, Fair Play, Moose, Neosha, Silver Lake, Reindeer and the Victory.

As the sun went down, Thomas wired Halleck: "*If Hood attacks me here, he will be more seriously damaged than he was yesterday. If he remains until Wilson gets equipped, I can whip him.*"

Thomas was far from ready to deliver an offensive. At 48, he was quite aware of the redoubtable Forrest. He meant to be well-prepared before riding out to meet such dynamite on horseback, and said so:

"*I have two ironclads here, with several gunboats, and Commodore (Leroy) Fitch assures me Hood can neither cross the Cumberland nor blockade it. I therefore think it best to wait until Wilson can equip his cavalry . . .*"

Until then, Thomas was retiring into the fortifications of Nashville. He'd wait for the horses.

Meanwhile, Hood has assigned the blockade attempt to Col. D. C. Kelley, the "Fighting Parson" of Forrest's "Old Brigade." Kelley heads for Bell's Bend with his guns. He will try for a spot on the river bluff near Bell's Mills, 12 miles below Nashville (four miles from the city by road).

Jitters began in Washington. To Lincoln's Secretary Stanton, Thomas' proposed delay looked like a "*strategy of do nothing.*" Stanton sent one of the messages to Lincoln who considered it overnight.

On Dec. 2 Stanton wired Grant at his City Point, Va., headquarters: "*The President feels solicitous about the disposition of Thomas to lay in fortifications. . . . 'until Wilson gets equipment.' . . . The President wishes you to consider the matter.*"

Thomas was in for it now. Patient, thorough-going, judicious, he was the exact opposite of the Rebel fire-eater then deploying his ragged vanguard on the southern hills. By nightfall, Hood's campfires would be twinkling on the uplands, like tiny stars of hope.

Maybe the contrast between the two, just a few miles apart, helped tear Grant's nerves to tatters.

Grant was usually calm. His calm was gone. Within an hour he was pouring advice to Thomas:

"*If Hood is permitted to remain about Nashville, we will lose all the roads back to Chattanooga. . . . Arm and put into the trenches your quartermaster employes, citizens—*" In other words, make the clerks help hold a line! Use the white-collar boys!

Then another message, hot on the heels of the first: "*With your citizen employes armed, you can . . . force the enemy to retire or fight. . . .*" And watch your railroads!

Thomas held his temper. Patiently he replied:

"*. . . I have enough infantry to assume the offensive if I had more cavalry . . .*"

Thomas hoped to give Hood a fight within "*a few days more.*"

As the wires hummed, Hood's campfires were twinkling brighter and brighter on the hills beyond Brown's Creek. His men were still arriving. They were digging in.

Soon they would be building breastworks. On the hilltops, five redoubts will rise, along Hillsboro—three on the west side, two on the east. Can they be finished before Thomas strikes? (Not all will be.)

The first week of December brought good working weather. Hood began a four-mile defense line. It would be too thin, not stoutly fortified. To some it will look more like a skirmish line. Its infantry will end along Hillsboro. From there on to the river . . . well, the cavalry will try. Its assignment will be too big.

Hood will take advantage of terrain—Brown's Creek, the ridges, hills, stone walls. Gen. B. F. Cheatham will be at the right, Lee at center, Gen. A. P. Stewart at left. Gen. James R. Chalmers will do his best over by the Cumberland.

This vast stretch, from Hillsboro to the river, will be Hood's weakest spot. (Here Wilson will hit and go roaring through, to curve back at the Rebel flank and cinch the Battle of Nashville.)

Looking west from Capitol. Near house in foreground spectators watched the first day's battle. This picture, made in 1868, shows old roundhouse and depot.

Travelers' Rest, Hood's headquarters. Drawn from a photograph taken in 1884.

—From Century Magazine

The Maxwell House at the close of the war. A watchmender's
sign hangs outside the shop where Life & Casualty Tower now
stands.

WHY DIDN'T Hood spread his infantry farther? He simply didn't have the
men. And he preferred to snap Federal communications lines with what
he had.

Brown's Creek, at his right front, gave additional strength. Behind it, south
of the city, Hood held two railroads and two pikes. Westward he held two more
pikes—again, south of the city. Thomas held their urban ends, of course. Hood
had cut off their outward traffic.

Along Hillsboro ran more than 1,000 yards of stone fencing. This would offer
cover and shelter rifle pits. (Until fairly recent years, one stretch ran through
the present Green Hills Village.)

And over these walls on the afternoon of Dec. 15 will blaze the rifles of Gen.
Edward C. Walthall's men, at Yankee hordes streaking southeastward; and the
frame plantation house where Walthall made his headquarters—until driven out
on that afternoon of smoky thunder—still stands on the east side of Hillsboro,
not far south of Castleman Drive, about a mile from Green Hills. This was the
Felix Compton house on the December afternoon 100 years ago when lead was
splatting against the stone fence.

Hood's right will rest in a deep cut of the Nashville & Chattanooga Railway.
From there his line will swing souhtwestward, behind Brown's Creek, crossing
the Nolensville and Franklin pikes. Then it will straighten out a bit, cross Brown's
Creek and Granny White Pike, and tilt slightly northwest toward Hillsboro Pike.

There, almost at a right angle, the Rebel line will fold sharply backward, with
Walthall's division—of Stewart's corps—on the extreme left of the southward fold.
The five redoubts will dot Stewart's front.

Hood set up headquarters at Travelers' Rest, the home of John Overton on
Franklin Pike (now the cherished museum house of the Tennessee Society of
the Colonial Dames of America). Here he found welcome in the home of the
Tennessee colonel who had inherited 105 pieces of Nashville real estate from his
father, Judge John Overton, a friend and adviser of Andrew Jackson.

Night is falling. As Hood lay down to sleep, and perhaps to dream uneasily
of Sally Preston, he might have rested better could he have known that, 13 days
hence, the nearby slopes of the Overtons' "peach orchard hill" would "look blue"
with Federal dead. At least, he would have some luck.

Many of his generals would dine with him here, in the busy two weeks ahead.
"The proudest day of my life," the Civil War mistress of Travelers' Rest would
say, "was when seven Confederate generals sat down to dinner at my table in full
uniform."

She was the Colonel's lady, Mrs. Harriet Maxwell Overton, for whom the
Maxwell House was named. Her husband, the hotel's builder, had given it her
maiden name.

The hotel was incomplete. Federals had commandeered it, as a convalescent
hospital and temporary prison. To much of the Nashville public, during the war
years, it was known as Zollicoffer Barracks, after Felix Zollicoffer.

From the Overtons', Hood soon will issue orders for the forming of his line:
"Gen. Lee . . . Stewart . . . Cheatham . . The entire line will curve forward
from Gen. Lee's center so that Gen. Cheatham's right may come as near the
Cumberland as possible below Nashville . . ."

Ah, little line! Its reach will exceed its grasp. "As nearly as possible"—
how bravely put! Stewart's left, hardly to Hillsboro, will lack four miles reaching
the river on the west. Cheatham's right, just crossing the Nolensville Pike, will
lack a mile reaching the river on the east.

The two gaps total five miles. How fill them? Hood will attempt it with
cavalry.

Mrs. John Overton
The Maxwell House was named for her, the former
Harriet Maxwell

—Courtesy Lanier Merritt

Huge warehouses held Yankee supplies here. Is this the northwest corner of McGavock Street and
Fifth Avenue?

Edwin M. Stanton
Secretary of War

THE SIEGE OF NASHVILLE.

Scene of the Operations of General Thomas and General Hood---The Rebel Line of Works in Front of Nashville.

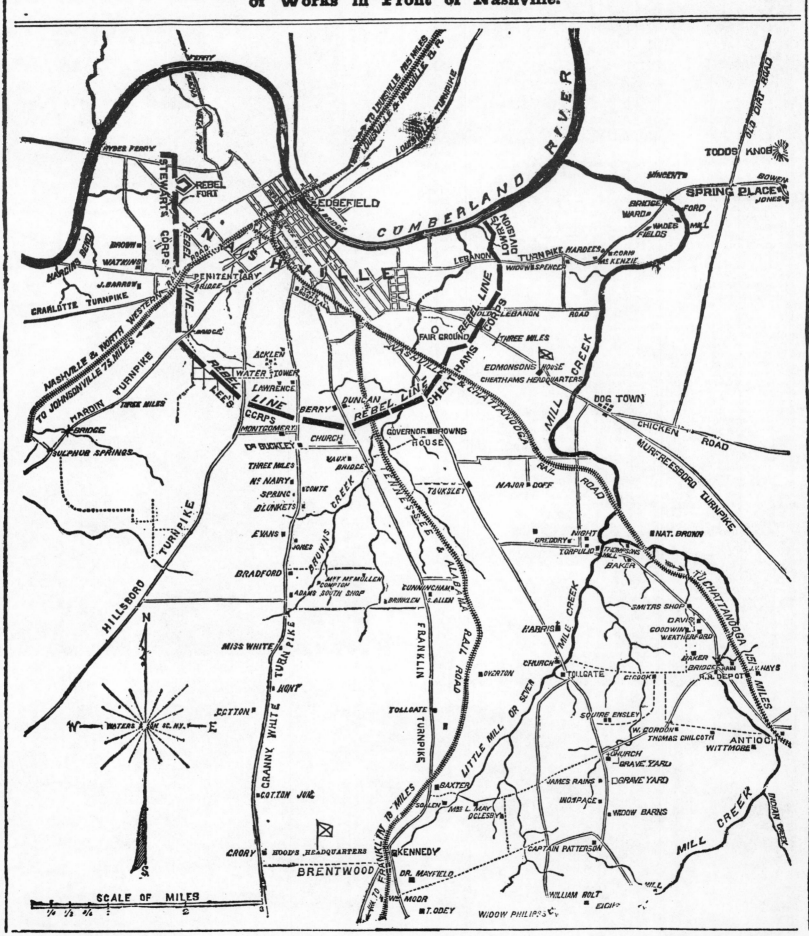

—Courtesy of the **New York Herald**

THE "SIEGE" OF NASHVILLE was no siege at all. Hood didn't have enough men to lay "siege." His thin line lacked miles of encircling the city to the river. But the North didn't know that. And this old map was enough to scare the daylights out of any apprehensive Yankee. It looks as if Hood has a castiron grip, ready for the city's throat. It is reprinted here unretouched, misspellings and all, that you may see it as New Yorkers saw it . . . On next page, a Confederate map of the battlefield, by a man who was there—Maj. Wilbur F. Foster of Nashville.

MAP OF THE
Battlefield of Nashville.
Dec. 15-16th, 1864.
Drawn by Wilbur F. Foster,
Major Engineer Corps, C. S. A.

EDGEFIELD

Scale of Miles.

EXPLANATIONS.

Confederate Advanced Lines. •••••••
Confederate Lines, Morning, ———
Dec. 15th.
Confederate Lines, 1 P.M., +++++×
Dec. 15th.
Confederate Lines from Morn
to 4 P.M., Dec. 16th.
Federal Lines 3 P.M., Dec. 15th. ▟▟▟
Federal Lines, 4 P.M., Dec. 16th. ▟▟▟

Rand, McNally & Co., Engr's, Chicago.

Seizing Horses—(sketched by W. D. Matthews).

INTO THE FOUR-MILE stretch he sends the cavalry division under Gen. Chalmers. He will make his headquarters at the Belle Meade mansion of Gen. W. G. Harding on the Harding Pike. Chalmers has a grim task for one division of just two brigades. These are commanded by Col. Edmund W. Rucker and Col. Jacob B. Biffle.

Chalmers is already 300 men short—the regiment of "Fighting Parson" Kelley on the bluff.

Into the one-mile stretch, at Cheatham's right, Hood sends Forrest's two other divisions, under Gen. Abraham Buford and Gen. William Hicks Jackson.

Cheatham's infantry is also diminished, by 1,600 men—an infantry division under Gen. William F. Bate, now heading toward Murfreesboro (unaware that the town is stoutly held). As Bate goes, he is to destroy, along the way, the railroad to Nashville.

Meanwhile, in City Point, Grant has come up with an idea which will resolve the horse problem for Thomas: Let Thomas impress horses anywhere below the Ohio. Simply take them from civilians. The legal power will be granted as a war-time emergency.

Years later, Wilson will call it "a stroke of genius for which Grant and Thomas—and not Stanton—deserve the credit." (The order will come through Stanton.)

Union soldiers will walk into the streets and take horses from shaves. Unhitch, please. Government orders.

It is night, Dec. 2. Thomas orders Wilson: Round them up. Take them to Edgefield with those you have. Give owners vouchers. No money. They can sue the government later.

It is Dec. 3. Hood's 23,000 has arrived in force. To the west, 2,000 impressed slaves are swinging picks and shovels, helping on the Yanks' outer line. To the south, there's a sound of heavy skirmishing. The Yankees are greeting Hood sourly and the Rebels are digging their line. To the east, there's a thunder of hooves. Wilson is crossing the river.

In downtown Nashville, horses are being taken from carriages, buggies, wagons; from streetcars, livery stables and carriage houses.

A circus is raided for "everything except its ponies." A heartbroken equestrienne-trainer follows behind her old white trick horse, pleading. She is brushed aside.

She doesn't give up. She keeps knocking on doors and pulling strings in an effort to save her horse. At last she finds mercy, from "Wilson's adjutant general," whom she "convinced" that old Whitey was "unfit for cavalry service."

Wilson is playing no favorites. Gov. Johnson, the vice president-elect, has a fine span. Wilson takes them.

Wilson further infuriated Johnson by taking his so-called "bodyguard"— 12 local cavalry units, loosely organized and somewhat footloose.

Wilson thought them a lazy crowd of good-for-nothings. He called them a bunch of drunken rowdies, on the Federal payroll, scattered close to home to make votes for Johnson. He ordered them to duty with Northern regiments. He court-martialed some of their officers.

Johnson raged. So did Wilson. They met. Words flew between the 27-year-old West Pointer and the East Tennessee Yankee, a former tailor . . . who would become President within four months (after the assassination of Lincoln).

Wilson was playing with political fire. He was going to get burned for it . . . in the years ahead. Johnson would not forget. One day in the White House he would take his revenge upon the sincere young officer.

Just now, Wilson was getting a big job done in a hurry. For the next seven days, he will acquire an average of 1,000 horses daily, 7,000 in a week.

The majority of his mounted men will have repeating rifles. He's hoping for 12,000 horsemen by the time the bugle sounds . . .

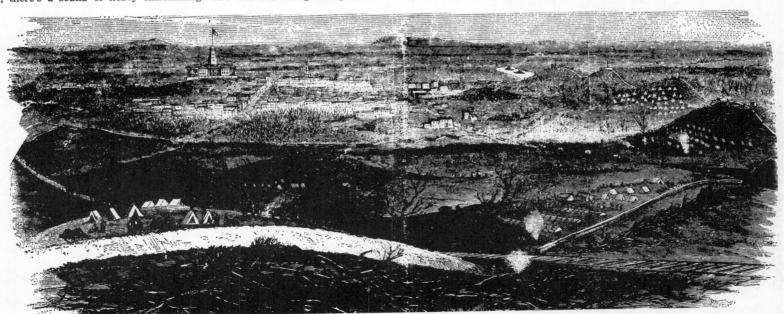

"Nashville and Its Fortifications." Some Civil War buffs think this drawing highly inaccurate. They ask: Do the hilltop forts represent Negley and Casino, near the river, then Morton and Houston? If so, shouldn't Casino be farther right? And Houston much farther left? Whose big house at center? And the railroad—a wartime spur track?

Burning Steamers on the Cumberland River. (But the artist may have let his imagination run away when he drew the side-wheeler. The stern-wheeler is far more typical of the narrow Cumberland.)

—From *Annals of the Army of the Cumberland*

IT WON'T BE easy. For one thing, there's a shortage of hay. (Forrest had destroyed enormous quantities when he burned Johnsonville, a few weeks earlier.)

But the horses keep coming, many from Kentucky, into whose lower counties Wilson has sent four regiments for impressment.

In Edgefield, anvils ring. Blacksmiths sweat. Wilson is trying to repair, in haste, the damage of Schofield's slambang retreat. Gen. Donaldson, the quartermaster, has placed orders with his out-of-state contractor for thousands of mules.

How many? the contractor asks, and he looks cheerful. (He must know where to find them.)

"As many as you can get," Donaldson replies. *"Just get 'em!"*

On Dec. 3 Thomas wired Halleck he hoped to have *"10,000 cavalry mounted in less than a week, when I shall feel able to march against Hood."*

Then incredible news. The Cumberland has been blockaded after all. Kelley is on the bluff and spitting fire. He has captured two Federal transports, the Prairie State and Prima Donna. Aboard are 197 horses and mules. Kelley has them, plus 56 prisoners. The two steamers are being unloaded of other cargo.

Commotion must have struck in Thomas' headquarters. Fitch! Where is Fitch?

Fitch was steaming down from Nashville. With him went the ironclad Carondolet and four tinclads, the Fair Play, Moose, Reindeer and Silver Lake. In a midnight battle he retook the transports before the Rebels could get them completely unloaded. But the Rebels have the horses, the mules and also the 56 Yanks.

Kelley's blockade held. If it continued to hold, Nashville's 100,000 population might soon be needing biscuits. Flour could no longer be brought up the river.

But Kelley had one regret. He had not been in time to blast Smith's men as they came steaming in from Missouri.

Sunday, Dec. 4, was a fair and balmy day. Up the road from Franklin comes an exhausted little group—Rebels who have helped to bury the dead.

Take a look at one, in a tattered shirt. His socks are almost footless but the **tops** still keep his legs warm. The welting of his shoes has given out. The uppers and soles are tied together with string. (That same day in Edgefield, Wilson was writing in irritation, *"Most of my horses are barefooted—"*)

Pity the hooves of the Federal horses! Pity the feet of the Rebels themselves! The nearly barefoot Rebel is a chaplain, the Rev. James Hugh McNeilly of

Gen. Walthall's division. He will become one of Tennessee's most notable Presbyterian ministers. Today he is no different from the others—except, perhaps, for the look on his face. Among the dead he buried was his brother, killed near the Franklin gin.

On this quiet Sunday morning Hood received bad news from Bate. Murfreesboro is strongly held, Bate says. Around 8,000 Yanks are there, under Gen. Lovell H. Rousseau.

Hood replies that he will send Forrest to help.

What utter folly is this? Hood is making perhaps his biggest mistake for the coming Battle of Nashville.

He is sending Forrest to Murfreesboro, 28 miles away, when one of the biggest cavalry invasion forces America has ever known is being assembled just across the river!

On this Sunday Wilson wrote, *"I think the Murfreesboro garrison is apt to 'go up.' It can do no good where it is, and here it might help to overwhelm Hood."*

Did Wilson know·of the departure of Forrest? Almost certainly not. He could not have believed that Hood would let Forrest remain in Murfreesboro.

Not until the Battle of Nashville was ending would the Federals become definitely convinced that Forrest, the wizard, was not upon the field. Had Forrest been present, the outcome might have been different.

This poses an old question: Why didn't Hood strike first at Murfreesboro, snap the railroad and then, if successful, turn on Nashville?

The suggestion was made. Hood put it aside. He did, however, send two infantry brigades to augment Forrest. With Forrest go Jackson and Buford. Thus the cavalry is peeled away from the eastern gap. (Forrest will assume command of the 6,000 men.)

Hood's head stayed high that Sunday afternoon. There was a sudden sound of music from Rebel camps. Out they came, ragged and strutting, with every brass band tooting.

Tattered flags were flying and bands all blaring "Dixie" as Hood marched his little army up to within 600 yards of the enemy's advanced salient. Defiantly he deployed, as smartly as if on drill, along Montgomery Hill (west of Belmont Boulevard, near Cedar Lane).

—From *Annals of the Army of the Cumberland*

YANKEES IMPRESSING NEGROES at church in Nashville. They were forced to work on the line.

—From **History of Homes and Gardens of Tennessee,** by the Garden Study Club

Rokeby
"Haunted"

—Courtesy Mrs. Paul E. Purks

Hillside
The line ran by its front door

—State Library and Archives

Wood's Watchtower
(Belmont's water tower)

ACROSS THE valley the music rolled, beating at Rebel hearts, and beating at the windows of a handsome house called Hillside. It stood near the very center of the lines for the coming struggle.

This was the home of William L. B. Lawrence and his lovely wife, Corinne. They were not at home. Hillside had been commandeered. About it Yankees lolled, members of the staff of Gen. Samuel Beatty, an Ohio banker turned able officer.

Beatty commanded Wood's Third Division. Beatty had made Hillside his headquarters. His staff and servants occupied every room of the house, which stood on a rocky hill west of Granny White.

Federals called the place Laurens Hill, (often spelling it that way on their maps). *"The Federal line of works ran transversely across my place and just by my front door,"* Lawrence would write in his diary.

Here, at Hillside, was a Middle Tennessee way of life. Here was a gentleman of old Nashville who owned 176 acres on the edge of the city and, at the beginning of the war, 10 slaves, a barouche, a buggy, and two town lots. Corinne, who would bear him 10 children, had 640 acres of her own in Haywood County.

Corinne had been one of the "three fair maids of Rokeby," the 1,280-acre estate (of the late Oliver Bliss Hayes, brilliant Nashville attorney) over which gunsmoke soon would be drifting. Rokeby at one time had extended from Hillsboro Pike to Granny White Pike, and from near West End Avenue to Cedar Lane.

In the old plantation mansion, on an October night 10 years ago, Lawrence had received his answer from Corinne which caused him to write in his diary, *"The blind god is triumphant . . ."* Then, on Christmas Night, he wrote, *". . . one kiss."* Their engagement had become formal.

On a part of old Rokeby's lands the newlyweds had built their home, with seven bedrooms, double parlors, Italian mantels, graceful casement windows and a hot-and-cold shower—facilities which the Yankees were finding much to their liking.

Here, at Hillside, had been abundance, and it was nothing unusual when Lawrence, in 1858, had *"2,548 pounds of pork laid in for the coming year,"* at 5 cents a pound. (How times would change! In 1870, Lawrence will write, *"Killed six hogs of my own raising—the first since Hood's raid, five years ago."*)

Here, too, had been a carefree happiness, in the palmy days when Corinne's barouche could hasten, in a few minutes, down the slope and around the way to a more magnificent part of old Rokeby—an adjacent 180 acres of manicured lawn upon which stood Belmont, the mansion of her older sister, Mrs. Adelicia Franklin Acklen, Nashville's richest widow. (The house is now the main building of Belmont College.)

Belmont, too, had been commandeered. Corinne went there no longer. Gen. Wood had made his headquarters at Adelicia's Belmont, which boasted two grand pianos, panes of Bohemian glass and a treasury of rare paintings.

Up Belmont's long driveway, bordered by alternate cedars and magnolias, Wood's IV Army Corps had come thumping, into the grounds where every flower bed was watered by an underground water system, from an ornamental water tower, 105 feet tall. Wood used it as a watchtower.

—Courtesy Mrs. Paul E. Purks

Wm. L. B. Lawrence
Master of Hillside

—From Harper's Weekly

"To the Last Ditch" says the signboard. Jefferson Davis is shown as passenger.

—From Harper's Weekly (Sketched by A. W. Warren)

WRECKING RAILROADS. Rails were heated and bent.

Gen. Henry W. Halleck
"coolness at Corinth"

—U. S. Signal Corps Photo (Brady Collection)
in National Archives

Gen. Lovell H. Rousseau
at Murfreesboro

HOW LONG ago seemed 1862, when Lawrence had written as Nashville fell, *"The war may be long and bloody but we will never submit . . ."* Now, with his family, he was sheltered by friends. His slaves were gone. For lack of workmen, he had raised no crop this year, except a vegetable garden, in his old poultry yard. (The Yankees had taken his chickens.) His fields were unfenced. (The Yankees had taken his rails in '63.)

Now they were cutting down his beautiful trees for firewood and headlogs. Before the Yankees depart they will also use his furniture and outhouses (presumably for heat). They were eating his cattle, his hogs and pigs.

Let "Dixie" ring! Play on, Hood! Play on!

Some Nashvillians who took a Sunday promenade did not come leisurely home in the afternoon. Many were waylaid by Federal soldiers and impressed to work. Before the day was done, 5,000 persons, including Negroes, were laboring on the Federal line.

Next day, Dec. 5, Forrest reached Lavergne. There he joined Bate. Together they moved toward Murfreesboro.

In Virginia, Grant was stewing again. *"Is there not danger,"* he wired Thomas, *"of Forrest moving down the river where he can cross it? . . . Hood should be attacked where he is. Time strengthens him . . . as much as it does you."*

Thomas wired Halleck he hoped to attack on the 7th, *"if I can perfect my arrangements."*

Halleck was grumbling to Grant that around *"22,000 horses"* had been issued in the West since Sept. 22. If the war continued to gobble them up like that, Halleck said, *"the Army will never be mounted . . ."*

Years later Wilson would write, *"Grant may have been disturbed by the fear that Thomas would fail to hold Hood and that this would condemn both himself and Sherman for stripping Thomas . . ."*

—Courtesy Mrs. Paul E. Purks

Mrs. Lawrence
(The former Corinne Hayes of Rokeby)

—From Homes and Gardens of Tennessee, by the Garden Study Club

FABULOUS BELMONT, home of Mrs. Adelicia Franklin Acklen, sister of Mrs. Lawrence. Here Gen. Wood made his headquarters.

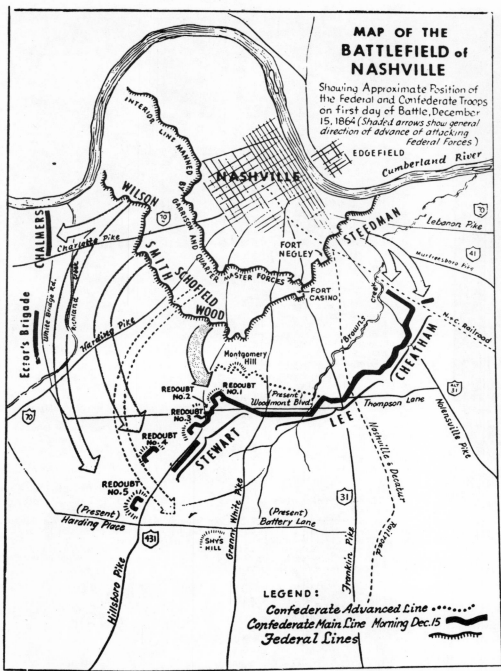

MAP OF THE BATTLEFIELD of NASHVILLE

Showing Approximate Position of the Federal and Confederate Troops on first day of Battle, December 15, 1864 (Shaded arrows show general direction of advance of attacking Federal Forces)

LEGEND:
Confederate Advanced Line ••••••••
Confederate Main Line Morning Dec.15 〜〜
Federal Lines

The Battlefield, First Day

Gen. Robert E. Lee

Knightliest of all commanders, Lee was held in his Petersburg works, vastly outnumbered, while disaster struck the Confederacy at Nashville. He foresaw that when Sherman reached the sea, swept northward and drew near, Petersburg and Richmond would have to be evacuated.

BLUNTLY GRANT now ordered Thomas: *"Attack Hood at once and wait no longer for a remount of your cavalry. There is great danger in delay resulting in a campaign back to the Ohio."*

It was 4 p.m., Dec. 6. Thomas had promised to attack next day, if ready. He wouldn't be. But things were better. Thomas has not yet received the "attack" order. Meanwhile, he answered Grant's earlier question about Forrest:

"As soon as I get up a respectable cavalry force, I will march against Hood. I hope to have some 6,000 to 8,000 mounted cavalry in three days . . . I do not think it prudent to attack Hood with less than 6,000 cavalry to cover my flanks, because he has under Forrest at least 12,000 . . ."

How mistaken was Thomas!

Hood had not more than 1,200 of Forrest's cavalry beside him in Nashville at that hour. Who could have guessed, however, that Hood would not call Forrest back?

Hood's secret service was more effective. After all, the city's secret heart was with him. On the day Grant gave his "attack" order, Hood warned his men to be ready on a moment's notice. Coincidence? Or able espionage?

The day brings more thunder from the bluff. Cmdr. Fitch again is trying to raise the blockade.

The ironclad Neosha is leading. Fitch is trying to run past Kelley's guns with a convoy. Kelley's guns are spouting fire. Splinters are flying from the Neosha's superstructure. Fitch is heading back toward Nashville.

He doesn't give up. On the same day, he steams back to the bluff, reinforced by the Carondelet. This time Kelley's guns whack the Neosha more than 100 times. The blockade holds for a day. The blockade holds.

At 6:30 p.m. Thomas received Grant's "attack" order. Immediately he replied:

"I will attack Hood at once . . . though I believe it will be hazardous with the small force of cavalry at my service."

Secretary of War Stanton exploded to Grant: *"If he waits for Wilson to get ready Gabriel will be blowing his last horn."*

Stanton's message was filed at 10:30 a.m., Dec. 7, the day Thomas had promised to attack. Grant waited for word of a battle. None came.

Wilson's horses were not yet in condition, although Wilson was working feverishly. Wilson needed more time.

Thomas, meanwhile, was acutely aware of his promise. But he didn't want to fiddle-faddle with the foe. When he struck, he meant to crush. With horses unready, he couldn't. He'd wait.

This delay? A hazard to his career? Thomas guessed it. He took the chance. He would attack on the 9th or 10th.

To his corps commanders, Thomas began to discuss his plan. They must turn Hood's left, which was, by now, being watched by just about all America. It was, so to speak, the only really threatening Rebel left on the western side of the mountains.

Thomas must get at Hood's rear, compress his line, roll it up, piece by piece, and dislodge him. When all was over, Thomas meant for the Rebel camp-fires, twinkling on the hills, to be gone and gone forever.

It would have to begin, no doubt, at dawn. Thomas didn't mention the date. His generals believed it would be Dec. 10. Intently they listened, as Thomas talked on:

From near the Murfreesboro Pike, Steedman would make a clockwise swing at the Rebel right. It would be a feint to veil the real sledge-hammer blows, to hit the Rebel left. Four sledge-hammer columns, swinging counter-clockwise, were to hit Hood's Hillsboro wing. And the four were to be so well-coordinated as to seem almost one. That is, if all went well.

They'd curve out southeastward, Wilson, Smith, Schofield, Wood, in that order. Wilson's cavalry, on the right, would be on the rim of the wheel, the outside pivot. Wood would be the pivot, the hub. Smith would be next to Wilson, with Schofield in reserve between Smith and Wood.

The biggest infantry assignment would go to Smith's salty men from beyond the Mississippi. They'll have the farthest to go and will make the grand wheel for the infantry. This should bring them crashing obliquely into Hood along Hillsboro.

Wood (riding away from Adelicia's Belmont) as corps commander at the pivot, will have the shortest path. He's to threaten Montgomery Hill. If possible, he's to take it. This means Wood should strike Hood's front while Smith hits Hood's left flank. Schofield will be ready, near left center, for use as the battle develops.

Wilson, on Smith's right, will help Smith carry the left. Wilson must send a division out Charlotte. (Look out, Chalmers!) He must "observe" in the direction of Bell's Landing. (Look out, Kelley!) Then Wilson must swing out, far and wide, and come crashing in at Hood's rear.

As Thomas talked, blood was running in Murfreesboro. Forrest has struck.

In their two years at the town, the Federals had made it a stronghold. Earthworks to the north and east enclosed 200 acres in which 57 guns were mounted. This was Fortress Rosecrans, too strong for direct assault.

Forrest and Bate had waited for a better chance, outside the fort. When it came, they tackled a column of 3,325 men under Gen. R. H. Milroy. The battle raged beyond the town, through cedar groves in which 100,000 men had struggled two years before at the Battle of Murfreesboro. This time the result will be a near rout for Bate's division.

Forrest is riding King Philip. He's whaling at fleeing Rebels, using the flat of his saber. He yanks a staff from a retreating color-bearer. He strikes with it at men beyond his reach. Stop and fight! They keep running. In disgust, Forrest hurls standard and all at a running Rebel beyond him.

Buford is riding into the town. Capt. John W. Morton is turning his guns on the Union garrison in the courthouse. The Yanks are striking heavily back at Morton's battery horses. The Rebels are stripping their dying steeds and retreating, pulling their caissons and guns away by hand.

Two days later, Dec. 9, Bate's division will be called back to Nashville. He will resume his position in Cheatham's line. Taking his place at Murfreesboro will be Col. Charles H. Olmstead, in charge of Gen. J. A. Smith's old brigade.

In Clarksville, the ironclad Cincinnati has arrived. Its commander is Rear Adm. Richard P. Lee. Like Fitch he hopes to break the blockade. He won't. Low water stops him.

Rain, snow, sleet. Nashville was frozen in. Battle-time was postponed.

GUNBOATS WILL continue to ply the river as far upstream as Carthage. Watch! Hood might try to cross. It's the hobgoblin of Federal thinking.

"The possibility," Wilson wrote later, *"was about the wildest . . . military undertaking possible to imagine . . . Grant lost his head."*

"He was misled," says Douglas, *"by the relatively minor raid of Lyon and the disposition of Kelley's battery. He thought these movements meant that Hood was about to move into Kentucky . . . He overlooked the threat of Murfreesboro to Hood."*

Thomas knew Murfreesboro was too strong to be yielded. Why present Hood with a fortified 200 acres? No, Thomas didn't mean to play Santa Claus, and leave an evacuated Murfreesboro in Hood's Christmas stocking.

In Washington, it's 1:30 p.m., Dec. 8. Grant has no word of the attack he thought Thomas would make on the 7th. All right, Thomas—step down!

Grant wires Halleck: *"If Thomas has not struck yet, he should be ordered to hand over his command to Schofield . . ."*

Halleck didn't jump like a frog. He conferred with associates for more than three hours.

Then he curtly informed Grant:

"If you wish Gen. Thomas removed, give the order . . . The responsibility, however, will be yours, as no one here, as far as I am informed, wishes Gen. Thomas removed."

Suddenly Grant shied, as if aware that he had been caught in the spotlight of history:

". . . I would not say remove him until I hear further from him." He still wanted Thomas reminded of the importance of *"immediate action."*

Thomas was spared. The worst was to come.

Years later, Wilson would say:

"Grant's telegrams of this fortnight . . . disclose a willingness, if not a settled purpose . . . to cause Thomas' removal and downfall, provided the authorities in Washington could be induced to take the responsibility . . ."

But, Wilson would add, when Grant was plainly told the responsibility was his, Grant *"hesitated and, while not abandoning his purpose, drafted orders to that end,"* which, luckily for Thomas and the Union, *"were not sent."*

It was within a few days of this troubled time that Gen. Donaldson encountered his mule-buying contractor on the street. (No specific date seems available for this meeting.)

Eagerly Donaldson inquired: How many mules have you procured?

"Twenty-five thousand or more," the buyer proudly replied.

Full skirts were ideal for smuggling. This happened in Nashville.

BLOOD IS THICKER THAN WATER. Tennessee relatives, often near hunger themselves, did their best to aid their Rebel soldiers.

133

—Library of Congress

Gen. James R. Chalmers

Capt. J. W. Morton
(Deserved Much Higher Rank)

—National Archives

General Abraham Buford

"A COZY SHELTER," by Forbes, from *30 Years After*

DID DONALDSON'S ears seem to pop and roar, in dazed disbelief? Would the buyer repeat?

"*Twenty-five thousand.*" The buyer was staring, puzzled, at Donaldson, who seemed about to fall.

"*I am a ruined man,*" Donaldson heard himself saying at last. "*I will be court-martialed and driven from the Army! You have procured many times more than I had any intention of purchasing!*"

Donaldson was trying to be calm, to get a grip upon himself and face the music of his own carelessness. "*The fault's mine, not yours. I ought to have been more particular in my order.*" It was too late now to limit this man.

Ooh . . . 25,000 mules! With hay short—and money short! What will Thomas say—Thomas, who thinks of everything! Shaken, Donaldson went to his residence.

A knock on the door. A messenger. How fast bad news travels! Report to the commanding general. Donaldson hurried to the Cunningham house.

Thomas sat waiting, deeply troubled. At once he asked, "*Donaldson, how many mules do you have?*"

Donaldson managed to speak. "*Upwards of 25,000.*"

Thomas echoed, "*Twenty-five thousand, did you say?*"

Donaldson repeated.

"*Donaldson!*" Thomas exclaimed. "*Accept my heartiest thanks! You have saved this army! I can now have transportation and can fight Hood, and will do so at once!*" (Remember, the precise date of this incident is unknown.)

On Dec. 8, Thomas set his zero hour for battle—daylight of the 10th. Be ready. In fact, on the afternoon of the 8th, an order went down the line, "*Be ready in two hours.*" Somebody wanted plenty margin.

At City Point, Grant is fuming. Night falls. Does the witch of fear now seem to be cackling gleefully around him, "*Hood's crossing, crossing—He's heading to Ohio, heading to Chicago—*"?

Grant fired another telegram at Thomas:

"*It looks to me evident the enemy are trying to cross the Cumberland and are scattered. Why not attack at once? By all means avoid the contingency of a footrace to see which, you or Hood, can beat to the Ohio.*"

Hood was not trying to cross. His main army was standing still before Nashville. There were two small exceptions. One was Kelley on the bluff. The other was Lyon, with two guns, heading for Kentucky.

On that day, Dec. 8, Lyon had crossed the Tennessee River into the Land Between the Rivers, where the two streams flow northward close together, toward the broad Ohio.

Lyon was heading toward Cumberland City, 30 miles below Clarksville and 10 below Fort Donelson.

And a cold, cold wind was heading toward Nashville . . . It would change the date for the battle.

An icy storm blew into the city after daybreak Dec. 9. A freezing rain fell, mixed with snow. Within a few hours Nashville was white and glittering. Ice sheathed it. Wind howled. The temperature plummeted. Streets, hills and fields turned slippery as glass.

Thomas couldn't strike. No army with big guns could move. He informed Grant:

"*. . . A terrible storm of freezing rain has just come on today . . . I am therefore compelled to wait for the storm to break.*"

Manfully, Thomas added, "*Gen. Halleck informs me you are much dissatisfied with my delay in attacking. I can only say I have done all in my power to prepare, and if you deem it necessary to relieve me, I shall submit without a murmur.*"

As Thomas wrote, the freezing moisture was still coming down. It would continue through the day and part of the night. It was one of the worst storms in years. ("*The Yankees,*" said Nashvillians, "*brought their weather with them.*")

Miles northward, in the Land Between the Rivers, Lyon was having difficulty making his recruits "*move away from the fires along the road.*"

They entered Cumberland City Dec. 9, captured a large streamer, and used it to ferry them across the Cumberland. That evening they seized two other steamers and four barges. All were burned and 50 prisoners taken.

The down-stream action by Lyon had been sketchily outlined to Washington in a telegram from Nashville at 8 p.m., Dec. 8. It went from Capt. John C. Van Duzer, Western Union's efficient man-of-all work in Nashville, to T. T. Eckert (later Western Union president). Such messages were part of the War Department's information arrangement.

"*. . . Enemy still in front,*" Van Duzer said, innocently. "*. . . One of our gunboats came to grief in exchange of iron at Bell's Ferry. Rebel Gen. Lyon holds same bank below Harpeth to Fort Donelson, but does not fight gunboats . . .*"

Van Duzer, not splitting hairs on details, was outlining generalities and intending no one harm. But events suggest that Grant, of course, saw the telegram.

Did Grant's worst fears erupt? In a nightmarish vision, did he see Hood's whole army spread out 70 miles along the Cumberland—ready to surge across? If so, maybe Grant felt that his hair was standing straight up. (When the message about Lyon came in, Grant had not yet heard of the Nashville storm.)

So, as ice deepened over Nashville, Grant swung the axe a second time at Thomas. He wired Halleck, at 11 a.m., Dec. 9:

"*Dispatch of 8 p.m. last night, from Nashville, shows the enemy 70 miles down the river from Nashville, and no attack yet made by Thomas. Please telegraph orders relieving him and placing Schofield in command.*"

Lyon's men were, indeed, about 70 miles down the river. But in between? Dreary miles of ice and snow . . . with a few foraging Rebels, or maybe hungry foxes on the prowl, after some misguided rabbit . . .

In Washington, the orders for Thomas' removal were made out. Schofield's chance of advancement seemed hanging high.

Then news of the storm arrived in Washington. Halleck asked Grant: Do you still want the removal orders forwarded?

Grant ducked again: "*. . . Suspend the order relieving him until it is seen whether he will do anything.*" This was sent at 5:30 p.m., Dec. 9.

Thomas was saved by the weather. That night Grant wired that he was suspending the order relieving him.

"*In later years Grant could ponder these mistakes,*" says Douglas, "*but before the Battle of Nashville his conduct toward Thomas was reprehensible. He was second-guessing a man who deserved his greatest confidence.*"

Five years would pass before Thomas learned that Grant had actually ordered that Schofield supersede him. (Halleck spilled the beans at a San Francisco dinner party in Thomas' honor in 1869.)

On the windswept hills, the shivering Rebels knew time was short. Hood's spy system was working. The city's Confederate heart was throbbing. News went straight to the hills.

In Nashville at night, many a wife, sweetheart and mother stood at their windows and looked out at the twinkling lights on the hills beyond Brown's Creek. Their men were there, hungry and ragged, blue-lipped. And as the women stood at the windows and watched, some of them knelt, prayed, and wept.

—U. S. Signal Corps Photo in National Archives

Gen. Edward Hatch

—Library of Congress

Gen. James F. Knipe

—National Archives

Gen. John T. Croxton

—National Archives

Gen. R. W. Johnson

Old foundry on Front Street (First Avenue). Yankees used it as a blacksmith and wagon shop.

—Courtesy of Lanier Merritt

—From *Old Glory, The True Story*
William Driver

—From *Old Glory, The True Story*
Driver's Home

Looking northeast toward railroad bridge, right of center, where the cavalry of Knipe and Croxton crossed from Edgefield, just before the battle. Linck's depot and hotel, left, and the Second Presbyterian Church (now on Belmont Boulevard) are prominent landmarks. 1868 photo.

THEY KNEW there was "a shoe shop in every brigade." They knew that whenever a beef was killed, the hide was saved. It was used to improvise shoes, at least to make something to go around a man's foot, moccasin-like, or to mend the worn-outs he might have. Many feet were bleeding.

The Rebels were still digging in, hacking at the frozen earth. Preparing for their desperate effort in behalf of the city now captive 33 months. They could see the lighted windows. My house . . . Oh, God, just take us there, in victory. It's warm, I hope. My wife. My children.

The women at the windows knew that while their men shivered and went hungry, there were in Nashville stores such things as fine French beaver cloth, for warm overcoats, which could be had for enough of the precious Yankee dollars, or for gold . . . There were English and French cassimeres . . .

Down at the Sign of the Big Horn, at 25 Church St., enough Federal money could buy the best cigars, and 13-year-old bourbon, and choice rye, and sparkling catawba, and powdered sugar and cherries. Down at the corner of Cedar and Cherry (now Fourth Avenue) there was Holland gin, and Jamaica rum, and Scotch ale, and jewelry and perfume.

"We're having a great time here," Rustling wrote, from Donaldson's quartermaster offices. "No danger or anything of that sort. But Hood pens us up here, and we haven't tried to prevent him as yet . . .

"Our line is immensely strong, crowned with forts and bristling with cannon, and both ends covered by gunboats. The Rebels might as well butt their heads against the Rocky Mountains . . .

"The troops on both sides have suffered terribly," Rustling continued. "The beautiful woods and groves, that make Nashville one of the most lovely towns I ever saw, are going remorselessly down before the axes of the soldiers . . .

"The Rebs must have wood too; and away it goes by the thousands of cord (sic) daily. If the Rebs coop us up here another fortnight, there won't be a tree left within five miles of Nashville . . ."

Prices were sky-high, Rebel "paper" dirt cheap. Until a better day, the Rebs would have to forego the luxuries of the Big Horn.

Salt was a different matter. Salt, man must have. The Rebels long ago had found the answer. Nearly everyone had a smokehouse. Upon its earthen floor, for years, the salt had dripped from curing meats. They dug up the dirt and boiled it, to extract the precious salt of yesteryear.

Kelley's blockade was leaving its mark. Flour was getting precious.

"We hear," said a letter to a Nashville editor, "that the special treasury agent has determined to revoke the permits of all (flour) dealers." That is, if they hiked prices after getting "a monopoly in their hands." The writer wanted more controls. "Why stop with the flour dealers?"

Another wrote, "Allow all who will to bring in cabbages, etc., to sell for the highest price they can get." This might attract fresh food to the city.

A merchant was commended in print for scattering 270 barrels of flour among his customers at "$15 per barrel," although offered $21 per barrel "before the price-fixing order." This meant U.S. currency.

The equivalent in Confederate money? A pat answer isn't easy. (In besieged Richmond, J. B. Jones wrote in his now-famous *A Rebel War Clerk's Diary*, on Jan. 18, "Flour is $1,250 per barrel today." This meant Confederate currency.)

Lyon, riding on, wouldn't be able to set mills grinding. But he would burn eight courthouses (some manned by Negro garrisons). He would keep McCook hopping. Finally, recrossing the Cumberland, Lyon will ride back into Tennessee, through Sparta—"to the utter consternation of Thomas, Lee and Fitch," Douglas says. (By that time, the Battle of Nashville will be over.)

Near Murfreesboro, Forrest around Dec. 11 captured a train of 17 cars, northbound toward Murfreesboro. Aboard were at least 60,000 rations. He took 200 prisoners. The train he burned.

Meanwhile, in Nashville, many a practical-minded Confederate father smuggled to his soldier son a bit of "Dr. Velloc's Pink Cerate." Made in Nashville, it was advertised for "extermination of body lice and other vermin, and for the cure of common itch, camp itch, barber's itch, psoriasis, scald head, tetter, and dandruff in the hair and beard."

For smuggling to the shallow trenches, shoes and medicine were perhaps the most desirable commodities. There was big risk.

On one earlier occasion a faithful Negro woman, aiding her mistress, was caught in the act. She jumped from a wagon as sentries approached. The precious shoes, dislodged as her feet hit the ground, shot from beneath her skirts. The Yankees kept them.

Dark days had come, for old-time Nashvillians. Nor were times easy for all new neighbors. All were not bad.

Most Nashvillians had remained, at heart, faithful to the Cause. Three years of domination and expediency is a long time. It had been too much for many—when there was money to be made, especially by meeting the needs of a Yankee quartermaster. Chickens? Eggs? What have you?

For the poorest, it was understandable, a livelihood. Others had dropped the Cause and made a fortune for fortune's sake. Others, from various pressures, had taken the Federal oath of allegiance—"swallowed the yellow dog"— in lip service only. Some could deceive. Some could dissemble. Some, without doubt, had taken the oath sincerely. To many it had seemed the only thing to do.

There was also a small minority, upright and courageous, which had been loyal to the Union from the first and made no bones about it. This group included the retired New England sea-captain, William Driver.

For years Capt. Driver had made Nashville his home. Years before, in 1831, back in old Salem, he had given the American Flag its name, "Old Glory." In Nashville, in February, 1862, when Yankees had first taken the city, Capt. Driver had proudly brought forth the original "Old Glory" (which he had kept safely hidden from Nashville's Rebels).

He took it to Capitol Hill. From the statehouse its aging folds had fluttered for several hours, until Driver took it down and ran up a substitute, lest the frayed old Flag be ruined.

Dissension had split his family. Three of his sons had enlisted in the Confederate Army. Driver's devotion to the Union never wavered. A number of Nashvillians knew similar heartbreak.

So it was that the twinkling lights of Hood's campfires set off many a different hope and prayer among the 100,000 who watched and waited.

Somebody's "comb was a-gonna get cut," yes, sir.

—U. S. Signal Corps photo (Brady Collection)
in National Archives
Gen. James B. Steedman

—Courtesy of the Benjamin Harrison Memorial
Home
Col. Benjamin Harrison
(later a general)
Future President

"SOUNDING THE CHARGE," by Forbes, from *30 Years After*

IT IS NIGHT inside the Cunningham mansion. A gas-lit chandelier is casting its soft radiance upon the Union commander. It seems to silver his hair. How gray he's getting!

Thomas is sitting by a window, looking out at the storm. It seems pressing at the panes, reaching for the prisms of light, as if to smother all brightness and life, as it has smothered the city, the armies, and the plans of men.

Did Thomas feel smothered, too? Was the room too hot? Did he long to open the window and let the storm rush in? To meet and deal with it directly, as he could not now deal with the foe, or with the wonky winds that blew from Washington and City Point?

And as if their smothering pressure were not enough, the Northern newspapers now were belaboring him for *"idle stupidity."*

Did he want to rise and cry out, *"Give me air!"* and throw open the big windows, and shout to the howling wind, *"To hell with all of you! I'll fight this battle my way!"*

Had it been ever thus, since boyhood? That he must always face the wind—or be smothered?

There had been those times when, as a boy, he'd wanted to teach the Negroes things. To read and write. His family had tried to smother the notion.

And on a day in his teens, in '36, when he was leaving for West Point, he'd gone by to thank his congressman for the appointment. And what a greeting he had received, from the congressman whose appointees in the past had always failed: *"If you fail to graduate, I never want to see your face again!"*

When the chips went down, Thomas had stuck with the Union which had educated him . . . And what had happened? The pressure again . . . and his picture, turned to the wall at home.

Must he always buck the wind? Why couldn't he turn his back sometimes and bend like other people?

Well, he'd bucked the wind before! Not for nothing had he earned the title, "Rock of Chickamauga." A rock could face the wind. And no matter what Grant said, the Nashville fight was off — until a thaw.

If they sacked him? Well, so be it! (A day would come when some people would also call him "The Sledge of Nashville.")

Thomas kept his own counsel. Not until the storm broke would he tell much of what Grant's telegrams said. He carried the whole burden himself. And he didn't mean to be pushed even now. He just kept on giving the orders for preparation.

Wilson, break camp in Edgefield. Cross the river. Take your position within the defenses of Nashville, between the Harding and Hillsboro turnpikes.

Until today, Dec. 9, Wilson had been preparing. Now he's ready. He'll manage to cross on the 12th. The army remains icebound.

Could Grant see all this, the Nashville weather? That at the first burst of battle fire, with men dodging, and horses falling, there would be one bloody avalanche after another, of men and beasts and guns and broken bones?

Grant was silenced—almost. The storm left him *"unconvinced, growling, waiting to strike and on the watch for an opportunity."* So Wilson would write.

Next day, Dec. 10, the storm spent its fury. The world started digging out. Hood is changing his original line. It seems too close. He is pulling back, withdrawing from the daring position on Montgomery Hill. He will keep the old entrenchments, however, as a thinly manned skirmish line.

How far back? Here is an instance: His first line had crossed Granny White at Gale Lane. The new line will cross the pike not very far south of what is now Woodmont Boulevard.

On Dec. 11 Hood pulled Buford's cavalry division from Murfreesboro. It will be sent to the Hermitage area, at the Confederate right wing, to picket the Cumberland and prevent flanking operations. And from Chalmers at Belle Meade, Hood sends Biffle to support Buford. (Jackson's division remains in Murfreesboro with Forrest.)

Chalmers will protest: I've four miles to cover, and only 900 horsemen! (In addition, he has to support Kelley on the bluff.) In response, Hood sends Chalmers the old infantry brigade of Gen. Matthew D. Ector, who had lost a leg at Atlanta. The Franklin slaughter has reduced it to 700 men. But the brigade has a brave new commander, Col. David Coleman of the 39th North Carolina Regiment.

Over the mud Ector's men will scurry, on the 14th, after the thaw, to their new position. They will take their stand in hurriedly made breastworks behind Richland Creek, north of Harding Pike. Across the turnpike they will throw their pickets. Across the creek, nearer Nashville, they will set up a skirmish line.

How thinly spread is Hood's cavalry now? On Charlotte Pike, where Wilson's horde will hit, there's one bold brigade of horsemen, under gallant Col. Edmund W. Rucker. (And one of its regiments, the Seventh Alabama, is spread between Harding and Hillsboro.)

Ah, Rucker, may the good Lord keep you . . .

To the south, a bitter wind whines at the Hillsboro hills. Up on their tops are the Rebels with purpling hands, hacking at the frozen ground, trying to complete their five western redoubts.

—Library of Congress
Thomas, watching the Battle of Nashville from his hilltop, may have looked much as he did in this painting of Missionary Ridge, by T. De Thulstrup. He's the large figure at left in long, dark coat, facing artist.

—Harper's Weekly

Afternoon, Dec. 15, '64: Col. Sylvester G. Hill (First Division, XVI Corps) received a Rebel shot in the head immediately after ordering his unit to take Redoubt 2.

STOUT NO. 1 is Hood's main salient, east of Hillsboro (west of Benham Avenue and north of Woodmont Boulevard), about where the infantry line bends southward. No. 2, also east of Hillsboro, is a little south of Woodmont. Nos. 3, 4 and 5 are west of Hillsboro, No. 3 at the approximate site of the Calvary Methodist Church, 3701 Hillsboro Road; No. 4 at the juncture of Hobbs and Trimble roads, a half-mile west of Hillsboro, and No. 5 farther south, the outermost of all, on a hill quite close to the road.

Oh, winds, blow gently . . .

That snowy night at the warm St. Cloud, Thomas called a conference of his corps commanders. They're clumping in, Schofield, Smith, Steedman, Wilson. They have heard rumors. Has someone been backbiting their chief to Washington and City Point? Is there a Judas among them?

What was said at the meeting? There is dispute.

Thomas disclosed a bit. He told them of Grant's attack order; of his own decision that *"obedience was impracticable."* With this all four agreed, according to one account.

The second account, by Wilson, says all agreed except Schofield, who sat silent.

Schofield would write a third and different account. He will assert that he did agree with Thomas. (To this Wilson snaps, *"On the testimony of all who were present . . . Schofield's advice . . . must have been given in private."*)

As the meeting broke up, Thomas asked his young cavalry general to remain. *"Wilson,"* Thomas says, *"the Washington authorities treat me as if I were a boy . . . But I am sure my plan of operation is perfect, and we shall lick the enemy, if he only stays to receive our attack."*

"I went to camp that night," Wilson wrote, *"with a higher opinion of Thomas . . . He was a patriot without flaw and a soldier without reproach."*

Grant's patience, if any, was snapping. Next day, Dec. 11, he wired Thomas: *"If you delay any longer, the mortifying spectacle will be witnessed of a*

rebel army moving for the Ohio . . . Delay no longer for weather or reinforcements."

Thomas answered:

"I will obey the order as promptly as possible, however much I may regret it . . . It is with difficulty the troops are able to move about on level ground." (On the icy hills, Wilson said, the Rebels could defend themselves with *"brickbats."*)

And to Halleck, Thomas wired, *". . . As soon as we have a thaw, I will attack Hood."*

By this time, Gen. William D. Whipple was asking: Who's backbiting Thomas? Steedman assigned a captain to do some quiet probing of outgoing messages. Soon there will be an answer.

It is morning, Dec. 12. Wilson's cavalry is crossing the Cumberland. Twelve thousand horses are beginning to string out of Edgefield, ever so slowly, over icy streets, toward two points on the Cumberland. There's slipping and falling. The lines keep moving.

A pontoon bridge has been constructed near the foot of Church Street. The railroad bridge, just downstream, has been planked over. Cross here? Yes, a portion, on the temporary flooring.

Two divisions cross on pontoons. These are the men of Gen. Edward Hatch, former Iowa lumberman, and Gen. R. W. Johnson (the same Johnson who had not fared so well near Gallatin two years ago, against Gen. John Hunt Morgan). (Part I.)

High above the water, on the planked crossties of the railroad bridge, go two divisions under Gen. Joseph F. Knipe and Gen. John T. Croxton, a tall and handsome man of coolness and courage, with a fierce hatred of slavery.

Meanwhile, some Nashvillians were wondering how long their food supply would last, *"should Peg-leg Hood keep his seat in our suburbs . . . We may all starve, Mr. Editor,"* said a letter to a newspaper, *"before Gen. Thomas thinks the time has come for him to assume the offensive . . ."*

BELMONT?

—Library of Congress

A view of Thomas' line during the battle—taken from Fort Casino, looking almost straight toward Belmont mansion? A silhouette strongly suggesting turreted and rectangular Belmont appears, in some reproductions, on skyline at arrow. To indicate, we have retouched.

—Library of Congress

Are those Gen. Wood's wagons, following his advance? (Note arrows.) Smoke still rises (right, background) from vacated outer line. This photograph was supposedly shot from Fort Negley, from which the picnic groves are now gone. Notice stumps.

—From Century Magazine

Through the fog came the well-clad Negroes, into slaughter by the railroad.

A THAW was near.

On the morning of Dec. 13 the temperature began to rise. A strong southwest wind sprang up. The ice began to melt. *"Before night,"* said a newspaper, *"the streets of Nashville were changed from solid ice to a sea of mud."*

The thaw is on. In Virginia, Grant doesn't know. He is dispatching Gen. John A. Logan for Nashville. If Thomas hasn't struck when you arrive—relieve him! Grant is preparing to leave for Nashville himself.

It is night. Logan is enroute to Cincinnati.

In Nashville, it is 8 p.m., Dec. 14. Thomas' last staff meeting is ending. His bouyancy returns. He wires Halleck: *". . . The enemy will be attacked tomorrow morning."*

Wires are down. The message won't be received and deciphered in Washington until around midnight, Dec. 15. (By then, the first day of the Battle of Nashville will have been fought. Grant will calm down a little. He will stop his journey in Washington and wait for news of the outcome. Logan will halt in Louisville.)

Midnight is near in Nashville. Wilson's cavalry is in bivouac, on the commons inside the entrenchments. It faces the ground over which he will advance. For some, it is the last night of life. Many an officer has made his will. Arrangements are complete. It is 11:40.

Wilson retires to his tent. Tomorrow is the day. He takes out paper and pen and begins to write a friend:

". . . Everybody else has made his last will and testament or written his wife or sweetheart, but, having nothing to dispose of, and neither wife nor sweetheart to write to, I give you about four minutes before preparing myself for sleep . . . The Rebels are quiescent . . ."

Many years later, in the military schools of Europe, wise warriors would be saying, *"There were only two perfect battles in the history of the world—Austerlitz and Nashville."* And the brain behind the "perfect" Battle of Nashville was "Old Slow Trot."

"It was Thomas," says Douglas, *"not Grant nor Sherman, who diagnosed the situation and made sure of victory."* Behind Thomas was the young horseman from Shawneetown.

And behind Thomas and Wilson; behind the lethal mobility of their 12,000? Behind them and the new cavalry concept was Forrest, their foeman; Forrest, the Middle Tennessean, and what they had learned from him . . .

McKinney says, *"For more than three years Nathan Bedford Forrest, the foremost leader of mounted troops in the English-speaking world, taught the Union commanders in the west the fine points of horse-fighting. Grant, Thomas, Sherman and Sheridan were four of his pupils. What they accomplished with Forrest's lessons is the history of the last months of the war."*

Bugles are blowing in the dense white fog. It's 4 a.m. in Nashville, Thursday, Dec. 15. All along the Yankee line reveille is sounding. Up! This is the day of the juggernaut. Orders: Be ready at 6.

A rain has ceased. It is much warmer. The ground has thawed. It will turn to mire. The fog begins a ghostly stirring at tent-level as about 66,000 warmly-clad Yankees bustle through it.

Of these, 54,881 are available for battle. They have three days' rations in their haversacks. Each infantryman has 50 to 60 rounds of ammunition.

Around 5,000 will hold the interior line from Hill 210 to Fort Negley. Six thousand more will cooperate. Hood has 23,053, ragged and underfed. Parched corn will be the breakfast for many.

Soon after 4 a.m. the fog begins its slow-motion swirl along the Federal outer line. Wood's IV and Schofield's XXIII Corps are moving. Steedman is preparing for his feint.

None goes far. They're simply moving out of the works into take-off positions beyond, ready to roll when the fog lifts.

Thomas, waking at the St. Cloud, has taken no chances with Nashville's safety. As the units move from the line, into the vacancies pour raw recruits, armed quartermaster forces and Nashville garrison troops.

Thus the Federal line stays intact. It covers all turnpikes to the city's heart. And nearly 56,000 men are freed for action.

Thomas, eyeing the fog at his windows, knows the four-jointed steam-roller at his right is being put together as one piece—Wood at the hub, Wilson on the rim, Smith on Wilson's left and Schofield's infantry (in reserve) next to Wood. It will swing in a giant quarter-circle, from the river to Hood's left at Hillsboro. When the quarter-circle reaches Hillsboro, the fatal hour will have come.

Wood, at the Federal center, has left Belmont. With 14,171 men, his is the largest corps in Thomas' army. It's closest of all to Hood's fortified Hillsboro line. Anything might happen here, if things went wrong.

Wood has thought of Adelicia's art treasures at Belmont. He has had them transported to town and stored at the home of Mrs. James K. Polk, widow of President Polk, at Union and Vine streets (Seventh Avenue today).

At much older Rokeby, no precaution is taken. The big house holds old treasures, but guards are needed elsewhere. There is one hope. Rokeby is "haunted." At least, so the Negroes say. Many Yankee soldiers share the superstition.

Will the "ghost" protect the house from looting as its mistress leaves, to seek safety during the battle?

—U. S. Signal Corps photo
Gen. B. F. Cheatham
Meets Steedman's Feint

COLLEGE STREET (today's Third Avenue S.) in 1868. At upper left is the old N&C Railroad along which, southeast of town, Steedman's Negro soldiers perished in the first overland movement of the battle. Against horizon: the Capitol, Downtown Presbyterian Church and the Maxwell House.

RIDE! Then dismount and fight! Out thundered Wilson's horsemen. (This painting of Yankee cavalry, by William T. Trego, portrayed an earlier scene near Murfreesboro.)

—National Archives, Record Group 111

SHE IS Mrs. Oliver Bliss Hayes, mother of Adelicia and Corinne. Rokeby is their girlhood home, named from a poem by Sir Walter Scott.

Rokeby's doors, even when bolted fast, reputedly had a way of suddenly flying open. Footsteps would patter up and down halls and stairway. Unknown faces would suddenly appear in mirrors over one's shoulder. But worst of all was the stumpy frightfulness of the ghost itself: only a floating head, with feet attached . . . and no body . . .

At least, such were the stories which would cling to the old plantation seat even after it had become, by 1875, the first dormitory of Vanderbilt University, housing divinity students and later law students at 1908 Grand Ave. (It was razed a number of years ago.)

Be watchful, ghost! For it's a perfect time for looting, in this fog which wraps all: the Capitol, where a man-to-be-President soon will begin his day; and the hills, the fields and the vital roads where another man-to-be-President is groping southward.

Benjamin Harrison, a young Indiana colonel, is moving through the eerie whiteness to block Granny White near the city. He's leading the Seventh Indiana Regiment, First Brigade, of the provisional division of Gen. Charles Cruft (Steedman's detachment). Harrison will go to the White House in 1889.

Just now his thoughts are pretty much like any other soldier's. He's fretted about the slowness of the mails. He's 31 and wants a letter from his wife.

He's hoping, too, for promotion to brigadier general and itching to talk with Thomas about it. He knows, however, that Thomas has enough on his mind, with this battle to be fought and all the harassment from Washington.

And Thomas now knows the probable cause of some of his troubles. At the telegraph office a message had been found, to Grant, in Schofield's handwriting. ("Many officers here," it said, think Thomas "certainly too slow.") They had brought it to Thomas. But why, Thomas asked, should Schofield do this?

Steedman asked, "Who would succeed you in case of removal?" Sadly Thomas shook his head. "I see." Schofield, his second in command; Schofield the ambitious, with a probable chip on his shoulder . . .

(Seventeen years after the Battle of Nashville, Gen. Steedman will declare in the New York Times, that three days before the battle, Thomas knew Schofield was "playing the part of Judas, by telegraphing Grant." Schofield denied it. Few historical writers seem to think Steedman cooked up the story.)

It's 5 a.m.

Thomas is mounting his horse, near what is now Church and Fifth. The gaslights, casting feeble nimbi in the mist, silhouette his staff on horseback about him. They are riding away. It's still a good while till sunrise.

There he goes, "Old Slow Trot," to the steady clatter of hooves. The master of detail, who wouldn't be rushed. The man with the steady blue eyes, who will take no wooden nickels from jumpy superiors or ambitious underlings.

Suddenly Thomas halts the cavalcade and beckons to a quartermaster major on the sidewalk. Quietly Thomas asks, "Have I drawn my allowance of coal for this month?"

No, says the puzzled major, in charge of fuel.

"Then will you please send 14 bushels of coal to my neighbor?" said Thomas. "I borrowed from him the other day."

Then Thomas rode on to his hilltop (between Hillsboro and Belmont Boulevard) to guide the battle destiny of 55,000 men. From this high spot, at the main salient of his outer works, Thomas would watch his corps move into their pre-battle line-up.

Out at 511 Summer St. (Fifth Avenue S.) Capt. Driver is coming down the steps of his home. The 61-year-old former sea captain has been pressed into duty to help man the guns of Fort Negley. It is said they commanded his house.

Above, the original "Old Glory" is stirring in the fog. Driver looks up, toward the second story window from which it hangs.

Does he think of the day he had named her, back in old Salem, when he was young and she was new, and she'd hung above his craft as the snow settled down through the rigging?

Does he think, too, of his own divided house and his three Confederate sons? Will somebody take down his Flag, while he's away? Well, they'd better not!

"If 'Old Glory's' not in sight," the captain shouts to those within his own house, "then I'll blow the house out of sight, too!"

Meanwhile, over by the Murfreesboro Pike and the railroad, Gen. Steedman is moving southeastward, clockwise, with 7,541 troops, mostly Negroes.

His troops were the first out of entrenchments. They will fire the first ground shots. (But the first shots of all will come from Yankee gunboats on the river.)

Steedman's detachment (according to McKinney) is made up of fragments from 200 regiments. Seven of his nine regiments are Negro. His command also includes persons who can neither speak nor understand English. He has two batteries of artillery.

Steedman has scouted the ground, appraised the terrain. He's to strike at 6:30, but the fog will prevent it.

Gen. Jacob D. Cox of Schofield's Third Division is moving along Hillsboro, forming at the rear of Wood's right. Gen. Darius N. Couch, of Schofield's Second Division, is coming out of the works on Harding Pike. He forms at the rear of Smith's left.

Into position about 10 a.m. will come Gen. Smith, with 10,461 men, for his stand between Wilson and Schofield. Smith has the biggest attack role. He's to form on and near the Harding Pike and, with Wilson's aid, make the main smash at the Rebel left.

Smith's Second Division, commanded by Gen. Kenner Garrard, is to link with Wood's right. At Garrard's right will be Smith's First Division, commanded by Gen. John McArthur. In Smith's rear, ready to aid either flank, will be Smith's Third Division, under Col. Johnathan B. Moore.

It is 6 o'clock. Most of Wood's IV Corps is settling into take-off location. It will become the link between Smith's left and Steedman's right.

But Wood's pivot corps, with the shortest distance to travel, must wait and wait, until noon, for the lining up of the far-traveling corps at their right.

When that fateful time comes, Wood's Gen. Washington L. Elliott will be in line with Smith's left. Next to Elliott will be Wood's Gen. Nathan Kimball, and next to Kimball, Gen. Beatty from Hillside.

As Smith's Mid-Westerners advance, Elliott will move with them; then Kimball, then Beatty. Thus the pivot will swing, pushed by events at its right.

Wagons and ambulances wait—10 ambulances, five ammunition wagons and others with entrenching tools—all set to go slopping through the mud behind each of Wood's three divisions.

Wilson is waiting, on the rim. His thousands of horses stand pawing the softening mud. He has eyed the goo. He's prepared. All artillery is double-teamed. At least four horses will pull even the smallest gun. Leave all other vehicles behind! When his cavalry moves, it must be as the wind.

—Library of Congress

Citizens and soldiers watch the first day's battle. (From the northwest corner of Capitol Hill?) They seem to be facing west, the camera facing northwest. At arrow is smoke of a train—about to start its curve into the station?

—U. S. Signal Corps photo, National Archives

Gen. James H. Wilson
(Forgotten Man of the Battle of Nashville)

Southwest front of Capitol, Dec. 15, 1864, looking toward the struggle. Near base of columns may be seen the Flag of Fort Negley in the distance.

WILSON WILL support Smith's right. Hatch's division, the cavalry left, will link with Smith's infantry. On Hatch's right, Croxton will conform with his movements. But Croxton has only one brigade. (His other two are in Kentucky, pursuing Lyon.)

Gen. Johnson's cavalry division is to fork off from Wilson's right and clear Charlotte. Johnson has three brigades, two unmounted. He's to hit the Rebel cavalry by the river.

Knipe's division, one brigade mounted and one not, is to move onto Harding Pike, follow the general advance and reinforce where needed.

In this almost perfect battle, there will be two slip-ups after all.

● From Gen. Smith's corps, Gen. McArthur's division (in coming out of the works) will cross Wilson's front instead of his rear. This will delay the advance of the cavalry column for an hour and a half. It will hold up the whole army. At least, so Wilson will explain the blunder.

And in front the infantry will go, while horses champ and whinny, and horsemen swear the air purple, waiting for the foot-soldiers to plod on out of the way.

● The other slip: Smith's column will swing farther left than Thomas planned. In the afternoon, to correct this, Schofield's XXIII Corps will be ordered from its dawn position (to fill in the space on Smith's right.)

It's sunrise, 6:50. The orb of the sun is blanketed by the fog. Heavy firing sounds from the river, the first gunfire of the battle. It's Fitch's gunboats, shelling the Rebels.

—From The Nashville Banner, May 13, 1928

CIVIL WAR "USO" in Nashville. Soldiers Home, it was called, at Deaderick and old Summer streets, now Fifth Avenue. Known as the Planters' Hotel to civilians, it stood next to St. Mary's Church (then a cathedral). Steeple of St. Mary's at upper left.

Then whoom! What's the new thunder? The guns of the "Fighting Parson," and Rucker and Chalmers, are talking back from the banks, far more effectively than Fitch ever thought they could.

All this was the big noise which actually opened the Battle of Nashville. Rebel guns were chewing into gunboats. Splinters and railings were flying. Then quickly the noise grew louder, more convulsive. Guns from the Yankee forts about town had begun to roar.

Fire and smoke were belching from the guns of Fort Negley and Fort Casino. It was throbbing from the other forts. Batteries in the Federal lines began banging away in the rising tumult, bringing answering fire from the Rebels.

Over by the railroad, Steedman is feeling his way southward. Using 3,200 men, he's pushing into the fog, through which a whitish glow is coming from the rising sun. The first overland advance has begun.

The Rebels see the vague mass coming. Who and what? They can't be sure, despite the ghostly light. For 30 minutes they peer, waiting, muskets ready. Then they see the faces of the Negro troops. They are headed for the railroad below Rains' cut. The Rebels keep silent.

Among them is Pvt. Charles B. Martin, First Georgia Volunteers. He wrote, "After crossing the railroad, the darkies formed a line of battle and, thinking they had not been discovered, prepared to surprise the men in our works by an attack on the rear."

The Negroes keep coming. Martin's account, from the Confederate Veteran Magazine, continues:

"When they had moved forward enough to enable our brigade to form in their rear, one of the divisions in the works about-faced. The other did likewise and wheeled to the left.

"We had the darkies in our trap. When we commenced firing on them, complete demoralization developed. We took no prisoners." Many of the Negroes died in their tracks, with brave astonishment. Others leaped into the railroad cut and were killed or crippled by their fall.

The first blood-bath of the Battle of Nashville had been in Negro blood, about 8:30.

"Not a single white man was seen among the killed," Martin wrote. "Where were their officers?"

Another account says: "We knocked down 800 of them and that was the end of it. They retired."

"This proves the manhood of the Negro," Gen. Thomas said when he rode over the field and saw the many Negro corpses. Clothing had been removed from many. Some ragged Rebels were, no doubt, better clothed next day.

One witness to the slaughter seems to have been a Negro man named Steve, from Charlotte. He had run away to "jine de Yankees" in Nashville. Whether he was driving a wagon for them or actually participated in the attack is not clear.

He went back to Charlotte, fast, and gave this account:

"Why, dey jes made breas'works of dem niggers. Dey took a brogan of niggers, dem Yankees did, and driv' 'em up to dem Rebels, and de Rebels shoot 'em down; and den dey driv up another brogan of niggers, and de Rebels dey shoot dem down. Den I lef'. And here I is, and here I stays."

Cheatham's skirmish line dropped back. His main line held. So did the brigade by the railroad. Steedman's demonstration continued.

Hood was undeceived. He recognized it as a cover for the up-coming push at his left. He had suspected such since Wilson's crossing at Edgefield.

For that reason Hood had sent Ector's brigade to back up Chalmers. From the Harding Pike, it now stretched thinly toward the Charlotte Pike.

There it waits. It is around 9 a.m. The sun is climbing the sky. The fog is turning to wisps. Big guns keep booming, with a background rumble of artillery. The river bluff is a sounding board for the gleeful fury of Kelley. He's having a magnificent time knocking showers of debris from Fitch's gunboats.

The Yankee cavalry, in a few hours, will be swarming at his rear . . .

Hood has left Travelers' Rest and gone to Lealand, the residence of Judge John M. Lea. Here, east of Granny White, Hood will establish new headquarters. The Yankee plan is clear: They're trying to roll up his left.

Vine Street (today's Seventh Avenue) when guns were booming.

Col. Datus E. Coon
Scourge of the Redoubts

SMITH'S INFANTRY is swinging on, connecting with Wood's right, wheeling south. Smith's vanguard is soon close to Harding Road . . . and, at last, Wilson's path is uncluttered by infantrymen. (Since 8:30, when the fog had cleared enough for advance, Wilson has had to cool his heels.) It's 10 o'clock or later.

One and a half hours lost! On a short winter day, when time is precious!

But the infantry, at last, is out of his way.

Out thunder the 9,000 horsemen. Out rumbles their artillery, eight horses pulling the big guns. In the pale winter sunlight the earth seems to shake. Mud is flying and falling from pounding hooves, falling like crazy black hail. Rich farmlands will be churned to loblolly. Through it, too, go 3,500 mud-splitters afoot, Wilson's unmounted men.

This is the enemy's iron rim, turning at last. This is the juggernaut's roller, the flesh and earth crusher, with Gen. Hatch on the inside, next to the infantry —nearly 23,000 men altogether. This is Wilson's theory, on the hoof at last and riding: a theory that the cavalry trooper should be "essentially an infantryman with four legs."

At Nashville, it's being put to the test for the first time, on a large scale, by the North. (Forrest has known all along.) At Nashville, Wilson is out to prove that the value of cavalry is vigorous offense—not defense.

At Nashville, Wilson is out to prove that the value of the horse is to get the trooper to the point of combat; to make him a mobile infantryman, who dismounts to fight, leaving his horse behind the scene, and becomes a cavalryman again to pursue.

Increased firepower is changing warfare. Wilson knows this. Massed cavalry charges can no longer do what they once did. One man with a Spencer repeating carbine is now *"equivalent to three with any other firearm."* And Wilson's men have Spencers. He's seen to that.

This is the landslide of horses, from plows and carriages and circus rings, and the stable of a vice president-elect; and there's neatly canned death in the guns of their riders.

It's a bright new day for Gen. Johnson—whom Gen. Morgan had captured near Hartsville on a hot August day out of Gallatin, more than two years ago . . . after Johnson had promised to "bring Morgan back in a bandbox."

Long since exchanged, Gen. Johnson is to sweep Charlotte of Rebels. How different from those audacious days of '62—when Morgan had merrily eaten the Hartsville hotel meal which Johnson had ordered!

Now Morgan is gone without his feathered hat, in a pine box down a mountain road in a one-horse wagon, gone with the Rebel laughter he knew in Rebel rooms that were 20 by 20 by 12. Such houses now need paint, their stables needs horses, the dogs need bones, and even death has become so hum-

drum that during the Battle of Nashville an enterprising undertaker will advertise, with bland impersonality, his willingness to *"attend promptly to the transportation of bodies."*

The undertaker must be faring well from Yankee trade, for he's offering *"zinc caskets"*—if you can afford one for your beloved. (Not many Rebels just then could afford even the black velvet with which to cover, in simple dignity, a plain homemade *"elbow-shaped"* wooden coffin.) Finally, at the end of the advertisement, the undertaker proudly offers as reference, *"Andrew Johnson, Military Governor."* (If in doubt, *"refer to me,"* says the vice president-elect!)

Death was abroad. It was riding with the horsemen. It was marching through the nearly-cleared fog. And although the Battle of Nashville would be a battle of maneuver, rather than colossal slaughter, death was reaching out, at this moment, toward Richland Creek . . .

Beyond the creek, Ector's men see the wave of Yankees, rolling at them from the northward. Smith's whole corps, supported by artillery and Wilson's horsemen, is about to hit the 700. The Rebels are still in breastworks north of Harding Pike. Their skirmish line still stretches across it. Against such numbers, they can only make a gesture of defense.

Not far away, the Rebels' only cavalry brigade (Rucker's, headed by Chalmers) is still on the high ground north of Charlotte.

Both units, Rucker's and Ector's, are under orders to drop back if need be. Fall back and run for it! That's for Ector's men. Run two miles or more, to the main Rebel line on Hillsboro. They wait—

In the skirmish line, they're bracing for the sea of horsemen. It's flooding out at them from the Yankee lines to the northeast, Wilson's men. At the same time, another flood is surging straight at them. This is the dismounted men of Col. Robert E. Stewart, from Hatch's cavalry division, supported by the mounted brigade of Col. Datus E. Coon.

Hold as long as you can! The order goes from Coleman to the skirmish line. Then retreat. Meet us at the main line on Hillsboro.

With the remainder, Coleman swung away, heading south for Gen. Stewart's left on Hillsboro. Two miles to go. Hatch's horsemen see them fleeing. What luck! Hatch sees his chance.

Out Harding Pike he roared and on into the grounds of Belle Meade plantation, overrunning Chalmers' headquarters while Chalmers still stood with Rucker's brigade from Charlotte to the river. The gunboats had been driven off a good while ago.

Worse was coming. Gen. Johnson's cavalry soon would be heading toward him. It too had been delayed, by the fog and the frontal crossing. Now go! It was well after 10 o'clock.

Col. Sylvester Hill
Take No. 2!

The three related scenes of these two pages, when viewed in sequence, provide the broadest known pictorial horizon of Nashville's battle-time.

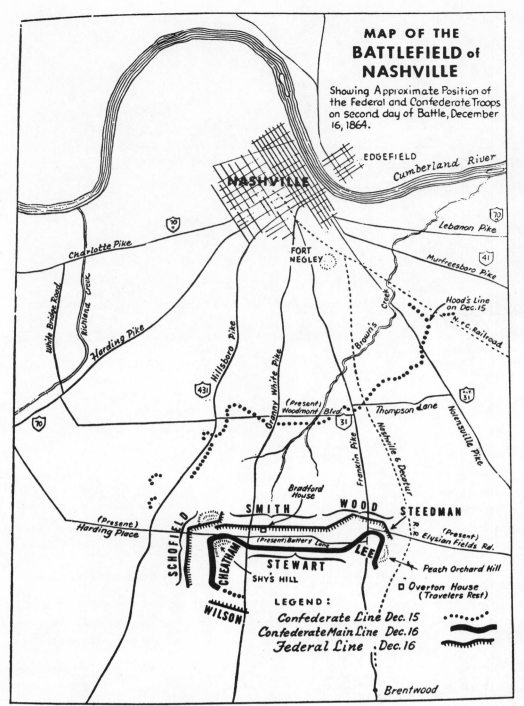

MAP OF THE
**BATTLEFIELD of
NASHVILLE**

Showing Approximate Position of
the Federal and Confederate Troops
on second day of Battle, December
16, 1864.

LEGEND:
Confederate Line Dec. 15
Confederate Main Line Dec. 16
Federal Line Dec. 16

The Battlefield, Second Day

Gen. E. C. Walthall
Hold the Wall!

Gen. W. W. Loring
At Redoubts 1 and 2

Capt. Charles L. Lumsden
*Hero of Redoubt 4
(Held three hours)*

CHALMERS' DAB of cavalry was now alone. He fought on, holding off the tidal wave of Johnson's men until the Rebel guns could be withdrawn. Then he fell back, two miles out Charlotte, opposite Bell's Mills.

The Rebel blockade of the Cumberland was about to end. But the Rebels would escape. "Fighting Parson" Kelley was still in the fight, with Rucker and Chalmers.

Johnson pursued. Gunboats followed, on Johnson's request.

Down-river they dropped, to lob big shells at Chalmers' changed position. The noise was terrific. Homes were damaged. The Rebels' stand was unshaken.

Once more, as two years ago at Hartsville, Johnson wasn't setting the woods on fire . . . and over the ridge to the south, Ector's men were panting on toward uncertain safety in the main Rebel line. Close behind, hot on their trail, came McArthur's 4,000 infantrymen.

Smith had begun to roll around 10 a.m. (About this time, on the Yankee left, Steedman was getting ready for his second strike. He would take some buildings on Rains' Hill. From there, sharpshooters would crack at the Rebs. For the remainder of the day, Steedman would be no great worry to Hood.)

Smith was soon south of the Harding Pike, lined up and moving on. He has begun his gigantic left wheel, with Gen. Garrard at the pivot. The Yankee steam-roller was really traveling now, rolling at the Rebel left and Gen. Stewart.

Smith's right guide, veering on left, seems to be paying no attention to Hatch's men on Smith's right. After the swing at Belle Meade, Hatch is trying to prolong the length of Smith's infantry line. But Hatch is on the outside. Can't Smith remember that? Hatch has the longer distance. Thousands of his men are soon running, to keep up with Smith's left-lunging infantry. (It is said that some of Hatch's men *"had to run three miles."*)

But they will keep up. And soon they will slam into the Rebel redoubts with the infantry. (Before they get to the top of the fortified hills, some will be crawling. For safety? Perhaps. And also because they were gasping for breath.)

The Yankees are wheeling through the weak Rebel gap, between the Reb left and the river. They're wheeling towards Hillsboro Pike, with Hatch and Col. Coon at Smith's right. Skirmishers are fleeing before them.

The big clash is near.

Stewart sees that his extreme left will soon be struck by a force stronger than Hood's whole army. He rushed a warning to Gen. Edward C. Walthall. Make ready!

Walthall sent men rushing to Redoubts 4 and 5. Hold against all hazards! Into each redoubt hurried a company of infantry and a battery of artillery. Two ragged little islands of courage—could they stem the tide?

It would not be their baptism of fire. Walthall and his men had been in the thick of the slaughter at Franklin. He's a fighter, determined, young— only 33, the youngest of all Hood's division commanders.

—Century War Book, 1861-1865

THE ROCK WALL, held by Walthall, had to be yielded at last. As night settled along Hillsboro Road, Dec. 15, 1864, the scene may have resembled this.

ACROSS FROM the redoubts ran the stone wall. Behind it, on the eastern side of the pike, Walthall put what was left of his division after the redoubts' manning—Quarles' (Gen. William A.) brigade at center, commanded by Gen. George D. Johnson; Cantey's (Gen. James) brigade at left, commanded by Gen. Charles M. Shelley, and Reynolds' (Gen. Daniel H.) brigade at right, connecting with Sears' (Gen. Claudius W.) brigade in the main line, at Gen. William L. Loring's left.

Stewart called on Hood for reinforcements. Hood will try to get them there in time, from Lee and Cheatham's corps. But time is running out once more. Hood has sown the wind. He's about to reap the whirlwind.

He's left Lealand. He's gone closer to the fighting. He's atop a high hill (now Shy's). It is two blocks west of Granny White (now crossed on its northern slope by Harding Place and accessible by steep footpath from Benton Smith Road). Here he has set up an observation post.

At his left, to the northeast, running Rebels are topping the ridge above Hillsboro. It's Ector's, pouring westward across the front of Smith's infantry. Some have their mouths wide open, gasping. Some look back. The 4,000 Bluecoats are closer. Ector's men are nearing Redoubt 4.

"Stay and help us!" cry the defenders. They have a wall about eight feet tall between the four embrasures. "Help us hold!"

"It can't be done!" cry the running men. "There's a whole army on your front!"

The cry is heard by the 148 men. They hold.

They'll write their courage upon a chapter of Nashville's story, as the heroes of No. 4—48 artillerymen, 10 to a gun, with extras to replace casualties—commanded by Capt. Charles L. Lumsden, and supported by 100 infantrymen in trenches three feet deep.

Lumsden is pleading with Ector's officers. Stand with us! Lumsden is an alumnus of Virginia Military Institute. The University of Alabama has known him. There, when war began, he had been commandant of cadets. His pleas are in vain.

On go Ector's men, downhill towards Hillsboro, heading for the rock wall. They will reach its brief shelter after noon. Walthall will place them on his left. The line still won't reach to Redoubt 5 where the Yankee hurricane is about to hit. (Some of Ector's men took shelter in No. 5.)

McArthur's men are nearing Redoubt 4. McArthur is wary. He's uncertain of No. 4's strength. It's no place to gamble. He halts on a ridge 1,800 feet to the west. He begins to shell Lumsden's position with three batteries of 24 rifled guns. Lumsden has only four smooth-bore Napoleons. All thunder defiance.

It is around noon. For nearly an hour the bombardment has roared. After the shelling—an attack by 4,000? Against 148?

Lumsden sends word to Stewart by horseback. A charge will come soon!

Stewart replied, about 12:30 p.m.: Tell Capt. Lumsden it is necessary to hold to the last minute.

Stewart needed men. He saw what was coming. The shadow of disaster was deepening at Redoubt 5, his outermost position. The first blow had fallen. No. 5—detached, without support—was being enveloped.

Wilson's cavalry had clattered to the slopes around it, the brigade of Col. Coon. His horsemen dismounted. They began to advance, their rifles spitting a seven-blast rhythm of death. An artillery battery supported them, McArthur's First Brigade.

It began an hour-long shelling of No. 5. The ridge guns of Gen. McArthur kept blasting at Lumsden's No. 4. Both kept holding, roaring back, each with only four smooth-bores. "Above our heads," wrote a survivor of No. 4, "was a network of shrieking steel."

—Courtesy State Library and Archives

Holy Trinity Episcopal Church, one of Nashville's most notable architectural gems, served as a powder magazine. The graceful stonework adorning its tower in this picture is, regrettably, no longer there—and silently beckons for a benefactor and restoration.

Mrs. W. H. Jackson
Mistress of Belle Meade
Stood Amid Gunfire

Miss Mary Bradford
(Later Mrs. John Johns)
Turn and Fight!

—Pictorial Field Book of the Civil War

Ruins on Montgomery Hill
(The mansion had burned before the battle)

IT IS 12:30 P.M. Three major units of the Yankee steam-roller are in precise position now—Smith, Wood and Wilson, with more than 30,000 men—moving to storm Hood's left, from Redoubt 5 to Montgomery Hill, where the Rebel line bends sharply eastward.

Hood's critical hour has come.

Gen. Wood gives a command. The Federal juggernaut moves.

Artillery thunders into crescendo. Rifles begin to crackle and the 30,000 swing forward in unison, *"a pageant . . . magnificently grand and inspiring,"* Wood would write. As far as *"the eye could reach, the lines and masses of blue moved forward in perfect order . . ."* Masses, yes. Including cavalry *"masses,"* which Wilson so long had advocated, to hurl *"into the bowels"* of the South.

Here it comes. And who can stop it? Where are Hood's dreams of glory now? And where the jitters of Gen. Grant?

Serene "Old Slow Trot" has them both in his pocket. Out there in the mud and through the timbered slopes, his castiron plan is coming into its full sweep of calculated power. And hundreds of Nashvillians watch.

The hills were *"black"* with spectators in the rear of Schofield's dawn position. They had come out from the city *"in droves."*

"Nearly all" were in *"sympathy with the Confederacy,"* one of Schofield's officers later wrote.

"The city was unusually quiet," one Yankee-influenced newspaper would say, *"notwithstanding that the rumble of artillery was constantly heard. The people went about as if nothing unusual were occurring . . . and gave themselves no uneasiness."*

This was a purely Federal view. Doubtless the city was quiet, but it was the quiet of a terrible foreboding.

Nothing was certain in the tense moments around noon when the great turning wheel brought the hub, Wood's Third Division, up before Montgomery Hill. How strongly was it defended? To Wood, the assignment looked rough.

(This hill, on which the Montgomery mansion had burned a few years before, did suggest strength. The masonry ruins, stalking out of once beautiful gardens, hinted at a stronghold. It wasn't.)

This was the lonely spot from which Hood, five days before, had pulled back. Only skirmishers remained in the line now crossing its top.

Wood commanded his gunners to chew up the heights. Two batteries shelled it.

Then, at 1 p.m., Col. P. Sidney Post's brigade swept up the slopes. From behind entrenchments the little band of Rebels stubbornly resisted. Over the blue wave came. They were swamped.

Wood is surprised. How easily taken! He makes a guess: It's Redoubt No. 1 on the nearby hill, not Montgomery Hill itself, which is the ace of this Confederate hand. Montgomery Hill is necessity's sham.

Redoubt No. 1 is the vital corner, where the Rebel line swings southward, toward Walthall and the outer redoubts. Along with Redoubt 2, it is the main Rebel stronghold. Both No. 1 and No. 2 are under the command of Gen. Loring, a one-armed veteran of the Mexican War.

His guns, for hours, have been hacking bloodily from No. 1 into the massing Federals. Shall Wood order its frontal assault?

No. Not now. That would be too costly. Wait. Bring up two batteries. Center their fire on No. 1's top. Bombard it to rubble. Then attack. (It has been written that Wood took a noontime *"breather"* before No. 1.) It was the pause of prudence.

The shelling began.

Reinforcements were now being rushed toward Hood's extreme left. They came from Lee's center where hostilities were not yet erupting, two brigades, and then two more.

The brigade of Gen. A. M. Maningault (wounded at Franklin) took its position behind the rock wall opposite Redoubt 4. Then the brigade of Gen. Zachariah C. Deas took its stand at Maningault's right. Sharp's (Gen. Jacob H.) brigade and Brantley's (Gen. William F.) brigade came up later.

Sources of Old Pictures

MOST OF THE illustrations in Part IV are credited individually. Many first appeared in *Harper's Weekly* and *Century Magazine.*

Again the works of Edwin Forbes and Gilbert Gaul appear. This time a Henry Mosler painting is included, by courtesy of the Andrew L. Todd Library, Murfreesboro.

The Banner is especially grateful to Lanier Merritt of Nashville and to Walter King Hoover of Smyrna for full access to extensive Civil War collections, and to Mrs. Paul E. Purks of Nashville for the use of both family documents and pictures, including the diary of her grandfather, W. L. B. Lawrence, master of Hillside.

From Mr. Merritt's large pictorial collection came such rarities as the Federal encampment at Nashville and pictures of many individuals.

From the trove of Civil War books and periodicals of Mr. Hoover (who has aided us on all four parts of this series) came many a hard-to-find illustration, such as the ruins of the Montgomery mansion.

All this took time. The die was well cast when they began to arrive.

Down at the left end of the line, Ector's men have taken their position. Their long race is over. They've escaped the frying pan. Soon they'll be in the fire. They're holding the feeble end in a desperate effort by Walthall to stretch his line as far as possible, a paper-shell dyke, against the wave. And before reinforcements arrive, the battered redoubts will begin to fall.

The great blue tide is almost cresting. Yankee infantry is crushing at Walthall's front and flank. Stewart's whole left, of which Walthall's men are the southern tip, is stretched out far too thin.

And now, to increase the enormous Federal odds, an order will go to Schofield's XXIII Corps of 10,207 men. Come forward! They've been standing idle since dawn.

There's a special need for them now. Smith, still veering too far left, has given the cavalry too broad a stretch to cover. Thomas sees this.

He's sitting his horse in the rear of Wood's right. With him is Schofield. Shells are dropping close. "Old Slow Trot" pays no attention except for the slightest movement of his bridle fingers, to quiet his mount.

Now and then, without a word, Thomas puts out his hand for Schofield's field glasses. *"Smith has not reached far enough to the right,"* Thomas says. *"Put in your troops."*

There they go, surging out toward Hillsboro at last. This will free Hatch, to cut loose from Smith and swing widely westward beyond Hood's outermost left.

The bombardment of Redoubt 5 has almost ceased. Are you ready, Col. Coon? His brigade has been ordered to charge it. His dismounted men start up. Rebel guns let go again with grape and canister. Yankee artillery answers.

Lead from the single-shot muskets is whining down the slope. The swarm of Coon's men, with their seven-shot repeaters, is too much. Up, too, comes McArthur's First Brigade.

No. 5 is being overrun. It's guns are seized. The hilltop is changing hands. Coon's men said they entered first. Smith's men said they arrived at the same time.

Hot lead hit both.

The deadly greeting is from Lumsden at No. 4. He's seen No. 5 fall. He's giving them flaming thunder from his own beleaguered hill to the north.

Below Lumsden, investing his slopes, swarms the remainder of Hatch and McArthur's divisions. Sixteen regiments are coming up after Lumsden—16 regiments, heading for what is left of 148 Rebels.

The guns of Redoubt 5 are turned upon Lumsden. His own four guns keep booming above the clatter of musketry. The Yankees are close enough to snatch at the end of a rifle. The network of overhead steel is still shrieking. A shell comes screaming low. Off goes the top of a gunner's head. Gore splats in Lumsden's hair.

He's standing by a gun, a charge in hand. Where's the man with the friction primers?

"Captain," yells Sgt. James R. Maxwell, *"he's gone with the friction primers!"* Somebody has run. It's high time. They have held for more than three hours. Down into the works slides a Yankee.

"Take care of yourselves, boys!" shouts Lumsden. The Rebels go sprinting downhill. Bullets whiz behind them. Redoubt 4 has fallen, second of the gallant five.

Sgt. Maxwell, tearing for the rock wall, saw a creek at the foot of the hill. *"Don't think I put a foot in the creek,"* he wrote.

It is 2 p.m. The bold little barriers are gone from Walthall's front. There is nothing now to hold back the Yanks. They come pouring across Hillsboro.

And Schofield's men are steaming up, eager and fresh. They're forming on Smith's right, as ordered. Wilson's big chance is at hand.

He must have smiled, almost gleefully. His cavalrymen can now swing far out from the fray, two miles beyond infantry gunfire, deep toward the Confederate rear, while Chalmers' Rebel horsemen still hold on Charlotte.

Many a Yankee infantryman will later marvel at what he has just seen—Northern cavalrymen dismounting and fighting like real infantrymen! How about that!

The theory of Wilson and Thomas is paying off. It's working.

Earlier, to protect the flank, as Hillsboro hung trembling under Federal pressure, Walthall had sent Ector's brigade down toward the Compton house. The effort was lost when Redoubt 5 fell. The dyke was gone.

Ector's men fell back eastward. A flying wedge slid between the brigade and Cantey's. Ector's unit was now cut off from Walthall, but uncaptured. (At the close of the day, a new assignment would be given them, by Hood himself.)

With two of the shielding redoubts gone, Smith can now blaze loose upon Walthall's line with a shattering bombardment. Walthall has no artillery. He must take it, die standing, surrender, or leave.

The Federal infantry rolling across Hillsboro is widening into a lake. It's engulfing the Compton house (now the home of A. M. Burton at 5050 Hillsboro). The Yanks take two hills, one to the southwest of the house, one to the west.

Walthall is hurling Reynolds' brigade from his right to his left, trying to plug the gap made by Ector's withdrawal. Into the gap left by Reynolds', Walthall thrusts the brigades of Quarles and Cantey. This try, too, will fail, after the Yanks pull guns to the top of the newly seized hills.

Fire from both hills will center upon Reynolds' new position. Both flanks are threatened.

The Rebel line is hair-hung. Reinforcements aren't helping much. Bravely Walthall has held his front. And a door for new slaughter is being opened at his rear . . . Reynolds is being driven back through the woods toward Granny White.

He's fighting at every step and falling back. Walthall's time is short. The Yanks shan't have his men as prisoners. Soon he must pull out, and fast. But not yet, O God, not yet. Another shot and another, and another—

Gen. John McArthur
Hits the Redoubts — and Shy's Hill

Gen. Darius N. Couch
560 rounds at Shy's

—Cook Collection, Valentine Museum, Richmond, Va.

Gen. Stephen D. Lee
"Now is the time for brave men to die!"

Gen. William B. Bate
(Tennessee governor, 1883-87)

—Battles and Sketches of the Army of Tennessee

Gen. A. P. Stewart
Steady and Strong

—Courtesy Lanier Merritt

Col. E. W. Rucker
The bear of the barricade

REDOUBT 1 was still under bombardment. Infantry was not yet smashing heavily at it, and Stewart sped a battery to an eastward hill across the pike. The brigades of Deas and Maningault were sent to back it up. Soon they fled. Yanks took the hilltop.

Chaplain McNeilly is chasing with assistant surgeons to join Reynolds: *"We ran through a hazel thicket . . . The bullets seemed to cut every twig."* Then they were speeding across a field *"over which Deas' and Maningault's men had retreated."* Had they thrown away their equipment to run faster?

". . . Many frying pans were laying around loose," McNeilly wrote. *"My old pan was about worn out. I coveted one with a good long handle, and as I stopped to pick it up I would see another just ahead that suited my fancy better . . . and I continued my flight with my eyes fixed on another pan . . . until I had passed the zone of frying pans and failed to get one . . ."*

The whole Rebel left seemed blazing. McArthur's Third Brigade was plowing toward Redoubt 3. Yankees were falling and seemed barely missed. They had more and to spare.

Here come the Seventh Minnesota Volunteers, a most heroic crew. The guns of Redoubt 1 reach across and claw into them with deadly aim. They're coming up, into No. 3. It's theirs in the lengthening shadows. The afternoon is far along.

Smith's infantry horde is crowding Walthall's front and flank. His flank is being turned. Yankees are gaining the rear of both Walthall and Loring, pushing in toward the back of the stone wall where bleeding men still crouch and fire.

The guns of unconquered Redoubt 2 have opened on fallen Redoubt 3, slapping the victors down. Stop that Rebel fire! Take No. 2 quickly! The order goes from Col. Sylvester G. Hill of the Minnesota Volunteers. He is shot through the head the next moment.

As the colonel slumps, a major repeats the order. Take No. 2! The Federals are crossing the pike and going up once more, at No. 2 (which stood to the rear of 2021 Woodmont Blvd.).

The jig is up for No. 2. Get ready to go—

Redoubt 1 still holds, its earthworks smoking. Bombardment has ripped it. For 30 minutes two batteries have chopped at Loring's high hilltop with fiercely converging fire.

Gen. Stewart has no choice now. He sends orders for both Walthall and Loring to withdraw and form anew, along Granny White. Walthall was already pulling out, however, to avoid capture.

Loring's men, like Walthall's, have faced up to all frontal assault. The hurricane of Yanks is now at his rear.

It was 4 p.m. or a bit later when Thomas sent word for Wood's IV Corps to storm Loring's heights. The assignment went to Gen. Elliott. He was slow and had not advanced by 4:30. The order then went to Gen. Kimball. His division rushed eagerly up and into the entrenchments.

It didn't go up alone. Up and over with them went McArthur's Third Brigade whose Col. Hill had fallen. These were Smith's veterans who, a few minutes earlier, had stormed Redoubt 3. (Elliott made it, too, getting into action with Kimball.)

Loring's men were evacuating Redoubts 1 and 2 as the Federals poured over. Those lucky enough to get away were pulling back in order, through the pink-hued dusk. (Gen. Loring will live to serve as a Pasha in the service of the Khedive of Egypt.) In the chill hint of wintry night they began taking up their new position along Granny White.

The Rebel left is no more.

As it fell, the center and right had to yield, too.

Gen. Sears, in retreat, halted on a small elevation, astride his faithful mount, Billy, which had served him through the entire war. Sears was peering through his field glasses when a shell hit. It shattered one leg below the knee and killed Billy.

Sears stood on the tattering stump in the snowy slush and, ignoring his own condition, wept for his horse. *"Poor Billy,"* he said, tears streaming down his cheeks. *"Poor Billy!"* (Sears' leg was amputated soon afterwards. He survived.)

Darkness is beginning to settle over the smoking hills. Hood's entire army is dropping back. Soldiers go mud-splitting down Granny White.

Suddenly they see her, a girl, in this desolate hour of mud and smoke and disaster—a lovely girl, running from her home onto the lawn as Rebels reel across it. She's Mary Bradford. Tears glitter on her cheeks as she pleads with Deas' retreating men. Please stop! Turn back and fight! Bullets are flying about her.

Her plea is futile. The men run on. (Hood's own report of the battle would enshrine Mary's courage in history.)

The Rebs had a reason to travel. Wood was pounding east, toward the Franklin Pike, rolling up Hood's line as he went. Wood's orders were to take the pike. He won't, by three-quarters of a mile or more. By then it will be 6 o'clock and the sun an hour behind the hills.

The scattered Rebels are converging, heading for Granny White. Gen. Bate and his men are coming from the far Rebel right, Ector's from Hillsboro.

Hood sees Ector's coming in, moving eastward. He stops the weary band. He places them on his observation hill.

"Texans," he says, *"I want you to hold this hill regardless of what transpires around you."* They promise. (Hood had joined the Cause from Texas. They feel a special allegiance to him.)

"This hill . . ." Hood called it, on that chill afternoon. To some, it seems to have had no name. Others called it Compton's Hill. But by another nightfall it will begin to have a new name, synonymous with battle courage—*Shy's Hill*, for Col. William M. Shy, 26, from Franklin, who would die in its defense. Bate was sent atop another hill, north of Shy's.

Near the end of the day, Rucker had moved about a mile farther out

Charlotte. Just now in the last moments of daylight, however, Chalmers is yet to learn that his wagon train has been captured.

He sends Lt. James Dinkins to bring it in from the Belle Meade race track. An escort company goes along.

Dinkins and his company found the wagons in ashes. Yankees were swarming over the place. Dinkins men eased in behind the barn. Then they charged. Nine Yankees were killed or wounded, about 15 captured. The Yankees fled and the Rebs pursued, running into more Yankees.

The action reversed and the Federals chased, with Rebels passing near the mansion's front steps as they retreated. At least, Dinkins himself rode near the front steps—because he saw there, during the heavy exchange of shots, a young woman who *"looked like a goddess . . ."* She was Selene Harding, daughter of the plantation's master, *"standing on the stone arm of the steps"* and waving her handkerchief for the Rebels as bullets fell *"thick and fast about her."*

Dinkins rode past, caught her handkerchief and urged her to go inside. *"She would not, until the boys had disappeared behind the barn."*

Selene's future husband was Gen. Jackson, then in Murfreesboro with Forrest. Had Jackson been there, Wilson's cavalry might not have galloped so wildly through the lanes around Belle Meade. Jackson knew horses. He had to, with Forrest. At Belle Meade, Jackson would fit in superbly.

(After the war, the plantation's stables would come into full and fabulous flower as the home of thoroughbreds. Gamma would be its first foundation mare; and Bonnie Scotland, brought from England, would stand at stud for many years in the 1870s.)

Night was near. Along Hillsboro, the thunder of battle was fading. About this time Schofield's men, under Couch, came rolling up, itching for action. They pushed Bate from his hilltop.

It's not enough for Couch. He wants more blood. He eyes Shy's Hill. Why not attack Ector's, on top?

He didn't get the chance. Darkness fell. Couch bivouacked. The first day of the Battle of Nashville had ended.

—Courtesy of the Harvard College Library

"The Courier," by Gilbert Gaul

"Holding the Line at All Hazards," by Gilbert Gaul

THE YANKEE juggernaut had come to rest, at Granny White. Cold night forms the barricade—night and the brave men of Walthall and Loring.

They're at Granny White as ordered, after leaving the wall. There they halt, facing west.

Thomas is riding back toward the St. Cloud. By morning, he thinks, Hood will be in retreat. Thomas leaves orders with Schofield. Press them as they go!

Thomas' only regret, according to Wilson, was *"for the fog and the delay"* caused by McArthur's blunder. Thomas felt that, *"if our movement could have begun at 7 instead of 10, we should have had three more hours of daylight and might have . . . routed the enemy before dark."*

To those riding with him, Thomas says, *"Unless Hood decamps tonight, to-morrow Steedman will double up his right. Wood will hold his center. Smith and Schofield will again strike his left, while the cavalry works away at his rear."*

He's clattering past a band of prisoners from South Carolina. Negro guards are herding them towards Nashville. The Rebels appeal to Thomas. Will he show them a favor? They'd *"rather die"* than be led into Nashville by Negroes.

"Well," Thomas replied, *"you can say your prayers and get ready to die. These are the only soldiers I can spare."* And he rode on toward Nashville.

Lawrence is writing in his diary:

"The great battle of Nashville was fought today, in which the Confederates under Hood were completely overthrown. From my hillside I witnessed the engagement and listened to the incessant roar of artillery, the rattle of small arms and the shouts of the advancing columns." He, too, must have expected retreat.

At Glen Leven, on the east side of Franklin Road, moans are coming from the dining room. The residence (just south of Caldwell Lane) is serving as a field hospital. The piano is being used as an operating table.

Debris litters Westwood, off Franklin Road (one block east on Westwood Drive, in today's Melrose section). The house, in the line of fire of both armies, has been severely damaged. A cannon ball (said to have come from Fort Negley) fell through the roof of the dining room.

At the Church of the Holy Trinity (Lafayette Street at Ewing and Sixth avenues S.) the altar is being used as a meat-chopping block by the Federals. The baptismal font is their wash basin.

At stately Rokeby, all is quiet. Darkness reigns. All is perfect. No pane is broken, no door jimmied. Its silver, its bric-a-brac, its heirloom trinklets— all stand as its mistress left them. Has the "ghost" been keeping watch? Some homes in the area will be rifled. But not Rokeby.

East of Hillsboro, Schofield is reading his orders with dismay. Press the foe, if they flee? Why, Hood won't retreat! Schofield mounts his horse and rides into Nashville to see Thomas.

"You don't know Hood," (as I do) Schofield says. *"He'll be right there, ready to attack, in the morning . . . or even strike our exposed flank before we can renew the attack!"*

Schofield wants this, he wants that. Make Wilson remain where he is, until Hood's plan is clear. Order Smith to support me if necessary.

(Did Schofield recall the red Franklin meadows—from which he'd kept a safe distance—and the wild Rebels willing to die?)

Thomas listened. He ordered Wilson: Stand pat until sure. He gave Schofield reinforcements, and perhaps Schofield's jumpiness eased.

Then Thomas wired Halleck:

"I attacked the enemy left this morning and drove it from the river, below the city, very nearly to the Franklin Pike, a distance of about eight miles . . . I shall attack again tomorrow, if he stays to fight . . ."

Schofield was right. Hood stayed.

He dropped back two miles. He took his new stand on high ground four miles north of Brentwood. The higher Brentwood hills loomed up behind him, blackly foreboding against the night. Three roads of escape ran through them. These must be kept open, in case of the worst.

These were the Granny White Pike, the Franklin Pike, and a country road curving between them toward Brentwood. Grimly Hood held them. They were routes of escape.

Retreat had compressed him. His new position, by air, would be two and a half miles long, far shorter than the first day. With its curves, however, it stretched a mile longer.

His eastern salient would be the Peach Orchard Hill of the Overtons, just east of Franklin Pike. His western stronghold would be Shy's Hill. Both flanks bent southward. Terrain gave extra toughness.

Gen. Lee dropped back along the Franklin Pike, with all his guns, and became the new Rebel right. Cheatham's men were shifted from right to left. Stewart's men, battered and bruised, were shifted to center. His right connected with Lee, his left with Cheatham. The center would be weakest.

Lee took a stout stand on Peach Orchard Hill. His men, not much used Thursday, were in good shape. Their picks and shovels, biting into the hill, made fast-moving shadows under the leafless limbs. They built an abatis of fallen trees, with their sharpened boughs pointing hideously toward the foe.

All along the line the Rebels were digging in. No matter how weary, prepare for tomorrow!

Their new line swept through the Lea place, crossing Granny White to the scallop of hills east of Hillsboro Pike. Here Shy's Hill stood out as the northern-most of the group. Around its northern and western sides the line bent, turning almost due south. Wilson's cavalry was close to its end. Schofield, facing east, looked upon its western front.

In the darkness, Hood's engineers would blunder. Their breastworks would be set too far back from the brow of Shy's—so far back that, when morning came, Bate's heart must have sunk a little. His men would be so far back that their guns would have almost no command of the slope—in some places, a range as short as five yards.

By then it would be too late to change. Yankee sharpshooters would be peppering his front from neighboring hills.

It is late in the night. Chaplain McNeilly is standing under a big oak, across Franklin Pike from Travelers' Rest. He's one of six men. They stand in a group, *"all that remained of 1,000 men."* This morning there had been 35. The day had cost 29, and McNeilly's unit *"ceased here."* It would be reorganized.

Desolation fills the chaplain. The toll of the years! And suddenly he realizes he has not eaten in 24 hours. Does anyone have anything to eat?

They examine their haversacks. Out comes one slice of raw bacon and a small pone of bread. If that's all—well, the parson won't take it from fighting men. They need it more.

The five soldiers move aside and murmur. Then one steps forward, the bacon and bread outspread on his palm. He's Hughes Gold of Clarksville.

"Parson," Gold says, *"you take this and eat it right here. If you don't, it won't do us any good. For I'll throw it down, and we'll tromp it in the mud."* The parson ate.

Later in the night, Hood's cavalry rejoined his left. By fields and byroads they swung clear of the Yankees, to Hillsboro, near the intersection of the road to Brentwood (a portion of Old Hickory Boulevard today). Here Rucker's brigade would spend what was left of the dreary night. They would not see much action tomorrow, until the final hours. Then blood would gush in a rainstorm, at the fierce *"battle of the barricade."*

The Rebels were back together.

Hundreds of miles northeast, Grant didn't know the Battle of Nashville had begun. Wires to Nashville had been down for hours. Grant had reached Washington that afternoon. He conferred with Lincoln.

Shy's Hill, west of Granny White, where the Confederate line was broken and the stampede began.

I'M GOING to Nashville, Grant said, and take charge myself! Meanwhile, Schofield must take over.

Lincoln objected. So did Stanton. Grant had his way. He wrote his third order in six days for Thomas' removal. He gave it to Eckert. Send it! Grant prepared to resume his hurried journey.

Later in the night Eckert managed to get in touch with Pittsburgh. It could relay from Louisville. Eckert could now get a message through.

The future Western Union president made a big decision on his own. He would hold up the order removing Thomas (until it could be learned just what was what in Nashville). Has anything been delayed from there?

Yes, here it is: First, the telegram from Thomas, hours old, that he will attack "*in the morning.*" Why, he's already fighting! Then one from Van Duzer, detailing Thomas' first day's triumph.

Eckert ran toward the door. He saw an ambulance, jumped in, and soon was waking Stanton. They headed for the White House. Inside the rattling horse-drawn vehicle, Eckert admits he has held up the order. Stanton, in the rosy glow of good news, isn't mad at anybody.

The horses are pounding down Pennsylvania Avenue. Wake the President! Soon they see a candle's glow on the landing of the stairway. Lincoln stands there in his nightgown, candle in hand. He, too, approves what Eckert had done.

And so Abraham Lincoln received his first word of the Battle of Nashville. Next morning he would wire Thomas: "*. . . You made a magnificent beginning. A grand consummation is within your easy reach. Do not let it slip.*"

Easy? Perhaps Lincoln had been listening to Grant.

Over Nashville, dismal dawn is breaking. There's a chill in the air, a slight fog, a hint of rain. The Yankees can make an earlier start. Gen. Thomas, riding back to the front from the St. Cloud, sees a young woman standing by her window.

Suddenly she recognizes him and slams the window.

Thomas smiled faintly. (The smile might have been broader could he have known that, in a day of future peace, the young woman would become the bride of one of his officers.)

Soon the messages of congratulation would be on their way to him. From Grant: "*. . . Push the enemy now . . . Give him no rest . . . Render it* (Hood's army) *useless . . . Do not stop . . .*"

Would Thomas then wonder, how patronizing can some people be? Do they think I have no sense at all?

Thomas' plan was the same as yesterday's—almost. This time he would really smash at the Rebel right. It would be no feint. (Actually this would resolve into a deadly struggle for the Franklin Pike near which Lee was waiting in the orchard.)

The Federals had bivouacked where darkness caught them. Wilson, doubtless, would have a rough day. He must drive the enemy from those hills. He must get on around the Rebel left. He must push them "*as vigorously as possible*" in flank and rear. Not until then could the big all-out push begin, with the infantry at Hood's front and flanks.

Closest to Wilson would be Schofield's infantry, at the Federal right—east of Hillsboro, waiting to join Wilson. Gen. Couch, commanding Schofield's Second Division, was on a hill facing Shy's—on an east and west line—with Gen. Cox, of Schofield's Third Division, at right angles to Couch.

Smith and Wood remained at the Federal center. All was going as planned. Thomas was quietly confident.

He took the time, enroute to battle, to pause before a group of wounded Confederates who lay beside the road unattended.

Bring stretchers, Thomas said. Get ambulances. Orderly, stay with these men until they are given relief. Then he rode on, an able and noble foe, greater than many of his critics.

Soon it was 6 a.m. Steedman, Smith and Wood began to move their troops forward. On the Federal left, Steedman thought he was moving against the Rebels as he pushed along Nolensville Road, feeling for the enemy under Lee . . . and feeling in vain . . . for Lee was now in the Peach Orchard (which Steedman's scouts should have known). So Steedman, finding only footprints, fog and corpses, at length took up his position to the left of Gen. Wood who meanwhile had moved toward the Franklin Pike.

Steedman finally faced Hood's eastern flank. His movement had left part of the Nashville outer line uncovered. Into the Rains' Hill vacancy came Cruft from the inner line.

It was 8 a.m. when Wood knew Hood had pulled back. He ran into Lee's light line of skirmishers. They dropped back to the Franklin Pike and on across it, into their main line. Wood deployed three divisions in pursuit, into Lee's heavy skirmish line.

There the Federals reformed, about a half-mile out from Lee's solid grip on the Peach Orchard. Then they advanced in "*magnificent array,*" into a hail of small arms and artillery fire, driving Lee's men back into their line.

Lee's 28 guns roared back. Wood faced Lee's earthworks and stopped. He was balked. Nothing but frontal assault could take the position now. Let the artillery pummel it. For the Rebels seemed in no mood to yield one inch of their slopes, even to a "*magnificent array.*"

Gen. Henry D. Clayton's division manned the top of Peach Orchard Hill. Gen. James T. Holtzclaw's straddled the road. Around the eastern sides bristled brigades of Gen. Randall L. Gibson and Gen. Marcellus A. Stovall. Come on, if you dare!

The Federals would wait until around 3 p.m. for their master-stroke at Lee's hill. Their guns kept going. All day long they would batter Lee's position. They drew a flaming reply.

The artillery duel would go on until noon. It has sometimes been called an interlude of "*skirmishing*" or "*feeler*" attacks. It was more than that. Federal charges were made, in vain. White and Negro troops surged at the slopes, time and again, including a "*desperate*" charge at 10 a.m. ("*Never saw dead men thicker,*" wrote Holtzclaw.)

These attacks worried Hood, although they were thrown back with vim. They threatened his escape route to Brentwood. Was it with a penchant for folly that he withdrew three brigades from Shy's Hill?

Hood sent them to Lee, who didn't need them (by Lee's own account). These brigades, from the division of Gen. Patrick Cleburne (killed at Franklin) were now under Gen. J. A. Smith.

Three and a half hours later, as Lee sent the three brigades toward Brentwood, Shy's Hill would be in desperate need of them. Of Cleburne's troops on Shy's, only one brigade would then remain, Gen. Daniel C. Govan's.

At daybreak Gen. A. J. Smith, too, had begun a careful movement, from between the Hillsboro and Granny White pikes. Where are the Rebs? He kept advancing until he knew. They were on his front. Smith's right confronted the firm Rebel left.

Boldly Smith took his stand just 600 yards away, north of the present Battery Lane. Stewart's men, battle sore, were facing him.

On Smith's right were the entrenchments of Schofield's reinforced XXIII Corps, joining Smith almost at a right angle. And toward the center of the angle, southeast of their intersection, Shy's Hill-of-the-future stood out against the sullen sky that now held an even heavier threat of rain.

Along Smith's extreme left was the Seventh Minnesota Regiment, its banners snapping proudly as it surged into a sink which led toward the back of the house where courageous Mary Bradford lived with her widowed mother, Mrs. Edward Bradford, far back on the east side of Granny White, south of Glendale Lane. Both Smith and Wood faced south.

In and near the ravine the Minnesotans paused, panting, crouching for safety. Over their heads a cannonading began. Big Yankee guns had been pulled into position near the back of Mary's house. Shy's would be pounded all day, from three sides.

The Seventh went on, crawling sometimes, with the ceaseless covering of fire overhead. Pause now. Let the big guns shatter the heights. Let the smoke roll overhead, and the deadly hail. It's pounding the whole Rebel line. Be glad to be alive. Lie down. Hold. And wait. So long as you breathe, you're living.

The air is acrid, heavy. Smoke hangs close to the soggy ground. Shy's is being slammed in cross fire. How can anything live up there?

From the back of Mary's house, shells are dropping into the back of Bate's left brigade. On Schofield's right, another Federal battery thunders from a hillside.

Gen. Couch's men, from their hill, will boom 560 rounds into Shy's before the day is done.

Bate couldn't make a like reply. He lacked Lee's strong artillery. His few smooth-bores talked on, and his sharpshooters kept Yankee gunners jumping and praying on the hills, beside their roaring cannon. The bombardment went on, unending thunder, dwarfing the Rebel reply.

Did Hood sense disaster? Already—early in the morning,—he had sent his wagons south, back to the Harpeth. At 8 a.m. he sent a message to Stewart: "*Should any disaster happen to us today—*"

BELLICOSE APPEARANCE OF OUR BRAVE BOYS AFTER THANKSGIVING.

Plenty! The North could take a humorous view of the bountiful fare of its soldiers.

IF SO, Stewart must file south by the Franklin Pike. Lee must hold it open until Stewart's men were safe. Cheatham must retreat by Granny White. This should reduce chances of melee in exit.

Chalmers and Rucker were on Hillsboro, guarding the intersection of the road to Brentwood. All day they would hold it.

Stewart comprehended. He sent word to Walthall at his left, on the west side of Granny White, *"Should Bate fall back, keep your left connected with him . . . falling back and forming a new line extending to the hills in the rear."*

Thomas comprehended, too. He knew Lee was holding the Rebel gate to safety. Thomas meant to take and close it—the Franklin Road, near the Peach Orchard. Steedman and Wood would cooperate in the effort.

Thomas comprehended more. Hood's weak spot was the center. Thomas didn't mean to push it in. No, sir—that would send the Rebels southward by both pikes, while the gate was open. Thomas didn't mean for them to get away.

He meant to roll up Hood's line, west to east, and have the Rebels in his bear-trap. It was to be snap shut when Wilson, in their rear, cut off retreat, and held them until the Union infantry could come up and strike.

This meant that Schofield, nearest Wilson; Schofield—with the chip on his shoulder—should make the first infantry strike at Shy's Hill, while Wilson pressed in from the rear. (But Schofield won't.)

It was a mid-morning of smoke and roar. Shelling still ranged from right to left. Through the morning there would be skirmishes, sporadic attacks, but as yet no general push. They were waiting on Wilson. Isn't he behind Hood yet?

Since 9 a.m. Wilson's men had been trying to thrust through the densely wooded hills at the Rebel left. The Rebel flank was alert, quick. It was taking a toll for his efforts. It was no longer like a door hook. It wouldn't stand still. It was bending back, now like a fishhook. How could he pass?

He was having to go uphill, over ridges. The upward struggle, over slippery slopes, clogged with underbrush, had almost come to a standstill. Within the woods the Rebels lurked, still throwing lead.

Like Wood before Peach Orchard Hill, Wilson faced a problem. This Rebel left, though freely moving, seemed granite hard, far stronger than Wilson had anticipated. So why not try their right?

He sent a message to Thomas: Their left *is "too difficult for cavalry operation . . . If I were on their other flank . . . I might do more . . ."*

No! said Thomas. Keep trying, on the left, right where you are.

Wilson obeyed. He was determined, bursting with energy and initiative, this youngster who had been at Yellow Tavern in the spring, when Jeb Stuart's

—Library of Congress
Gen. Thomas Benton Smith
59 years of shadows

—History of 20th Tennessee Volunteer Infantry
Col. W. M. Shy
"His finger still on the trigger"

plumed hat had rolled in the dust, and Stuart had fallen (with a rose in his gray jacket).

Wilson sent reinforcements to Gen. Hatch on Schofield's right, and to the brigade of Gen. John H. Hammond, who linked Hatch's division with Knipe's. Doggedly, they stuck to the slopes. They were gaining, just a little. Another hour passed, and another. More of Wilson's men lay dead in the bramble.

By noon, more than 4,000 of his dismounted cavalrymen were pushing their way up over the ridge. Their rifles soon would be pointing at the very backs of Bate and Walthall's men. Just look at 'em down there! Like fish in a barrel!

Wilson was ready to move in, with the terrible rifles. He was ready to jump on the Confederate backs. He sent word to Thomas and Schofield: The cavalry is ready! This was to be the signal for the big push. Schofield was to come forward against Shy's Hill.

But Schofield stood motionless on the east. What was wrong? Why wasn't he moving? Wilson's 4,000 soon would be facing Nashville. They would soon be stretched out a mile and a half on Schofield's right, diagonally across the Granny White. They were behind Hood.

Smith, Wood, Steedman—all faced south, head-on. They were waiting for Schofield to act.

—The Century War Book, 1861-1865
The first startled moment at the "Battle of the Barricade" may have looked much like this old drawing.

Hood saw his danger. Quick! *"For God's sake, drive the enemy cavalry from our left or all is lost,"* he said in a message to Chalmers.

It was captured by Wilson's troops. Wilson rushed it to Thomas. The time is now. Schofield's infantry would rush forward . . . so Wilson thought.

He waited, poised to strike. (*"But nothing whatever was done to support my movement,"* he wrote.) What's holding Schofield? Why doesn't the infantry come forward?

Wilson fumed. Night was coming. Finally, he sent an officer to Schofield, urging attack.

Hood played what has been called *"his last card."* In an effort to stall the threatening Federal cavalry, he pulled Ector's (Coleman's) brigade from his Shy's Hill front. There it had supported Bate's rear.

Hood sends it speeding to a hill east of Granny White. Form a new line! With your backs toward Shy's! Face the cavalry, to the south! Then, around 3 p.m., he sent Reynolds' brigade to aid Ector's. Both will do their work superbly. They will stand like a wall, blocking Wilson so stoutly that most of his men will have to stay west of Granny White as they move northward behind Hood.

Nevertheless, their removal from Shy's left Bate in deeper trouble. Ector's brigade had been taken from support of his angle. Bate protested to Cheatham. Reinforce me! (Reynolds' had been taken from Walthall's line.)

Cheatham couldn't. Ector's removal had been from the western side of Shy's where the line formed a right angle with Gen. Benton Smith's men. Bate must fill in with Smith's men, thinning out for the stretch. So into the place of Ector's men went part of Smith's. There, on top of the hill, they saw the poorly placed guns.

Meanwhile, around noon, Gen. Thomas had joined Gen. Wood on the Yankee-held section of Franklin Pike. Be alert, said Thomas, for a *"more decisive effort"* against Lee's Peach Orchard hold on the pike.

Then Thomas rode east and Wood west. Cold rain was falling. Through it Thomas went calmly clopping, inspecting his line. His troops at last were deployed as he wished.

His skirmishers now knew the full stretch of Hood's line. Union artillery was blasting its length. Thomas eyed his batteries. Is the firing rhythmic and even? He would tolerate no show-off blamming. Hit your target!

Wood, riding east, met Steedman. Could they, together, carry Peach Orchard Hill? If so, they could turn Hood's right and block his get-away path. They could then roll west, taking his line in reverse. If they could take the peach orchard.

Careful reconnaissance followed. They decided Lee's hill could be taken. In a massive onslaught, they struck around 3 p.m. Leading was Col. Post's brigade, of Beatty's division, supported by the brigade of Col. Abel D. Streight.

—Staff Photo by Vic Cooley
COL. SHY'S HOME, on Del Rio Road, near Franklin, now the residence of J. W. Buford. Col. Shy is buried nearby.

Steedman's two brigades demonstrated on the eastern side, advancing on Post's left.

Canister, grape and musketry tore at them. Many an officer fell beside his men. Down went Col. Post, slashed by grape. His horse was killed.

The battalions, thinned and bloody, were paces from Lee's works, now a gushing sheet of flame. Suddenly Lee's reserves on the slopes stood up and poured new fire.

Men in blue were falling across one another at the very edge of the Rebel abatis. The wall of fire was too deadly. Could any man survive it?

Steedman's shock brigade, of raw Negro recruits, was moving boldly on. Excitement gripped them. Their demonstration became an attack. They poured toward the Rebel works, forking their surge in half around a fallen tree. It thinned their mass, as Post's brigade was retreating.

The curtain of lead fell upon them. Again Negro blood poured.

Retreat is sounding. The Yanks are pulling back (*"with nothing of panic,"* according to Wood, but *"in great disorder,"* according to Lee).

Lee has held. It is well after 3 p.m. Cold rain is drumming upon the dead, the wounded and the dying. One is Lt. Peter G. Tait of Beatty's 89th Illinois Regiment. A cannon ball has pierced his left side. As he fell, his heart and left lung dropped out upon his right arm, across his body. For 20 minutes, a comrade said, the heart continued to beat.

In spots on the rain-whipped slope, a reddish wash is trickling downhill through the brownish stubble. White and Negro corpses lay so thick upon the hillside that the slopes, according to tradition, *"looked blue."*

And the road of escape was still open. Thomas hasn't broken the gate.

From Hillsboro, Chalmers and Kelley have moved over to Granny White. Again they hold the intersection of the road to Brentwood. Cheatham's ambulances are rolling through toward Franklin.

For a while, Rucker's horsemen remain on Hillsboro. But Gen. Johnson will soon cross from Charlotte to hit Rucker.

Then Rucker will join Kelley and the regiment will form before Brentwood to protect the ambulances and wagons.

Far on the Rebel left, Cheatham's plight was desperate. He was almost boxed, closely confronted on three sides. He could see Wilson's men at his rear, ready to swoop down. Schofield's infantry stood massed to the west, unmoving but doubtless ready, Smith's infantry to the north. Cheatham's line was bent far back, into the fishhook shape, and Wilson's men were pushing around the hook's point. The parapet of Shy's Hill was being shot away.

There is an old controversy on details of what was now about to happen in the Federal high command. The reports of honest men often differ. Events were, perhaps, something very close to this:

Sometime around 3 p.m. or earlier, Thomas joined Smith. An hour later, Thomas will be with Schofield, farther west.

It is while Thomas is with the Mid-Westerners of the XVIth Corps that Smith shows him a request from the commander of his First Division, Gen. McArthur. McArthur has sent Smith word:

The parapet of Shy's Hill is down. Blown off. It's open for infantry attack. Let me take it! McArthur, like Wilson, is acutely aware that darkness will be coming early.

The bitterness of defeat. Gen. Hood's men, retreating toward Brentwood, doubtless saw sights akin to this.

—From The Century War Book, 1861-1865

BUT THOMAS, like Wilson, is still waiting to hear from Schofield.

"The prescribed order of attack," said Thomas, "gives the initiative to Gen. Schofield, in conjunction with the cavalry. I'll ride to Gen. Schofield and hasten his attack."

It is well along toward 4 p.m. There's a hint of the early dark.

Through the rain and smoke, two horsemen are now riding toward Schofield, by different roads. One is Thomas, riding west, after the failure to dislodge Lee. The other is Wilson.

On a gray named Sheridan he's galloping hard around the enemy's flank. He wants to find out what's wrong.

Wilson has sent three officers, "one after another," begging Schofield to come up. Instead, at 1 p.m., Schofield had requested reinforcements. Thomas had sent him a division from Smith and was about to send more when Smith's protest caused Thomas to dispatch his chief-of-staff to Schofield. Look and see. Does he really need more? The answer was No, from Gen. Whipple.

And at 1:30 Schofield had sent Thomas a message, "I have not attempted to move my main line today, and I do not think I am strong enough to do so."

Wilson's patience had ended. Whatever Schofield thought or didn't think, it was time to advance! That was Wilson's mood as he pounded on through the rain that freely spilled, then drizzled, stopped, and started again.

Nor was Wilson the only impatient man. Smith was waiting, too. So was Mc-Arthur, itching for Shy's. McArthur's patience, like Wilson's, was nearing an end by the time Wilson, on his faithful gray, clattered up beside Thomas and Schofield.

Wilson found them on the side of a small hill. Over its top could be seen a higher range, less than a mile away. There Wilson's dismounted men were "in plain sight," their guidons fluttering as they advanced against Hood's left and rear. They were flanked and covered by two batteries of their horse artillery.

To Wilson, before his commander, it must have been a proud moment. Some of the shots of his men, too high, were even falling in front of Schofield's corps.

But Schofield was "reluctant" to move, for fear of the loss of men it might entail. Thomas looked at the young general he had known as a cadet. Gravely Thomas said, "The battle must be fought, if men are killed."

Thomas was lifting his field glasses toward the distant ridge where guidons fluttered in the rain and smoke. Was Wilson sure those men were his?

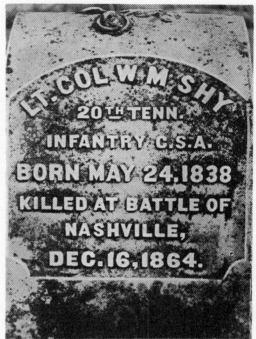

—Staff Photo by Vic Cooley

Col. Shy's Grave

—From The Century War Book, 1861-1865

The Retreat. Down the road they were going, battered, cold and hungry. But some were singing . . . Hope lived on.

"Peace"

—From Harper's Weekly

—From photograph taken by M. Miley, 1866

Gen. Robert E. Lee on Traveler

WILSON WAS *"dead certain,"* and rearin' to go. And over there—Look! McArthur had started for Shy's Hill. It was 4:15.

Thomas saw.

McArthur's patience has snapped. (Acting on his own, McArthur has given orders to *"take that hill."*) He was moving southeast, with Smith's First Division. McArthur was attacking Shy's.

Thomas turned to Schofield: *"Gen. Smith is attacking without waiting for you. Please advance your entire line."*

Schofield disputed this—33 years later. *"He (Thomas) gave no order, nor was there time . . ."* Schofield would declare in his book, *Forty-six Years in the Army,* published in 1897.

Schofield would write that he had earlier ordered Cox to advance his Third Division. (Cox would say otherwise—that no order for the big push was given until around 4:30, after Wilson had *"pushed past"* Hood's left flank.)

Whatever the precise truth, one thing was clear: The big push was on. Schofield was moving at last, southeastward, toward Hood's left flank. Wilson sprang to his horse and tore back toward his horsemen.

Artillery thunder broke out with a new intensity all along the Union line. More than one ammunition team was mud-stuck. Soldiers grabbed shells and ran with them to batteries. Uphill went two artillery pieces pulled by Hatch's men.

All the Federal right was moving—Smith southward, head-on; Wilson's men at Hood's rear. The bear-trap's jaws were closing on Cheatham and Bate. Still they stood and fought.

Wilson's men, curving across Granny White behind Cheatham, were now bending his extreme left so far back that Cheatham's men in the hook-shaped line at one place were firing north, and on the opposite line were firing south, with only a few hundred yards between them.

The sky is dark, above flame and smoke. Bate, on Shy's Hill, rushes along the trenches dug by Ector's men, in the light works now occupied by the infantrymen of young Gen. Thomas Benton Smith. Many are being shot in the back. Bate is urging them to hold—and they're holding, amid fire from three directions.

"Grape and canister shrieked and whizzed," Gen. Rustling wrote. *"The whole battlefield at times was like the grisly mouth of hell, agape and aflame with smoke, alive with thunder and death-dealing shots. The hills and slopes were strewn with dead; ravines and gorges crowded with wounded."*

The brigade on Bate's extreme left has been driven downhill, into mucky fields at his rear. The men in the trenches see the left give way. It's Gen. Govan's, breaking under Wilson's pressure. (No wonder! Govan's brigade was holding a space intended for a division—most of which Hood had sent to Lee hours ago.)

The gap is refilled, but briefly. The enemy is taking it over. And Col. Shy, at the brow of the hill, is fighting calmly on; handsome Shy, the man everybody liked, of *"unusually quiet disposition, not much given to words"* . . . on the hill now without obstructions.

"I saw men with their heads or limbs shot off," Rustling continued, *"others blown to pieces. I rode by a tree behind which a Confederate had dodged to safety, and a Union shell had gone clear through both tree and soldier and exploded among his comrades."*

Then the Rebels see it—a brigade with fixed bayonets, coming uphill at their front. Coming silently, without yells and without firing a shot. For that was the order of Col. W. L. McMillen, of the 95th Ohio Infantry. It's McArthur's First Brigade, under cover of their artillery. This is the attack McArthur had ordered, unleashed when his patience ended.

They had formed in two lines, outside the works of Couch's division. It hits the slopes, under the smoking, red-ribbed umbrella of fire. And Shy's Hill itself is smoking as it lets go again at its attackers, with shell, canister, musketry.

Yankees are dropping and bayonets clatter, spilt from star-fingered hands. Men squirm and kick and roll, hitting the clumping feet of their fellows who evade the thresh of the dying. They're going up, brave as they come, and some are tall blond men, like stalwart Vikings . . . Who? Many come from Minnesota, and their blood will wash Shy's Hill as will no other state's . . .

There's something eerie, too, in their silence, unreal except for the throbbing grunt of animal sounds and the startled quick howl of the stricken. Their ranks are thinner, thinning. They're holding their fire. They're traveling.

Orders are that, when the First Brigade is halfway up, the Second Brigade shall follow. But the First has hardly begun its ascent when the Second comes closely behind, followed alike by the Third. Behind swarms the whole Second Division.

With the First Brigade is the 10th Minnesota Regiment, on the left where death is roaring; and with the Third Brigade goes the Seventh Minnesota, which has lain skirmishing in the rain near Mary Bradford's house until 3 p.m.

It's the 10th Minnesota, together with others in the front line, which first springs over the Rebel works, into the stronghold of Shy's. It's hand to hand, for a twinkling, and eternity's doors are swinging, in the splatter and clutter of dying. Flesh sways and pounds and explodes or not, in a cold and high excitement that is not excitement at all but something beyond each man, the plateau of never-never, from which any man, descending, may never fear death as before.

In Appreciation

FOR AID in preparing this narrative and assembling illustrations, The Banner expresses its gratitude to Col. Campbell H. Brown, state executive director, Civil War Centennial Commission, and Thomas A. Wiggington, assistant director; to Dr. Robert H. White, state historian; Robert T. Quarles Jr., state archivist, retired; Stanley F. Horn, Nashville's distinguished historian; Dr. A. L. Crabb, noted author of many historical novels; Paul H. Beasley, Lanier Merritt and Mrs. Paul E. Purks;

To Mrs. Gertrude Parsley, Mrs. Hermione Embry and Miss Kendall Cram, State Library; Miss Bettye Bell of the Tennessee Room, Nashville Public Library; Miss Catherine Clark, Andrew L. Todd Library, Middle Tennessee State College; to the Joint University Libraries, the Nashville Public Library, the New York Public Library, The Library of Congress and the University of Alabama.

The Banner is deeply grateful for material used and permission to quote from:

Education in Violence, the *Life of George H. Thomas* and the *History of the Army of the Cumberland,* by Francis F. McKinney, Wayne State University Press, Detroit, 1961, particularly concerning the career of Thomas as a professional soldier, his family background and youth, interchanges with Gen. William T. Sherman in late 1864 and data concerning Thomas' final honors;

Steamboatin' on the Cumberland, by Judge Byrd Douglas, Tennessee Book Company, 1961;

A Diary from Dixie by Mrs. Mary Boykin Chesnut (Ben Ames Williams, ed.) Houghton Mifflin Co., 1949, concerning Hood's romance with Sally Preston, and *A Rebel War Clerk's Diary,* by J. B. Jones, Lippincott;

Most frequently consulted were the works of Mr. Horn, *The Army of Tennessee,* Bobbs-Merrill; *The Decisive Battle of Nashville,* Louisiana State University Press, and also his article, "Nashville During the Civil War," in the *Tennessee Historical Quarterly,* March, 1945.

To Mrs. Purks we are grateful for material from the diary of her grandfather, W. L. B. Lawrence of Hillside.

Other works frequently consulted were:

"First With the Most" Forrest, by Robert Selph Henry, McCowat-Mercer Press; *The Gallant Hood,* by John P. Dyer, Bobbs-Merrill Company, Inc.; *Story of the U.S. Cavalry, 1775-1942,* by John Knowles Herr and Edward S. Wallace, Little, Brown, 1953; *Marks, Landmarks and Markers—a Guide to the Civil War in Nashville and Davidson County,* by Paul H. Beasley; *Guide to the Civil War in Tennessee,* by the Civil War Centennial Commission;

Messages of the Governors of Tennessee, 1857-1869, Vol. V, by Dr. White, Tennessee Historical Commission, 1959; *Hood's Tennessee Campaign,* by Thomas Robson Hay, Neale, New York, 1929; *Maj. Gen. George H. Thomas* by T. B. Van Horne, New York, 1882; *Rock of Chickamauga,* by Freeman Cleaves, University of Oklahoma Press, 1949; *General Thomas,* by Henry Coppee, New York, 1893; *Gen. George H. Thomas,* by Donn Piatt and H. V. Boynton, Cincinnati, 1891; *Gen. George H. Thomas* by John Watts DePeyster, 1875; *Memoir of Maj. Gen. George H. Thomas,* by Gen. Richard W. Johnson, Lippincott, 1881;

Official Records of the War of the Rebellion, Washington; *A History of Lumsden's Battery,* by George Little, Tuscaloosa, Ala.; *Under the Old Flag,* by Gen. James H. Wilson, Appleton-Century-Crofts, Inc., 1912, 2 vols.; *Men and Things I Saw in the Civil War,* James F. Rustling, New York, 1899; *Under the Stars and Bars,* Walter A. Clark, Augusta, Ga., 1900;

Co. "Aytch"—First Tennessee Regiment, by Samuel R. Watkins, Nashville, 1882; *Battles and Sketches of the Army of Tennessee,* Bromfield L. Ridley, Mexico, Mo., 1906; *Annals of the Army of the Cumberland,* Nashville, 1878;

Life of Gen. N. B. Forrest, by John A. Wyeth, New York, 1899; *The Campaigns of Lt. Gen. N. B. Forrest,* by Gen. Thomas Jordan and J. P. Pryor, Blelock, New Orleans and New York, 1868; *Bedford Forrest and His Critter Company,* by Andrew Lytle, McDowell, Obolensky, New York, 1960; *The Artillery of Nathan Bedford Forrest's Cavalry,* by John W. Morton, Nashville, 1909;

Advance and Retreat, by Gen. John B. Hood, New Orleans, 1880; *Narrative of Military Operations,* Gen. Joseph E. Johnston, Appleton; *Forty-Six Years in the Army,* Lt. Gen. John M. Schofield, Century, New York, 1897; *History of the Twentieth Tennessee Regiment,* W. J. Murray, Nashville, 1904; *The Southern Bivouac,* Louisville, 1886-1887 (six volumes); *The Confederate Veteran,* Nashville, 1883-1932 (40 volumes) and *Century Magazine.*

FROM OUR SPECIAL WAR CORRESPONDENT.

"CITY POINT, VA., *April —*, 8.30 A.M.
"All seems well with us."—A. LINCOLN.

—Harper's Weekly, April 15, 1865

"ALL SEEMS WELL." On the very day this hopeful cartoon appeared, Lincoln died of an assassin's bullet.

THE COOL WIND of death is still blowing, seductive and soft in the thunder, as more Yanks crowd at the works. A Yankee captain is up and coming over, gun in hand. It blazes and a Rebel's left ear goes silent from the explosion. He's unhit but stunned and sagging, grasping for clarity, reeling—Harry K. Moss, in a smokily reddish world that melts and swims and clears again, with a color-bearer now over the works and the captain inside, too, with a Rebel's gun at his chest.

It's the gun of James W. McFerrin, friend of the shaken Moss, and McFerrin is squeezing the trigger. The gun is failing to fire and the color bearer is swinging, knocking McFerrin down. Then a slashing swing of bayonets as six men lunge, but the captain quickly stops them. McFerrin rises, in heaven or hell? With Moss, he's taken prisoner. The Yankee captain had saved him.

Shy is down. So are nearly half his men. Death is crowding in upon the larger part of the three right companies of the 37th Georgia Regiment, at Bate's extreme left. They are still contesting the ground, despite the break. This command, under Maj. H. C. Lucas, includes the consolidated fragments of the Second, 10th, 15th, 20th, 30th and 37th Tennessee Regiments.

The blue horde has them. They're almost wiped out. Only 65 will escape, each on his own. A few minutes more and they're leaping their dead and fleeing downhill, then climbing over the rugged hills to their rear and sprinting and stumbling on into the short valley which leads toward Granny White and the Franklin Road.

On either side of the break, the others must need fall back. The great blue sea is washing all along the left now, a left that's broken in a dozen places; and suddenly the whole line lifts.

The Rebels are running downhill. The Yanks are cheering. Then the Rebel *"multitude"* was swarming up the slope, as one Yankee officer put it, toward the valley of escape beyond.

Col. Shy lies limp on the hill, a Minie ball in his brain, dead at 26. His hand is still grasping the Enfield, his finger still set on the trigger. About him lie many of Smith's veterans, dead so far from home.

It has been said that in the taking of Shy's Hill, Minnesota's losses were the greatest suffered by the state in any Civil War engagement—302 men killed, wounded or missing, from the Fifth, Seventh, Ninth and 10th Minnesota Regiments.

Among the captured Rebels is young Gen. Smith. He is only 26. They are leading him toward the rear. As he goes, a saber-wielding Yankee officer strikes him over the head, three times. The officer is not a Mid-Westerner. According to strong indications, his regiment was from Ohio. There is virtually no doubt about his identity.

Smith did not die. (The injury will affect his mind. Much of his next 59 years will be spent in a Tennessee mental institution. Death will come in 1923, at 85.) He's walking on with his captors, blood streaming down his face.

The break at the right had come too quickly for anyone to be prepared. Even the men on Bate's own right were startled. Suddenly they heard the Yankees hurrahing, the splutter of mud from hundreds of feet, the rumble of guns and cries of *"Surrender!"*

Then they, too, went racing toward Franklin Pike, where Lee still held the road. Hood, still strapped to his horse, was watching from the Lea place.

He saw the left break, only minutes after the Rebels had been bravely shouting, *"Come on!"* The Yanks had come on, by thousands.

"I beheld for the first time," Hood wrote, *"a Confederate army abandon the field in confusion."*

Not long afterwards he reached the Franklin Road, trying to rally his men. They could not be halted long. Cheatham, stopping one man, turned to halt another. The first darted under Cheatham's horse and fled on.

Through the icing rain and sucking mud the Rebels kept coming, over the hills and on. They were running. They were whipped. Hood rushed a message to Chalmers:

"Hold the Granny White Pike at all hazards." Down the Granny White, Hood knew, Hatch's mounted men would soon come thundering, after this fleeing mass.

And if Hatch got through, into this tumult of infantry, abandoned wagons, rearing horses, jerking artillery, and cast-aside equipment—if Hatch got through into this, with his murderous seven-shot rifles, the slaughter and capture would be sickening.

Chalmers received the message in Brentwood. There, with nearly all the Rebel cavalry, he was protecting the ice-covered wagons and ambulances until they could file on toward Franklin.

He sped northeast. He took his stand on the Granny White just north of the eastward-going road to Brentwood. Along this stretch Hatch would soon come pounding, trying to reach and block the Franklin Road—his slaughter-pen, his jackpot.

Chalmers' meager cavalry began construction of a barricade. Hurry! Use anything. Fence rails, logs. Whatever will move. Block the path. Hold Hatch off, just as Lee has held Peach Orchard Hill.

—Century War Book, 1861-1865

Grand Review of Troops in Washington at the Close of the War.

President Lincoln leaving the White House of the Confederacy. Richmond has fallen.

LEE WAS still holding the orchard when Shy's Hill fell. He was getting his breath, so to speak, from beating back Wood and Steedman.

Chaplain McNeilly had come to a *"field infirmary on the Franklin Pike, not far from Col. Overton's house."* He wrote, *"There did not seem to be much doing. The ambulances and wagons, with teams harnessed, were standing in the road. In a little while . . . I saw men running toward us in confusion. It was plain that our line had broken and that the enemy would soon be upon us. At once the teams were hitched and they moved off at a gallop."*

Lee was caught by surprise. The left and center—going or gone? It couldn't be true. It was. Of a sudden, he was without support. His left was being struck. Bring up the horses—save the guns! There was no time to bring all horses forward.

"Directly the retreating soldiers were upon us," McNeilly wrote. *"Then I realized it was a panic. I could not find what had happened. Every man seemed anxious to save himself. I ran with them; and as the mass of fugitives increased, the panic grew.*

"Every man had some dreadful tale. According to these stories, the Yankee batteries would soon be in a position on a rise in the road just behind us and would blow us all to smithereens, and there were at least 100,000 Yanks on our track. I ran as fast as I could; and the faster I ran, the worse I was scared. I could almost feel the grape and canister plugging me in the back . . ."

Lee was astride his horse near Clayton's division. He spurred his horse and went flying east through the misting sleet, taking both fences of the Franklin Pike, and on into the midst of his faltering men. He seized the standard of a color-bearer and rode on with it.

"Rally, men, rally! For God's suke, rally! This is the place for brave men to die!"

Backbones stiffened. Men halted and stood together in little groups. Courage had clogged the path.

The advancing Yankees hesitate. Bullets fly at their leading horsemen. Behind the vanguard, the forward thumping of feet dies away.

It was the pause that Gen. Henry D. Clayton needed. Coming down from Peach Orchard Hill, he seized the minutes to fall well to the rear in good order. With part of Gen. Carter L. Stevenson's division, Clayton's men formed a new line on one of the Overton Hills.

The welcome new runnel of life-or-death is crossing the Franklin Pike and extending on into the woods near Travelers' Rest. Gen. Lee returns.

The brigade of Gen. Randall L. Gibson is pulling up to join. He has a few guns. And—look! Beside a wheel of one of the now pitifully few artillery pieces stands a little drummer boy, a *"mere lad."*

He's brave as the calmest man.

He's beating *"the long roll in perfect time, without missing a note, as Gibson's brigade comes up and forms a rear guard."*

Who was he? No monument marks the spot where he stood, this brave and nameless lad, as Hood's house of cards came tumbling down . . . This boy who stood and beat on his drum, to give courage to fleeing men . . . Tr-r-r-rr!! TR-R-R-RR! Pass on, a world is ending. But the road to tomorrow is open. Lee still guards the retreat. There'll always be a tomorrow. Tr-r-r-rrrrrr!

Pass on. To Brentwood.

The Battle of Nashville has been lost.

The Granny White barricade is not complete. Hooves are sounding, thousands. Hatch's horsemen are on a dead run for the Franklin Pike. *"Woah!"* What's this? Barricade!

Guns roar. Riders pitch and fall. Rain is pouring in the darkness. It's hand to hand, to and fro, *"one of the fiercest conflicts that ever took place in the Civil War,"* according to Wilson.

Rucker grabs a bridle. *"You are my prisoner!"* he shouts.

"Not by a damned sight!" answers Col. George Spalding of the 12th Tennessee (U.S.A.) Cavalry. He breaks free. A Yankee captain grabs Rucker's saber. Rucker grabs the captain's. They slash. A pistol shot strikes Rucker's arm, from another Federal. Rucker is captured and taken before Hatch.

"Forrest has just arrived," Rucker boasts. Wishful thinking? It wasn't true. *"He'll give you hell tonight."*

This unretouched Harper's Weekly drawing is from a much worn old page in the Nashville Public Library.

AND ABOUT that time one more flank attack broke loose, from an Alabama cadet company. The coincidence gave the Federals concern. Was it Forrest?

His absence had been observed. No prisoners had been taken from the cavalry of either Jackson or Buford. Was Forrest dead?

"Killed certainly at Murfreesboro," Schofield had told Thomas—incorrect information from citizens.

Rucker's survivors withdrew from Granny White. They were not pursued. They moved over to the Franklin Pike. When the last Rebel had passed the horsemen encamped on the freezing ground.

They had kept Hatch from his jackpot. Had Hatch made it about 900 yards farther down the road, he could have gained the passage eastward. Or had he been an hour earlier—

It was too late now. His men were spent. So were their mounts. The risks were unknown. Around midnight, Wilson ordered bivouac wherever the order was received. Pursuit would resume in the morning.

(The Rebels would always have a notion that Rucker's remark, plus the uproar of cadets, helped bring Wilson's order to halt.)

Soon afterwards, Wilson heard the gallop of a heavy rider on Franklin Road. *"That you, Wilson?"* a voice boomed. It was Thomas. *"Dang it to hell, Wilson, didn't I tell you we could lick 'em? Didn't I tell you?"*

Then Thomas galloped back toward Nashville. Just about everything had gone as planned. Not all, but nearly. His loss had been small, 387 killed, 2,562 wounded, 112 missing. Hood, behind his works, had lost only half as many by death and injury. But 4,500 had been captured. And he had lost the battle.

In the morning, Wilson's deadly rifles would be at Hood's heels.

Forrest was, indeed, on his way to help. But he was not heading for Nashville. He was cutting across country with his wagon train; with his prisoners and great droves of cattle and pigs, to join Hood's retreat at Columbia and take over the rear guard. (As usual Forrest, with all his livestock, was remembering: An army must eat!)

As Forrest rides through the rain, the unsleeping Rucker is occupying the same room with his captors, Hatch and Wilson. Hatch has given up his bed to Rucker. Hatch will sleep on the floor. Through the long night, he will get up to bring Rucker water.

(Rucker's arm will be amputated in a Nashville hospital. Twenty-five years later, his sword will be returned to him.)

At Brentwood, a wounded Rebel is stumbling through the downpour. He wants a certificate of discharge. Is this the right tent? Cold rain is drumming upon it.

He opens a flap, from which water drips. Did he quickly drop it? The sight he saw!

Never would the wounded soldier forget. It was Hood's tent. Inside sat Hood, one-legged, his limp arm sagging beside him. Frantically he was running the fingers of his good hand through his mass of hair. Tears was slipping down his long cheeks, into his tawny beard.

Hood was whipped, his chances gone.

Gone! The chance of freeing Nashville. Gone! The chance to sweep east and aid Lee. The chance to justify the faith of his friend, President Jefferson Davis—one man who had believed in him. Gone!

Davis would be blamed for this failure, wouldn't he? Davis, who had enough troubles, with Yankee teeth waiting for the throat of Richmond, and some vague paralysis creeping at his own face, affecting one of the President's eyes—

"Poor Hood went on a fool's errand, and Jefferson Davis sent him." So *Harper's Weekly* would say, Dec. 31. Tomorrow the Yankee-minded *Nashville Union* would exult, *"The failure of the (Tennessee) campaign will disgrace him (Hood) and he will not go down without sinking his army with him."*

(*"I alone am responsible for its conception,"* Hood would soon declare of his tragic campaign, in a sweeping attempt to absolve Davis.)

And Sally, his fiancee? With whom he had left the diamond-studded star of his hat . . . Could Sally bear it, this failure?

Outside in the freezing rain, Hood's shattered army was streaming down the pike. Most of them had no tents. And there was no time for tents. Sludge on, before the dawn. Before pursuit. On, with our 54 guns behind, captured. That, too, was shocking, irreparable.

"THE LOST CAUSE," by Henry Mosler, first American to have a painting bought by the French government for the Luxembourg Museum.   (When about 13, in 1854, the noted genre painter lived for a year in Nashville, with German parents. His father was a lithographer.)   The painting was a gift to the Todd Library from the home of the late Judge W. C. Houston, Woodbury, Tenn.

WHEN "OLD JOE" Johnston came to Nashville, May 20, 1880. It was a big day, of many dignitaries, for the unveiling of the statue of Andrew Jackson (still veiled, against tree, right).

—From History of Henry County Commands
"Old Joe" Johnston

NEVER BEFORE this day had the Army of Tennessee been known to break and run. Never, never. What, oh, what, would Sally think of that?

If, by rare chance, the *Nashville Daily Union* reached Hood for that day, he may have seen a sardonic poem on love, which Nashvillians were reading as he wept out his heart:,

> *He promised to love me only,*
> *I promised to love but him—*
> *Till the moon fell out of the heavens*
> *And the stars with age grow dim . . .*
> *He found a gold that was brighter*
> *Than that of my floating curls,*
> *And married a cross-eyed widow*
> *With a dozen grown-up girls.*

It was no solace for a troubled heart. Nor was the song Hood must have heard, as his men went sludging past his tent. Some were thinking wistfully of Gen. Joseph E. Johnston, who had commanded them before Hood. Through the bleak night came the song, a parody of "The Yellow Rose of Texas":

> So now we're going to leave you,
> Our hearts are full of woe;
> We're going back to Georgia,
> To see our Uncle Joe.
> Talk about your Beauregard,
> And sing of Gen. Lee,
> But the Gallant Hood of Texas
> Played hell in Tennessee!

Eh, what's that? Did Hood's ears prick up? "Uncle Joe"? So they're thinking of him, are they . . . Johnston, and his nimble strategy? So they prefer him, do they—to me and my frontal assaults?

No wonder Hood wept.

(Hood had treated Johnston, in a way, much as Schofield had treated Thomas. The chickens had come home to roost.)

Around 10 p.m. Lee began to form a rear guard at Hollow Tree Gap, seven miles north of Franklin. By 2 a.m. it was complete.

At daylight Wilson's horsemen began pursuit. For 10 days they would follow and strike at the mass of bleeding, freezing men. For 10 wretched days the Confederate rear guard would magnificently fight them off.

On Dec. 17 the broken army reeled through Franklin, making for the West Harpeth River. Its cavalry made a stand at the crossing. Three Union horsemen thundered at Gen. Buford. He shot one, clubbed the second with his empty pistol and dragged the third from the saddle by the hair of the head.

Get out of the way! We're heading south!

On the afternoon of Dec. 18 Forrest rejoined the army at Columbia. He took command of the rear guard. Its barefoot infantry he put into wagons. They were rolling south, through mire and sleet. When the enemy approached again, out hobbled the shoeless men from the wagons, to fight on call once more. Again the ruts were red.

In one of the jolting wagons a man sits strangely still. He tightens his rags about him and his hands are seen to fumble. It's Chaplain McNeilly. He is blind. (The cause? We do not know.) He's sticking with the Rebels. He offers prayer when they ask.

They cross the Duck, burning its bridges. Here Hood had hoped to make a stand for the winter.

He changed his mind. His losses had been too severe. Forrest agreed. Let's put the Tennessee behind us. Push on!

Freshets came. Snow melted. Prayers seemed answered. The Duck rose. The Federals had to pause for pontoons. (Their own, by error, had been sent toward Murfreesboro instead of Columbia!)

On Dec. 23 the Army of Tennessee passed through Pulaski, heading for the Tennessee at Bainbridge, Ala., near Florence.

In Georgia, Sherman was entering Savannah. A swath of ashes lay behind him. He wired Lincoln on Christmas Day, *"A Christmas gift of the City of Savannah."*

Thomas, in Pulaski, received a gift by telegram. He has been nominated as a major general. He sits in silence. *"What do you make of that?"* he says finally, to Chief Surgeon George E. Cooper, who thought it better late than never.

"I suppose it is better late than never," Thomas replies. *"But it is too late to be appreciated. I earned this at Chickamauga,"* 16 months before.

On the same Christmas Day, Hood's army began to cross the Tennessee. Once across on the pontoon bridge, they should be reasonably safe—if they could take up the pontoons in time to thwart capture.

—From Hale and Merritt's History of Tennessee and Tennesseans
Gen. Forrest, in later years

—From Battles and Sketches
Gen. Stephen D. Lee, in old age

—Courtesy Tennessee Historical Society
Gen. Thomas, from the portrait which some Tennesseans wanted to sell.

BATTLE
OF
NASHVILLE
1864

—Staff photo by Vic Cooley

The Peace Monument, on Franklin Road, honors both the Blue and the Gray.

"Struggling for the Works"

—The Century War Book, 1861-1865

FORREST managed. The crossing continued through the 27th. On the morning of the 28th he even got his droves of cattle and hogs across, with which he had left Murfreesboro. The pontoons were yanked up . . . as Federals appeared on the north bank.

That day Thomas called off the southward chase, after 120 miles. (From the east, however, Col. William J. Palmer, under Steedman, will soon strike at Hood's pontoon train in Alabama.)

In 10 days the Yankee cavalry had broken down 5,000 horses. Still it had failed to bring the Rebels to bay.

It had, nevertheless, won the Battle of Nashville for Thomas. At least, so old timers say: *"Wilson's cavalry did it! The infantry didn't scratch 'em! (the Rebels). They had held against all frontal assault and didn't budge a step, till Wilson got behind 'em."*

The view, for a thumb-nail sketch, is in the right direction. Wilson virtually confirms it. He says, rather rosily:

"If I had had the use and help of McCook's division (absent, chasing Lyon)

—Harper's Weekly, Dec. 24, 1864

MAKING CORN MEAL.   In the South, food was desperately short.

it is doubtful whether any of the enemy would have been left to tell the tale. It is also well known that all prisoners taken primarily passed through the hands of the cavalry or were picked up by the infantry because their escape had been cut off by the cavalry.

"My report shows that the cavalry actually captured 32 field pieces, 11 caissons, 3,232 prisoners, one general officer and 12 battle flags . . ." The prisoners were sent north.

Boxcars are rumbling through Edgefield, loaded with captive Rebels. McFerrin stands near a door. He hasn't been home in two years. Soon the freight will pass the home of his father, the Rev. John B. McFerrin.

"Henry," McFerrin says to Moss, *"a little farther on I'll show you the dearest place on earth to me."*

A guard overhears. He orders McFerrin to the back of the car. He keeps him there, until long after the train has passed his old home.

Ah, victory!

The war in Middle Tennessee is ending.

The last significant action of the Civil War in Tennessee had been fought at Sugar Creek the day after Christmas. Forrest, concealed in dense fog, had driven Yankees into the creek, capturing men and horses.

It was during the crossing of the Tennessee that a Rebel fell in the mud. He scrambled up and spoke his mind:

"Now ain't we in a hell of a fix! A one-eyed President, a one-legged general and a one-hoss Confederacy!"

Hood's army was hurrying on toward Tupelo, Miss.

To the east, Col. Palmer crossed the Tennessee at Decatur. Striking westward, on Dec. 31 in Northern Alabama he overtook and wrecked Hood's pontoon train. Next day Palmer shattered a supply train of 110 wagons and 500 mules. Two weeks later he captured 80 of Gen. Lyon's remaining raiders who had dropped down out of Kentucky.

The last blow at Hood had been struck, 200 miles from Nashville.

Grant still growled. He had congratulated Thomas. Guns had boomed in Thomas' honor. Grant still thought him *"sluggish."* (Years later, Thomas would criticize himself for the *"grave error"* in not having sent a mobile force to block Hood on the night of Dec. 15, after the first day of the Battle of Nashville.)

In Nashville, the *Daily Union* was gleefully quoting a captured Rebel's letter: *"To be candid with you, I am afraid the Confederate cause is about 'gone up' . . ."*

It was true. The twilight of the Confederacy was at hand. But not the twilight of the Southern spirit.

Hood's battered men reached Tupelo Jan. 10. He would resign Jan. 23. Gen. Pierre G. T. Beauregard saw Hood's troops Jan. 15. *"If not . . . a disorganized mob,"* he wrote, *"it was no longer an army."*

And Chaplain McNeilly would see again. In Tuscaloosa, a noted surgeon heard of the blind parson and his faithful work among the Rebels. He sent for McNeilly. What the surgeon did is not recorded. The chaplain's sight was restored.

How many reached Tupelo? Estimates differ. About 18,000, according to Hood. There were assignments elsewhere, furloughs. This accounted for 7,500. There were desertions.

Soon their beloved "Old Joe" would be back in the saddle as commander. At least 5,000 from Tupelo—the last of the heroic Army of Tennessee—would reach Johnston in North Carolina to fight again.

They would go afoot, by train, by steamer and train again. On March 27 Mrs. Chesnut would see Gen. Stephen D. Lee's corps—men from the Nashville peach orchard—come swinging down the main street of Chester, S.C.

They were singing. *"There they go,"* Mrs. Chesnut wrote, *"the gay and gallant few, doomed, the last gathering of the flowers of Southern pride, to be killed, or worse, to prison. They continue to prance by, light and jaunty. They march with as airy a tread as if they still believe the world was all on their side, and there were no Yankee bullets for the unwary. What will Jo Johnston do with them now?"*

"WINTER CAMP," by Forbes, in *30 Years After*

"**O**LD JOE" will use them to try to stop Sherman, now thumping northward out of smoking Georgia, in a move to join Grant. (On March 19, at the Battle of Bentonville, N.C., "Old Joe" had given the South its last triumph of Confederate arms—15,000 against Sherman's 60,000.)

For the South, the sun was going down . . . Soon "Old Joe" and Gen. Robert E. Lee would face even more insuperable numbers.

President Davis was in church when he received Lee's word that Petersburg and Richmond would have to be evacuated. Davis left at once.

Tumult shook Richmond. Trains pulled out loaded with archives, treasure, the Davis family.

Union troops occupied the fallen Confederate capital April 3. Lincoln paid the city a visit. He was not bitter. He was in no humor to. "*hang*" anyone. The Rebels weren't too sure of that. There was talk of "*going to Mexico.*" The Davis family was fleeing southward. The last candles of hope were flickering low.

In Nashville, on April 5, Brownlow was inaugurated governor. Radical Unionists now had the state by the throat.

In Virginia, Lee is speeding along the Appomattox River, still hoping eventually to link his army with "Old Joe's." Grant pursued. Gen. Philip A. Sheridan raced ahead. Soon Lee was blocked. Further bloodshed was useless.

It is April 9 at Appomattox, a cold and dreary morning. A handsome man sits waiting by a window, wearing his last clean linen. He has new boots, trimmed with red satin. He carries a beautiful saber, an ivory lion's head on its handle. This is Gen. Lee, waiting to surrender.

Afternoon comes. There is a pounding of hooves and Grant takes the fence, astride Cincinnati. He hitches him in the yard of Wilmer McLean's home, near a dappled gray. This is Lee's horse, Traveler.

The two men meet in the parlor. Grant is not too tidy. He explains that he had not been able to find his baggage train. The small talk ends. Aides begin to copy the surrender terms.

Lee corrects his own aide. "*Don't say, 'I have the honor . . .'* (to accept the terms). "*Just say, 'I accept the terms.'*"

Grant permits the Rebels to keep their own horses. The two men shake hands. Lee departs. As he leaves, men take off their hats . . .

In Alabama, Forrest never actually "*surrendered*" at all. He was never captured. But he and his army were surrendered by Gen. Richard Taylor, President Davis' brother-in-law (son of former President Zachary Taylor) on May 6, in a regional truce.

"*That we are beaten is a self-evident fact,*" Forrest told his men on May 9. "*Reason dictates and humanity demands that no more blood be shed . . .*"

Next day President Davis, fleeing on into Georgia, was captured near Irwinsville. (For two years he will be imprisoned. Old-time Yankee opponents will go his bail.)

Two weeks pass. It is late May in Grenada, Miss. Forrest is riding home, back to his old plantation. With him go seven Federal officers . . . and 20 Negroes. To the Yankees he will rent plantations. The Negroes are free, his former slaves, but they're going back, whence they came.

Forrest has kept a promise to them: When he entered the army as a private, 45 of his slaves had come along as teamsters. He had promised to free them if the war were won; then, 18 months later, fearing he might be killed, he had freed them anyway.

Now he's a lieutenant general (or was)—the only private in all the armies of the Civil War to rise to such a rank; and "Old Joe" will call him "*the greatest soldier the war produced.*" No doubt he was . . . but weary now, aging, riding home . . . broke; a man who'd been a millionaire.

The tide of disaster was roaring on. The night of April 14, at Ford's Theater in Washington, Lincoln had been assassinated—shot from the back, by John Wilkes Booth, an actor. Death came next morning to the Great Emancipator.

"*No greater disaster could have befallen the South,*" said "Old Joe," in tribute to the man whose bigness of heart would have embraced the South with compassion and understanding.

Andrew Johnson, Tennessee's war-time governor, is now President. And Hood . . . ?

In South Carolina, he has seen Sally. Before heading for Texas without her, Hood paused at Mrs. Chesnut's to say goodbye. In the buzz of conversation someone asks quietly, not intending that Hood should hear, "*Is his engagement broken?*"

Hood overhears. Significantly, he answers, "*Is my neck broken, did you ask?*"

Deep in reverie, in the long hours ahead, Sally will sit on the piazza, seldom speaking; and one day, against Mrs. Chesnut's knee, Sally will sob out her own distress:

—Harper's Weekly

Interior of a Federal hospital tent and wagon. Notice how the wagon has been backed up to the tent to serve as a dispensary.

Lincoln's Funeral Procession

—Harper's Weekly, May 13, 1865

"... A SICKENING, almost insane longing comes over me just to see him once more, and I know I never will! He is gone forever! If he had been persistent—if he had not given way under Mama's violent refusal to listen to us (months before);—If he had asked me (instead of bowing before family opposition) ... Well, I would have married him in a moment, if the parson could be found to do it! I was ready to leave all the world for him—to tie my clothes in a bundle and, like a soldier's wife, trudge after him to the ends of the earth! Does that sound like me? Well, it was true that day!"

A few weeks later Sally will sail for Paris with her family. Upon return in 1867 she will be married to another faithful Confederate, Rollins Lowndes, long a suitor. He's handsome, rich, and much in love. (His family fortune, invested in English securities at the beginning of the war, was intact.)

Later in the same year Hood will be married in New Orleans to lovely Anna Maria Hennen, granddaughter of a Louisiana Supreme Court justice.

In Nashville, as the autumn comes, the Rev. James Hugh McNeilly will begin an inspiring 10-year pastorate at Woodland Presbyterian Church. It was Nov. 7, 1867.

And in Louisville, that same year, Hood and Thomas will happen to stop at the same hotel. Friends will arrange a meeting.

Thomas hears Hood coming, clattering down the hall on his crutches. The Virginian flings the door wide. He throws his arms around Hood. For an hour they talk.

"Thomas is a grand man," Hood said, upon return to his room. "He should have remained with us, where he would have been appreciated and loved."

For several years thereafter, bad luck left Hood alone. He did well in a brokerage and commission business. He dealt in cotton and also had an insurance firm. Within 10 years, Hood and Anna had 11 children, including three sets of twins.

Then yellow fever struck New Orleans in 1878, and 3,000 persons died. The cotton exchange closed and most life insurance companies failed, including Hood's. By the next summer he was broke and, for the first time, unable to take his family to the uplands.

Yellow fever returned. It killed only six persons. But three of those were Hood, his wife and a daughter. Hood, dying, hoped his old Texas brigade would take care of his children, and it was promptly willing. Other arrangements were made, however, and good homes were found for every child. Offers of adoption poured in from all over America.

Ever so little, the bitterness of Reconstruction was beginning to yield. Almost every Middle Tennessee family had known its anguish, its anger, and at least something of its poverty, far back in the quiet wings of time, which only elder kinsmen truly know, and sometimes tell, when the hair is white, and the nights are long, and a child sits down to ask ... of some beloved voice that shan't have long to answer ...

But the jackbooted men in the spotlight, the famous names, the winners—did they escape all its sting? No.

Grant, in the interlude, had become President, 1869-1877. Schofield, in 1868 and '69, had served as Secretary of War. They found many an aspect of the Battle of Nashville transformed into political gunpowder.

One such little explosion went off at Gen. Thomas on Nov. 11, 1869, after the Democrats had begun to edge their way back to Nashville's Capitol Hill. W. F. Hinkle of Hardin County offered a joint house resolution to sell the portraits of both Thomas and Brownlow.

B. A. Enloe of Madison County offered an amendment. It provided that if proceeds "of said sale shall not be sufficient to pay the auctioneer, he shall have no recourse upon the State."

It was all tabled. But Thomas eventually learned. He was insulted, of course. Angrily he offered to buy the picture, for its $1,000 cost. And Tennesseans could have back the gold medal he had been given—by Tennesseans of Brownlow's ilk. Yes, just as soon as he could get it out of a vault in New York—

It was not to be. The offer of purchase was declined. A more somber event was impending. Politics, meanwhile, had uncorked the old controversy of what Grant and Schofield did or didn't do just before the Battle of Nashville.

It had flared afresh in the New York Tribune in March, 1870. Thomas was in San Francisco. He read it, two whole columns. He looked grim.

He entered his office and began to write, write, three long hours, composing his reply. It was March 28. As he wrote, perhaps he was recalling the agony of old, the endless pressure, from boyhood on, do this, not that; the disownment by his family, his picture to the wall, his portrait unwanted; the harassment by Grant, and the hours of waiting in the Cunningham mansion in Nashville, with the driven ice pressing and pressing against the panes, as if to shut out all life and smother him.

Was there no freedom for Yank or Rebel, anywhere, ever, unless a man fought for it?

Thomas rose. He moved toward a door.

"I want air," he said and fell.

It was apoplexy. He died at 7:25 p.m.

Cannon boomed from Army posts as his funeral train moved across the breadth of America. It was taking the Virginian's body to Troy, N.Y., home city of Mrs. Thomas. Armloads of flowers were put aboard at every stop. In Chicago, 50,000 persons lined the tracks as the train chugged slowly through the city for which Grant once thought Hood was headed—with only Thomas and his army at Nashville standing between the possibility.

"The Bivouac of the Dead"

—Forbes, in 30 Years After

The McLean residence, where Gen. Lee surrendered.

—A Narrative of the Civil War

"A Deserted Picket Hut"

TWENTY-FIVE passenger cars of national guardsmen were brought to Troy to pay Gen. Thomas homage. In the procession were 145 carriages. In one rode President Grant. Four brass bands played. Schofield—ah, irony!—was a pallbearer. Twenty-five of Mrs. Thomas' relatives were there.

But no one came, no one, from the big white house in Virginia beside the almost perfect oak.

O bitter years . . . Is there an answer?

Today in Nashville a monument stands on Franklin Road, where Gen. Stephen D. Lee bestrode the pike 100 years ago, Dec. 15, 1864. There, in statuary, the Spirit of Youth holds apart two fighting steeds.

The inscription reads:

O Valorous Gray, in the grave of your fate,

O Glorious Blue, in the long dead years.

You were sown in sorrow and harrowed in hate,

But your harvest today is a nation's tears.

For the message you left through the land has sped,

From the lips of God to the heart of man:

"Let the past be past, let the dead be dead—

Now and forever American!"

END of WAR

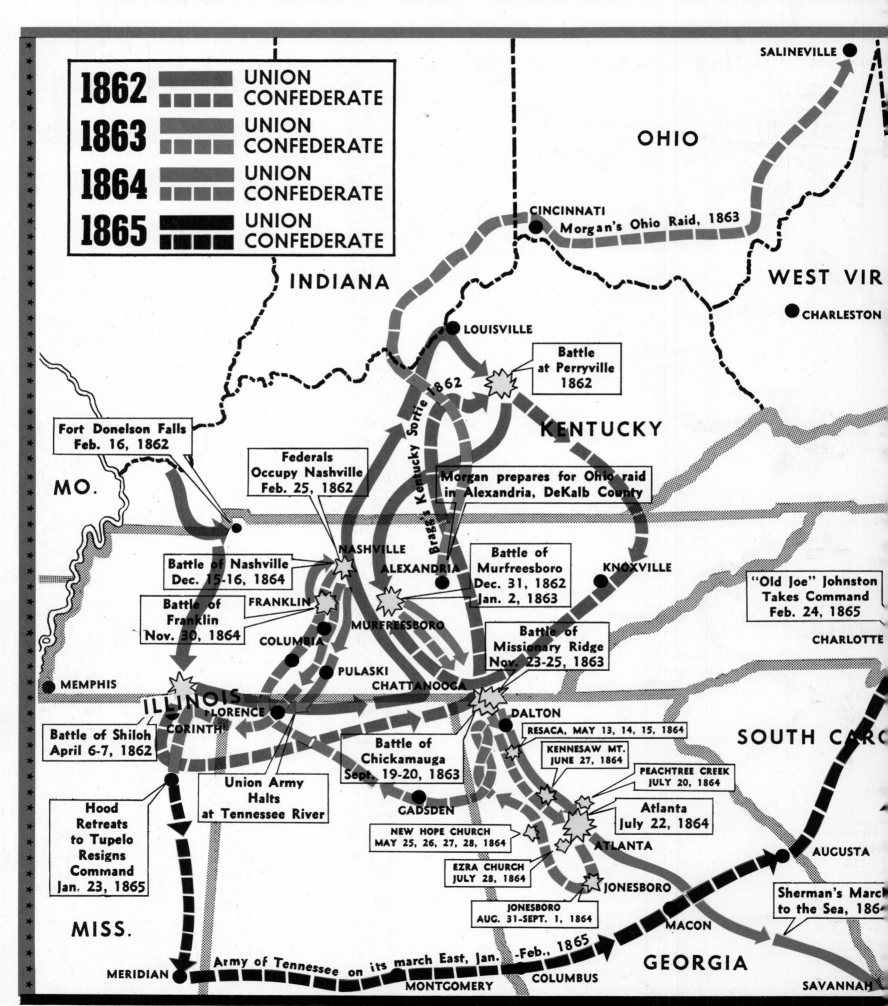

THE CIVIL WAR IN MI...

1862 UNION / CONFEDERATE
1863 UNION / CONFEDERATE
1864 UNION / CONFEDERATE
1865 UNION / CONFEDERATE

OHIO

SALINEVILLE

CINCINNATI
Morgan's Ohio Raid, 1863

WEST VIR...

CHARLESTON

INDIANA

LOUISVILLE

Battle
at Perryville
1862

KENTUCKY

Fort Donelson Falls
Feb. 16, 1862

MO.

Federals
Occupy Nashville
Feb. 25, 1862

Morgan prepares for Ohio raid
in Alexandria, DeKalb County

Bragg's Kentucky Sortie 1862

Battle of Nashville
Dec. 15-16, 1864

NASHVILLE

ALEXANDRIA

Battle of
Murfreesboro
Dec. 31, 1862
Jan. 2, 1863

KNOXVILLE

"Old Joe" Johnston
Takes Command
Feb. 24, 1865

Battle of
Franklin
Nov. 30, 1864

FRANKLIN

MURFREESBORO

CHARLOTTE

COLUMBIA

Battle of
Missionary Ridge
Nov. 23-25, 1863

MEMPHIS

PULASKI

CHATTANOOGA

ILLINOIS

FLORENCE

CORINTH

Battle of Shiloh
April 6-7, 1862

DALTON

RESACA, MAY 13, 14, 15, 1864

SOUTH CAR...

Union Army
Halts
at Tennessee River

Battle of
Chickamauga
Sept. 19-20, 1863

KENNESAW MT.
JUNE 27, 1864

PEACHTREE CREEK
JULY 20, 1864

Hood
Retreats
to Tupelo
Resigns
Command
Jan. 23, 1865

GADSDEN

NEW HOPE CHURCH
MAY 25, 26, 27, 28, 1864

Atlanta
July 22, 1864

ATLANTA

AUGUSTA

EZRA CHURCH
JULY 28, 1864

JONESBORO

Sherman's Marc...
to the Sea, 186...

MISS.

JONESBORO
AUG. 31-SEPT. 1, 1864

MACON

Army of Tennessee on its march East, Jan. -Feb., 1865

GEORGIA

MERIDIAN

MONTGOMERY

COLUMBUS

SAVANNAH